Criminology and Public Policy

Edited by

Hugh D. Barlow *and*
Scott H. Decker

Criminology
and Public Policy

Putting Theory to Work

TEMPLE UNIVERSITY PRESS
Philadelphia

TEMPLE UNIVERSITY PRESS
1601 North Broad Street
Philadelphia, Pennsylvania 19122
www.temple.edu/tempress

Library of Congress Cataloging-in-Publication Data

Criminology and public policy : putting theory to work / edited by
Hugh D. Barlow and Scott H. Decker.
   p. cm.
  Includes bibliographical references and index.
  ISBN 978-1-4399-0006-2 (cloth : alk. paper)
  ISBN 978-1-4399-0007-9 (pbk. : alk. paper)
  1. Criminology. 2. Crime—Government policy. 3. Crime prevention.
4. Criminal justice, Administration of. I. Barlow, Hugh D. II. Decker,
Scott H.

  HV6025.C7458 2009
  364—dc22   2009018647

Printed in the United States of America

2 4 6 8 9 7 5 3 1

Contents

PART II   The Policy Implications of Theory Applied to Specific Crime Types

Foreword

Mass incarceration has been the lynchpin of American crime control policy over the past three decades. It is the elephant in the policy room; it dominates our attention and shows little inclination to leave. Commentators now repeat with numbing regularity that, on any given day, nearly 2.4 million people are institutionalized. Next year or soon thereafter, the count will be 2.5 million, and then 2.6 million, and likely 3 million.

Many factors have fueled this penal harm movement, as Todd Clear poignantly terms it. But one suspects that it would not have been possible if correctional institutions were not brimming mainly with the poor and with people of color. It is not that imprisoned offenders are blameless; life-course criminology shows that most have violated the law many times over. Still, prison inmates often are nastily portrayed as "the Other"—as shrewd calculators undeserving of our help or as super-predators beyond redemption. This imagery inspires relief that this dangerous class sits safely away from us and behind the prison's high and sturdy walls. However, if offenders were more like "us"—a bit more affluent, members perhaps of our neighborhood or church—our capacity to turn a moral blind eye would not be so easy. We might ask more often whether, beyond slamming prison cell doors shut, something else might be done to save our wayward brethren from lives in crime.

In this context, we are fortunate that criminologists serve the crucial role of stubbornly challenging the hegemony of get-tough thinking. As professionals, criminologists sometimes commit the error of over-identifying with offenders, of seeing the bad hand they have been dealt in life and thus of ignoring their pathology and the harm they visit on others. But if occasionally guilty of political correctness, criminologists also have the imagination—rooted, I believe, in a collective empathy for the plight of offenders that comes from studying them up close—to envision a different future in which crime control involves far more than mass incarceration. The reductionist trap of seeing offenders as "the Other" is avoided, and the complexities surrounding their lives are appreciated.

The profession's excursion into the policy domain, however, would be like wandering in the dark if the pathway were not illuminated by criminological theory. In any applied venture, theorizing is not some quaint, esoteric undertaking that is divorced from the real world. Rather, at the core of scientific criminology are the ideas that specify causal relationships and, ultimately, the factors that must be transformed if crime is to be reduced. A-theoretical interventions—such as boot-camp programs, to give but one recent example—are doomed to failure. They are the twenty-first-century equivalent of bloodletting in which common-sense folk ideas lead to quackery.

In the current policy landscape, criminological theory has had an important impact in at least three notable areas. First, life-course and developmental criminology has pushed interest into the beginning years of life and identified key risk factors that can be targeted for change. Early-intervention programs are thus gaining in credibility. Second, social learning theory underlies the principles of effective intervention developed by Don Andrews, James Bonta, and Paul Gendreau. Correctional treatment programs based on these ideas are being implemented successfully across North America. Third, routine activity/opportunity theory has informed a lengthy roster of situational crime prevention initiatives. Results drawn from across nations and diverse contexts are promising.

These interventions are increasingly influential for a trinity of reasons: They reduce crime, are cost-effective, and are supported by the public. Alternatives to penal harm are possible; in fact, the recipe for success is emerging. Thus, programs that reflect sound theoretical principles and are evidence-based, that can be shown to be a worthy investment of the public treasury, and that earn the trust of the citizenry have the chance to shape crime policy in meaningful ways.

Criminology and Public Policy enriches this ongoing conversation about the future of crime control in the United States. An unexpected benefit is that within its covers, prominent scholars provide parsimonious and accessible summaries of their theories. In a very real way, this is a theory book first and foremost—and a policy book thereafter. Beyond this special feature, the volume is invaluable in showing why mass incarceration and naïve get-tough policies have only a limited impact on the crime rate. In chapter after chapter, the authors illuminate the intricate sources of crime that rest far beyond the reach of a punitive state and its harsh legal sanctions. The scholars also reveal, however, why certain current programs (e.g., early-intervention initiatives) are effective: They target for change the factors that theories argue are central to crime causation.

The book also is sobering. It cautions that ingrained structural factors and political interests conspire to sustain get-tough policies and to limit more progressive approaches to reducing crime. These admonitions are important, for they discourage utopian thinking and let those with reformist impulses comprehend the daunting obstacles they are likely to confront.

In the end, however, *Criminology and Public Policy* is an optimistic venture. The contributors offer a roster of fresh, innovative ideas on how crime might best be understood and addressed. Their collective criminological imagination thus energizes the mind and inspires thought about how a better world might be constructed. I trust that this will be a gift that all readers will receive from the pages that follow.

—*Francis T. Cullen*
University of Cincinnati

Preface

The central argument of this book is that crime policy ought to be guided by science rather than by ideology. This provides a vital role for criminologists—one that has largely been ignored, especially by theorists, who "rarely contemplate the policy implications" of their work (Barlow 1995, 7). This book seeks to change that trend by having a group of the field's most acclaimed scholars identify the policy implications of major theories, often their own.

The policy implications of criminological scholarship have been getting more press in recent years, at least within the field. The American Society of Criminology (ASC) established a new journal, *Crime and Public Policy*, with the first issue published in November 2001. This was a step in the right direction, certainly, but the new journal has focused on the link between empirical research and policy, with no space set aside for papers on the policy implications of criminological theory.

Since 1995, outgoing ASC presidents have given public policy issues greater attention in their annual addresses, which are subsequently published in the ASC journal *Criminology*. In the past fourteen addresses (1995–2008), ten presidents brought up the topic of crime policy, and six made it a major theme of their talk. Freda Adler, for example, reminded the criminologists in attendance that it was their "obligation" to reach out to policymakers on a global scale. Optimistically, she asserted that the ASC "had an ear at the highest level" of national criminal justice policy (1996, 2). An ear, of course, is not the same as the pen with which to write policy. The pen remains firmly in the hands of politicians and legislators, whose allegiance is less to the products of science— for example, how to deal with the AIDS pandemic, warnings about global warming, and the ineffectiveness of the Strategic Defense Initiative, or SDI (otherwise known as "Star Wars")—than to the whims of voters and the personal agendas of their counselors and financial supporters.

It should come as no surprise, therefore, that current crime policies are far from benign in their social consequences. In his 2007 address, Michael Tonry (2008) explored the violation of human rights resulting from American public policy, particularly that dealing with crime control. Trends such as the increasing emphasis on imprisonment, life sentences without the possibility of parole, "three-strikes" laws, the prosecution of juveniles as adults, and the weakening of procedural protections since 1970 all exemplify the harshness of American crime control policy compared with the policies of European countries, Australia, Canada, and New Zealand. Further, Tonry showed how American policies systematically undermine the welfare of already disadvantaged black Americans. For example, even with declining racial disparities in arrests for serious crimes since 1987, black imprisonment rates remain seven times higher than those of whites, and a similar disparity exists for those on Death Row. In large measure, Tonry argued, this situation is explained by cultural and historical traditions in America that support the strategic regulation and control of marginalized groups through harsh criminal justice practices that are reinforced by the intolerance arising from paranoia and religious fundamentalism.

So it remains important to ask *how* criminology can turn its products into action. Frank Cullen addressed just this question, saying that the "science of criminology is capable of making an important difference in the correctional enterprise, if not far beyond" (2005, 1). He went on to suggest five ways that this could occur, the first being to develop a "theory of when criminology makes a difference in policy and/or practice" and the second being to engage in rigorous science. "Why should anyone listen to criminologists?" he asked, rhetorically. Because, he explained, "as scientists, we have a form of knowledge—scientific knowledge—that has a special legitimacy" (27).

The special legitimacy of science comes not just from its emphasis on systematic research methods but also from the core of theory that not only drives the research but is also, in turn, advanced by it. As John Laub noted in his presidential address, "Successful theories organize the findings of an area, attract the attention of a broad spectrum of researchers and scholars, and provide influential guides to public policy." Thus, he observed, "in order to enhance policy and practice one needs not only sound research but strong theory" (2004, 18). Fittingly, the 2003 ASC meeting was titled "The Challenge of Practice, the Benefits of Theory."

The policy implications of the interplay between theory and research in good science had come up in Lawrence Sherman's discussion of restorative justice the year before. With illustrations from New Zealand, Australia, the United Kingdom, Indianapolis, and Pennsylvania, Sherman described a cyclical pattern, "with research informing theories, changes in theories guiding changes in innovations [read "policy and practice"], and research on innovations leading to further modification of theory" (2003, 12). This model encourages the formation of global links between theorists, researchers, practitioners, and policymakers of the sort proposed by Adler and subsequently illustrated by David Farrington (2000) in his remarks on the "risk factor prevention paradigm." Experiments designed to assess different technologies of intervention (e.g., improving parental supervision of at-risk children) "ideally" also test causal hypotheses.

The idea that criminologists could (even should) be in the business of transforming the lives of people and places through effective and just crime policy is not new. But the idea has gained momentum in recent years, in part because ASC presidents have taken their annual address as the opportunity to show American criminologists—and their colleagues abroad—that thinking about policy is part of the field's scientific mission. The costs of *not* addressing the policy implications of our work can be seen in the remarks of ASC President Charles Wellford:

> Our field should help people understand the consequences of their actions and how their actions relate to their values and standards. . . . Our work should assist people in assessing the degree to which what we are doing in the area of crime is *effective* and *just*. . . . Until we accept our transformative mission we will support reward systems that emphasize only what we produce not what the knowledge we produce produces. (1997, 3)

Acknowledgments

The editors thank the contributing authors for their hard work—and their patience. The result is a volume we are very proud of. Hugh Barlow owes a special debt to Scott Decker, who first suggested this revision, then took the lead in producing it. We are also indebted to Melanie Taylor for her work in proofreading and developing the index, as well as Jessica Knoerzer for her work in proofreading.

References

Adler, F. 1996. 1995 presidential address: Our American Society of Criminology, the world, and the state of the art. *Criminology* 34:1–9.

Barlow, H. D. 1995. *Crime and public policy: Putting theory to work.* Boulder, Colo.: Westview Press.

Cullen, F. T. 2005. The twelve people who saved rehabilitation: How the science of criminology made a difference. The American Society of Criminology 2004 presidential address. *Criminology* 43:1–42.

Farrington, D. P. 2000. Explaining and preventing crime: The globalization of knowledge. The American Society of Criminology 1999 presidential address. *Criminology* 38:1–24.

Laub, J. H. 2004. The life course of criminology in the United States. The American Society of Criminology 2003 presidential address. *Criminology* 42:1–26.

Sherman, L. W. 2003. Reason for emotion: Reinventing justice with theories, innovations, and research. The American Society of Criminology 2002 presidential address. *Criminology* 41:1–37.

Tonry, M. 2008. Crime and human rights: How political paranoia, Protestant fundamentalism, and constitutional obsolescence combined to devastate black America. The American Society of Criminology 2007 presidential address. *Criminology* 46:1–33.

Wellford, C. F. 1997. 1996 presidential address: Controlling crime and achieving justice. *Criminology* 35:1–11.

I

The Policy Implications of General Theories of Crime

HUGH D. BARLOW AND SCOTT H. DECKER

Introduction to Part I

Putting Criminological Theory into Practice

Generaly theories purport to explain a broad range of facts about crime and criminality that are not restricted to any one time or place. This does not mean they have to explain all crime, and a general theory that accounts for individual differences might not apply at group or societal levels. There are even some theories that are rightly called "general" yet have little or nothing to say about why people commit crimes, focusing instead on the situational forces that make criminal events more or less likely.

Because of their broad applicability, general theories should have wide-ranging implications for crime control and prevention. But spelling them out is not always easy, particularly if a theory is highly abstract. Indeed, Charles Tittle writes in Chapter 1 that general theories have "no necessary connection to the real world they purport to explain." The intellectual exercise that creates theory is driven by science, the goal of which is knowledge, rather than policy, the goal of which is to do something.

Even so, contemplating (and evaluating) the practical implications of general theories may help uncover inconsistencies within, and overlap among, them, thus advancing knowledge. Furthermore, what appears at first to be a logical and sensible policy application of a theory may turn out to have negative consequences, to make things worse. Tittle discusses this problem in terms of control imbalances, and in Chapter 6, Marcus Felson and Ronald Clarke address it in the context of routine precautions.

The overlap among theories is demonstrated time and again in these six chapters. For example, Robert Agnew's general strain theory (Chapter 2) shares much with Tittle's control balance theory, which in turn shares the key variable "self-control" with the general theory of crime proposed by Michael Gottfred-son and Travis Hirschi and discussed in Chapter 4 by Alex Piquero. Not surprisingly, the overlap among theories is reproduced in their policy implications.

But the reader will also discover that similar policy implications sometimes flow from distinctly different theories. Piquero argues that a long-term strategy of crime prevention stemming from control theory is to improve child-rearing practices through more effective parenting; a similar strategy is drawn from the social learning theory advanced by Ronald Akers in Chapter 5. Intervention programs that integrate elements of competing theories show considerable promise, though Akers is quick to point out that "no program has been found always to be highly effective, and even the successful programs have modest effects."

Some of the policy implications of general theories are so profound that they are unlikely ever to see the light of day. This is the case with the institutional anomie theory of crime advanced by Richard Rosenfeld and Steven Messner in Chapter 3. They theorize that the comparatively high rates of crime in the United States are "normal," given the domination of a free-market economy and resulting imbalance among the society's core institutions. The policy implication is that real crime reduction would "require fundamental changes to American society and culture." A similar policy implication can be drawn from strain theory, at least in its focus on manipulating the social environment to reduce objective strain. This leads Felson and Clarke to aver that much modern criminology does not try to solve crime problems and thus "avoids the opportunity for its own improvement." They go on: "Most crime theories are so remote from real life that such evasion is built into their very structure. For example, the policy implication of strain theory is a complete restructuring of society, which in reality is not likely to occur anywhere."

When it comes to proposing an effective crime policy drawn from their own or others' general theory, the authors of these six chapters exude modesty in the face of their own skepticism. Tittle suggests that development of a culture of sensitivity (a kinder, gentler world) might help. Felson and Clarke propose a public health approach: change the minds of organizations about the importance of situational prevention rather than focus on the routine precautions of individuals. Agnew puts his money on restorative justice and the creation of "strain responders" and "social support centers" to help people identify and cope with strain. Rosenfeld and Messner like the promise of prisoner reentry programs to address recidivism, a policy that has bipartisan support. Piquero looks to better child-rearing practices and short-term strategies such as target hardening, which makes crime more difficult to commit, an approach drawn from rational choice theory and also dear to Felson and Clarke. Akers is clearly the most confident in his theory's promise for reducing and controlling crime:

When he applies the "practicality test" to social learning theory, he claims that much empirical evidence supports it, and there is "little research evidence that runs counter to social learning hypotheses." He ends with a plea that those responsible for policy and practice make clear the theory behind their efforts. Using the popular DARE (Drug Abuse Resistance Education) program as an example, Akers argues that its poor record of achievement over the years might be changed if the organizers clearly articulated the theoretical principles underpinning it.

CHARLES R. TITTLE

Control Balance Theory and Social Policy

This chapter spells out some of the policy implications of control balance theory. However, it is important for the reader to recognize that this theory was intended strictly as a scientific instrument. As such, it does not lend itself readily to policy application. Scientific accounts are designed to help explain things within given domains of interest. That is, scientific theories try to provide answers to questions of "why" and "how" that are deemed satisfactory by a critical audience of scientists who expect such a theory to provide the means for predicting aspects of the phenomena of interest. Scientific predictions are quite different from prophecy. A scientific prediction is of the form, "Given conditions x, y, and z, one should expect to find q," which may be applied to events in the past as well as in the present. A prophecy, by contrast, is a projection into the future. Scientists do not issue prophecies except in the form of conditional statements, such as, "If conditions x, y, and z continue or emerge, then q is likely to happen."

Scientific explanations can be freestanding, applying to a specific phenomenon, often at a particular time and place, with quite concrete elements. But the best explanations are embedded in general theories setting forth abstract principles from which explanations of many separate phenomena can be derived. Science strives for such general theories because they are more efficient than myriad specific explanations. In addition, general theories make it possible to organize and summarize large bodies of knowledge as well as to derive explanations of phenomena that previously have not been explained. Finally, general theories serve the ends of science because they identify common causes of various phenomena, thereby guiding the identification of the unity in nature on which science is built.

Theories, however, are intellectual accounts with no necessary connection to the real world they purport to explain. Theories may be intellectually excellent— well structured, logical, comprehensive, and the like—at the same time that the predictions they suggest about the empirical world may be incorrect. Science strives to produce theories that are good intellectual products and that are also empirically faithful. Ultimately, the point is to explain aspects of the domain covered by the theory. To determine whether a theory is empirically correct, and to provide the means for improving it when evidence shows that it is not fully correct, scholars must assess how well it fits appropriate data about the real world. Research is about testing the match between the intellectual world of a theory with the empirical world supposedly being explained.

The research process requires, first, derivation of specific, reality-oriented hypotheses, the validity of which can be compared with concrete information. A theory cannot be tested directly because it is composed of abstract notions that are stated generally rather than specifically. Moreover, a theory typically cannot be tested in its entirety because it is composed of many potential causal parts that must fit together in particular specified ways. For instance, a given theory may suggest that A (a general, abstract concept) causes B (another general abstract concept) and that C (a general, abstract concept) causes D (a general, abstract concept), as well as many other relationships and causal connections. In addition, that theory might imply that A indirectly affects D because A affects C, which in turn affects D. As long as these implied relationships concern abstract phenomena they stand simply as intellectual puzzles. An empirical test, however, requires that the general, abstract concepts of A and B be reduced to concrete instances of the general categories of A and B and that the theoretical relationship between those general categories be specified in empirical terms. But usually the whole set of relationships cannot be tested at once. Instead, scientists focus mainly on more limited empirical statements, called hypotheses. Hypotheses are statements of relationship among concrete referents for theoretical concepts. By testing a large number of such hypotheses derived from a theory, scholars can indirectly test the accuracy of the entire theory.

However, because the same abstract principles can yield many hypotheses, and because abstract concepts can be expressed in many concrete variables, no particular test of a hypothesis provides all, or even a substantial amount, of the information needed to evaluate a theory. Correct evaluation requires many tests of many hypotheses in many different circumstances. At any given time, the status of a theory depends on the weight of evidence compiled up to that point. No theory is ever completely proved, because even if all prior tests have been supportive, there is no guarantee that the next test, with different variables, different samples, and in different parts of the world, will also be supportive. And when a theory enjoys numerous successful tests, it is likely to provoke closer attention to detail that reveals other possibilities that need testing. Hence, the validity of a theory is always tentative, resting on the collective judgment of scientists who express various degrees of confidence in it at any given point in time. Theories are not deemed to be right or wrong; they simply enjoy different amounts of support.

Scientific Theory and Policy

Before a theory can be used for policy, it should be well tested, modified in response to contradictory evidence, and have achieved a position of wide support from the scientific community. However, even such a theory might not yield useful implications for ameliorating social problems. Indeed, there is disagreement among scholars about the appropriate role of science in policymaking.

Most scientists think that the ultimate goal of their work is to explain the phenomena in their arena, but not all agree. To some, explanation is simply a midpoint, with the final objective being the application of knowledge to solve practical problems or to control the domains being explained. Whether they are scientists or not, such individuals can be characterized as "policy oriented." Policy-oriented scientists often eschew the process of theory building, instead focusing their attention directly on problems or issues, and policy-oriented laypeople often demand and expect scientists to show the policy implications of their work.

Some science scholars are reluctant to recommend policy because they think policy issues are largely, if not entirely, subjective in character and vulnerable to influence by interest groups, while science is rooted in objective reasoning, testing, and analysis. Those reluctant to draw policy implications point out that identifying practical or social "problems" is judgmental, informed by the individual's personal philosophy or ideology. A theory may yield different directives, depending on what practical thing one wants to accomplish, and what one wants to accomplish reflects personal orientations. To some, then, the more that science is driven by the goal of practical application, the less objective and the less scientific it becomes.

For instance, some view crime and deviance as "bad." They want theories that contain the knowledge necessary to reduce or eliminate criminal or deviant behavior, and they have no patience with theories implying that non-normative behavior may not always be disadvantageous for a society or other social group or that preventing it may be impossible. Others regard some criminal and deviant behavior as a "good" thing, sometimes as an essential or inherent element making organized social life viable and other times as an important counterweight to laws expressing the interests of dominant elements in a population. Different theories have been formulated on each side of this issue, but their empirical validity remains in doubt, so policy based on them is problematic.

The various theories of crime and deviance simply have not yet been tested often enough and well enough to judge accurately the import of crime and deviance or whether they can be prevented. Further, judging "good" or "bad" are moral issues, not scientific ones, so whether crime and deviance "should" be prevented is not an element of science. Therefore, those who are committed to policy-driven work may have trouble thinking outside their own preferences or ideologies to design and execute crucial research. Moreover, their orientations sometimes incline them to reject research or evidence out of hand if it contradicts their goals. In other words, policy orientations can get in the way of science.

A second reason that some resist policy-driven directives in knowledge building is that practical applications are not always, or even usually, apparent at the time that scientific work is being produced. Often, knowledge produced in the pursuit of what at the time seems like non-practical scientific objectives later turns out to have practical import. In many such instances, realization that the information would be useful for policy was unknown ahead of time, so had scholars who produced the knowledge heeded the mandates of policy orientation, the knowledge that ultimately proved beneficial would not have been produced. As a result, some believe that even for policy application, the most useful knowledge is precisely that which is developed theoretically for scientific purposes and honed through objective empirical research guided strictly by scientific objectives. That is, policy is best made from knowledge that at the time of its compilation was not developed with policy concerns in mind. From such a perspective, effective policies, whatever their goal, can be fashioned only from well-developed, verified general theories that explain how and why things produce various outcomes.

There is one way, however, that the tension between policy concerns and science can be reconciled. It may be possible to improve scientific theories by spelling out their logical implications, even if those logical implications are not strictly scientific but instead bear on various potential practical problems. The intellectual exercise of drawing potential policy implications may help theorists and consumers of theories identify logical problems in theoretical accounts. After all, imagining the consequences of different explanatory processes may stretch the intellectual limits of a theory in ways not possible in ordinary scientific manipulation. Moreover, if attempts are actually made to implement various theoretical principles, such social experiments may provide empirical feedback that otherwise might not be available. For instance, the attempt in decades past to apply the principles of labeling theory through the development of diversionary programs in juvenile justice, ostensibly to steer troubled youth away from the formal labeling, provided massive amounts of evidence relative to the validity of that theory. Though the evidence was crude in the sense of not being based on well-honed applications, its volume was far greater than otherwise would have been possible through normal channels of theory testing.

It is with a view to these potential advantages of thinking about social policy that I set forth in the following pages what I believe to be the main implications of control balance theory.

A Brief Overview of Control Balance Theory

Control balance theory contends that deviant behavior results when an individual experiences an imbalance of control (those with balanced controls are unlikely to engage in deviant behavior), becomes motivated to do something to alter that imbalance, perceives that deviant behavior may have advantages in that respect, is in a situation where opportunity to commit deviance exists, and perceives that the gain in control from some deviant behavior is greater than the loss of control that may result from that deviant act. The theory further attempts to specify the type of deviant behavior a person is likely to choose when faced with opportunities for different kinds of misconduct in his or her efforts to alter a control imbalance.

The causal sequence of the theory can be stated in general terms in the following way: a control imbalance makes people sensitive to provocation. When provocations are encountered, the person realizes anew that his or her controls are imbalanced, and he or she may grasp the notion that deviance may alleviate the problem. If so, he or she becomes motivated toward deviance. The greater the provocation relative to the control imbalance, the stronger and more probable the likely motivation, and the greater the chances the person or entity will engage in some form of deviant behavior. This greater probability of misbehavior, however, does not imply that the person will commit a specific form of deviance. From the control ratio and provocation alone we cannot predict, say, the chances that the person will commit an assault. However, if a researcher were to measure perhaps thirty different kinds of deviance, it could be expected that the probability of committing a total of one or more of them would be predictable from the control ratio and provocation alone. Moreover, we could predict that the deviant act chosen would fall within a somewhat restricted range of "control balance desirability" (to be described later) that is associated roughly with the person's control ratio.

To bring the theory down to specifics, consider the following situation. A man is fired from his job. This is naturally upsetting to him, for a lot of reasons—such as loss of income, humiliation, decrease in credit rating, and the like. The theory, however, interprets the underlying issue as being a loss or a challenge to the individual's control. Without income, he cannot control economic circumstances; humiliation reminds him that he did not have much control of things in the first place; and a decline in credit rating means he

cannot arrange things for future benefit. In other words, being fired is a provocation that reminds this individual that he is not fully in control of circumstances. Since people inherently desire to control things (an assumption of the
theory), this reminder of inability to control things generates an urge to try to
fix the problem.

The fired individual contemplates what he can do to gain more control. He
can, of course, do nothing, look for another job, or assert his autonomy through
deviance. Deviance is likely to appear attractive, mainly because it is potentially
the quickest and most effective way to reestablish control. The fired worker
might assault the foreman as a way to say that he is in control of things. He
might steal something from the company, which not only asserts that he is in
command after all but provides economic resources that enable him to control
some other important things in his life. Or he might go home and assault his
wife or abuse his children as a way to show that he is a master of his domain.
However, all of these means of gaining control raise the possibility of counter-
control. The man could be arrested and jailed for assault, or he might face
physical retaliation by the foreman, either of which would further erode his
control. He might get caught stealing and suffer great loss of freedom as well as
jeopardize future employment opportunities. And assaulting his loved ones may
undermine their cooperation in accomplishing his goals. This individual quickly
contemplates, though not necessarily in a rational manner, the potential gains
in control from these possible actions as opposed to the potential losses in
control their commission might imply. When the balance appears favorable for
a gain in control, the individual engages in some opportune deviant behavior.

In brief, given a control imbalance, a provocation, and an acute awareness
that deviant behavior can alter the situation, an individual is likely to choose
some form of deviant behavior. However, he or she also has to consider the
possibility of counter-control. Some forms of deviance imply greater and more
likely potential counter-control than others. Therefore, a motivated individual
will likely seek some form of deviance that is perceived to provide the maximum
of control gain with the least chance of reactions that might reduce overall control ratios. The extent to which rationality is exercised in this decision depends
on the individual's self-control and beginning control ratio. The higher the control ratio and self-control, the more likely is the person to choose an act with
high "control balance desirability" (a quality of an act representing a long-range
gain in control and the degree of indirect involvement in accomplishing it).

The basic process of control balancing is subject to "contingencies" (conditions or circumstances that influence the degree to which the full control-
balancing process unfolds). While there are, in fact, many such contingencies,
two are particularly important and can be thought of as illustrative. First, some
people, during the course of their socialization, come to internalize certain moral
standards concerning specific deviant acts. For those with moral commitments,

contemplating or actually doing various deviant acts stimulates an uncontrollable internal emotional punishment in the form of feelings of guilt or personal shame. Such individuals have greater difficulty in weighing the gain in control from deviance against potential losses. They may even have difficulty in imagining that deviance might help rectify a control imbalance or the humiliation of provocation. Therefore, for the highly moral, the control-balancing process will not unfold with as much certainty, or as completely, as for others.

Similarly, individuals differ with respect to their social environments. Some are surrounded by people, sometimes even by people they admire, love, or respect, who readily employ deviant behavior to solve control problems. The more an individual observes deviance as a culturally appropriate response to provocation, or observes that his or her role models resort to deviance, the greater the likelihood that he or she will also contemplate or employ deviance in solving problems associated with an imbalanced control ratio. Thus, extensive exposure to deviant role models distorts the control-balancing process because individuals so exposed are likely to become motivated toward deviance more quickly than normal and to discount potential counter-control to a greater degree than is normal.

Therefore, correct application of control balance theory requires attention to the basic model as well as to potential influences that affect the extent to which the basic model is likely to operate in a specific instance.

The key variables in the theory are control ratios, provocation, motivation, opportunity, potential counter-control, control balance desirability, and self-control. All but one of these variables potentially can be manipulated through carefully managed social policies to alter the chances or type of criminal or deviant behavior. Control balance desirability is a characteristic associated with a deviant act. Control balance desirability incorporates the chances and degree to which the act will have a long-range effect in altering a control imbalance and the degree to which the act requires personal, direct involvement by the perpetrator. Control balance desirability is to a large extent inherent in particular types of deviant behavior, and so it cannot really be manipulated. The other six variables might be alterable by government or citizen action.

First, individuals' control ratios differ. A control ratio is the degree of control over various aspects of the world (other people, physical things, and circumstances) that an individual has relative to the control various aspects of the world have on him or her. Such control ratios vary from large deficits, in which a person is almost totally controlled without being able to control anything, to large surpluses, in which the individual has almost total control over things while having little vulnerability to being controlled. The greater the control ratio, the more likely is a person, when provoked and motivated toward deviant behavior, to choose deviance high in "control balance desirability," although that probability can be upset if the person has low self-control or happens to be characterized by variables such as morality that can play a contingency role.

Provocation occurs when some situational event reminds the person of his or her control deficit or surplus. Insults, for instance, remind people with low control ratios that they cannot control things, while insults remind people with control surpluses that they should have control but it is not being honored. In both instances, the individuals are likely to feel some negative emotion, often in the form of humiliation, and to think about ways to gain in control. People who are insulted often consider the possibility of deviant behavior. Being fired from a job is another reminder to those with weak control balances that they are subordinate, while losing a contract may remind those with strong control balances that they are not all-powerful. Here, too, the urge to gain control is likely to stimulate thoughts of deviant behavior. Deviant motivation is simply the realization by an individual that deviant behavior can help rectify the provoking or humiliating situation or the control imbalance that is recalled by the provocation. Deviant motivation does not always follow when provocation takes place, but it usually does.

When people are provoked and come to realize that deviant behavior can be helpful in gaining or restoring control, they cannot necessarily contemplate committing just any deviant act. Some deviant acts simply are not possible, either because they cannot be accomplished physically in a given context or because the person's circumstances (implicated in the control ratio) will not permit them. Thus, a worker cannot contemplate firing a boss, although a boss can contemplate firing a worker. Similarly, a worker may not be able to contemplate using a piece of company equipment (such as a computer) for his own purposes if he cannot operate it, while a boss may not be able to imagine beating up a physically superior worker. The physical possibility of various deviant acts (opportunity) is crucial and is an essential element in the chances of deviant behavior.

In addition, not all deviant acts are realistic for a provoked individual to contemplate. Deviant acts usually involve harm or inconvenience to others, or they tweak moral concerns. That is, any deviant act carries some potential for counter-control, and sometimes counter-control is so likely and so potentially constraining that any gain in control from a given deviant act would be threatened by the consequences of the act. Provoked/motivated individuals must engage in "control balancing" in which they weigh the gains in control from deviance against the potential loss in control that might be brought about by the deviant act.

However, a provoked person is likely to think first of opportune deviant acts that have immediate consequences and that involve direct, hands-on action by the individual, such as punching somebody, vandalizing something, or cutting off an offending driver. Such acts are likely to be most satisfying emotionally, but they are also most likely to bring about strong counter-control, so they are less effective in the long run for gaining in control balance. The most "control balance–desirable" acts have the maximum long-range impact in altering control imbalances, and they are most impersonal (can be accomplished without direct, hands-on action). For example, a powerful corporate executive might be able to damage an insulting rival's economic future without being obviously and directly involved, thereby gaining a lot of control but avoiding the costs that would have accrued had he or she directly yelled at or punched the competing executive. The higher the control ratio, the greater the potential for engaging in the more desirable control-balancing acts. Finally, the degree to which control balancing is conducted rationally depends on the self-control of the individual. Those with high self-control are more likely to refrain from acts with high potential counter-control, while those with lower self-control are less likely to refrain.

Overall, then, control balance theory predicts that the greater the control imbalance (either a deficit or a surplus) the greater the chances of provocation and deviant motivation, inspiring control balancing in deciding what to do. The greater the motivation, the greater the chances of some form of deviant behavior—selected with respect to opportunity and potential counter-control and guided by the person's self-control. But those with high control ratios are more likely to select deviant acts high in potential long-range positive conse-quences for control gains and involving the least direct personal involvement. Hence, there is a predicted correlation between control ratios and control balance desirability of deviant acts likely to be committed.

However, the alleviation of feelings stemming from provocation or from a control imbalance is usually not dependent on the commission of a specific deviant act, because any one of several may accomplish the same purpose. So the theory does not predict the selection of a specific deviant act. Instead, it predicts that a motivated individual will select some deviant act from among several possibilities within a range of similar control balance desirability.

Intervention Policies Suggested by the Theory

Before identifying specific approaches for changing criminal or deviant behavior using the principles of control balance theory, it is critical to recognize that the theory portrays the variables affecting crime in a hydraulic relationship. Hence, if one thing implicated in the production of crime or deviance is altered, it is likely to lead automatically to the alteration of other relevant things. Thus, an action that reduces the chances of one kind of crime or deviance may lead to an increase in the chances of another kind of crime or deviance. For example, if the potential counter-control (say, the probability or magnitude of legal penal-ties) is increased for some acts, motivated individuals are likely to choose other deviant acts rather than simply to refrain altogether from misconduct. The net result of a policy intervention, therefore, may be more undesirable than the original conditions, depending, of course, on the specific acts that are counter-controlled and the opportunities for committing acts in specific circumstances that involve less chance of counter-control. For that reason, one must be very careful in assessing potential outcomes, taking into account not only the direct implications of policy but also the indirect ones. However, since it is often impossible to assess accurately either direct or indirect possibilities, much policy intervention, even if guided by the principles of control balance theory, may be counterproductive to the goals of a policy—that is, policy intervention may sometimes be dangerous.

Nevertheless, as noted before, alteration in any one of six variables central in the theory might change the probability of some criminal or deviant behavior, and alteration in two or more simultaneously may have even greater effects. The following paragraphs indicate certain effects that should be expected when one or another of the key control balance variables is changed. However, a net ameliorating effect stemming from the manipulation of each of the key control balance variables is likely to be complex and problematic, and sometimes undesirable in the long run.

Control Ratios

The most important variable in control balance theory is the control ratio. It is theorized to affect how and why provocations leading to criminal or deviant motivation emerge, the nature and degree of constraint an individual might face in committing deviance, and the kind of deviant behavior one is likely to pursue in efforts to overcome a control deficit or extend a control surplus. The variables of control balance theory that affect criminal or deviant behavior converge in a sequential causal chain beginning with control imbalances. Therefore, if one wishes to have the maximum effect on crime or deviance, altering control ratios is first and foremost.

According to the theory, people with balanced control ratios are least likely to offend, because they are less vulnerable to provocation, less likely to become motivated toward deviance, and more likely to face counter-control for deviant actions that might be undertaken to change their control situations. This does not mean that such people will never offend; it means only that their chances of offending are lower than for others. Thus, crime/deviance rates will be lower when the proportion of the population with balanced control ratios is greater, and such rates will be higher when the proportion of the population with unbalanced control ratios is larger. An interventionist's dream, based on control balance theory, would be to change things so that every person has a balanced control ratio.

Achieving such a goal would not be easy. Control ratios are complex phenomena, made up of relative controls of all kinds in numerous domains, and
there are both global and domain-specific control ratios. Many of the controls
implicated in overall control ratios cannot be manipulated. For instance, all
people are sometimes controlled by weather conditions, by structural factors
such as population size, and by actions of foreign governments. Moreover,
control is, at least partly, dependent and reciprocal. Part of any person's control
stems from others' having less control; if one individual gains or loses control,
it will be to some extent because somebody else or some other entity gains or
loses it.

For example, if a society is transformed so that some of those with unbalanced control ratios move closer to balance, making them less liable for deviance in general but more liable for certain kinds of deviance than before, other
people may come to have more unbalanced control ratios, thereby increasing
their chances of deviance and shifting the zone of control balance desirability
within which a likely act of misbehavior will fall. Hence, unless efforts to move
people toward balanced control ratios are totally successful (which is impossible
to imagine), they will result in shifts all along the control ratio continuum,
implying gains for some and losses for others, with accompanying changes in
probabilities of deviance and in types of likely deviance. Some of those effects
may even involve the unintended consequence of knocking some who are currently in the balanced zone into imbalance, with resulting increases in the
chances of misbehavior. While some of these changes may bring about a lower
probability of criminal or deviant behavior, others may increase that probability.
Moreover, the shifts that decrease the chances of one kind of deviance may at
the same time increase the chances of other kinds of deviance, depending on
control balance desirability. Control balance–desirable deviance is not necessarily less damaging to society or others. A massive effort by a person in a corporate leadership job to wipe out a competitor by lowering prices below costs
may produce more overall harm than would have been produced by another
deviant act by that person had he or she been in a position with less surplus of
control. Simply stated, lower rates of some kinds of deviance may be achieved
at the price of higher rates of other kinds of deviance, some of which may be
more dangerous.

Moreover, equalizing control ratios might necessitate massive changes, such
as altering the distribution of wealth, creating more equal access to institutions
to protect the autonomy of individuals (such as the police and courts, arbitration
schemes in the workplace, and the like), or accomplishing more equal outcomes
by institutions conferring the means of achieving autonomy (such as places of
employment, or educational and financial institutions). Equalizing control ratios
would also imply cultural alterations to reduce status differentials between various social groupings, such as by race, ethnicity, gender, socioeconomic category,

and age. However, some, maybe most, elements going into control ratios probably cannot be altered, even in an ideal world. For instance, it is hard to conceive how equality of control can be achieved in courtship, family, organizational pursuits, or interpersonal relationships. For example, would a workable society in which parents and young children exercised equal control or where businesses or armies did not grant more control to some than to others be possible? It even stretches the imagination to think of effective educational institutions in which teachers and students share equal control. And as hard as it is to imagine such things, it is even harder to conceive of social policies to bring about such social arrangements. Moreover, as noted above, efforts to alter control ratios can backfire, especially if they are not completely successful in producing balanced control ratios for all.

Provocations That Remind People of Control Imbalances

According to control balance theory, the starting point for a causal sequence ending in criminal behavior is an acute reminder to an individual of his or her control imbalance. Such provocations can include words from other people, such as insults; being told that one's work is poor; receiving bills that cannot be paid easily; being rejected by a lover; or failing to win a promotion. Borrowing from strain theory, one might call such provocations "noxious stimuli." They are noxious because they remind a person of an inability to control his or her world. Even if a person has an unbalanced control ratio, no criminal behavior is likely without provocation. Therefore, attempting to alter provoking conditions is a logical policy to pursue in attempting to reduce crime or deviance.

One can idealize "a kinder and gentler world" in which no person's behavior offends any other person, where success in courtship is guaranteed, where every person gets the job he or she seeks, where failure never happens, where all debts are payable and loans are equally available, and the like. It is completely unrealistic, however, to think that most provocative situations actually can be eliminated. For one thing, provocation for one person may actually reduce the chances of provocation for another, so removing the provocative circumstances for the first person may mean creating provocations for the second one. A professor may contradict a student's argument or idea, thereby reminding that student that in the classroom he or she has less control than the professor. Under specified conditions, such provocation may lead to misbehavior by the student. To reduce that possibility, one might say that professors should never contradict students. But if the student's argument contradicts the professor, then the student's words constitute a provocation for the professor, which increases his or her chances of deviant behavior. Similarly, being reminded of a deficiency in work performance may constitute a provocation for a worker, but the inability to point out such deficiency may constitute a provocation for a boss.

Despite the two-edged sword implied by trying to reduce some provocations that remind people of control imbalances, and despite the fact that some situations are inherently provoking for one or another party, it nevertheless remains true that a culture more sensitive to the emotional feelings of others might be beneficial. While professors may need to correct students, they can learn to do it in a less provoking manner, and bosses may find it necessary to call attention to poor work but can do it in ways that reduce the sting. Similarly, business transactions, such as sending bills for services rendered, may be essential, but arranging terms for easier payment may be less provocative than threatening immediate repayment on pain of lawsuit. And a general culture of sensitivity might encourage potential lovers to reject their suitors in kinder terms, while parents could learn to correct and supervise their children in more ameliorative ways.

Criminal and Deviant Motivations

In control balance theory, the motivation to employ misbehavior in dealing with an unbalanced control ratio results when the person encounters some provocation that brings to mind his or her control shortfall and, at the same time, he or she comes to realize that deviant (or criminal) behavior may permit the control imbalance to be alleviated, at least temporarily. Motivation does not always follow provocation, but most of the time it does. Moreover, when an individual perceives that deviance may help, the kind of deviance most attractive to him or her at the time is likely to be of the most serious form. But a motivated individual, unless crippled by low self-control, will weigh the advantage of the misbehavior against the potential loss of control likely to stem from its commission. If the potential loss of control exceeds the potential gain in control, a less serious crime or act of deviance is likely to be committed than a more serious act. Motivation, then, is a key variable implicated in the production of criminal or deviant behavior. Therefore, effective social policy to reduce crime and deviance might be aimed at preventing provocations from resulting in criminal or deviant motivation.

Some of the contingencies that make it more or less likely that the full sequence of control balancing will take place bear on the likelihood that provocation will stimulate deviant motivation and so are relevant to policy. For instance, a person exposed to role models who frequently use deviance to gain additional control will be more likely to think of deviant behavior as an option than are those without deviant role models. In general, greater familiarity with deviance will more quickly bring its possibility to mind when a person is experiencing humiliation. In addition, individuals with deep-seated moral objections to various kinds of deviance will be less likely to imagine that those forms of deviance will help overcome provocations or alter the control imbalances at their root. Therefore, a society that wishes to reduce criminal or deviant behavior may want to reduce the chances that provocations will lead to deviant motivation by de-emphasizing deviance as a method for solving control problems and by endeavoring to build moral consciences against resorting to deviance.

One way a society can try to de-emphasize deviance is by changing the content of popular entertainment; by reducing publicity about politicians, athletes, teachers, corporate executives, or family members who use deviance to try to solve control imbalances; by inspiring parents to increase their discouragement of associations with peers known to practice criminal or deviant behavior; and by teaching coping skills so that the alternative of deviance does not loom so large. Promoting popular entertainment without heavy doses of deviance may be difficult, but if control balance theory is correct, it is important to try to do so. But messages suggesting criminal or deviant behavior as a possibility may stimulate deviant motivation even when the misbehavior is shown to be costly—because such messages feed into observers' repertoires of possible behavioral alternatives to be recalled when provocations occur. Moreover, a social policy mandating the reduction of criminal or deviant examples itself would probably involve coercion. Introducing coercion, even to reduce deviant examples, could have the ancillary consequence of increasing control imbalances, thereby helping to provoke additional criminal or deviant behavior.

Another possibility is to reduce public knowledge of misdeeds among citizens, because it might minimize the extent to which provoked individuals think of deviance as a possible solution. Thus, public relations campaigns that lead citizens to believe that deviance is rare might have a modulating effect. Though citizens might still learn about misconduct through gossip and rumor, they would be less convinced of its prevalence and probably less likely to bring it to mind as a potential tool. Such approaches, however, may be contrary to notions of freedom of the press and open democratic exchange of information (and likely would be opposed for those reasons), and their dishonesty might lead to their own long-term ineffectiveness. Similarly, isolating delinquents for individualized schooling and living arrangements could reduce their influence as models for criminal or deviant behavior that might be employed as a ready remedy for control issues. But, such possibilities would be expensive and would no doubt generate all manner of additional social issues.

Societies trying to reduce the chances that provocations surrounding control imbalances will lead to deviance could also conduct massive campaigns to teach conventional coping skills. Such training, which could be undertaken at various points in the educational process as well as in job situations, in the military, and in open programs for whole communities, might involve learning about the circumstances in which humiliation is likely to be felt. In addition, the training might drill people in conventional methods of overcoming such humiliation or of enhancing their control within approved channels.

Here, too, it is important to note that all of these possibilities would likely simply reduce deviant motivation; they would not eliminate it. Moreover, so much effort devoted to managing control imbalances might backfire by making people more aware of the control imbalances they normally experience but usually routinize or ignore. After all, most people learn to suppress their awareness of lack of control, allowing it to spew forth only when cast into acute situations or when facing potent events. If people were talking a lot about provocation and were pointing up the likelihood of humiliation in programs to train people to deal with such situations, people might actually become even more sensitized to control imbalances than they are now and might be primed to interpret more situations and events as potentially humiliating. In other words, the potential solution might actually enhance the problem.

Finally, morality as a defense against deviant motivation might well involve a change in child-rearing practices as well as in general cultural themes. U.S. society appears to be mainly a utilitarian society, dominated by notions of business efficiency and personal decision making in which individual choices motivated by rational calculations of cost and benefit are glorified. Issues of right and wrong, moral and immoral, and of just or unjust take a back seat, and when they do emerge, they usually do so in distorted form aimed at narrow abstractions such as denying artificial life supports, stem cell research, or abortion. In this context, actions resulting in suffering by millions, such as careless war making, failure to install known safety devices in automobiles, neglectful attention to natural disasters, denial of routine health care for those who have no money or insurance, and countless others are not evaluated in moral terms. More pointedly, illegal and harmful acts by role models are excused as "mistakes," not moral wrongs, as if the acts were simple miscalculations rather than deliberate actions. Without widely shared moral notions, it is little surprise that criminal or deviant actions easily come to mind when people are humiliated or made aware of a control imbalance.

Criminal Opportunity

In control balance theory opportunity to commit a criminal or deviant act after having balanced the potential gain in control against the potential countercontrol implied by that act simply means that the act is possible. One cannot steal cars if there are no cars, if all cars are unalterably locked, or if one cannot move the car. One cannot assault a person who is physically superior and on guard. Robbing a bank after hours is practically impossible for those without knowledge of safe cracking. So some dent in deviant probability could be made simply by reducing the opportunities for various undesirable behaviors. Fewer homes would be burgled if they were better fortified; fewer cars would be stolen if specified hand prints were necessary to start them; fewer women would be raped if they avoided being alone with men capable of overpowering them; and fewer people might be assaulted if they were known to carry weapons (although advertising that one is carrying a weapon might also inspire some others to try to establish their dominance even in the face of danger, and it might lead to accidental injuries).

Note, however, that a motivated person theoretically is likely to commit some kind of deviance. If the opportunity for assault is not available, a person is likely to turn to another form of deviance with a similar control balance desirability—perhaps an act of road rage—and if the opportunity to vandalize an automobile is not available, a motivated person might turn to arson of a building. Whether the alternative chosen has an overall salutary effect may be problematic.

Potential Counter-Control

Control balance theory contends that people weigh the gain in control to be realized from various forms of deviance against the potential consequences of committing those acts, conceived in terms of loss of control. While this seems to imply a certain amount of "rationality," the theory actually maintains that such "balancing" often occurs quickly, semiconsciously, even habitually, and that it is often driven by emotion. As a result, most control balancing does not involve careful estimates of potential consequences. More often than not, the person is in an emotional state, and often such individuals lack self-control. Therefore, they take into account only the most glaring, obvious potential costs. It is only those who have large control surpluses and a high degree of self-control who can appreciate the more subtle likely consequences of deviance, and it is they who are likely to select deviant acts that are high in control balance desirability, involving less chance of counter-control. Nevertheless, social policies to increase the costs of deviance, thereby making counter-control more likely and more consequential, is one way that deviance might be reduced.

Our society already provides large legal penalties for some criminal offenses, but it neglects to provide such penalties for all types of criminal offenses, and the certainty of experiencing penalties of any kind is not generally very high. Moreover, there is often a dearth of informal costs for criminal or non-criminal acts of deviance. One ameliorative approach might be to bring more things under the criminal umbrella and to increase the chances of experiencing legal costs (perhaps by suspending constitutional protections or beefing up police forces), especially by stronger enforcement of those acts that now escape attention. An alternative solution is to bring more things within the domain of informal control. For instance, domestic violence may be more responsive to greater public awareness than to criminal penalties, and deviant acts of everyday living (such as breaking into a line, yelling at a subordinate, or betraying a lover) are generally affected only by informal responses. But informal sanctioning depends on a favorable culture, demographic circumstances (such as the size of the population), and dependence of individuals on social networks (those not integrated into such networks are not subject to control), all of which are hardly capable of being manipulated. Moreover, all efforts to increase costs of deviance also, ironically, feed into the general pool of control, shifting the control ratios of numerous individuals, which, as noted previously, affects the chances of provocation and deviant motivation.

Self-Control

As currently formulated, control balance theory treats self-control, a personality-like characteristic that individuals possess in greater or smaller amounts, as a central variable that influences crucial processes of control balancing. Self-control refers to the ability and tendency of people to be contemplative and restrained in their actions. Self-control is potentially important because it affects whether individuals anticipate provoking conditions and act to avoid them. It also influences whether individuals place themselves in situations where opportunities for deviance of various types are present. Finally, self-control affects the extent to which people act impulsively in response to criminal or deviant motivation either without taking into account potential counter-control or in defiance of potential costs. Thus, self-control is instrumental, though not necessarily determinative, in whether deviantly motivated individuals resort to misconduct that is less control balance desirable than implied by their control ratios. Therefore, one possible avenue for affecting deviance or crime is to increase self-control among individuals.

Theorists contend that self-control is largely learned, with most of the learning occurring in childhood, and that self-control is a product of the socialization practices of childhood caregivers. Theoretically, self-control does not change much once the child leaves the home, remaining relatively constant during the life course, at least in comparison with others from a given cohort. However, even if self-control is learned in the childhood context, there is some possibility of policy manipulation to spread successful child-rearing techniques more widely among caregivers or to help create familial circumstances conducive to effective child rearing. Presumably, self-control is maximized among children when caregivers love them enough to monitor their activities and act when misbehavior is discovered. Effectiveness, of course, assumes that loving caregivers also have the resources and are in circumstances that permit actual monitoring, but it also assumes that caregivers recognize misbehavior when it occurs. Finally, those who would produce strong self-control must express disapproval, correct the child, or impose punishments.

One potential flaw in modern societies, particularly in the United States, is the absence of training for parenthood. Strangely enough, individuals must be certified for all manner of occupations, they must demonstrate skills to drive legally, and they must be licensed even to marry. However, any person is permitted to produce and raise children without authorization or demonstrated skill, provided he or she does not abuse or neglect them. Most people deal with children the way they were dealt with—that is, if their parents employed techniques producing weak self-control, so do they. Moreover, circumstances of life often prevent caregivers from employing effective techniques even when they know how to do otherwise. For example, employment outside the household may restrict parents' ability to monitor children. Single parenthood, especially of more than one child, may have the same effect. Thus, not only is weak self-control likely to be reproduced from one generation to another, but the conditions of modern living in which both parents participate in the labor force or there is only one caregiver likely increase the pool of individuals with weak self-control.

Policy, then, might require that individuals who want to produce children undergo training for child rearing, and it might provide public support to ensure that parents are capable of exercising the correct techniques. In effect, the state might require a license for child rearing, contingent on training. Children born to parents without prior authorization or whose caregivers, even though authorized, were found to use destructive child-rearing practices might be declared wards of the state to be placed with trained adoptive or foster parents. In addition, if authorized parents were financially unable to monitor the child, the state might provide subsidies. If self-control is a result of parenting, then such policies might help improve self-control in a society. And if self-control is crucial in control balancing, as the theory contends, then such policies might have long-range indirect effects on the possibility of criminal or deviant behavior, especially on the types of deviance employed.

Such policies, especially those involving governmental intervention in the child-production process, would violate deeply felt and widely shared notions about human rights and personal freedom and for that reason would be difficult to initiate. Similarly, government programs to provide aid to parents have not been popular in the United States, mainly because of the ideology of personal responsibility and the suspicion that recipients of aid are "undeserving." Furthermore, the idea of official approval of specific child-rearing techniques assumes a degree of consensus among the population that is highly unrealistic. But more important from a control balance perspective is that such policies themselves imply an additional level of control imposed on potential parents. As we have already seen, any form of control plays into the general repertoire of control ratios and thus may have unintended, perhaps destructive, consequences.

For instance, these additional controls might shift some would-be parents into different zones of imbalance where they might engage in more or different kinds of deviance than before—even while helping to produce better self-control among their offspring. Whether the trade-off would be favorable is unknown.

Summary and Conclusion

Scientific theories, even if correct, do not always imply practical policy applications. Control balance theory in particular deals with variables that are difficult to manipulate and that have hydraulic relationships with each other. Consequently, it is difficult to imagine policy innovations that might have large ameliorative effects that are both politically and socially feasible. Moreover, even if changes in crucial variables were possible, their alteration might produce changes in other variables relevant to the production of deviant behavior, sometimes increasing the chances of deviance and at other times changing the nature of the deviance likely to be committed. Such outcomes may not have a net desirable effect.

Nevertheless, it is possible to imagine, at least in the abstract, potential modifications in things affecting control ratios of a population, the chances of circumstances arising that remind people of control imbalances, the likelihood of deviant motivation emerging, opportunities for deviance of various types, the potential for counter-control, and the prevalence of low self-control among individuals in a population. Addressing the full causal chain implied by control balance theory is far more complicated, however. Perhaps the most practical, though limited, potential policy intervention would be to train people to anticipate and manage provocation to avoid becoming motivated for deviance. It is an intervention likely to be accepted by the public; the institutional mechanisms are in place to implement it (especially in schools); and it appears to be a policy with minimal chances of adversely affecting other variables in the control-balancing process while offering some hope for reducing at least some of the more undesirable forms of deviance.

2   ROBERT AGNEW

Controlling Crime

Recommendations from
General Strain Theory

The core idea of general strain theory (GST) is quite simple: when people are treated in a negative manner, they often become upset and may respond with crime (Agnew 1992, 2006a, 2006b). GST, however, elaborates on this idea in several ways. It describes (1) the types of negative treatment or strains most likely to result in crime; (2) why these strains increase the likelihood of crime; and (3) why some people are more likely than others to respond to strains with crime. These elaborations are summarized in the first section of this chapter, as is the evidence on GST.

The core policy recommendations of GST are likewise quite simple: we can reduce crime by reducing exposure to strains and the tendency to respond to strains with crime (Agnew 1995, 2006a). There are several ways to reduce exposure to strains, certain of which involve altering the social environment. In particular, we can (1) eliminate strains conducive to crime; (2) alter strains to make them less conducive to crime; (3) make it easier for people to avoid strains; and (4) remove individuals from strains. While we can accomplish these objectives in a variety of ways, three general strategies involve creating "strain responders," setting up "social support" centers, and altering the larger social environment. These efforts to reduce exposure to strains are described in the second section of the chapter.

It is also possible to reduce exposure to strains by working with individuals. In particular, we can (1) equip individuals with the skills and resources to better avoid strains; and (2) teach individuals to interpret the social environment in ways that minimize "subjective" strain. These strategies are described in the third section of the chapter. It is important to note, however, that the second strategy should be used with great caution. We do not want to teach individuals to accept or tolerate strains that should be altered.

Finally, we can control crime by reducing the likelihood that individuals will cope with strains through crime. In particular, we can (1) improve the coping skills and resources of individuals; (2) provide individuals with more assistance in coping; (3) increase their levels of social control; (4) reduce their disposition for criminal coping; and (5) reduce their exposure to situations conducive to crime. The fourth section of the chapter describes strategies in these areas.

Certain of the strategies described in this chapter are already in use and have shown some success in reducing crime. None of these strategies was explicitly inspired by GST, but they nevertheless reduce exposure to strains or the likelihood of coping with strains through crime. These strategies are described in detail in numerous places, so this chapter simply presents brief descriptions (for more detailed descriptions and reviews of the effectiveness of these strategies, see Agnew 1995, 2005, 2006a; Andrews and Bonta 2003; Aos, Miller, and Drake 2006; Currie 1998; Farrington and Welsh 2007; Greenwood 2006).[1] Other strategies are based explicitly on GST but have not yet been employed to any significant degree.

An Overview of General Strain Theory

Strains Most Likely to Increase Crime

Strains refer to events and conditions disliked by individuals (Agnew 1992, 2001, 2006a, 2006b). Examples of strains include child abuse, unemployment, and the failure to achieve one's monetary goals. GST makes a distinction between "objective" and "subjective" strains. Objective strains refer to events and conditions disliked by most people in a given group. Subjective strains refer to events and conditions disliked by the particular people who have experienced them. People differ in their subjective reaction to the same objective strains. For example, some people may experience a divorce as quite upsetting, while others may experience it as a cause for celebration. This fact suggests one mechanism for reducing crime: reduce the likelihood that people will subjectively evaluate objective strains in a negative manner (see below).

GST classifies strains into three groups: the failure to achieve valued goals (e.g., monetary success, masculinity goals); the actual or threatened loss of positively valued stimuli (e.g., financial loss, the death of a friend); and the actual or threatened presentation of negatively valued stimuli (e.g., verbal and physical abuse). Literally hundreds of specific strains fall into these broad categories. Not all of these strains are conducive to crime, however. Rather, strains

---

[1] See also the Blueprints for Violence Prevention Web site at www.colorado.edu/cspv/blueprints and the Campbell Crime and Justice Group Web site at www.campbellcollaboration.org/CCJG.

are most likely to lead to crime when they are high in magnitude, are perceived as unjust, are associated with low social control, and create some pressure or incentive for criminal coping.

A strain that is high in magnitude has several characteristics. It is high in degree (e.g., a large financial loss, severe physical abuse). It is frequent, of long duration, and recent (e.g., chronic unemployment, ongoing abuse). And it is high in centrality. That is, it threatens the individual's central goals, values, needs, identities, or activities. For example, a central goal for most people in the United States is monetary success. As a consequence, individuals often become quite upset when the achievement of this goal is threatened (e.g., they lose their job, experience a significant financial loss).

Strains are likely to be seen as unjust when they involve the voluntary and deliberate violation of a relevant justice norm. To illustrate, the voluntary and deliberate infliction of strains is more likely to be seen as unjust in the following circumstances: Victims believe the strain they experienced is undeserved and not in the service of some greater good (e.g., children are punished for misdeeds they did not commit). No rationale for the infliction of the strain is provided, and victims had no voice in the decision to inflict the strain (e.g., victims did not have the opportunity to tell "their side of the story" before being punished). The strain violates strongly held social norms or values (e.g., child abuse). And the strain is very different from the past treatment of the victim in similar circumstances or from the treatment of similar others (e.g., a teacher punishes the victim more harshly than others who engage in similar misbehavior).

Social controls refer to those factors that restrain individuals from engaging in crime (see Agnew 2005). Many individuals do not engage in crime because they are high in direct controls—that is, they are surrounded by others who set clear rules that prohibit misbehavior, closely monitor behavior, and consistently sanction violations of rules in an appropriate manner. These others may be parents, teachers, neighbors, employers, and police. Individuals also refrain from crime because they have strong emotional bonds to conventional others, such as parents, spouses, and teachers. Individuals do not want to hurt these others or jeopardize these bonds by engaging in crime. Further, individuals refrain from crime because they have a large investment in conventional activities, such as school and work. For example, they have good grades or "good" jobs. Again, they do not want to jeopardize this investment through crime. Finally, individuals refrain from crime because they have been taught that crime is wrong or immoral. Some strains are associated with high social control—for example, parents impose rules that juveniles do not like and sanction juveniles for violating those rules. Other strains are associated with low social control. For example, individuals who are chronically unemployed have little investment in conventional activities. These strains are more likely to result in crime, since individuals who experience them face weaker restraints to crime.

Finally, strains differ in the extent to which they create pressure or incentive for criminal coping. Certain strains are more easily resolved through crime than others, creating more incentive for criminal coping. For example, the strain involving a desperate need for money is more easily resolved through crime than is the strain involving the inability to do well in school. Also, certain strains involve exposure to others who model crime, reinforce crime, teach beliefs favorable to crime, or otherwise pressure individuals to engage in crime (see Agnew 2005, 2006a). For example, individuals who are bullied by peers are exposed to others who model crime.

Drawing on these criteria, GST lists several strains that are conducive to crime:

- Parental rejection
- Supervision/discipline that is erratic, excessive, or harsh
- Child abuse and neglect
- Negative secondary-school experiences (low grades, negative treatment by teachers, experiencing school as boring and a waste of time)
- Abusive peer relations, including verbal and physical abuse
- Work in the secondary labor market (jobs involving low pay, no or few benefits, little opportunity for advancement, unpleasant working conditions)
- Chronic unemployment
- Marital problems, including frequent conflicts and verbal and physical abuse
- Failure to achieve selected goals, including thrills/excitement, high levels of autonomy, masculine status, and the desire for much money in a short period of time
- Criminal victimization
- Residence in very poor communities
- Homelessness
- Discrimination based on race/ethnicity, gender, and religion

Research suggests that these strains increase the likelihood of crime, with certain of these strains being among the most important causes of crime (Agnew 2001, 2006a, 2006b). It should be noted, however, that other theories also predict that certain of these factors increase the likelihood of crime. For example, social control theories predict that chronic unemployment increases crime, because unemployed individuals have less to lose by engaging in crime. GST is distinguished from these other theories not only in terms of the causes of crime that it examines, but also in terms of its explanation of why these causes increase crime.

Why Strains Increase the Likelihood of Crime

GST states that strains contribute to a range of negative emotions, such as anger, frustration, and depression. These emotions create pressure for corrective action: people feel bad and want to do something about it. The emotion of anger is especially conducive to crime because it energizes the individual for action, lowers inhibitions, and creates a desire for revenge. Individuals may turn to crime as a way to reduce or escape from their strains (e.g., theft to achieve monetary goals, running away to escape abuse at home), seek revenge against others (e.g., assault the peers who abuse you), and alleviate negative emotions (e.g., through illicit drug use).

Strains may also lead to crime for other reasons. They may reduce the types of social control described above, thereby making it easier for individuals to engage in crime. For example, individuals who are abused by parents may come to dislike their parents. Individuals who find school boring and are harassed by teachers may come to hate school. Individuals who are chronically unemployed may come to believe that theft is not very bad.

Strains may also foster the social learning of crime (see Agnew 2005). Strained individuals may sometimes band together to reduce their strain. For example, juveniles who are threatened by others may form a gang. These individuals then encourage one another to engage in crime. Also, strains may lead individuals to develop beliefs favorable to crime. Individuals who are unable to achieve their monetary goals through legal channels, for example, may come to believe that theft and drug selling are sometimes justified.

Research provides some support for these arguments, with studies suggesting that negative emotions such as anger partly explain the effect of strains on crime. There is also evidence that strains may reduce social control, lead to beliefs favorable to crime, and increase association with delinquent peers (Agnew 2006a, 2006b).

Why Are Some Individuals More Likely than Others to Cope with Strains through Crime?

Most individuals do not respond to strains with crime. Rather, they cope in a legal manner. For example, they may negotiate with the peers who harass them, work harder in an effort to obtain the money they desire, report the criminals who victimize them to the police, or simply endure their unpleasant working conditions. GST states that several factors increase the likelihood that individuals will cope with strains through crime.

Criminal coping is more likely among individuals with poor coping skills and resources. For example, it is more likely among individuals who have poor problem-solving and social skills, who have limited educations and financial resources, and who have personality traits such as negative emotionality and low constraint. Individuals with these traits are easily upset, are quick to anger, are impulsive, like to take risks, and have little concern for the feelings or rights of others. Criminal coping is also more likely among those who are low in conventional social support. Such individuals do not have others they can turn to for help, including emotional support, advice, financial assistance, and direct assistance in coping.

Criminal coping is more likely among those who are low in social control. Such individuals have less to lose when they cope with strains through crime. Further, criminal coping is more likely among those who hold beliefs favorable to crime. Such beliefs, in fact, often define crime as a justifiable or excusable response to a range of strains, such as provocations by others and the inability to obtain money through legal channels. Related to this, criminal coping is more likely among those with criminal friends. Such friends often reinforce criminal coping, model criminal coping, teach beliefs favorable to criminal coping, and otherwise encourage such coping. Finally, criminal coping is more likely among individuals who are exposed to situations where the costs of crime are low and the benefits are high. For example, criminal coping is more likely when strained individuals encounter attractive targets for crime and no one is around to sanction crime.

Research on the factors that influence the response to strain has produced mixed results (Agnew 2006a, 2006b). Some studies find that strained individuals are more likely to engage in criminal coping when they possess the factors listed above, such as the personality traits of negative emotionality/low constraint, beliefs favorable to crime, and association with delinquent peers. Other studies, however, fail to find this. Agnew (2006a, 2006b) suggests that these mixed results stem from methodological problems in the research in this area (also see Mazerolle and Maahs 2000).

Policy Implication of GST:
Reducing Strains by Altering the Environment

The most obvious policy recommendation of GST is to reduce the exposure of individuals to strains—for example, the extent to which individuals are abused by parents, bullied by peers, or chronically unemployed. Several strategies for reducing exposure to strains are described below and involve altering the social environment.

Eliminate Strains

There is little justification or necessity for most of the strains that are conducive to crime. We should therefore make an effort to eliminate these strains.

It is, of course, unlikely that we will be entirely successful in doing so. Nevertheless, many programs have tried to reduce the likelihood that people will treat others in a negative manner. Certain of these programs have been able to substantially reduce the incidence of some strains—such as child abuse, the use of harsh or erratic discipline by parents, negative treatment by teachers, and bullying (see the references cited in the introduction). These programs typically address some or all of the reasons people mistreat others.

People may mistreat others because they have personality traits conducive to mistreatment—for example, they are easily upset, become quite angry when upset, and are unable to exercise much self-control. People may mistreat others because they themselves are under much strain or stress. A parent, for example, may be struggling with a range of financial problems, may be trying to raise a "difficult" child who frequently misbehaves, and may herself be the victim of spousal abuse. These strains increase the likelihood that the parent will engage in harsh, even abusive, behavior toward the child. People may mistreat others because they have been taught to do so, perhaps by their parents, peers, or community residents. Related to this, people are sometimes differentially reinforced for such behaviors. An individual who bullies others, for example, may be praised by friends and seldom sanctioned. Finally, people may mistreat others because they have little knowledge of alternative behaviors. Some parents and teachers, for example, engage in harsh disciplinary methods partly because they have never been taught alternative methods.

A range of programs attempt to address these causes of mistreatment. Certain of these programs focus on individuals who have already engaged in negative treatment or are at high risk of doing so (e.g., offenders, teenage parents in poor communities). Other programs focus on broader groups, such as all of the teachers or students in a school. These programs may teach these people to better control their anger and exercise more self-control. They may attempt to reduce the strains faced by these people. For example, they may attempt to solve certain of the financial, child-care, or spousal-abuse problems faced by parents. These programs may attempt to end the differential reinforcement of negative behaviors. Individuals will be taught that such behaviors are wrong. The behavior of individuals will be monitored, and negative behaviors will be sanctioned. At the same time, individuals will be taught more appropriate behaviors, such as more effective ways to discipline children and students. Individuals will be reinforced for the use of such behaviors. These behaviors are also typically self-reinforcing in that they allow individuals to better achieve their goals (e.g., better maintain discipline in the classroom).

Not all such programs are successful. Successful programs are typically intensive, involving much contact with the participants and lasting several months or longer. They employ a variety of instructional techniques, including direct instruction, demonstrations, role-playing, and real-world applications with feedback. They provide some opportunity to monitor the behavior of participants. And there is typically a good rapport between the program staff and participants. Further, even well-designed programs sometimes have trouble enrolling those individuals who need them the most. It is often possible, however, to entice individuals to participate through various incentives or to compel them to participate if they are under the control of some agency, such as the school system or the courts.

Alter Strains to Make Them Less Conducive to Crime

Certain strains are difficult to eliminate because they serve useful functions or because larger social forces make their elimination difficult. For example, it is likely that teachers will continue to give out low grades, people will continue to work in the secondary labor market, and some individuals will be unable to achieve their economic goals. While we cannot eliminate such strains, we can alter them in ways that make them less conducive to crime. As indicated, strains conducive to crime are high in magnitude, perceived as unjust, associated with low social control, and create some pressure or incentive for criminal coping. Altering one or more of these characteristics, then, can reduce the likelihood that strains will lead to crime.

The magnitude of strains can be reduced through a focus on their degree, frequency and duration, and centrality. For example, we might improve the conditions of work for those in the secondary labor market by raising the minimum wage and requiring the provision of certain benefits, such as health insurance. We might reduce the severity of sanctions administered by parents and teachers by banning or discouraging the use of such practices as corporal punishment. Or we might reduce the duration of unemployment by expanding the use of job training and creating jobs in the public sector. It is more difficult to reduce the centrality of strains, because this involves altering the core goals, values, or identities of individuals. Nevertheless, it is possible to envision efforts in this area. For example, steps might be taken to encourage individuals to place less emphasis on certain goals, such as monetary success and masculine status.

Second, efforts can be made to reduce the perceived injustice of strains. Consider, for example, sanctions administered by parents, school officials, employers, and criminal justice officials. Such sanctions are often perceived as unjust and sometimes increase the likelihood of subsequent crime. We might reduce the perceived injustice of sanctions by teaching sanctioning agents to (1) provide individuals with the opportunity to state their side of the case; (2) treat individuals in a respectful manner, avoiding verbally and physically abusive behavior; (3) explain the rationale behind sanctions, making the case that the sanctions are deserved or for some greater good; and (4) ensure that their sanctions are consistent over time and across individuals who engage in similar misbehavior.

Third, efforts can be made to increase the level of social control associated with strains such as low grades, unemployment, and work in the secondary labor market. For example, students who receive very low grades or severe sanctions at school might be targeted for a range of interventions designed to increase control. In particular, they might be matched with mentors and placed in special programs, such as recreational and job-training programs, in an effort to increase bonding to conventional others, opportunities for success, and direct control (e.g., monitoring). A type of strain normally associated with low social control, then, may act as a trigger to increase social control. Similar strategies can be developed for those who lose their jobs, work in the secondary labor market, or experience other strains associated with low control.

Fourth, we can reduce the extent to which certain strains create some incentive or pressure for criminal coping. One way to do this is to make it more difficult to resolve these strains through crime. For example, we might target individuals who experience certain strains for increased monitoring. At the same time, efforts can be made to increase opportunities for resolving these strains through conventional channels. Students who receive low grades, for example, might be provided with tutoring, opportunities for extra-credit work, or alternative avenues for achievement. These activities, along with efforts to increase social control, should also reduce the likelihood that these strains will increase association with delinquent peers.

One approach that attempts to accomplish many of the above goals is the restorative justice initiative (Braithwaite 2002). This initiative essentially proposes an alternative way to officially sanction individuals. The sanctions now imposed by the criminal justice system generally do little to reduce subsequent offending and may even increase such offending (see Agnew 2005). This occurs in part because such sanctions often function as strains conducive to crime. The sanctions are often high in magnitude and administered in ways perceived as unjust. Offenders, for example, may be treated in a gruff manner and given little opportunity to tell their side of the story. The sanctions often isolate offenders from conventional others and make it difficult to find employment, thereby reducing social control. Partly as a consequence, the sanctions may increase association with criminal peers.

The restorative justice approach avoids these negative effects. At the heart of the approach is a conference involving the crime victim, the offender, selected associates of the victim and offender, and community residents. The victim and others describe the harm caused by the crime and have the opportunity to question the offender. The offender, in turn, has the opportunity to tell his or her side of the story. All of the involved parties then develop a plan for repairing the harm that was done. This plan typically involves such things as an apology and restitution to the victim, as well as community service. An effort is made to avoid harsh sanctions such as incarceration. Once the harm is repaired, the offender is forgiven. Efforts are also made to address the offender's problems and reintegrate him or her back into conventional society. The restorative justice approach, then, reduces the magnitude of sanctions, increases the perceived justice of sanctions, and takes steps to enhance social control and reduce the likelihood of association with delinquent peers. Research suggests that this approach is somewhat effective in reducing subsequent offending (Braithwaite 2002).

Make It Easier to Avoid Strains

In addition to eliminating and altering strains, we can make it easier for people to avoid strains. In particular, people are sometimes unaware that certain behaviors on their part might result in negative treatment. We can take steps to make them more aware of this fact. Parents, teachers, employers, criminal justice officials, and others can be taught to more clearly state rules for behavior and the consequences of violating those rules. This will not only help individuals avoid acts that might result in negative treatment; it will also increase the perceived justice of the sanctions that are administered.

People are also sometimes unaware that negative treatment is more likely in certain circumstances—including certain places, certain times, and around certain people. We might also make people more aware of this fact so they can avoid such circumstances or take other precautions to reduce the likelihood of negative treatment. This already occurs on an informal basis. Some individuals, for example, know that they should avoid certain areas at night or avoid certain people if they want to escape negative treatment. In certain cases, however, we might better warn people about circumstances in which the likelihood of strain is high. This was done in Newport News, for example, when sailors and businesspeople were warned about the dangers of soliciting prostitutes in certain areas of the city where the prostitutes were often men in disguise who robbed their customers (Spelman and Eck 1987). Care, however, must be taken in issuing such warnings. Labeling someone a dangerous person or a certain area a dangerous place can have negative consequences (Agnew 2005), so the potential benefits of such labeling must be compared with the costs.

Even when people are aware that negative treatment is more likely in certain circumstances, they may be unable to avoid such circumstances. This is particularly true of adolescents, who are generally forced to interact with a given set of peers, teachers, and community residents. Adolescents who are negatively treated by these people generally have few legal options for avoiding them (see Agnew 1985). We might provide adolescents with more such options. For example, we might make it easier for adolescents to change classes or even schools when they cannot "get along" with their teachers or certain peers.

Or we might create supervised recreational programs that will provide adolescents with a safe haven from the dangers of the street.

Finally, we might attempt to isolate those places where strain is likely and those people who frequently inflict strain. For example, we might attempt to isolate certain high-risk businesses in a "red light" district, confine drug markets to certain areas, or place belligerent students in special classes or schools. We might also place students and groups with ongoing disputes in separate classes or even schools. It is possible, then, to take a variety of steps that make it easier for people to avoid strains.

Remove Individuals from Strains

In those cases where we cannot eliminate, alter, or make it easier to avoid strains, we might remove individuals from strains. This is already done to a limited extent. Children are sometimes removed from abusive families. Families are sometimes given the option of transferring their juveniles from schools designated as dangerous. And some programs have made it possible for poor families to move out of impoverished, high-crime communities (see the references cited in the introduction). Certain of these programs have been successful at reducing subsequent crime. Such programs, however, should be used with caution. Individuals removed from their families are sometimes placed in situations where they continue to suffer abuse, although steps can be taken to minimize this risk. And programs that allow individuals to leave high-risk schools or communities have the potential to make conditions worse for those who are left behind.

Create "Strain Responders"

In sum, we might eliminate strains, alter strains to make them less conducive to crime, make it easier for individuals to avoid strains, and—if necessary—remove individuals from strains. Several strategies for achieving these goals have been described, and many are already in use, although none was explicitly designed to reduce exposure to strains. There is, however, a general strategy for achieving all of these goals that is not in use. This strategy involves the creation of "strain responders." Strain responders play a role similar to the role played by many parents with young children.

Parents often keep close watch over their young children and their children's environment, in large part to protect their children from harm or strains. Parents may eliminate strains or potential sources of strain in the environment. For example, they may remove hazardous objects from their homes. Parents may help their children avoid strains. For example, parents may tell their children that certain activities are risky or that they should not associate with certain dangerous others. And parents may intervene when strains occur in an effort to end or alleviate the strains. For example, parents may intervene to end a dispute with another child. Parents, then, act like "strain responders." (I might mention that this critical parental role is often overlooked by criminologists, who instead focus on parents as sources of social control or social learning for conformity [see Agnew 2005].)

Parents, however, dramatically reduce these behaviors as their children become adolescents. This is partly due to the fact that adolescents spend much less time at home and are more reluctant to share information with parents, making monitoring difficult. It is also due to the fact that adolescents are expected to cope on their own. And it is due to the belief that others, such as teachers and the police, are acting as strain responders when necessary. Unfortunately, adolescents often lack the skills and resources to cope effectively on their own. Adolescents often spend much time away from adults who might act as strain responders. And many adults fail to act as strain responders. These facts may help explain why crime increases as juveniles move from childhood to adolescence (see Agnew 2005).

It is possible, however, to create strain responders who perform many of the same functions as parents. We cannot place these responders everywhere, of course. But such responders can focus their efforts on the "hot spots" for strain—that is, those places, times, people, and events that are at high risk for strain. One central task of the responders, in fact, would be to determine the hot spots for strains conducive to crime. They may discover, for example, that much peer abuse occurs in and around schools during certain times of the day, such as immediately after school. They may further discover that peer abuse is common among certain individuals and groups, such as juveniles on probation, gang members, and people with a history of repeat victimization. Further, the likelihood of peer abuse may be especially high when these individuals and groups are in the midst of certain "storylines," such as ongoing disputes (see Agnew 2006c). Criminologists can assist strain responders in identifying the hot spots for strains in both general and particular communities.

In addition to monitoring, strain responders would engage in the other activities that parents perform. In particular, responders would attempt to eliminate strains when possible, alter strains to make them less conducive to crime, help individuals and groups avoid strains, remove individuals from strains when necessary, and arrange for the delivery of outside services when necessary. Further, responders would try to equip individuals with the skills and resources to reduce exposure to strains on their own and to minimize the strain they inflict on others (see below). Strain responders might be specially hired to perform these tasks, and we might train teachers, community activists, religious figures, police, and probation officers to better engage in these tasks. It is, of course, important that the monitors have a good rapport with and be respected by those they are monitoring.

We might also take steps to increase the extent to which people in the environment "naturally" engage in strain responding. For example, we can encourage adolescents and other high-risk individuals to spend more time in locations where they are supervised by conventional adults. Such locations might include supervised recreational programs and shopping malls. Related to this, we might take steps to increase the "collective efficacy" of community residents so they intervene more often when strains occur (see Geason and Wilson 1998; Sampson 2002).

As an illustration, a strain responder might be assigned to a school with a high rate of crime. The responder might be a former gang member who has become active in community affairs and has a good rapport with the students. The first task of this responder would be to identify those places or times, people, and events where the likelihood of strain is greatest. The responder might do this by, among other things, talking with students, teachers, police, and others; reading material prepared by criminologists; or working with others to conduct a local survey. The responder would then attempt to monitor these hot spots. This might involve developing an ongoing relationship with high-risk individuals and groups, and it might involve spending time at the locations and events where the risk of strain is highest (e.g., the school cafeteria during lunch, the school grounds after school, football games). The responder would attempt to reduce exposure to strains in all of the ways indicated above. For example, the responder might attempt to resolve disputes between individuals and gangs; provide advice on avoiding or alleviating strains; and obtain mentors, tutoring, and other services for students in need.

Create "Social-Support Centers"

A second general strategy for eliminating, altering, avoiding, or removing individuals from strains involves the creation of "social-support centers" (see Cullen 1994). Individuals who are experiencing or who anticipate experiencing strains are often unable to cope on their own, and they frequently lack others they can turn to for assistance. We can help these individuals by creating readily available social support centers that offer a range of services designed to reduce exposure to strains. These centers would be easily accessible, would provide a range of supportive services under one roof, and would match individuals with case managers who provide or facilitate access to appropriate services. The strain responders described above might be employed by such centers and would certainly use the centers as a resource.

Suppose, for example, that a woman is experiencing spousal abuse. She might go to a social support center on her own or be referred to the center by a strain responder, police, or others. A case manager at the center would talk with the abused individual to learn more about her background and the strains she is experiencing. The case manager might then engage in one or more of the following activities: notify the police, arrange anger-management therapy and other services for the abuser, arrange marital counseling for the couple, closely monitor the home environment for evidence of further abuse, place the abuse victim and her children in a safe location, or arrange job training and child care for the abuse victim. To give another example, suppose an individual anticipates severe financial problems, such as the inability to pay his rent. A case manager might do such things as arrange an emergency loan or grant, provide credit counseling, help him secure subsidized housing, or arrange educational or vocational training. Note that case managers attempt not only to resolve current strains but also to equip individuals with the resources and skills to avoid future strains.

Alter the Larger Social Environment

The strategies listed above focus on the individual's immediate social environment, including his or her family, peer, classroom, and work environment. Reducing exposure to strains, however, also requires that we change the larger social environment, which directly contributes to the negative treatment that individuals experience. For example, values in the larger society may contribute to racist and sexist behavior. A shortage of decent jobs may contribute to unemployment and the inability to achieve economic goals. The larger social environment may also contribute to negative treatment in an indirect manner. Most notably, problems in the economy contribute to a range of family, school, and other strains—including family violence and poor academic performance (see Agnew 2005; Currie 1998). Certain criminologists have suggested a number of social changes that should do much to eliminate or alter many of the strains conducive to crime. These changes involve attracting more jobs to poor communities through a variety of incentives; creating new jobs in the public sector, including jobs that focus on child care, health care, education, and public safety; requiring that all jobs pay a "living wage"; and increasing social services, including health-care, child-care, and housing assistance.

Policy Implication of GST: Reducing Strains by Altering the Characteristics of Individuals

Individuals are not passive entities who all react in the same way to a given social environment. Individuals differ in terms of how they perceive, experience, and respond to the environment. There is good reason to believe that such differences influence the amount of strain experienced. In particular, some individuals are more likely than others to experience certain events and conditions as negative, to elicit negative treatment from others, to select or sort themselves into environments where the likelihood of negative treatment is high, and to have difficulty achieving their goals in a given environment. Given these facts, we can reduce exposure to strains by altering the characteristics of individuals—as well as by altering the environment to which individuals are exposed.

Equip Individuals with the Traits and Skills to Avoid Strains Conducive to Crime

Some individuals act in ways that increase their exposure to strains. This is particularly true of individuals who possess the traits of low constraint and negative emotionality (see above). In popular terms, such individuals might be described as "mean" or "nasty" and "out of control." It is also true of individuals with poor social skills and problem-solving skills. And it is true of individuals who lack traits, such as intelligence and good study skills, that are necessary to do well in school and on the job.

Such individuals often elicit negative treatment from others, including parents, teachers, peers, and employers. Parents, for example, may become frustrated with the behavior of such individuals and respond by employing harsh, even abusive, disciplinary techniques. Teachers may give such individuals low grades. Peers may regularly get into conflicts with such individuals that involve verbal and physical abuse. And employers may fire or regularly reprimand such individuals.

In addition, such individuals may select or sort themselves into environments where negative treatment is common. Juveniles who are low in constraint and high in negative emotionality, for example, may be rejected by conventional peers and decide to associate with delinquent peers, who engage in the risky and aggressive behaviors they prefer. Delinquent peers, however, are more likely to abuse one another and elicit abuse from others. Juveniles with weak academic skills may drop out of school and find that the only jobs available to them are in the secondary labor market. And individuals with poor social skills and problem-solving skills may develop romantic involvements with people like themselves, increasing the likelihood of relationship problems of various sorts.

Finally, individuals with these traits have more trouble achieving many of their goals through legal channels. For example, they have more trouble achieving monetary success through such accepted methods as getting a good education and then a good job.

A number of programs have shown some success in equipping individuals with the traits and skills that allow them to better avoid strains. Some programs attempt to teach juveniles to better control their anger and exercise more self-control, thinking before they act. Other programs teach juveniles a range of social and problem-solving skills. And still other programs attempt to equip juveniles with the academic and vocational skills they need to do well in school and get good jobs. Many of these programs have shown some success in reducing crime (see the references cited in the introduction).

The extent to which the success of these programs is due to the fact that they reduce exposure to strains is not clear. These programs also increase control and sometimes reduce exposure to delinquent peers. Nevertheless, such programs are quite compatible with GST. In fact, such programs have a critical role to play in reducing exposure to strains. While it is important to alter the individual's environment in the ways described above, the effect of such alterations may be short-lived unless we also alter the individual traits that increase exposure to strains.

Teach Individuals to Interpret/Perceive the Environment in Ways That Minimize Subjective Strains

All of the above strategies attempt to reduce the individual's exposure to events and conditions that are generally disliked by others (i.e., objective strains). As indicated earlier, however, individuals sometimes differ in their subjective evaluation of the same events and conditions (i.e., their subjective strain). For example, two individuals may be bumped by another person while walking down the street. The first individual may interpret the bump as an accident and dismiss it as unimportant. The second individual may interpret the bump as deliberate and view it as a significant challenge to his masculinity. The second individual, therefore, is higher in subjective strain—interpreting the bump as a strongly disliked event. This difference in interpretation suggests a final strategy for reducing exposure to strains.

We can teach individuals to perceive or interpret the environment in ways that reduce their level of subjective strain. For example, an individual may believe she is being mistreated by her spouse. Rather than change the behavior of her spouse, we may attempt to convince her that she is not being mistreated. This strategy, of course, must be used with great caution. Many individuals are experiencing strains that most people would define as severe (i.e., major objective strains). We do not want to convince people to define these strains as minor. We do not, for example, want to convince someone that being abused by her spouse is a minor event. Some individuals, however, are not experiencing objective strains but are nevertheless high in subjective strain. That is, some individuals strongly dislike events and conditions that most people would define as trivial. This may occur for several reasons.

As Kenneth Dodge and others have found, some individuals have an "attributional bias," such that they are more likely to attribute hostile intentions to the acts of others (Dodge and Schwartz 1997). They are more likely, for example, to interpret a bump while walking down the street as a deliberate provocation than as an accident. Also, some individuals possess personality traits that increase their sensitivity to perceived slights and provocations. This is especially true of individuals high in negative emotionality. Finally, some individuals may be especially sensitive to certain events and conditions because they place a relatively strong emphasis on certain values, identities, or goals. Individuals who are highly concerned about their masculine status, for example, may be more likely to interpret certain acts as challenges to their masculinity and to become very upset at such challenges. For example, such individuals may interpret a stare from another as a major provocation.

Given these arguments, we can reduce subjective strain in several ways. We can reduce the attributional bias of individuals so that they are less likely to attribute hostile intentions incorrectly to the acts of others. We can reduce the individual's level of negative emotionality through anger-management and other programs. And we can attempt to alter certain of the individual's values, goals, and identity. We might, for example, attempt to convince individuals to place less emphasis on monetary success, or we might attempt to alter their masculine identity so they are not so sensitive to minor slights and provocations.

Policy Implication of GST: Reduce the Likelihood That Individuals Will Cope with Strains through Crime

There is much we can do to reduce the exposure of individuals to objective and subjective strains. It is unlikely, however, that we can eliminate all exposure to strains. It is therefore important that we also try to reduce the likelihood that individuals will cope with strains through crime. A number of strategies are available here. Certain of these strategies overlap with those described above. For example, providing individuals with training in social skills and problem-solving skills not only helps them avoid strains; it also reduces the likelihood that they will cope with the strains they do encounter through crime. In addition, the strain responders, social support centers, and alterations in the larger social environment described above may reduce not only exposure to strains but also the likelihood of criminal coping. Strain responders, for example, may help individuals cope with strains in a legal manner by providing advice and other assistance.

Coping Skills and Resources

One obvious way to reduce the likelihood of criminal coping is to improve the coping skills and resources of individuals. A number of programs have shown some success in this area, including programs that attempt to improve social skills, problem-solving skills, and the ability to control one's anger. Such programs teach juveniles appropriate ways to handle a variety of strains, such as teasing by peers, criticism by teachers, and encounters with the police. These programs may also teach more general problem-solving skills. For example, they may teach juveniles the steps involved in evaluating a problem, developing possible solutions to the problem, and evaluating the desirability of the solutions. And programs may teach individuals how to recognize the early-warning signs of anger and take steps to control their anger. Still other programs attempt to improve the academic and vocational skills of individuals. Examples include preschool enrichment programs such as Head Start and vocational programs such as Job Corps.

Social Support

We can also attempt to increase the individual's level of social support so that others are available to help him or her cope in a legal manner (see Cullen 1994). In this area, some programs have attempted to teach parents and teachers how to provide more support to juveniles. Certain of these programs focus on juveniles at high risk for strain, such as those who are making the transition from correctional institutions back to the community. Other programs have provided juveniles with mentors, such as the Big Brothers Big Sisters program. Still other programs have provided help to individuals facing certain strains with government assistance, including unemployment and welfare assistance. Many of the programs in this area have shown some success at reducing crime.

Social Control

A range of programs also attempt to increase the individual's level of social control. These include parent-training programs that, among other things, aim to strengthen the bond between parent and child and improve parental supervision and discipline. They include school-based programs, which aim to enhance school performance, improve monitoring and discipline, and strengthen the bond to teachers and school. They also include vocational-training programs, which increase the individual's stake in conformity. As indicated earlier, individuals with a high level of social control are less likely to cope with strains through crime.

Beliefs and Criminal Peer Groups

Still other programs have attempted to change the individual's beliefs so they are less conducive to criminal coping. Related to this, certain programs have attempted to remove individuals from criminal peer groups or to change the nature of such groups. Programs in these areas have been less successful than programs in other areas, but some programs have shown signs of success. For example, certain programs have been able to alter beliefs favorable to crime, particularly programs that employ peer educators, actively involve juveniles in the instructional process, teach juveniles the skills to resist peer pressure, and try to get groups of juveniles—such as classroom groups—to take a public stand against crime.

Costs and Benefits of Crime.

Finally, some programs have tried to reduce the likelihood that individuals will be exposed to situations where the costs of crime are low and the benefits are high. After-school recreational programs are an example, since they increase the supervision to which individuals are subjected. Numerous other examples are provided in discussions of "situational crime prevention" (e.g., Eck 2002).

Conclusion

A range of strategies for reducing exposure to strains and the likelihood of coping with strains through crime were described. These strategies focus on both the individual and the individual's environment, including family, peer, school, work, community, and the larger society. The effectiveness of certain of these strategies in reducing crime has already been demonstrated, although it is not clear whether these strategies reduce crime for reasons related to general strain theory. Other strategies have not been tried, including the general strategies of creating strain responders and social support centers. It is clear, however, that GST offers a wealth of suggestions for reducing crime in our society.

References

Agnew, R. 1985. A revised strain theory of delinquency. *Social Forces* 64:435–451.

———. 1992. Foundation for a general strain theory of crime and delinquency. *Criminology* 30:47–87.

———. 1995. Controlling delinquency: Recommendations from general strain theory. In *Crime and public policy: Putting theory to work.* Ed. H. D. Barlow, 43–70. Boulder, Colo.: Westview Press.

———. 2001. Building on the foundation of general strain theory: Specifying the types of strain most likely to lead to crime and delinquency. *Journal of Research in Crime and Delinquency* 38:319–361.

———. 2005. *Juvenile delinquency: Causes and control.* Los Angeles: Roxbury.

———. 2006a. *Pressured into crime: An overview of general strain theory.* Los Angeles: Roxbury.

———. 2006b. General strain theory: Current status and directions for further research. In *Taking stock: The status of criminological theory,* Vol. 15. *Advances in criminological theory.* Ed. F. Cullen, J. Wright, and K. Blevins, 127–148. New Brunswick, N.J.: Transaction Publishers.

———. 2006c. Storylines as a neglected cause of crime. *Journal of Research in Crime and Delinquency* 43:119–147.

Andrews, D. A., and J. Bonta. 2003. *The psychology of criminal conduct.* Cincinnati: Anderson Publishing.

Aos, S., M. G. Miller, and E. Drake. 2006. *Evidence-based public policy options to reduce future prison construction, criminal justice costs, and crime rates.* Olympia: Washington State Institute for Public Policy.

Braithwaite, J. 2002. *Restorative justice and responsive regulation.* Oxford: Oxford University Press.

Cullen, F. T. 1994. Social support as an organizing concept for criminology. *Justice Quarterly* 11:527–559.

Currie, E. 1998. *Crime and punishment in America.* New York: Owl Books.

Dodge, K. A., and D. Schwartz. 1997. Social information processing mechanisms in aggressive behavior. In *Handbook of antisocial behavior.* Ed. D. Stoff, J. Breiling, and J. Maser, 171–180. New York: Wiley.

Eck, J. E. 2002. Preventing crime at places. In *Evidence-based crime prevention.* Ed. L. Sherman, D. Farrington, and B. Welsh, 241–294. London: Routledge.

Farrington, D. P., and B. C. Welsh. 2007. *Saving children from a life of crime.* Cambridge: Cambridge University Press.

Geason, S., and P. R. Wilson. 1998. *Designing out crime.* Canberra: Australian Institute of Criminology.

Greenwood, P. 2006. *Changing lives: Delinquency prevention as crime-control policy.* Chicago: University of Chicago Press.

Mazerolle, P., and J. Maahs. 2000. General strain and delinquency: An alternative examination of conditioning influences. *Justice Quarterly* 17:753–778.

Sampson, R. J. 2002. The community. In *Crime.* Ed. J. Wilson and J. Petersilia, 225–252. Oakland, Calif.: ICS Press.

Spelman, W., and J. E. Eck. 1987. *Newport News tests problem-oriented policing.* Washington, D.C.: National Institute of Justice.

3

RICHARD ROSENFELD AND STEVEN F. MESSNER

The Normal Crime Rate, the Economy, and Mass Incarceration

An Institutional Anomie Perspective on Crime Control Policy

> Crime . . . must no longer be conceived as an evil that cannot be too much suppressed. There is no occasion for self-congratulation when the crime rate drops below the average level, for we may be certain that this apparent progress is associated with some social disorder.
>
> —Emile Durkheim, *The Rules of the Sociological Method*

When we turned in a draft of the first edition of *Crime and the American Dream* (Messner and Rosenfeld 1994), our very supportive editor was surprised to learn that the manuscript had almost nothing to say about criminal justice policy. This was the early 1990s, and crime rates were on the rise across the United States. Surely we must have something to contribute to the national debate over crime control, our editor advised. Frankly, we didn't think we did. We already had published an essay by the same title without a word on criminal justice policy (Rosenfeld and Messner 1994). But our editor insisted, and every edition of *Crime and the American Dream* since the first one has contained a discussion of the "policy implications" of our theory of crime (Messner and Rosenfeld 1994, 1997, 2001a, 2007).

Why were we reluctant to spell out the policies implied by our explanation of the American crime problem? It was not as if we had no ideas about how to reduce crime; we did, and those ideas flowed logically from our explanation of the causes of crime in the United States. But our views on crime reduction did not fit easily within the terms of the crime control debates of the early 1990s, and fifteen years later they still do not quite square with conventional criminal justice policy analysis.

That is because, in keeping with our explanation of the causes of crime, we believe that comparatively high levels of serious criminality are "normal" in the United States, and enduring crime reductions will require fundamental changes to American culture and society. Changes of that sort are simply not what most people have in mind when they think about the police, courts, jails, prisons, and other aspects of the criminal justice system. The changes we believe are necessary do not ignore conventionally defined criminal justice agencies and processes, but they are broader and go deeper than criminal justice. They involve alterations in the entire range of social institutions that make up American society, from the economy to the political system, the educational system, and the family. They transcend "policy," defined as improved means for achieving predetermined goals, and entail a rethinking of deeply rooted and widely cherished cultural goals, as well as the means for attaining them. The way we think about crime reduction involves nothing short of transforming the American dream itself.

So in a volume devoted to criminal justice policy, we have a rather unconventional story to tell. We begin by presenting the classical sociologist Emile Durkheim's ideas about the social normality of crime and discuss some of the implications of those ideas for crime control. We then summarize the main tenets of our theory of crime, termed "institutional anomie theory," and set forth our thesis that comparatively high rates of serious crime are a normal feature of the organization of American society. We conclude by describing the differences between social change and social policy but also discuss prisoner reentry policies that are consistent with our theory and could point the way toward the more fundamental changes that the theory entails.

The Normal Crime Rate

Institutional anomie theory and Robert Merton's anomie theory of crime before it (1938) were inspired by the insights of the founders of modern sociology, most directly by Emile Durkheim. Durkheim introduced the concept of "anomie" into modern social thought and insisted that, from a sociological perspective, crime is a normal social fact. As Durkheim observed a century ago, all societies necessarily contain some level and type of crime. "There is no society," he wrote (1966 [1895], 65–66), "that is not confronted with the problem of criminality. Its form changes; the acts thus characterized are not the same everywhere; but, everywhere and always, there have been men who have behaved in such a way as to draw upon themselves penal repression." Durkheim maintained that crime is not only universal; it is "normal" in the sense that "it is bound up with the fundamental conditions of all social life" (70). If crime is normal, what does that make of the criminal? "Contrary to current ideas, the criminal no longer seems a totally unsociable being, a sort of parasitic element, a strange and unassimilable body, introduced into the midst of society. On the contrary, he plays a definite role in social life" (72).[1] Writing about seventy years later, and speaking more generally of the "deviant" rather than the "criminal," Kai Erikson (1966, 19) echoed Durkheim's provocative insight: "[the deviant] is not a bit of debris spun out by faulty social machinery, but a relevant figure in the community's overall division of labor."

Three important implications for crime control follow from the idea that crime is normal. First, if crime is part of the "conditions of social life," its form and frequency should vary with changes in social conditions. This might be termed the first sociological principle of crime. Different societies, then, should have characteristically different patterns and levels of crime, as should the same society during different historical periods. Another way to state the latter point is that differing patterns and levels of crime are products of *social change.*

A second consequence of the social normality of crime is that the crime rate can never be driven to zero. Even if a particular type of crime is extinguished, another type will take its place. To take an obvious example, stealing horses is not prevalent in modern, industrial societies, but stealing automobiles is. Violent crime rates have fallen in most Western societies since the Late Middle Ages, but rates of property crime have risen over the same period (Eisner 2001, 2003; Gurr 1989). In each instance, it took fundamental social changes (e.g., new modes of transportation and economic organization) to eliminate or reduce one type of crime and to foster the ascendance of the other.

A final implication for crime control of the social normality of crime, presaged in the quotation from Durkheim at the beginning of the chapter, is that crime rates can fall *too low* for the good of a society. This idea seems as curious, even pernicious, to contemporary sensibilities as it did to Durkheim's readers a century ago, but it follows directly from the premise that crime is a normal and characteristic feature of a society's basic make-up. It suggests that a lower-than-normal crime rate is symptomatic of some "social disorder" or abnormality that impedes the smooth operation of the social system. As an example, consider the low rates of robbery, burglary, and other forms of street crime that prevailed in the former Soviet Union. A garrison state can suppress street crime, but at great social cost. Later we will ask whether the suppression of crime brought about by mass incarceration in the United States ought to be regarded in a similar light, but first it is necessary to forestall possible misconceptions about the meaning of crime as a normal social phenomenon.

The idea that crime is normal does not mean that high levels of crime must be tolerated as an inevitable and unchangeable fact of life. Rather, it directs

---

[1] Durkheim drew an important distinction between the social normality of crime and the possibly aberrant psychological characteristics of individual criminals. The latter issue, for Durkheim, is beyond the scope of sociological inquiry and has no bearing on crime as a social fact (see Durkheim 1966 [1985], 66n).

attention to the social conditions that produce crime and suggests that efforts to reduce crime *without altering the underlying crime-producing conditions* may prove futile, costly, or both. Durkheim compared the social functions of crime to the biological functions of pain in this respect. "Pain itself has nothing desirable about it," he pointed out. "The individual dislikes it as society does crime, and yet it is a function of normal physiology" (Durkheim 1966 [1895], 72n). Crime suppression that does not address the social conditions that produce crime, to continue the analogy, is like numbing pain with medication without treating the malady producing the pain.

Just as crime may drop to abnormally low levels, it also may rise above the rate that is normal for a given society. Determining when crime is above, or below, normal presupposes, of course, that the normal rate has been established. Durkheim does not offer much guidance about how to establish the normal crime rate, beyond the premise that it is the "average" level of crime associated with prevailing social conditions. Contemporary sociology and criminology also provide little practical assistance. In fact, with the exception of occasional references in introductory textbooks to Durkheim's ideas about crime, the concept of a normal crime rate is largely absent from current theory and research (see Messner and Rosenfeld 2004). We believe that institutional anomie theory offers a useful framework for linking the concept of the normal crime rate to the organization of American society and for evaluating the benefits and costs of American crime control policies—particularly the policy of mass incarceration.

Institutional Anomie Theory

The central idea underlying institutional anomie theory is that a society's level and types of crime are tied to how it is organized.[2] All societies, if they are to survive, must meet certain basic needs of their members. They must adapt to the environment, enable members to achieve collective goals, integrate members and their diverse activities around core values and beliefs, and maintain the fundamental cultural patterns over time. *Social institutions* are complexes of particular elements of culture and social structure that perform these basic functions of adaptation, goal attainment, integration, and pattern maintenance.[3]

Adaptation to the environment to meet the physical and material needs of a population is the chief function of the economy. Political institutions, or the

---

[2] Summaries of institutional anomie theory can be found in several sources (e.g., Messner and Rosenfeld 2001b, 2006, 2007; Rosenfeld and Messner 1997). The description in the text is adapted from Rosenfeld and Messner 2006.

[3] This description of the organization and survival requirements of societies comes from the sociologist Talcott Parsons (1951). See Turner 2003 for an application of this type of institutional analysis to the explanation of societal evolution.

"polity," enable a population to attain collective goals. Responsibility for social integration and the maintenance of cultural patterns falls to religion, education, and the family system. The interrelations among these institutions constitute a society as an ongoing concern and distinguish it from other societies. Although all institutions play a vital role in meeting basic material and social needs, they rarely play equal roles. In most societies, one or another institution dominates the others by commanding greater allegiance and resources and by forcing other institutions to accommodate to its particular functions at the expense of their own. All societies, in other words, demonstrate a distinctive *institutional balance of power* wherein some institutions are more equal than others.

We argue in *Crime and the American Dream* (Messner and Rosenfeld 2007) that the free-market economy dominates the institutional structure of American society. As a result, other institutions are more "market driven" than is the case in many other societies. Non-economic institutions bend to the economy as plants to sunlight; their rewards and routines conform to economic requirements, and the very language used to describe them has economic overtones. Think about the accommodations families make to economic requirements— how work hours determine household meal and vacation schedules; how an employer's permission is needed to tend to a sick child; how having a family above all requires having a job. Think about how the economy dominates American political life—how much attention during elections is devoted to the candidates' "tax and spend" policies; how much more efficient government would be, we are told, if it were run like a private business. Think about the sheer amount of money it takes to run for political office. Think about how much competition for grades in school mimics the competition for income in the labor market.

Now consider how such an institutional arrangement affects the level and nature of crime. In his classic essay published in the 1930s, Merton (1938) called attention to the pervasive "anomie" in American culture. Anomie refers to a condition wherein the moral foundations of social norms have eroded. "Efficiency norms" reign supreme in an anomic context, encouraging people to achieve goals (primarily monetary success) by any means necessary. We maintain that the dominance of the free-market economy in the institutional structure reinforces anomic cultural tendencies that elevate the goal of material success above others and de-emphasize the importance of using the legitimate means for attaining success. Under such cultural conditions, people tend to cut corners and may disobey the law when it gets in the way of the pursuit of economic gain. At the same time, the *social control* exerted by the polity, family, education, and religion is diminished when the institutional balance of power favors the economy. The *social support* institutions provide also weakens (cf. Cullen and Wright 1997). Diminished social control frees people from normative restraints; weakened social support pushes people to meet their material and other needs however they can. Both lead to high rates of criminality.

The Crime Decline of the 1990s, Economic Growth, and Mass Incarceration

From the vantage point of institutional anomie theory, then, there is nothing surprising about high rates of serious crime in the United States. Comparatively high rates of crime are the normal, expected product of American social organization. For at least a century, and perhaps longer, American crime rates, especially rates of serious violent crime, typically exceeded those of comparably developed European nations, Canada, Australia, and Japan (Archer and Gartner 1984; Messner and Rosenfeld 2007). But beginning in the early 1990s, the gap between crime rates in the United States and other developed countries began to narrow and in some cases disappear. The United States no longer leads the developed world in rates of burglary and robbery, and although the American homicide rate remains higher than the homicide rates of "old" Europe and other developed nations, the difference diminished during the 1990s (Messner and Rosenfeld 1997, 20–26).

What accounts for the shrinking "crime gap" between the United States and other developed nations? To some extent, the cross-national convergence in crime rates has resulted from increases in crime elsewhere, but the main reason the gap has closed is the dramatic drop in crime that took place in the United States during the final decade of the twentieth century (see Blumstein and Wallman 2005; Zimring 2006). American homicide, robbery, and burglary rates were nearly cut in half between 1992 and 2000 (Rosenfeld 2004). The causes of the American crime drop are not fully understood and are subject to continuing debate, but it would be surprising if the robust *economic expansion* during the 1990s had no effect on crime rates. The relationship between economic growth and crime remains a contested issue in criminology, with some analysts suggesting that economic growth reduces crime and others maintaining that it has little impact on or may even increase crime rates (Cantor and Land 1985; Chiricos 1987; Cook and Zarkin 1985; Levitt 2004). But in light of recent research showing sizable effects of economic growth, declining unemployment, and rising consumer confidence on the crime drop of the 1990s (Arvanites and Defina 2006; Raphael and Winter-Ebmer 2001; Rosenfeld and Fornango 2007), it seems wise to consider the role of the 1990s economic expansion in narrowing the crime gap between the United States and other developed nations.

A second contributing factor, the importance of which is now widely accepted among criminologists, is the rise of *mass incarceration*. Escalating incarceration rates may reduce crime by deterring people from committing crimes, by rehabilitating imprisoned offenders, or simply by incapacitating offenders. Most criminologists think that incarceration cuts crime mainly through incapacitation. The number of persons serving time in state and federal prisons in the United States quadrupled between 1980 and 2000 and continues to grow.[4] The United States holds a larger fraction of its population in prisons and jails than any other nation in the world, and it has widened its lead during the past quarter of a century. So while the crime gap has narrowed, the "imprisonment gap" separating the United States and other countries has greatly expanded.

Institutional anomie theory suggests two questions to guide our discussion of how economic expansion and mass incarceration contributed to the crime drop in the United States: (1) were declining crime rates during the 1990s "abnormal" in the sense of falling below levels expected on the basis of prevailing cultural and social conditions in the United States? (2) should economic expansion and mass incarceration be considered products or aspects of prevailing conditions, or should they, too, be considered abnormal social phenomena? Neither question can be answered easily or definitively in this essay, and each raises additional questions that require further theoretical and empirical inquiry. In considering possible answers and additional research issues, we wish simply to highlight the policy, as well as the theoretical, implications of institutional anomie theory and the idea of the normal crime rate for controlling crime in the United States.

Was the Crime Drop Abnormal?

Crime rates have fallen periodically in the United States during the past century, but the magnitude and duration of the 1990s crime drop were unprecedented (see Zimring 2006). Another notable feature of the crime drop was its breadth. Crime rates fell in large cities, suburbs, and small towns; in every region of the country; in both violent and property offenses; and in nearly every age, sex, and race category (Rosenfeld 2004). In many places, crime rates fell to levels not seen since the 1960s. By 2000, the national homicide rate had reached a thirty-four-year low of 5.5 homicides per 100,000 population. Robbery rates also dropped to a thirty-one-year low by the end of the twentieth century (see Figure 3.1).

The crime drop was not the product of fundamental changes in prevailing social conditions. Social institutions did not become notably more controlling or supportive during the last decade of the twentieth century. In fact, with the end of "welfare as we know it" during the mid-1990s, a good case can be made that American society had become much *less* supportive of the poor (Eckholm 2006). The emphasis on the value of monetary achievement in American

---

[4] State and federal prisons in the United States housed roughly 1.4 million persons in 2000, compared with about 330,000 inmates in 1980. The prison population grew by another 200,000 inmates between 2000 and the end of 2007 (West and Sabol 2008).

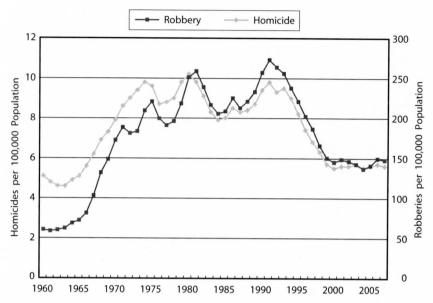

FIGURE 3.1   Homicides and Robberies per 100,000 Population in the United States, 1960–2007

Source: Trends are based on the FBI's Uniform Crime Report (UCR) crime data gathered from police agencies across the country and published on the U.S. Bureau of Justice Statistics Web site, http://bjsdata.ojp.usdoj .gov/dataonline/Search/Crime/State/StateCrime.cfm.

culture certainly had not disappeared at the end of the decade. Judging by the speculative fever that gripped the stock market during the 1990s, Americans' devotion to quick and easy financial success remained quite strong. By December 1996, Alan Greenspan, chairman of the Federal Reserve Board, had become sufficiently concerned with overvaluation in the stock market that he coined his highly publicized term "irrational exuberance" to warn investors of the speculative bubble and perhaps to let some air out it. It worked. The stock market fell 2 percent at the opening of trade the day after his speech, but only momentarily.[5]

The American dream and the institutional arrangements that support it were alive and well in the 1990s. But perhaps, in seeming contradiction to our argument in *Crime and the American Dream,* it was the prosperity stimulated by the pursuit of the American dream during the booming 1990s that produced the crime drop. This explanation has the virtue of squaring with much conven-

---

[5] The full text of Greenspan's "irrational exuberance" speech can be found on the Federal Reserve Board's Web site, available online at http://www.federalreserve.gov/boarddocs/speeches/19961205 .htm (July 12, 2009). The stock market's response to the speech is described by the economist Robert Shiller (2005).

tional wisdom and sociological thinking about the relationship between economic opportunities and crime: When jobs become more plentiful and incomes rise, fewer people will resort to crime to supplement their incomes or vent their frustrations (see Rosenfeld and Fornango 2007). But explanations that link crime with economic opportunity are actually consistent with our argument in *Crime and the American Dream*. In fact, institutional anomie theory explains why we should expect to observe a particularly strong association between normal economic cycles and crime rates in American society.

The Booming 1990s

The American economy grew at record pace during the 1990s. The opening page of President Bill Clinton's 1999 *Economic Report of the President* hit the high points:

> I am pleased to report that the American economy today is healthy and strong. Our Nation is enjoying the longest peacetime economic expansion in its history, with almost 18 million new jobs since 1993, wages rising at twice the rate of inflation, the highest home ownership ever, the smallest welfare rolls in 30 years, and unemployment and inflation at their lowest levels in three decades. (Office of the President 1999, 1)

Like the crime drop, the economic expansion was wide, deep, and prolonged. It lasted nine years, from 1992 to 2000, and produced sizable wage gains and reductions in unemployment, even among the most disadvantaged groups in American society. Without question, the great majority of Americans were better off economically at the end of the decade than at the beginning.

There is good reason to expect that the booming economy contributed to the crime drop, not simply because of the scale of the 1990s economic expansion, but because crime rates typically respond to cyclical fluctuations in the American economy. When the economy expands, crime rates tend to fall, and when the economy contracts, crime rates tend to rise. Not surprisingly, not all crimes are affected equally by the state of the economy. Prior research indicates that the crime reduction effects of the business cycle are limited to property crimes and to robbery—that is, to offenses with a transparently economic motive (Arvanites and Defina 2006; Cook and Zarkin 1985).

Business cycles can be measured using a variety of indicators (e.g., income levels, unemployment rates, measures of total output), but a particularly useful measure for studying the effects of economic conditions on crime is *consumer sentiment*. Each month, researchers from the University of Michigan survey a national sample of adults to gauge current economic conditions and consumers'

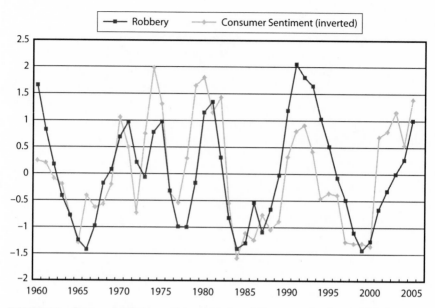

FIGURE 3.2 De-trended Robbery Rate and Index of Consumer Sentiment (ICS), Inverted, in Standard Measures, 1960–2005

Source: UCR robbery rates are from the U.S. Bureau of Justice Statistics Web site, http://bjsdata.ojp.usdoj.gov/dataonline/Search/Crime/State/StateCrime.cfm, and the Index of Consumer Sentiment from the University of Michigan's Surveys of Consumers, available online at http://www.sca.isr.umich.edu.

expectations for the future. Economic indicators based on the consumer survey data are closely watched by economists and typically outperform standard economic models in forecasting inflation rates, unemployment rates, and related economic changes (Curtin 2002, 2003).

Fluctuations in consumer sentiment also are associated with crime trends (Rosenfeld and Fornango 2007). Figure 3.2 shows the relationship between yearly changes from 1960 to 2005 in robbery rates and the Index of Consumer Sentiment (ICS), a summary indicator of consumer sentiment developed from the monthly consumer surveys. Each series has been de-trended to reveal cyclical changes and is expressed in units of standard deviation from its mean value. The ICS has been inverted so that high values reflect consumer pessimism and low values reflect consumer optimism.

The figure reveals a very close and consistent association between cyclical changes in robbery and consumer sentiment over the forty-five-year period. When the ICS deviates from its underlying trend, robbery rates do as well, in recurring oscillations between 1960 and 2005. The oscillations correspond with periods of economic expansion and contraction. Consumer sentiment fell and robbery rates rose during the recessions of 1969, 1974–1975, 1980–1981,

1990–1991, and 2001.[6] Robbery rates fell with expansionary periods and rising consumer sentiment in the early 1960s, late 1970s, early 1980s, and nearly the entire decade of the 1990s. Rates of burglary, larceny, and motor-vehicle theft show the same cyclical pattern, and the relationship between economically motivated crimes and consumer sentiment withstands controls for other conditions affecting crime rates, such as imprisonment, police per capita, and population composition by race and age (Rosenfeld and Fornango 2007). When viewed in the context of prior research on crime rates and cyclical economic change (Arvanites and Defina 2006; Cook and Zarkin 1985; Raphael and Winter-Ebmer 2001), these results suggest that the ups and downs of the business cycle over the past four decades in the United States have produced comparable changes in robbery and property crime rates.

How can the evidence on the relationship between economic cycles and crime rates be rendered compatible with institutional anomie theory? Why doesn't economic prosperity reinforce the dictates of the American dream and thereby promote higher rather than lower crime rates? We suggest that the business cycle has paradoxical consequences for the cultural and institutional order of American society. As explained above, anomie encourages people to pursue goals "by any means necessary." Behavior is governed by "efficiency norms;" people select means for pursuing success that are technically expedient without regard to their normative status. The manifestation of an anomic ethic in criminal behavior depends, however, on the extent to which illegitimate means are in fact technically expedient relative to legitimate means. When the economy is booming, legitimate means become more widely available, and criminal behavior becomes less attractive from a purely calculative, tactical standpoint. Conversely, when the economy contracts, access to the legitimate means is restricted, and the technical superiority of the illegitimate means increases. Thus, in a society where behavior is governed by "efficiency norms," the level of criminal activity should respond to economic opportunities.

There is another, less obvious way in which economic prosperity might mitigate rather than exacerbate the social pressures for crime in the United States. The dominance of the economy in the institutional balance of power implies that non-economic institutions are subservient to, and dependent on, the economy. Non-economic roles must accommodate to economic demands. The need for such accommodation is likely to be lessened when the economy is booming because economic resources are more plentiful. To illustrate, the pressures to make family schedules conform to work schedules are more intense when people have meager prospects of finding a new job if they are let go.

---

[6] See Federal Deposit Insurance Corporation 2006, charts 1, 3, for the timing of economic recessions since 1960.

Similarly, the need to work overtime and to adjust family schedules accordingly is less pressing when wages are high. The ironic implication is that non-economic institutions are stronger and more capable of fulfilling their distinctive functions, including that of promoting non-economic goals and orientations, in times of economic expansion than in times of economic contraction. Thus, economic prosperity not only alters the opportunity structure in ways that diminish the likelihood that anomic individuals will select criminal means to achieve their monetary goals; it also mitigates—at least, to some extent—the cultural emphasis on monetary-success goals to the exclusion of others.

From the perspective of institutional anomie theory, then, the crime reductions that occurred in the 1990s were the normal, expected product of the expansion of the American economy. If the crime drop of the 1990s lasted longer than previous crime reductions, that was in part because it was driven by the longest peacetime economic expansion on record. But only in part. The business cycle is not the only source of variation in crime rates over time, and by definition its effects are more-or-less short-lived. Other factors also were implicated in the 1990s crime drop, including the rise of mass incarceration in the United States.

The Rise of Mass Incarceration

During the 1970s several criminologists sought to explain the remarkable temporal stability in imprisonment rates in the United States and other nations on the basis of Durkheim's idea that societies stabilize levels of crime and punishment to maintain social solidarity (Blumstein and Cohen 1973; Blumstein, Cohen, and Nagin 1976). No sooner had the "stability of punishment" hypothesis been advanced than imprisonment rates in the United States began climbing to historically unprecedented levels. So much for the normality of punishment in the United States (see Figure 3.3).

From an institutional anomie perspective, the dramatic growth in incarceration suppressed crime rates in the United States below their normal levels—that is, the expected levels given the cultural stimulation of criminal propensities, weak social controls and supports in the American social structure, and the normal oscillations of the business cycle. To understand the role of incarceration in suppressing crime, it is useful to distinguish between crime rates and *criminality* (see Gottfredson and Hirschi 1990). A crime rate is the observed level of crime of a particular type during a particular period per unit of population. Criminality, by contrast, refers to the propensity of individuals to engage in criminal behavior. For criminality to give rise to criminal acts, opportunities to commit crimes must exist. Incarceration is a potent method of suppressing criminal acts by denying would-be offenders the opportunity to commit crimes against the general public.

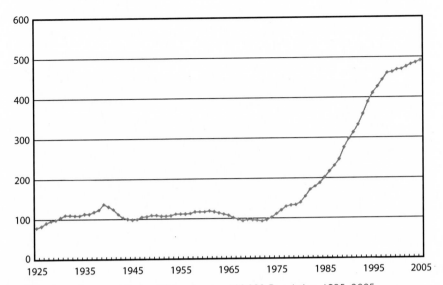

FIGURE 3.3 State and Federal Prisoners per 100,000 Population, 1925–2005

Source: State and federal imprisonment rates are from the *Sourcebook of Criminal Justice Statistics,* available online at http://www.albany.edu/sourcebook.

In principle, incarceration suppresses crime not only by incapacitating offenders but also by deterring prisoners from committing crimes once they are released, which is termed "specific" deterrence, or by deterring others from committing crimes through the threat of imprisonment, termed "general" deterrence. Whether incarceration has much of a deterrent effect on criminal behavior, either specific or general, remains uncertain (see Nagin 1998). Few criminologists believe that imprisonment reduces crime by rehabilitating criminal offenders—in other words, by reducing criminality. But the incapacitation effects of incarceration are beyond dispute, even if the magnitude of those effects is subject to debate and the impact of incarceration on crime has grown over time with escalating rates of imprisonment.

Like most sociological theories of crime, the institutional anomie perspective is mainly a theory of criminality. The theory specifies the cultural and social conditions under which levels of criminality are expected to be high and those expected to reduce criminality. The theory largely omits consideration of the distribution of *criminal opportunities* across space and time, and it has yet to be sufficiently elaborated to offer an explanation for the rise of mass incarceration in the United States.[7]

---

[7] See Cohen and Felson 1979 and Felson 2002 for an explanation of crime that highlights the role of criminal opportunities. Garland 2001 offers a cogent account of the sociocultural forces underlying social control practices in the advanced societies. See Messner et al. 2008 for a preliminary effort to elaborate institutional anomie theory to explain punishment polices such as mass incarceration.

The increase in American incarceration rates beginning in the 1970s was anything but normal, but does it reflect a permanent alteration in American crime control policy? After thirty years of escalating rates, should we expect incarceration to return to pre-1970s, historically normal levels anytime soon, or has the nation entered a new era of permanently high imprisonment rates?

Mass incarceration is not a discrete policy. It is the result of several policies intended to "get tough" on crime and illegal drugs (Messner and Rosenfeld 2007, 115–118). It is fair to assume that few policymakers intended or foresaw a quadrupling of the prison population as a consequence of the mandatory minimum sentencing and truth-in-sentencing laws passed over the last thirty years, but once the dramatic escalation in incarceration became evident, if policymakers were inclined to limit future imprisonment growth, presumably they would have done so by now. That incarceration levels have continued to increase even during a period of record declines in crime suggests that mass incarceration is here to stay.

Perhaps rattled by the unexpected takeoff in incarceration thirty years ago, few criminologists have offered forecasts of the future of incarceration. Our view, admittedly speculative and based largely on a theory of criminality rather than punishment, is that mass incarceration at levels unknown elsewhere in the world is becoming institutionalized in American society and is not likely to subside anytime soon. That is because a permanently high level of incarceration is the only means policymakers have found—or have been willing to try on a large scale—to limit crime rates. Monetary and fiscal policies in the United States are not intended to reduce crime, and even if they were, they could at best do little more than extend the upside of the business cycle a little longer than it otherwise might last. Short of qualitative changes in American economic and social institutions, mass incarceration seems to be the only politically feasible means by which relatively permanent crime reductions can be achieved. But, as we will see, policies such as mass incarceration that merely remove the opportunities to commit crime and leave the social pressures toward criminality intact are often costly and limited in effectiveness (Liedka, Piehl, and Useem 2006). They contradictorily signal the need for social change and the desire to maintain existing institutional arrangements, even at great cost.

Social Policy versus Social Change

Mass incarceration is an example of a broader class of policy initiatives that seek to influence some social outcome—in this case, crime rates—without fundamentally changing the cultural and social conditions that generate that outcome. Like advertisements that promise weight loss with minimal exercise or dieting, such policies are limited by their failure to tackle the causes of the problem. We might term them "policies without change" and distinguish them from policies that emerge from and are designed to implement social change. Examples of the latter include antidiscrimination policies resulting from the Civil Rights and Women's movements during the 1960s and 1970s and legislation guaranteeing workers' collective-bargaining rights passed during the Great Depression of the 1930s. Such policies alter social goals regarding fundamental rights and liberties and not merely the means of realizing pre-established goals. Mass incarceration, by contrast, does not represent new goals for criminal justice but revised means for achieving the traditional goals of crime control and punishment. Mandatory minimum sentences and truth-in-sentencing laws reduce the discretion of judges and corrections officials in setting criminal sentences and releasing inmates from prison, thereby insuring that larger numbers of convicted offenders are imprisoned for longer periods of time. These policies probably do strengthen the hand of prosecutors at the expense of the discretionary authority traditionally granted to judges and corrections managers in the sentencing process, but they do not alter the basic character or goals of criminal sentencing and related institutional practices.

Mass incarceration, we have argued, is a stopgap policy for reducing crime—by how much and for how long remain uncertain—without having to change the conditions that produce criminality. Pursuing crime control exclusively through incarceration is akin to managing illness and disease exclusively through hospitalization without treating the underlying medical conditions that make people sick. A rich society could continue to store the sick in hospitals for a long time, but at tremendous cost and with diminishing benefits.

We should expect policies that in effect substitute for rather than implement social change to exact a high price in economic, political, and social capital. The economic costs of mass incarceration can be reckoned in two ways: first, by the amount of money spent to build the jails and prisons and hire the staff needed to guard the growing number of prisoners; and second, by what economists term the "opportunity" costs of these outlays—that is, what we might have done with the money had we not spent it on mass incarceration. Direct expenditures on corrections in the United States increased to $68.8 billion in 2006 from $9 billion in 1982, or by 664 percent.[8] This increase does not take population growth or price inflation into account, but inflation-adjusted per capita expenditures on corrections grew substantially over the twenty-two-year period, as well (Hughes 2006).

The United States is a rich nation and can afford to maintain a huge corrections complex, even though mounting corrections expenditures have far outstripped the overall growth in the U.S. economy. But corrections costs are

---

[8] The expenditure figures reported in the text include the costs of the probation and parole as well as those for prison and jail confinement. The expenditure data are from the Bureau of Justice Statistics Web site, available online at http://www.ojp.usdoj.gov/bjs/glance/exptyp.htm (July 13, 2009); Hughes 2006.

borne primarily by state and local governments, and they have grown at roughly double the rate of state and local outlays for education, health care, and policing over the past thirty years (Hughes 2006). Each additional dollar spent on prisons, jails, and community corrections is money that states and local areas cannot devote to other pressing needs, including improvements in education and early-childhood interventions that hold some promise for reducing criminality and not just containing crime rates (Greenwood et al. 1998).

As costly as mass incarceration is in purely economic terms, it also has significant political and social costs that researchers only recently have begun to analyze in depth, including destabilizing effects on families and communities, a growing population of permanently disenfranchised former prisoners and other convicted felons, and, quite possibly, higher crime rates over the long term (Liedka, Piehl, and Useem 2006; Manza and Uggen 2006; Pattillo, Weiman, and Western 2004; Travis and Visher 2005). Moreover, the political and social costs of mass incarceration are not spread evenly across the population but are borne disproportionately by African Americans. Fully 10 percent of African American men between the age 25 and 29 resided in a state or federal prison in 2002, compared with 2 percent of Hispanic men and 1 percent of white men of the same age (Messner and Rosenfeld 2007, 5). Arrest rates for many serious offenses also are higher among African Americans than other groups, but only a small part of the growth in incarceration over the past thirty years has resulted from a rise in crime. Most of the growth is from changes in sentencing and recommitment policies that, whether intended or not, have disproportionately affected the life chances of African Americans (Blumstein and Beck 2005; Tonry 1996).

In summary, the costs of mass incarceration are high, growing, and multifarious, and they are borne unequally. A natural question is whether the costs of a policy equal or exceed the benefits. This question proves to be a very difficult one to answer in the case of mass incarceration. For one thing, the magnitude and duration of mass incarceration's effects on crime remain uncertain. But more important, it is far from clear how we should weigh the benefits of less crime against the escalating costs of mass incarceration. How much are we willing to increase community instability or voter disenfranchisement to avert one additional robbery or burglary (or ten or one hundred) through increased incarceration? How much less should we spend on education or health care to avert an additional homicide? The costs and (possible) benefits of mass incarceration simply do not share a metric against which such tradeoffs can be reconciled.[9]

---

[9] It should be apparent that simply adding up the economic losses from crime (medical expenses, time lost from work, etc.) and comparing them with the economic costs of incarceration does not capture the full range of costs associated with either crime or incarceration. Nor is it clear how economists' efforts to fully "monetize" the costs of crime (i.e., to assign a dollar value to all costs,

It is nevertheless useful to consider whether many of the purported benefits of mass incarceration can be achieved through alternative means. Can we achieve whatever crime reductions are attributable to mass incarceration by implementing programs and policies that are less costly to the public purse, the affected families and communities (of both offenders and victims), and a democratic polity? We believe that we can, but doing so will require public policies that address the causes of criminality and not just the opportunities to commit crimes. If, as institutional anomie theory proposes, the causes of criminality in American society lie in a cultural ethos that elevates the goal of monetary success above other forms of achievement and an institutional order that does not adequately protect people from the normal oscillations of a free-market economy, reducing criminality will require cultural and social changes that broaden the goals to which we aspire and soften the blows of market forces. We have outlined these changes elsewhere (Messner and Rosenfeld 2007, 112–124) and do not discuss them here. Rather, we conclude this essay by discussing a more immediate and feasible policy initiative for limiting the growth in imprisonment without unduly jeopardizing public safety.

Prisoner Reentry

We have argued that high levels of crime are normal in the United States, which led the developed world in rates of violent and many property crimes until American crime rates plummeted in the 1990s. The crime drop resulted from, among other factors, the economic boom of the 1990s and escalating imprisonment rates—that is, from the normal oscillations of the American economy and the extraordinary increase in imprisonment beginning in the 1970s. Incarceration rates in the 700–800 per 100,000 range, unknown anywhere else in the world, may represent a new crime control equilibrium in the United States. Because about 95 percent of people who enter prison are eventually released, mass incarceration has produced a corresponding increase in the number of former prisoners living in the community. What should be done with them?

As evidence of the economic, political, and social costs of mass incarceration has begun to accumulate, political pressures to limit the growth of imprisonment have emerged in the form of a "prisoner reentry" movement that initially attracted the attention of the second Bush administration and state legislatures across the country at the time (see Petersilia 2003; Travis 2005).[10] The new

---

no matter how intangible) can help policymakers and informed citizens make the difficult political and moral tradeoffs inherent in deciding how many people to incarcerate to lower the crime rate. On the economic losses from crime, see Klaus 1994. See Cohen 2005 on monetizing the costs of crime and criminal justice.

[10] For information about the federal government's Serious Violent Offender and Reentry Initiative, see http://www.reentry.gov/whatsnew.html (July 13, 2009).

emphasis on supervision and support of former prisoners in the community is consistent with the Durkheimian idea of the criminal as a normal, if troublesome, member of society and not some "strange and unassimilable body" incapable of personal reform or social reintegration.

Advocates of prisoner reentry point to the limited employment and housing, health, and social services available to people returning home from prison and the spotty and inconsistent supervision of many former prisoners in the community as primary reasons for their high recidivism rates. Well over six hundred thousand persons are released from prison each year in the United States, roughly two-thirds of whom are rearrested and fully half of whom are reincarcerated within three years (Langan and Levin 2002; Travis 2005). To protect the communities into which they are released and stanch the flow of offenders back to prison, reentry advocates call for sharply lower parole caseloads and enhanced supportive services for former prisoners and their families. It is too early to tell whether current reentry programs reduce recidivism rates, but if they are found to be effective and are widely implemented, they could limit the overall growth in imprisonment for the simple reason that most people entering prison in recent years have been there at least once before (Blumstein and Beck 2005). The essential challenge to prisoner reentry programs is finding the right mix of incentives, supports, and controls that will reduce the chances that people who have already been in and out of prison and then are reincarcerated will not return to prison yet again when they are released.

Reducing the recidivism rates of this population of "repeat prisoners," who constitute a growing fraction of released prisoners, will not be easy. By definition they have already demonstrated that they are poor reentry bets. An analysis of recidivism among people released from state prisons in 1994 and followed over the next three years found significantly higher rates of rearrest, on the order of 18 percent to 25 percent, among those who had been in prison before than among those released from prison for the first time, even with age, arrest history, and other predictors of recidivism controlled (Rosenfeld, Wallman, and Fornango 2005; cf. Tonry 2004, 189). Having served time in prison, in and of itself, appears to be a major risk factor for committing new crimes and returning to prison.

Despite the difficult challenges it poses for parole agencies and service providers, the emphasis on prisoner reentry is a bright spot on the current crime control policy horizon. It addresses head-on the immense needs of the more than 1,600 persons released from prison each day in the United States and the risks they pose to their communities if those needs remain unmet. It reminds us that our prisons do not adequately prepare inmates for the rigors of life on the outside. It encourages collective responsibility for the destructive consequences of our policy of mass incarceration, especially those heaped on the already fragile communities in which high crime and incarceration rates are concentrated. And unlike other policy initiatives that have a decidedly partisan or ideological cast, prison reentry has been embraced by policymakers across the political spectrum. Improving the transition from prison back to the community will not by itself markedly reduce the normally high levels of criminality in the United States, but it may ameliorate the costs of mass incarceration. Unless or until we are willing to transform our crime-producing cultural values and social structure, that may be the best we can do.

References

Archer, D., and R. Gartner. 1984. *Violence and crime in cross-national perspective.* New Haven, Conn.: Yale University Press.

Arvanites, T. M., and R. H. Defina. 2006. Business cycles and street crime. *Criminology* 44:139–164.

Blumstein, A., and A. J. Beck. 2005. Reentry as a transient state between liberty and recommitment. In *Prisoner reentry and crime in America.* Ed. J. Travis and C. Visher, 50–79. New York: Cambridge University Press.

Blumstein, A., and J. Cohen. 1973. A theory of the stability of punishment. *Journal of Criminal Law and Criminology* 64:198–207.

Blumstein, A., J. Cohen, and D. Nagin. 1976. The dynamics of a homeostatic punishment process. *Journal of Criminal Law and Criminology* 67:317–334.

Blumstein, A., and J. Wallman (Eds.). 2005. *The crime drop in America.* 2nd ed. New York: Cambridge University Press.

Cantor, D., and K. C. Land. 1985. Unemployment and crime rates in the post–World War II United States: A theoretical and empirical analysis. *American Sociological Review* 50: 317–332.

Chiricos, T. 1987. Rates of crime and unemployment: An analysis of aggregate research evidence. *Social Problems* 34:187–212.

Cohen, L. E., and M. Felson. 1979. Social change and crime rate trends: A routine activity approach. *American Sociological Review* 44:588–608.

Cohen, M. A. 2005. *The costs of crime and justice.* New York: Routledge.

Cook, P. J., and G. A. Zarkin. 1985. Crime and the business cycle. *Journal of Legal Studies* 14:115–128.

Cullen, F. T., and J. P. Wright. 1997. Liberating the anomie-strain paradigm: Implications from social-support theory. In *The future of anomie theory.* Ed. N. Passas and R. Agnew, 187–206. Boston: Northeastern University Press.

Curtin, R. T. 2002. Surveys of consumers: Theory, methods, and interpretation. Paper presented at the meeting of the National Association for Business Economics. Washington, D.C.

———. 2003. Unemployment expectations: The impact of private information on income uncertainty. *Review of Income and Wealth* 49:539–554.

Durkheim, E. 1966 [1895]. *The rules of the sociological method.* New York: Free Press.

Eckholm, E. 2006. A welfare law milestone finds many left behind. *New York Times,* August 22. Available at http://www.nytimes.com/2006/08/22/us/22welfare.html?pagewanted =1&ref=us.

Eisner, M. 2001. Modernization, self-control and lethal violence. The long-term dynamics of European homicide rates in theoretical perspective. *British Journal of Criminology* 41:618–638.

———. 2003. The long-term development of violence: Empirical findings and theoretical approaches to interpretation. In *International handbook of violence research*. Ed. W. Heitmeyer and J. Hagan, 41–59. Dordrecht: Kluwer Academic Publisher.

Erikson, K. 1966. *Wayward puritans: A study in the sociology of deviance*. New York: John Wiley and Sons.

Federal Deposit Insurance Corporation. 2006. *Scenarios for the next U.S. recession*. Available at http://www.fdic.gov/bank/analytical/fyi/2006/032306fyi.html.

Felson, M. K. 2002. *Crime and everyday life*. 3rd ed. Thousand Oaks, Calif.: Sage.

Garland, D. 2001. *The culture of control: Crime and social order in contemporary society*. Chicago: University of Chicago Press.

Gottfredson, M., and T. Hirschi. 1990. *A general theory of crime*. Stanford, Calif.: Stanford University Press.

Greenwood, P. W., L. C. Model, P. Rydell, and J. Chiesa. 1998. *Diverting children from a life of crime*. Santa Monica, Calif.: RAND Corporation.

Gurr, T. 1989. Historical trends in violent crime: Europe and the United States. In *Violence in America*. Vol. 1, *The history of crime*. Ed. T. Gurr, 21–54. Newbury Park, Calif.: Sage.

Hughes, K. A. 2006. *Justice expenditure and employment in the United States, 2003*. Washington, D.C.: U.S. Department of Justice.

Klaus, P. A. 1994. *The costs of crime to victims*. Washington, D.C.: U.S. Department of Justice.

Langan, P. A., and D. A. Levin. 2002. *Recidivism of prisoners released in 1994*. Washington, D.C.: U.S. Department of Justice.

Levitt, S. D. 2004. Understanding why crime fell in the 1990s: Four factors that explain the decline and six that do not. *Journal of Economic Perspectives* 18:163–190.

Liedka, R. V., A. M. Piehl, and B. Useem. 2006. The crime-control effect of incarceration: Does scale matter? *Criminology and Public Policy* 5:245–276.

Manza, J., and C. Uggen. 2006. *Locked out: Felon disenfranchisement and American democracy*. New York: Oxford University Press.

Merton, R. K. 1938. Social structure and anomie. *American Sociological Review* 3:672–682.

Messner, S. F., and R. Rosenfeld. 1994. *Crime and the American dream*. Belmont, Calif.: Wadsworth.

———. 1997. *Crime and the American dream*. 2nd ed. Belmont, Calif.: Wadsworth.

———. 2001a. *Crime and the American dream*. 3rd ed. Belmont, Calif.: Wadsworth.

———. 2001b. An institutional-anomie theory of crime. In *Explaining criminals and crime*. Ed. R. Paternoster and R. Bachman, 151–160. Los Angeles: Roxbury.

———. 2004. 'Institutionalizing' criminological theory. *Advances in Criminological Theory* 13:83–105.

———. 2006. The present and future of institutional-anomie theory. *Advances in Criminological Theory* 15:127–148.

———. 2007. *Crime and the American dream*. 4th ed. Belmont, Calif.: Wadsworth.

Messner, S. F., H. Thome, and R. Rosenfeld. 2008. Institutions, anomie, and violent crime: Clarifying and elaborating institutional-anomie theory. *International Journal of Conflict and Violence* 2:163–181.

Nagin, D. S. 1998. Criminal deterrence research at the outset of the twenty-first century. In *Crime and justice: An annual review of research*, Vol. 23. Ed. M. Tonry, 1–42. Chicago: University of Chicago Press.

Office of the President. 1999. *Economic report of the president*. Washington, D.C.: U.S. Government Printing Office.

Parsons, T. 1951. *The social system*. New York: Free Press.

Pattillo, M., D. F. Weiman, and B. Western (Eds.). 2004. *Imprisoning America: The social effects of mass incarceration.* New York: Russell Sage Foundation.

Petersilia, J. 2003. *When prisoners come home: Parole and prisoner reentry.* New York: Oxford University Press.

Raphael, S., and R. Winter-Ebmer. 2001. Identifying the effect of unemployment on crime. *Journal o f Law and Economics* 44:259–283.

Rosenfeld, R. 2004. The case of the unsolved crime decline. *Scientific American* (February): 82–89.

Rosenfeld, R., and R. Fornango. 2007. The impact of economic conditions on robbery and property crime: The role of consumer sentiment. *Criminology* 45:735–769.

Rosenfeld, R., and S. F. Messner. 1994. Crime and the American dream: An institutional analysis. *Advances in Criminological Theory* 6:159–181.

———. 1997. Markets, morality, and an institutional-anomie theory of crime. In *The future of anomie theory.* Ed. N. Passas and R. Agnew, 207–224. Boston: Northeastern University Press.

Rosenfeld, R., J. Wallman, and R. Fornango. 2005. The contribution of ex-prisoners to crime rates. In *Prisoner reentry and crime in America.* Ed. J. Travis and C. Visher, 80–104. New York: Cambridge University Press.

Shiller, R. J. 2005. *Irrational exuberance.* New York: Doubleday.

Tonry, M. 1996. *Malign neglect: Race, crime, and punishment in America.* New York: Oxford University Press.

———. 2004. *Thinking about crime: Sense and sensibility in American penal culture.* New York: Oxford University Press.

Travis, J. 2005. *But they all come back: Facing the challenges of prisoner reentry.* Washington, D.C.: Urban Institute Press.

Travis, J., and C. Visher (Eds.). 2005. *Prisoner reentry and crime in America.* New York: Cambridge University Press.

Turner, J. H. 2003. *Human institutions: A theory of societal evolution.* Lanham: Rowman and Littlefield.

West, H. C., and W. J. Sabol. 2008. *Prisoners in 2007.* Washington, D.C.: U.S. Department of Justice.

Zimring, F. E. 2006. *The great American crime decline.* New York: Oxford University Press.

4

ALEX R. PIQUERO

A General Theory of Crime and Public Policy

In *A General Theory of Crime,* Michael Gottfredson and Travis Hirschi (1990) argue that self-control is the principal cause of criminal and analogous activity over the life course. According to the theorists, self-control is formed via a three-pronged parental socialization process in the first decade of life that includes parental monitoring of offspring, parental recognition of deviant behavior, and appropriate parental punishment associated with deviant behavior. Once formed by age 10–12, self-control is believed to be relatively stable over the life course, impervious to change by external sources of social control. Moreover, the effect of self-control infiltrates other life domains, including work, employment, education, and relationships. Those with low self-control are expected to have a higher likelihood of engaging in crime and deviant behavior and to have little success in other life domains (i.e., poor jobs, low education, poor relationship quality, etc.).

Much has been written about the general theory of crime, and researchers have subjected the theory to theoretical and empirical research (see reviews in Goode 2007; Pratt and Cullen 2000). And while Gottfredson and Hirschi have described some of the public policy implications of their theory, such discussion has been relegated to difficult-to-find publications, which has likely resulted in there being little debate in the more general, mainstream literature about the implications of their theory for crime control. This is an unfortunate happenstance. Discussions of theory and policy must be closely intertwined, because good theory abounds with policy implications, and good policy is guided by sound theory.

After identifying the key postulates and summarizing the strength for each postulate emerging from related research on the general theory of crime, the purpose of this chapter is to bring to the forefront a discussion about the public policy implications emanating from the general theory of crime generally, and from the key postulates in particular. The chapter closes with a reflection on the likelihood of achieving the specific policy implications, as well as their successful implementation.

Key Postulates in the General Theory of Crime

To be sure, Gottfredson and Hirschi constructed their theory largely in response to what they perceived the facts of crime to be. According to the theorists, the key facts are that (1) differences between high- and low-rate offenders persist over the life course; (2) efforts to treat or rehabilitate offenders do not produce the desired results; (3) intervention in childhood offers the greatest promise of success in crime reduction; (4) police and the more general criminal justice system have little effect on crime; (5) crimes may be prevented by increasing the effort required to commit them; (6) crime declines with age among all offenders and in almost all types of offending; (7) offenders do not specialize; (8) offenders have higher rate of accident, illness, and death than do non-offenders; (9) offenders are more likely than non-offenders to use drugs; (10) offenders are more frequently involved in non-criminal forms of deviance; (11) offenders are more weakly attached than non-offenders to restrictive institutions and long-term careers (families, schools, jobs); (12) offenders are disadvantaged with respect to intellectual and cognitive skills; and (13) family structure, family relations, and child-rearing practices are important predictors of deviant behavior because they operate through self-control (Hirschi and Gottfredson 2001, 91).

From these facts, one can deduce the key postulates emerging from the general theory of crime. Before these postulates are reviewed, it is important to remind readers that Gottfredson and Hirschi came to their general theory (and their image of the offender) largely as a result of looking at the various crimes to determine what they had in common.[1] Their study of this indicated that crimes were all quick and easy ways to get what one wants, and in the long run they are all dangerous to one's health, safety, reputation, and economic well-being (Hirschi and Gottfredson 2001, 82). With this image of crime, Gottfredson and Hirschi's image of the offender is one where individuals differ in the likelihood that they will take the quick and easy way regardless of the long-term risks. This enduring difference between people is called self-control, or

---

[1] As Hirschi and Gottfredson (1995, 138) recollect, "When we first attempted to understand the correlates of delinquency from a theoretical point of view, we decided that versatility was the primary or central issue, that our first task was to understand the source of versatility, to find what seemingly diverse behaviors have in common that accounts for their tendency to appear together in the behavioral repertoires of individuals."

the tendency to avoid acts whose long-term costs exceed their immediate or short-term benefits. Thus, the theorists contend that they need to be able to distinguish between crime and criminality (i.e., need something that changes with age—crime, but something that does not, criminality, or the tendency of people to engage in or refrain from criminal acts).

As originally described by the theorists, three critical interrelated postulates are associated with the general theory of crime (Gottfredson and Hirschi 1990, 253): (1) the age postulate (where composite measures of crime follow a predictable path over the life course, rising to a peak in late adolescence and declining sharply thereafter throughout life); (2) the stability postulate (where composite measures of crime are highly stable over time—people who have a high degree of criminality at one time will tend to have a high degree of criminality later in life); and (3) the versatility postulate (where indicators of crime, deviance, and analogous acts are consistently positively correlated among themselves).

The first postulate is the invariance of the age–crime relation (Hirschi and Gottfredson 1983). The distribution of age with respect to crime and delinquency is such that it increases throughout early to mid-adolescence, peaks in late adolescence, and then begins a precipitous decline throughout early adulthood. According to Gottfredson and Hirschi (1990, 124), "The shape or form of the distribution has remained virtually unchanged for about 150 years," leading them to conclude that "the age effect is everywhere and at all times the same." The theorists also extend the age postulate to include acts that are equivalent to crime, including prison infractions, motor-vehicle accidents, and the like.

Gottfredson and Hirschi (1990, 254) contend that because the causes of crime do not vary by age, they may be studied at any age. Perhaps there is no better or stronger statement of the age postulate than the following: "The empirical fact of a decline in the crime rate with age is beyond dispute" (131) and "is due to the inexorable aging of the organism" (141).

The second postulate is a fundamental assumption of control theory in that relative differences in the tendency to engage in deviant behavior are stable over the life course (Hirschi and Gottfredson 2000, 58). This postulate emerges from two strands of empirical data: (1) the relative invariance of the age effect on crime from which it follows "that differences in criminality between individuals at one point in time must be present at subsequent points in time as well" (58) or that "differences between people in the likelihood that they will commit criminal acts persist over time" (Gottfredson and Hirschi 1990, 107); and (2) the strong positive correlation between prior and future crime and delinquency.

According to the theorists, "Stability lies at the heart of the concept of self-control, and justifies our emphasis on early childhood socialization" (Gottfredson and Hirschi 1990, 58–59).[2] In fact, it could be stated that a major finding in criminology—that of stability—is one that had routinely been ignored or denied by extant theory until Gottfredson and Hirschi proposed the general theory of crime. Perhaps there is no better or stronger statement of the stability postulate than Hirschi and Gottfredson's (1995, 134) point, akin to David Farrington's (1992, 258) similar claim, regarding the stability evidence: "There is clear continuity over time in antisocial tendency. In other words, the antisocial child tends to become the antisocial teenager and the antisocial adult. . . . The relative orderings of any cohort of people on antisocial tendency is significantly consistent over time." And as Hirschi and Gottfredson surmised, "Differences between high- and low-rate offenders persist during the life course. Children ranked on the frequency of their delinquent acts will be ranked similarly later in life" (2001, 91).

The third postulate, regarding the versatility of offending, covers the idea that offenders are involved in a wide range of deviant, criminal, and analogous acts such that one need not to consider them as specific outcomes. In other words, individuals who engage in criminal acts, drug use, and other, more traditional crimes are also more likely to be involved in accidents, quit their jobs, fail to do their homework, engage in sexual promiscuity, engage in excessive gambling, and so forth. According Hirschi and Gottfredson, "Research ha[s] for some time shown that the behavior of offenders covers a broad range of criminal, deviant, and reckless acts. Indeed, the versatility finding is so widely accepted by the research community that [they] no longer feel compelled to defend it" (2000, 64). In making this claim, they are clear in noting that some specific crimes, such as "white-collar/corporate" crimes like tax evasion, stock swindles, and medical-billing fraud, are so "few in number and of limited interest to a behavioral theory" (65) that they need not be explained. Perhaps there is no clearer statement of the versatility postulate than the following: "Theories that assume specialization in particular forms of crime or deviant behavior are seriously at odds with good evidence" (Gottfredson and Hirschi 1990, 119). And consider these two statements made by Gottfredson and Hirschi:

---

[2] It is important to remind readers here that Gottfredson and Hirschi do not discount the possibility of changes in absolute levels of self-control within individuals. As they note, "Combining little or no movement from high self-control to low self-control with the fact that socialization continues to occur throughout life produces the conclusion that the proportion of the population in the potential offender pool should tend to decline as cohorts age. . . . Even the most active offenders burn out with time. . . . Put another way, the low self-control group continues over time to exhibit low self-control. Its size, however, declines" (1990, 107–108). Elsewhere they point out that "individual differences in self-control are established early in life (before differences in criminal behavior, however the state defines it, are possible) and are reasonably stable thereafter" (177).

Our portrait of the burglar applies equally well to the white-collar offender, the organized-crime offender, the dope dealer, and the assaulter; they are, after all, the same people. . . . They seem to do just about everything they can do: they do not specialize. (74, 190)

In short, after explicitly identifying the invariance of the age–crime relationship, Gottfredson and Hirschi's general theory of crime explicitly addresses the stability and versatility findings from extant criminological research and accounts for such findings with the concept of self-control (Gottfredson and Hirschi 1990, 119). As they surmise, "Both the stability of differences between individuals and the versatility of offenders can be derived from the fact that all such acts follow a predictable path over the life course, peaking in the middle to late teens, and then declining steadily throughout life" (Hirschi and Gottfredson 1994, 2).

To this list of Gottfredson and Hirschi's original postulates, I would argue that one more needs to be added: the generality postulate. This postulate contends that as a general theory of crime, with self-control as the principal correlate, self-control should be implicated in all sorts of deviant, criminal, and analogous acts, as the versatility postulate suggests. However, the generality postulate advanced here covers the theorists' expectation that the theory will be applicable across demographic groups and invariant across cultures, societies, times, and places. In this regard, Gottfredson and Hirschi are clear in noting that "the important correlates of crime do not vary across cultures" (1990, 178) or "social conditions" (128); "available data suggests that the age–crime relation is *invariant* across sex and race" (126; emphasis in the original); and "the age effect is everywhere and at all times the same" (124) and is for all people, irrespective of race, class, and other demographic characteristic (149–153). Perhaps there is no better summary statement of the generality postulate than this:

Tests of generality or scope are, in our view, easy to devise. In criminology, it is often argued that special theories are required to explain female and male crime, crime in one culture rather than another, crime committed in the course of an occupation as distinct from street crime, or crime committed by children as distinct from crime committed by adults. . . . [W]e intend our theory to apply to all of these cases, and more. It is meant to explain *all crimes, at all times,* and, for that matter, many forms of behavior that are not sanctioned by the state. (117; emphasis added)

How has the general theory of crime held up with regard to research on these three postulates? The next section documents this accumulated knowledge base.

Strength of Empirical Support regarding the General Theory's Postulates

A number of high-quality reviews exist regarding the general theory's empirical record (see Goode 2007; Pratt and Cullen 2000). Here, a brief overview of the empirical support regarding the general theory's key postulates will be highlighted. This will be followed by a more expansive discussion of the public policy implications emanating from the general theory, as well as the extent to which such policy implications could be fruitful if applied in a policy context.

With respect to the age postulate generally, and the invariance thesis in particular, a wide range of studies have generated discrepant results. For example, some studies have shown that the relationship between age and crime is not precisely the same for all crimes and for all populations (Greenberg 1985; Steffensmeier et al. 1989). At the same time, there is much evidence in favor of shape invariance—that is, that the relationships between age and many kinds of crime across different populations adhere to the single, mid- to late-adolescence peak, followed by a decline in early adulthood (Farrington 1986). At the same time, a recent strand of research that employs advanced statistical and methodological tools (e.g., semi-parametric mixed Poisson model) that parcels out the aggregate age–crime curve into distinct trajectories of similar offenders often reveals that the unique trajectories do not resemble the aggregate age–crime curve (see Nagin 2005; Piquero 2007). In particular, several of these empirical studies show substantial and significant deviations from the aggregate trend (peaking in late adolescence and dropping in early adulthood). One study in particular, using data from criminal offenders in the Netherlands, shows that there is a small group of offenders who offend at relatively stable rates into middle to late adulthood (Blokland, Nagin, and Nieuwbeerta 2005). Further, John Laub and Robert Sampson's (2003) recent analysis of the official arrest records of the Glueck delinquent sample showed unique age–crime curves for different trajectory groups in general and across crime type, with the common finding that by age 70, most offenders had desisted from crime.[3]

One recent study that deserved further discussion comes from an analysis of survey data from Oklahoma. Here, Charles Tittle and Harold Grasmick (1997) provided three advances over the previous age–crime research: (1) data were based on subjects age 18–90; (2) data contained several indicators of crime; and (3) data contained several important and competing theoretical variables, in addition to self-control, that had not been previously used in tests

---

[3] True to form, Gottfredson and Hirschi dismiss the evidence that does not comport with their view of the age–crime relation in the following manner: "The question for criminology is whether the glass is 97 percent full or 3 percent empty—that is, whether to pursue the important implications of a remarkably robust age effect or to continue to revel in the statistical noise generated by atheoretical research" (1990, 134).

of the general theory of crime. In total, their analysis yielded a mixed bag of results. First, with regard to the "invariance hypothesis," they found fairly strong evidence, with the exception of tax cheating, of a single peak in late adolescence (when their data began) and a linear negative trend of offending into adulthood. Tittle and Grasmick interpret this result as one of generalizability but not necessarily complete invariance. Second, they found mixed results with regard to the "inexplicability hypothesis" regarding the ability of social variables to explain the age–crime relationship. That is, they were unable to explain most of the age effect. Third, their assessment of the "non-interaction hypothesis" that the correlates of crime do not interact with age also showed mixed results but that most variables did not interact with age. Finally, Tittle and Grasmick's analysis, in contrast to Gottfredson and Hirschi, found that low self-control varied with age (i.e., it demonstrated a U-shaped relationship with age).

Regarding the stability postulate, some of its support (or lack thereof) was reviewed in the above section on age and crime, For this reason, this section focuses more on the assessment of the stability postulate within the context of two strands of literature: the relationship between past and future crime and the stability of self-control within individuals.[4]

Gottfredson and Hirschi (1990) are clear in noting that the best predictor of future criminal behavior is past criminal behavior. One of the first studies to directly assess this issue was Daniel Nagin and Raymond Paternoster's (1991) longitudinal analysis of the linkage between four self-reported delinquency acts in a two-wave panel of high-school students. Nagin and Paternoster cast their study within the two-pronged perspective of persistent heterogeneity and state dependence as the causal underpinning of the relationship between past and future delinquency, the former noting that unmeasured differences across individuals account for the relationship and the latter noting that prior offending alters the individual's situational or moral constraints in some fashion, which in turn increases their future offending. Results indicated more support for the state-dependence argument. In another study, Nagin and Farrington (1992) assessed a similar question with data from the Cambridge Study in Delinquent Development, a longitudinal study of 411 men in South London age 10–32. Results from this study showed strong support for persistent heterogeneity over state dependence. Several other studies yield similarly conflicting results, with Raymond Paternoster and Robert Brame (1997) finding support for state dependence; Shawn Bushway, Robert Brame, and Raymond Paternoster (1999) and Alex Piquero, Chris Gibson, and Stephen Tibbetts (2002) finding support for

---

[4] According to Hirschi and Gottfredson, "The positive correlation between past and future measures of crime net of the effects of other variables does not deny the influence of some enduring individual difference, such as level of self-control. On the contrary, such a correlation is 'fully consistent' with the idea that a 'latent behavioral trait' accounts for both measures" (2000, 64).

state dependence even in the wake of strong controls for persistent heterogeneity (which itself was important). This has led some scholars to call for a theory that is friendly to an integrated persistent heterogeneity and state dependence perspective to explain the relationship between prior and future delinquency generally and to account for crime over the life course in particular (see Laub and Sampson 2003; Paternoster et al. 1997).

Four studies have specifically examined the stability of self-control, using some type of attitudinal/behavioral measure, within and across persons over time. Bruce Arneklev, John Cochran, and Randy Gainey (1998) employed data on college students who were assessed at the beginning and end of a semester (four months apart) to examine the stability issue. Their analysis indicated that overall self-control was quite stable (test–retest correlation of .82), but that separate analyses of the self-control components showed somewhat less stability within persons. Michael Turner and Alex Piquero (2002) used data from a large sample of children followed through late adolescence in the National Longitudinal Survey of Youth (NLSY) and compared changes in self-control generally and among offenders and non-offenders in the NLSY in particular. Using both attitudinal and behavioral measures of self-control, four findings emerged from their effort: (1) prior to age 8, offenders and non-offenders did not differ significantly on self-control, but after age 8, offenders showed lower self-control than non-offenders; (2) self-control increased with age for both offenders and non-offenders; (3) within groups, the correlations between measures of self-control were positive and modest though not overly strong; and (4) when they isolated offenders and non-offenders in the bottom quartile on the behavioral measure of self-control during early adolescence and then compared these individuals with other sample members in the same group at three subsequent time periods, they found evidence of both stability and change in self-control. Ojmarrh Mitchell and Doris Layton MacKenzie (2006) used data from a two-wave panel of incarcerated offenders to examine two hypotheses regarding the stability postulate: (1) that after early childhood, interventions aimed at reducing antisocial behavior will be unsuccessful, as self-control is believed to be resilient to such efforts; and (2) that self-control was relatively stable among individuals over time. Their analysis indicated that self-control was not stable (in absolute or relative terms) during a short period of time, but that it was resilient to participation in a treatment-oriented boot camp program. Moreover, some of the components of their self-control measure actually fared worse during the imprisonment experience. Finally, L. Thomas Winfree, Terrance Taylor, Ni He, and Finn-Aage Esbensen (2006) examined self-control levels, self-reported illegal behavior, and supporting attitudes in a longitudinal study of youth from six cities at five points in time. Several key findings emerged from their effort, but I focus here on their specific findings with respect to the stability postulate. Importantly, their analysis did not find evidence for the hypothesis that self-control is an "immutable and stable propensity" (278). Specifically, levels of self-control generally, and of impulsivity in particular, declined throughout the study period (as individuals aged), and this decline was more consistent in each year for offenders compared with non-offenders. Splitting the sample into offenders and non-offenders did little to change the overall conclusions from the study: that self-control is not a stable, immutable construct.[5]

The empirical record on the versatility postulate is probably the one area where Gottfredson and Hirschi's theory has received the most empirical support. Prior to the delineation of their theory, researchers had long been interested in the patterning of offenses within offenders over the course of their criminal careers (see Blumstein et al. 1986; Farrington, Snyder, and Finnegan, 1988; Wolfgang, Figlio, and Sellin, 1972). This line of research generated the summary conclusion that there was very little evidence of specialization among offenders and that versatility was a characteristic of offenders' careers—and, in fact, was used as a large cornerstone of the general theory.

Since the publication of *A General Theory of Crime*, a number of scholars have continued to assess the versatility issue. In fact, empirical tests of the versatility postulate are clear and straightforward to conduct because one is interested in knowing simply where those who engage in one crime are more likely to engage in other deviant or criminal activities. In general, results continue to remain supportive of Gottfredson and Hirschi's contention that individuals involved in one form or type of deviant or criminal behavior are likely to be involved in other forms and types of deviant behavior over the life course. The versatility postulate is perhaps the one part of the theory that most criminologists accept, yet some continue to question whether particular crimes, such as terrorism and tax evasion, fall under the theory's purview and whether these acts, as Hirschi and Gottfredson (2000, 65) suggest, are "few in number and of limited interest to behavioral theory."

For example, Chester Britt (1994) used three different data sources (offense-specific data from the Uniform Crime Reports, data from the Bail Decision-Making Study, and self-reported data from the Seattle Youth Survey) to assess the specialization question and failed to find any evidence that offenders specialize in the types of crime they commit. David Evans, Francis Cullen, Velmer Burton, R. Gregory Dunaway, and Michael Benson (1997) used self-reported data from a sample of Midwestern individuals and found that offenders were more frequently involved in non-criminal forms of deviance than non-offenders and that the effect of self-control on crime and analogous behaviors was virtually

---

[5] They also found that the relative intergroup rankings for impulsivity and risk seeking (when comparisons were made between offenders and non-offenders in the lowest quartile and then among offenders and non-offenders in the highest quartile) did not change over time (Winfree et al. 2006, 279).

identical.[6] Using data from the Cambridge Study in Delinquent Development, Paternoster and Brame (1998) examined the empirical association between self-control at age 8–9 and self-reported involvement in a variety of criminal and analogous acts during adolescence. Their analysis indicated that self-control was associated with both outcomes, as Gottfredson and Hirschi would suggest, but that the covariance between criminal and analogous behaviors could not be explained entirely by self-control.

Other research has linked self-control to myriad deviant and antisocial outcomes, including accidents and illnesses (Robins 1978), death (Piquero et al. 2005), binge drinking and assorted alcohol-related consequences (Piquero, Gibson, and Tibbetts 2002), and differential sanction threat perceptions (Piquero, Gomez-Smith, and Langton, 2004). Even further, some researchers have found very little evidence for specialization in sexual (Lussier, LeBlanc, and Proulx, 2005; Zimring 2004) or violent (Capaldi and Patterson 1996; Farrington 1989; Piquero 2000) offending. In general, these efforts have shown that the best predictor of a particular crime type is the frequency of offending.[7]

With this review in hand, the next section of the chapter focuses on the policy implications that emanate from the general theory of crime generally, and from each postulate in particular.

Policy Implication Emanating from Each Postulate

It is the case that Gottfredson and Hirschi (1990, 1995; see also Hirschi and Gottfredson 2001) have devoted some time to public policy implications throughout their collective works. Instead of listing such implications within a postulate framework, they do provide a more general listing that is useful to reproduce here. This will present a good overview before turning to the postulate-specific policy implications. It is important to note that the theorists are just as clear about what they think will be effective with regard to crime control as about what they believe will be ineffective (criminal career programs, modifications in policing, selective incapacitation, and so on; Gottfredson and Hirschi 1990, 274).

---

[6] To be sure, several of the acts in the Evans et al. (1997) analogous behavior index were actually criminal offenses (e.g., drunk driving, use of illegal drugs).

[7] Clearly, some researchers still do not view the evidence in favor of versatility in the same light. For example, Gilbert Geis concludes, "Research indicates, however, that criminal offenders are not necessarily polymorphously perverse. . . . Offenders often specialize" (2000, 43). Some studies do offer evidence of some level of specialization in offending. For example, in their analysis of white-collar offenders, Benson and Moore (1992) find that those who commit garden-variety white-collar crimes can, as a group, be distinguished from those who commit more general street offenses. Richard Wright and colleagues' (1995) analysis of residential burglars makes the specialization claim as a function of the acquired expertise gained by burglars as a result of the commission of that specific crime type.

The policy implications arising from the general theory of crime stem directly from Gottfredson and Hirschi's image of the offender (youthfulness, limited cognitive skills, and low self-control) and of crimes (which provide immediate, obvious benefit; are easily accomplished; and require little skill, planning, or persistence). Recall that offenders are believed to be easily deterred by increasing the immediate difficulties and risks of criminal acts and are generally unaffected by changes in the long-term costs of criminal behavior. To Gottfredson and Hirschi, steering wheel locks (which increase certainty) are more effective than increased penalties (severity) in reducing auto theft. Such a view is entirely consistent with evidence on deterrence theory, which shows that the certainty of punishment is a more effective inhibitor of crime than its severity (Nagin 1998). Thus, within the context of the general theory of crime, crimes can be prevented in part by making them more complex or difficult to commit.

Borrowing from the rational choice framework (Cornish and Clarke 1987), the general theory of crime supports an offense-specific approach to crime prevention. Offense-specific approaches begin by analyzing the conditions necessary for a particular act to occur. As Hirschi and Gottfredson (2001, 93) note: "Efforts directed at offenders—treatment, deterrence, incapacitation—will be highly inefficient compared to programs that restrict access to [committing crime]." Thus, consistent with more general evidence on crime control (Sherman et al. 2002), more impact in crime reduction will emerge from making crime harder to commit than from anything else and from keeping offenders guessing (Koper 1995). Thus, according to Hirschi and Gottfredson:

> Self-control theory leads to the conclusion that the formal criminal justice system can play only a minor role in the prevention and control of crime. Because potential offenders do not consider the long-term consequences of their acts, modification of these consequences will have little effect on their behavior. Because criminal acts are so quickly and easily accomplished, they are only rarely directly observed by agents of the criminal justice system. As a result, even large increases in the number of such agents would have minimal effect on the rates of most crimes. (2001, 93)

These and other considerations led the theorists to advance the following eight recommendations for crime control policy (Gottfredson and Hirschi 1995; Hirschi and Gottfredson 2001, 93–94).

1. Do not attempt to control crime by incapacitating adults; this is so because by the time offenders are identified and incarcerated in

adulthood, they have already finished the brunt of their criminal activity.

2. Do not attempt to control crime by rehabilitating adults; this is so because the age effect makes treatment unnecessary and no treatment program has been shown to be effective.

3. Do not attempt to control crime by altering the penalties available to the criminal justice system; this is so because legal penalties do not have the desired effect because offenders do not consider them. Increasing the certainty and severity will have a highly limited effect on the decisions of offenders.

4. Restrict unsupervised activities of teenagers; by limiting teens' access to guns, cars, and alcohol, opportunities become restricted.

5. Limit proactive policing, including sweeps, stings, intensive arrest programs, aggressive drug policies.

6. Question the characterization of crime offered by agents of the criminal justice system and repeated by the media; this is so because evidence suggests that offenders are not dedicated, professional.

7. Support programs designed to provide early education and effective child care; this is so because prevention [and] intervention in the early years are most important. Programs that target dysfunctional families and seek to remedy lack of supervision have shown promise.

8. Support policies that promote and facilitate two-parent families and that increase the number of caregivers relative to the number of children; this is so because large and single-parent families are handicapped with respect to monitoring and discipline (the key elements in producing adequate socialization and strong self-control). Programs to prevent teen pregnancies should be given high priority.

With this listing in hand, let us turn now to a postulate-specific review of policy implications arising from the general theory of crime.

Age Postulate

Because Gottfredson and Hirschi believe the age–crime relation to be invariant across time, space, place, and people, and because they believe the age–crime relation to be inexplicable by any theory, they contend that time is the best healer of criminal activity. In other words, with the aging of the person, crime will inevitably decrease. Thus, for Gottfredson and Hirschi a clear policy implication is that lengthy incarceration stints, mandatory maximum penalties, and associated three strikes laws will do little to alter criminal activity at the aggregate or individual level.

Stability Postulate

Gottfredson and Hirschi contend that the best predictor of future criminal behavior is prior criminal behavior, that self-control is relatively stable between individuals (though absolute, within-person levels of self-control may change), and that self-control is impervious to change from external sources of social control after the first decade of life. The policy implication stemming from this stability postulate is such that if one wants to achieve any measure of lowering the chances of criminal activity, attention must be focused on the first ten to twelve years of a child's life. Gottfredson and Hirschi paint a very dismal portrait for the prospect of change after this dynamic time period lapses. There is good evidence with respect to the success of early childhood intervention and prevention efforts from various sources. For example, David Olds and colleagues' (1998) nurse home-visitation program uncovered strong results (lower crime, lower drug use, better school performance) for mothers and their children who participated in a nurse home-visitation program in the first two to three years of life. Similar positive results were obtained by children participating in the Perry Preschool Program (Schweinhart et al. 2005), where a longitudinal follow-up of a small sample of African Americans born in poverty and at high risk of failing in school who received a high-quality preschool program were found at age 40 to have higher earnings, were more likely to hold a job, had committed fewer crimes, and were more likely to have graduated from high school than adults who did not have preschool. Finally, Richard Tremblay and colleagues' (1996) Montreal Longitudinal-Experimental Study combined child skills training and parent training to identify disruptive (aggressive/hyperactive) boys at age 6 and randomly allocated more than three hundred of them to experimental or control conditions. In the following two to three years, the boys in the experimental group received training designed to foster social skills and self-control, while the parents were taught how to provide positive reinforcement, use non-punitive and consistent discipline practices, and develop family-crisis-management techniques. Follow-up analyses at age 12 showed that, compared with boys in the control group, the boys in the experimental group committed less theft and burglary, were less likely to get drunk, and were less likely to be involved in fights. Other findings showed that the boys in the experimental group had higher school achievement and were less likely to be gang members, get drunk, or take drugs. All of these studies provide support for what has come to be known outside the general theory of crime parlance as developmental crime prevention (Farrington and Welsh 2007; Tremblay and Craig 1995).

Although good evidence exists on the malleability of self-control in the first decade of life, it is important to return to Gottfredson and Hirschi's stance that self-control is unlikely to change after this time period in response to external sources of social control. Thus, they contend that rehabilitation efforts and cognitive skills training will have little success for individuals in the teenage and adult years. What is the evidence with respect to the changeability of self-control after childhood? The record on this point is unfriendly to Gottfredson and Hirschi. In fact, a number of prevention and intervention efforts in childhood and adulthood do hold some promise for both altering self-control and reducing criminal behavior. Moreover, external sources of social control have shown alterations with respect to individual self-control, including schools (Gottfredson 2001; Turner, Pratt, and Piquero, 2005), neighborhoods (Pratt, Turner, and Piquero 2004), correctional facilities (Mitchell and MacKenzie 2006), and several treatment efforts (see, e.g., Sherman et al. 2002).

Versatility Postulate

Gottfredson and Hirschi contend that the evidence with regard to versatility is such that offenders engage in all sorts of deviant, antisocial, and criminal acts and that they will not respond to specific points of intervention other than to shift to another type of crime when opportunities for a certain one are limited. There is some evidence with respect to how offenders choose crime targets (Cornish and Clarke 1987; Jacobs 1996; Piquero and Rengert 1999; Wright and Decker 1994, 1997) but little by way of information at the individual, perceptual level about differential responses to perceived constraints on and blockages of criminal opportunity and how offenders react to them. More generally, the issue here with respect to crime prevention is such that because Gottfredson and Hirschi believe the within-person causes of a deviant act such as truancy are the same as the within-person causes of drug use, aggravated assault, tax evasion, and so forth, the criminal justice system will have little effect on any of them. Instead, efforts should be aimed at dealing not necessarily with specific crimes (though making some crimes more difficult to commit may have some modicum of success) but instead at dealing with the origins of criminal behavior: self-control. Thus, to deal with the versatility problem, Gottfredson and Hirschi suggest that efforts must be aimed at the offender; if self-control is instilled, then a reduction in the range of deviant, antisocial, and criminal acts is likely to follow. Efforts aimed at improving self-control appear to have success in reducing various forms of deviant, antisocial, and criminal activity (Farrington and Welsh 2007; Tremblay et al. 1996), as Gottfredson and Hirschi hypothesize.

What Is the Likelihood of Achieving These Policy Implications?

Achieving policy implications is one thing; getting them to the discussion table in the first place seems like a good place to start. So let us begin there.

Many of the specific policy implications emerging from the general theory of crime are intuitive; are easily grasped by academics, policymakers, and citizens alike; and are likely to be embraceable (though not necessarily embraced). Some readers may have qualms about Gottfredson and Hirschi's specific recommendations or about those inferred from the theory's postulates. For example, although Gottfredson and Hirschi claim that the police have no effect on crime, there is ample evidence to suggest that in some contexts the police do have some effect on crime, but it should be remembered that what the police do on the street is the most important—that is, keeping offenders guessing, rotating crackdowns, and the like (Koper 1995; Sherman 1990). To say that the police have no effect on crime, as Gottfredson and Hirschi do, is an overstatement. Similarly, there is good evidence that some rehabilitation and intervention efforts and programs can increase self-control, improve decision making, and reduce crime regardless of whether the effort is instilled in childhood, adolescence, or even adulthood. So some of their strong statements about what does not work are likely to be met with serious disagreement backed by empirical research.

Boiled down to its core, Gottfredson and Hirschi's general theory of crime really has two key policy prescriptions: a short-term strategy that makes criminal events less attractive to potential offenders by making them more difficult to commit successfully (increase certainty); and a longer-term strategy that focuses prevention and intervention efforts that improve child-rearing practices (which produce more self-control) in the first decade of life. Good evidence exists on both of these fronts, and the costs are not as exorbitant as are the costs associated with the continued incarceration binge that the United States currently faces and will continue to face in the years to come. These efforts, many of which are described more specifically in other sources (for efforts to increase certainty of detection and punishment, see Nagin 1998; for efforts to improve child-rearing practices, see Tremblay et al. 1996), have been found to be successful and not cost-prohibitive. With a short- and long-term focus, there is something for everyone. The cost of instilling these efforts is small, and the rewards may be great. Given the knowledge of weak effects at high costs for mass incarceration, it seems prudent to give serious consideration to the short- and long-term strategies that emanate from the general theory of crime with respect to crime control.

References

Arneklev, B. J., J. K. Cochran, and R. R. Gainey. 1998. Testing Gottfredson and Hirschi's "low self-control" stability hypothesis: An exploratory study. *American Journal of Criminal Justice* 23:107–127.

Benson, M. L., and E. Moore. 1992. Are white collar and common offenders the same? *Journal of Research in Crime and Delinquency* 29:251–272.

Blokland, A. J., D. S. Nagin, and P. Nieuwbeerta. 2005. Life span offending trajectories of a Dutch conviction cohort. *Criminology* 43:919–954.

Blumstein, A., J. Cohen, J. A. Roth, and C. A. Visher (Eds.). 1986. *Criminal careers and career criminals.* Washington, D.C.: National Academy Press.

Britt, C. L. 1994. Participation and frequency. In *The generality of deviance.* Ed. T. Hirschi and M. R. Gottfredson, 193–213. New Brunswick, N.J.: Transaction Publishers.

Bushway, S. D., R. Brame, and R. Paternoster. 1999. Assessing stability and change in criminal offending: A comparison of random effects, semiparametric, and fixed effects modeling strategies. *Journal of Quantitative Criminology* 15:23–61.

Capaldi, D. N., and G. R. Patterson. 1996. Can violent offenders be distinguished from frequent offenders: Prediction from childhood to adolescence. *Journal of Research in Crime and Delinquency* 33:206–231.

Cornish, D., and R. V. Clarke. 1987. Understanding crime displacement: An application of rational choice theory. *Criminology* 25:933–947.

Evans, T. D., F. T. Cullen, V. S. Burton Jr., R. G. Dunaway, and M. L. Benson. 1997. The social consequences of self-control: Testing the general theory of crime. *Criminology* 35:475–501.

Farrington, D. P. 1986. Age and crime. In *Crime and justice: An annual review of research.* Vol. 7. Ed. M. Tonry and N. Morris, 189–250. Chicago: University of Chicago Press.

———. 1989. Self-reported and official offending from adolescence to adulthood. In *Cross-national research in self-reported crime and delinquency.* Ed. M. Klein, 399–423. Dordrecht: Kluwer.

———. 1992. Explaining the beginning, process, and ending of antisocial behavior from birth to adulthood. In *Facts, frameworks, and forecasts,* Vol. 3, *Advances in criminological theory.* Ed. J. McCord, 253–286. New Brunswick, N.J.: Transaction.

Farrington, D. P., H. N. Snyder, and T. A. Finnegan. 1988. Specialization in juvenile court careers. *Criminology* 26:461–487.

Farrington, D. P., and B. C. Welsh. 2007. *Saving children from a life of crime: Early risk factors and effective interventions.* New York: Oxford University Press.

Geis, G. 2000. On the absence of self-control as the basis for a general theory of crime. *Theoretical Criminology* 4:35–53.

Goode, E. 2007. *The general theory of crime, a review of the issues.* Palo Alto, Calif.: Stanford University Press.

Gottfredson, D. C. 2001. *Schools and delinquency.* New York: Cambridge University Press.

Gottfredson, M. R., and T. Hirschi. 1990. *A general theory of crime.* Stanford, Calif.: Stanford University Press.

———. 1995. National crime control policies. *Society* 32:30–36.

Greenberg, D. 1985. Age, crime, and social explanation. *American Journal of Sociology* 91: 1–21.

Hirschi, T., and M. R. Gottfredson. 1983. Age and the explanation of crime. *American Journal of Sociology* 89:552–584.

——— (Eds.). 1994. *The generality of deviance.* New Brunswick, N.J.: Transaction.

———. 1995. Control theory and the life-course perspective. *Studies on Crime and Crime Prevention* 4:131–142.

———. 2000. In defense of self-control. *Theoretical Criminology* 4:55–69.

———. 2001. Self-control. In *Explaining criminals and crime.* Ed. R. Paternoster and R. Bachman, 81–96. Los Angeles: Roxbury.

Jacobs, B. A. 1996. *Dealing crack: The social world of streetcorner selling.* Boston: Northeastern University Press.

Koper, C. 1995. Just enough police presence: Reducing crime and disorderly behavior by optimizing patrol time in crime hot spots. *Justice Quarterly* 12:649–672.

Laub, J. H., and R. J. Sampson. 2003. *Shared beginnings, divergent lives.* Cambridge, Mass.: Harvard University Press.

Lussier, P., M. LeBlanc, and J. Proulx. 2005. The generality of criminal behavior: A confirmatory factor analysis of the criminal activity of sex offenders in adulthood. *Journal of Criminal Justice* 33:177–189.

Mitchell, O., and D. L. MacKenzie. 2006. The stability and resiliency of self-control in a sample of incarcerated offenders. *Crime and Delinquency* 52:432–449.

Nagin, D. S. 1998. Criminal deterrence research at the outset of the twenty-first century. In *Crime and justice: A review of research.* Vol. 23. Ed. M. Tonry, 1–42. Chicago: University of Chicago Press.

———. 2005. *Group-based modeling of development.* Cambridge, Mass.: Harvard University Press.

Nagin, D. S., and D. P. Farrington. 1992. The stability of criminal potential from childhood to adulthood. *Criminology* 30:235–260.

Nagin, D. S., and R. Paternoster. 1991. On the relationship of past and future participation in delinquency. *Criminology* 29:163–190.

Olds, D., C. R. Henderson Jr., R. Cole, J. Eckenrode, H. Kitzman, D. Luckey, et al. 1998. Long-term effects of nurse home visitation on children's criminal and antisocial behavior: 15-year follow-up of a randomized controlled trial. *Journal of the American Medical Association* 280:1238–1244.

Paternoster, R., and R. Brame. 1997. Multiple routes to delinquency: A test of developmental and general theories of crime. *Criminology* 35:49–84.

———. 1998. The structural similarity of processes generating criminal and analogous behaviors. *Criminology* 36:633–670.

Paternoster, R., C. W. Dean, A. R. Piquero, P. Mazerolle, R. and Brame. 1997. Generality, continuity, and change in offending. *Journal of Quantitative Criminology* 13:231–266.

Piquero, A. R. 2000. Frequency, specialization, and violence in offending careers. *Journal of Research in Crime and Delinquency* 37:392–418.

———. 2008. Taking stock of developmental trajectories of criminal activity over the life course. In *The yield of longitudinal studies of crime and delinquency.* Ed. A. Liberman, 23–78. New York: Springer.

Piquero, A. R., C. Gibson, and S. G. Tibbetts. 2002. Does low self-control account for the correlation between binge-drinking and alcohol related behaviors? *Criminal Behavior and Mental Health* 12:135–154.

Piquero, A. R., Z. Gomez-Smith, and L. Langton. 2004. Discerning unfairness where others may not: Low self-control and unfair sanction perceptions. *Criminology* 42:699–734.

Piquero, A. R., J. MacDonald, A. Dobrin, L. E. Daigle, and F. T. Cullen. 2005. Self-control, violent offending, and homicide victimization: Assessing the general theory of crime. *Journal of Quantitative Criminology* 21:55–72.

Piquero, A. R., and G. F. Rengert. 1999. Studying deterrence with active residential burglars. *Justice Quarterly* 16:451–471.

Pratt, T. C., and F. T. Cullen. 2000. The empirical status of Gottfredson and Hirschi's general theory of crime: A meta-analysis. *Criminology* 38:931–964.

Pratt, T. C., M. G. Turner, and A. R. Piquero. 2004. Parental socialization and community context: A longitudinal analysis of the structural sources of low self-control. *Journal of Research in Crime and Delinquency* 41:219–243.

Robins, L. N. 1978. Sturdy childhood predictors of adult antisocial behavior: Replications from longitudinal studies. *Psychological Medicine* 8:611–622.

Schweinhart, L. J., J. Montie, Z. Xiang, W. S. Barnett, C. R. Belfield, and M. Nores. 2005. *Lifetime effects: The High/Scope Perry Preschool study through age 40.* Monographs of the High/Scope Educational Research Foundation, 14. Ypsilanti, Mich.: High/Scope Press.

Sherman, L. W. 1990. Police crackdowns: Initial and residual deterrence. In *Crime and justice: A review of research,* Vol. 13. Ed. M. Tonry, 1–48. Chicago: University of Chicago Press.

Sherman, L. W., D. P. Farrington, B. C. Welsh, and D. L. MacKenzie. 2002. *Evidence-based crime prevention.* New York: Routledge.

Steffensmeier, D. J., E. A. Allan, M. D. Harer, and C. Streifel. 1989. Age and the distribution of crime. *American Journal of Sociology* 94:803–831.

Tittle, C. R., and H. G. Grasmick. 1997. Criminal behavior and age: A test of three provocative hypotheses. *Journal of Criminal Law and Criminology* 88:309–342.

Tremblay, R. E., and W. M. Craig. 1995. Developmental crime prevention. In *Crime and justice: An annual review of research.* Ed. M. Tonry and D. P. Farrington, 151–236. Chicago: University of Chicago Press.

Tremblay, R. E., L. C. Masse, L. Pagani, and F. Vitaro. 1996. From childhood physical aggression to adolescent maladjustment: The Montreal Prevention Experiment. In *Preventing childhood disorders, substance use, and delinquency.* Ed. R. D. Peters and R. J. McMahon, 168–298. Thousand Oaks, Calif.: Sage.

Turner, M. G., and A. R. Piquero. 2002. The stability of self-control. *Journal of Criminal Justice* 30:457–471.

Turner, M. G., T. C. Pratt, and A. R. Piquero. 2005. The school context as a source of self-control. *Journal of Criminal Justice* 33:329–339.

Winfree, L. T., T. J. Taylor, N. He, and F. A. Esbensen. 2006. Self-control and variability over time: Multivariate results using a five-year, multisite panel of youths. *Crime and Delinquency* 52:253–286.

Wolfgang, M. E., R. M. Figlio, and T. Sellin. 1972. *Delinquency in a birth cohort.* Chicago: University of Chicago Press.

Wright, R. T., and S. H. Decker. 1994. *Burglars on the job: Streetlife and residential break-ins.* Boston: Northeastern University Press.

———. 1997. *Armed robbers in action: Stickups and street culture.* Boston: Northeastern University Press.

Wright, R. T., R. H. Logie, and S. H. Decker. 1995. Criminal expertise and offender decision making: An experimental study of the target selection process in residential burglary. *Journal of Research in Crime and Delinquency* 32:39–53.

Zimring, F. E. 2004. *An American travesty: Legal responses to adolescent sexual offending.* Chicago: University of Chicago Press.

5

RONALD L. AKERS

Nothing Is as Practical as a Good Theory

*Social Learning Theory and the Treatment
and Prevention of Delinquency*

I concluded a recent article on the relationship between theory and practice by outlining some questions to ask when examining existing programs and policies for theoretical linkages. These included the following questions regarding past and current programs for control, treatment, or prevention of crime and delinquency (Akers 2005, 34–36):

1. Which of these programs and policies are based explicitly and clearly on a theory of crime and delinquency? . . .
2. Which policies and programs are based on a combination of different theories? . . .
3. Which programs are based only implicitly on theoretical assumptions, not recognized or articulated by those who put the program into place or operate it? Can the underlying theoretical principles behind the program be identified?

These questions are related to the purposes of this chapter. I begin with a review of some basic assertions about the relationship between theory and practice in criminology. Then, after providing an overview of social learning theory of crime and delinquency, I review prevention and treatment programs that are self-consciously and clearly based on the cognitive-behavioral principles and processes in social learning theory (whether or not they are combined with other compatible theories) relevant to questions 1 and 2. Programs based on

---

This is a revised version of a paper presented at the Academy of Criminal Justice Sciences, Seattle, March 2007.

these principles have been shown by good research to be at least moderately effective, and I include references to that research. I give somewhat more detailed descriptions of some good examples of theory-based programs taken from the work of the Oregon Social Learning Center (OSLC) and from the work of the Social Development Research Group (SDRG) in Seattle. The OSLC programs are explicitly founded on social learning theory but also have elements that are consistent—at least, implicitly—with social bonding theory (Hirschi 1969). The SDRG programs are explicitly based on a foundation of both social learning and bonding theories. Finally, I review Gang Resistance Education and Training (GREAT) and Drug Awareness and Resistance Education (DARE) as programs that relate to question 3. That is, as nearly as I am able to decipher them, neither of these programs is based on clear statements of principles or assumptions of a theory of crime and deviance. Neither has been found by sound evaluation research to be effective in producing the desired and expected outcomes. I draw directly from what I have previously written over many years on social learning theory—its empirical validity and its practical usefulness and issues related to theory and practice. I apologize for any overlap and redundancy to those readers who are familiar with the prior work (see Akers 1973, 1985, 1992, 1998, 2005, 2006; Akers and Jensen 2003; Akers and Sellers 2004; Akers et al. 1979; Sellers and Akers 2006).

Relationship between Theory and Practice in Criminology

I take the title of this chapter from a book by Hans Lennart Zetterberg (1962) that I read in graduate school many years ago in which he says:

> The phrase "nothing is as practical as a good theory" is a twist of an older truth: Nothing improves theory more than its confrontation with practice. It is my belief that the development of applied social theory will do much good to basic theoretical sociology. This is obvious enough as we deal with those parts of theoretical sociology that are put to practical use; they become refined in the process. (189)

Some forty years later, John H. Laub (2004) echoed this sentiment for criminology: "Despite efforts by many to divide theory and research from policy, the fact is theory, research, and policy are deeply intertwined and central to the lives of everyone involved in explaining crime and advancing justice and public safety" (18). The usual academic distinction between "pure" theoretical and "applied" practical social science has some validity and relevance for criminology and sociology. As these insightful quotes remind us, however, the distinction is flawed because it too often obscures the integral relationship between the two.

There are a number of scientific criteria for evaluating criminological theories, the most important of which is the extent to which an explanation of crime and deviance is consistent with the known facts of crime and is supported by empirical data from direct tests of its propositions. The usefulness or applicability of a theory to doing something about the problems of crime and delinquency is another important criterion (Akers 1994; Akers and Sellers 2004). Does the theory provide principles that can be used to control, prevent, or modify offending behavior? The question is most often asked with regard to actions, policies, or programs in the formal social control (criminal and juvenile justice) systems. But it can also be asked regarding informal social control that can be undertaken by parents, schools, churches, peers, and neighborhood and community groups and organizations, as well as by private practitioners and enterprises, to enhance conformity and prevent, change, or control criminal and deviant behavior.

All formal and informal efforts to prevent, deter, lessen, modify, or otherwise "do something about" delinquency, crime, drug abuse, violence, and other forms of antisocial and deviant behavior relate in some way to explanations of what causes that behavior at the individual or group level (Akers and Sellers 2004; Barlow 1995). Of course, the emphasis is on practicality and trying to find what works; programs rely on common-sense hunches, intuition, and guesses along with some mixture of theoretical insights. They are not meant to be, and we cannot expect them to be, theoretically pure. Too often, however, this pragmatism produces a combination of techniques and approaches in the same program or facility that is fraught with "paradoxes," conflict, and confusion (Abrams, Kim, and Anderson-Nathe 2005), and it is difficult to determine what exactly the theories are on which the practices might be based. This, in turn, makes it difficult to determine the conclusions that could be reached about a particular theory if the program were found to be a success or a failure. This unduly undermines the link between theory and practice and can be avoided by clearer articulation of theory when establishing or operating programs and policies. "Evidence-based practice" has become a catch phrase today in criminology and sociology, but it is a sound principle of application (see Welsh and Farrington 2006). Of course, certain practices should never be put in place because they do not conform to moral and ethical standards of fairness, justice, and human rights, regardless of how effective they might be or how much they are based on empirically validated theory. (For a more complete discussion of these issues, see Akers 2005.)

Brief Overview of Social Learning Theory

My version of social learning theory is an integration of Edwin H. Sutherland's (1947) sociological theory of differential association and behavioral principles of conditioning and reinforcement from psychology originally formulated by

Robert L. Burgess and Akers (1966) as "differential association-reinforcement" theory and as I have developed it since then (see Akers 1973, 1985, 1994, 1998; Akers and Sellers 2004; Akers et al. 1979; Jensen and Akers 2003). Social learning principles have been used to explain criminal and delinquent behavior. They have also been applied to treatment and prevention by other social behaviorists working with explanatory models that are compatible with and differ only somewhat from social learning theory as I have proposed it (see Andrews and Bonta 1998, 2003; Patterson and Dishion 1985; Patterson, Reid, and Dishion 1992; Reid, Patterson, and Snyder 2002).

Social learning is a general social-psychological theory that offers an explanation of the full range of criminal and deviant behavior (onset, persistence, desistence, and change) and embraces social, nonsocial, and cultural factors operating to both motivate and control criminal behavior and to both promote and undermine conformity. The social, cognitive, and behavioral principles in the theory "are fundamental principles of performance [that account for] . . . the acquisition, maintenance, and modification of human behavior" (Andrews and Bonta 1998, 150). They are not confined to accounting for learning and performing novel behavior. Contrary to the way it is sometimes depicted, the theory does not simply try to account for the "positive causes" of crime, which would thereby render it unable to answer questions of why people do not commit crime (Gottfredson and Hirschi 1990; Hirschi 1969). Rather, it offers answers to both the question of why people do and why people do not violate norms; it incorporates factors and variables that facilitate as well those that counteract crime and delinquency. The basic proposition is that the same learning process in a context of social structure, interaction, and situation produces both conforming and deviant behavior. The probability of criminal or conforming behavior is a function of the balance of these risk and protective influences on behavior—not only those that operate in an individual's learning history, but also on those that operate at a given time in a given situation and those that predict future behavior (Akers 1998, 59). Deviant and criminal behavior is acquired, performed, repeated, maintained, and changed through all of the same cognitive and behavioral mechanisms as conforming behavior.

Social learning theory accounts for the individual becoming prone to deviant or criminal behavior, stability or change in that propensity, committing the behavior in some situations and not others, and for processes of offense specialization (discrimination) and versatility (generalization). Therefore, the theory is capable of accounting for the development of stable individual differences, as well as for changes in the individual's behavioral patterns or tendencies to commit deviant and criminal acts over time and in different situations. In the Social Structure–Social Learning (SSSL) Model, the social learning process is hypothesized to mediate the effects of society, culture, and social structure on rates of crime, deviance, and delinquency (Akers 1998);

social learning processes are micro-level mechanisms most relevant to the macro-level mechanisms proposed in structural theories of crime (Akers and Jensen 2006; Jensen and Akers 2003).

While referring to all dimensions of the underlying behavioral process (e.g., operant and classical conditioning, reinforcement schedules, stimulus satiation and deprivation) I have relied mainly on four principal explanatory concepts: differential association, definitions (and other discriminative stimuli), differential reinforcement, and imitation to explicate the social learning process (Akers 1985, 1998; Akers et al. 1979).

Differential reinforcement, or instrumental conditioning, refers to the frequency, amount, and probability of experienced and perceived contingent rewards and punishment for behavior. *Imitation* refers to the process in which the behavior of others and its consequences are observed and modeled. *Stimulus discrimination/generalization* designates the process by which overt and covert stimuli, verbal and cognitive, act as cues or signals for behavior to occur. The reinforcement and discriminative stimuli are mainly social (such as socially valued rewards and punishments contingent on the behavior and other social stimuli), but they are also nonsocial (such as unconditioned physiological reactions to environmental stimuli and physical effects of ingested substances and the physical environment). The content of the learning by these mechanisms includes the simple and complex behavioral sequences and the *definitions* (beliefs, attitudes, justifications, orientations) that in turn become discriminative for the commission of deviant and criminal behavior. *Differential association* has both behavioral-interactional and normative dimensions and refers to the direct and indirect, verbal and nonverbal communication, interaction, and identification with groups and individuals that comprise or control the individual's major sources of reinforcement, most salient behavioral models, and most effective definitions for the commission and repetition of behavior. The most important of these groups are the primary ones of family, friends, and peer groups, though they may also be secondary and reference groups, including "virtual peer groups" formed through the Internet, land and cell phones, movies, television, and other social media (Warr 2002). The relative frequency, intensity, duration, and priority of associations affect the relative amount, frequency, and probability of reinforcement of conforming or deviant behavior and exposure of individuals to deviant or conforming norms and behavioral models.

There is a large body of research that typically finds strong to moderate relationships between social learning variables (singly and in combination) and criminal, delinquent, and deviant behavior, mainly in American samples but also in studies in European, Asian, and other societies. There has been little research evidence that runs counter to social learning hypotheses (see reviews in Akers 1998; Akers and Jensen 2006; Akers and Sellers 2004).

Social Learning Principles in Prevention
and Treatment Programs

Social learning theory proposes that criminal and delinquent behavior is acquired and sustained through association, reinforcement, definitions, imitation, and other learning processes. The application of social learning theory is found in programs designed, directly or indirectly, to affect associations, reinforcement, definitions and attitudes, modeling and imitation, discriminative stimuli, and other learning and variables by which behavior is acquired and changed. The general prediction is that the greater the degree to which an intervention project is designed or otherwise reflects these social learning principles, the greater the effectiveness of the program in preventing, controlling, or countering delinquent or criminal behavior.

Some Early Programs

Donald R. Cressey (1955) recognized more than fifty years ago, in his concept of "retroflexive reformation," that most group-based approaches to rehabilitation for juveniles and adults, whether those responsible for them recognized it or not, were based on the principle of differential association—that is, the assumption that group dynamics can be directed to influence individual offenders to change their definitions, attitudes, and orientations to make them less favorable to lawbreaking. Cressey argued:

> The most effective mechanism for exerting group pressure on members will be found in groups so organized that criminals are induced to join with non-criminals for the purpose of changing other criminals. A group in which Criminal A joins with some non-criminals to change criminal B is probably most effective in changing Criminal A, not B; in order to change Criminal B, criminal A must necessarily share the values of the anti-criminal members. (117)

A decade later, Don Gibbons (1965), in what may have been the first sociologically oriented book proposing general principles and treatment strategies for "changing the lawbreaker," made a similar argument:

> Group therapy encourages the participants to put pressure on each other for behavioral change and to get the group to define new conduct norms. . . . [G]roup therapy represents a kind of primary group relationship in which behavioral change is attempted through the same mechanisms by which attitude formation and behavioral change takes place in conventional primary groups. (151)

One of the first systematic uses of created peer groups to change delinquents' attitudes and behavior was in the Highfields project (Weeks 1958), which used Guided Group Interaction (GGI) in a residential facility for adjudicated delinquent boys. GGI reflects the principle of differential association applied in peer group (guided by adult staff) sessions in which common problems can be discussed in a group atmosphere that intends to encourage nondelinquent attitudes and behavior. At the end of the program, the Highfields boys had developed attitudes more favorable to obeying the law, and those who had changed their attitudes the most were more likely to succeed and stay out of trouble later. The Highfields boys did somewhat better than a comparison group of boys who had been committed to the state reformatory school (even when adjustments for in-program failures were made) in avoiding reinstitutionalization, but this was primarily due to the differences observed among the black youth.

The Provo Experiment (Empey and Erickson 1972) offered a semi-residential alternative to regular juvenile probation and to incarceration in a state training school for adjudicated delinquent boys. The boys assigned to the facility were subjected to group techniques similar to GGI that were meant, with guidance from adult counselors, to develop a pro-social, anti-delinquent peer culture in the facility and to use peer group interaction and influence to foster modifications in the boys' motivations and definitions toward conforming, and away from delinquent, behavior. The evaluation of the Provo project was designed to have court-adjudicated delinquent boys randomly assigned to one of the three conditions: (1) Pinehills, the semi-residential facility; (2) the secure-custody state training school; or (3) a regular juvenile probation caseload in the community. However, the experimental design did not last because the juvenile-court judge began purposely, rather than randomly, assigning boys to Pinehills once he learned that the Pinehills boys had significantly lower recidivism than those boys assigned to the state training school. The Pinehills boys did better than the state training school boys six months after release and even four years later. However, after four years the Pinehills boys did little better than the juveniles placed on community probation (Lundman 1993).

The Teaching Family model (and its predecessor, Achievement Place) operated in a home with a married couple as surrogate parents and six to eight delinquent or "at risk" youth living with them as a family. A "token economy" was installed in which the youth could earn reward points for proper behavior or have points taken away for improper behavior in the home or at school. The group home parents were responsible for teaching social, academic, and pre-vocational skills and maintaining positive, mutually reinforcing relationships with the adolescents. In addition, the youths operated a peer-oriented self-government system in the home. Thus, in addition to the shaping of behavior by the teaching parents (applying the principle of differential reinforcement), the Teaching Family model promoted conforming behavior through exposure to a pro-social peer group (applying the principle of differential association). The Teaching Family was quite effective in maintaining good behavior in the school and in the community while the youth were in residence. Outcome evaluations, however, found that the delinquency-inhibiting effects on the adolescents did not survive release from the environment of the Teaching Family homes back to their previous family and neighborhood environments because there was no after-care program (Braukmann and Wolf 1987).

Three Programs of the Oregon Social Learning Center

These earlier programs had some acknowledged and plain social learning underpinnings, but none was as able to tie theory and practice together as carefully and successfully over so many years as have Gerald R. Patterson and his colleagues at the Oregon Social Learning Center (OSLC; Dishion, McCord, and Poulin 1999; Dishion, Patterson, and Kavanagh 1992; Patterson 1975; Patterson and Chamberlain 1994; Patterson, Capaldi, and Bank 1991; Patterson, Debaryshe and Ramsey 1989; Reid, Patterson, and Snyder 2002; Snyder and Patterson 1995). The OSLC has conducted research on, and applied the principles of, social learning theory in family, peer group, and school programs for the treatment and prevention of childhood and adolescent misbehavior. The OSLC model proposes that the child's behavior and interaction with others are "learned in the family, and under more extreme conditions carr[y] over to a child's interactions with others outside the family, including peers and teachers" (Dishion, Patterson, and Kavanagh 1992, 254–255). This learning is more apt to result in misbehavior in the home and delinquency outside the home when the interaction between parent and child can be characterized as "coercive": "Poor parent discipline practices increase the likelihood of child coercive responses, and high rates of child coercion impede parents' attempts to provide evenhanded, consistent, and effective discipline. It is in this sense that parental limit setting for behaviors such as lying, stealing, or fighting often fail in the quagmire of the child's arguments, excuses, and counteraccusations" (258).

The OSLC's Adolescent Transition Program (ATP) was a successful intervention with at-risk youth that targeted family disciplinary and socialization skills in parent-focused and parent–teen groups compared with teen-focused groups and self-directed change. Parents were enlisted (voluntarily) into training sessions and provided services to help them develop more effective socialization and disciplinary skills to develop and maintain a home environment in which pro-social behavior is modeled and rewarded and aggressiveness or other misbehavior is punished. "Social learning parent training is a step-wise, skill-based approach for developing effective parenting skills and strategies for maintaining change." (Dishion et al. 1992, 263) In addition, at risk youth age 10–14 were involved in group and individual sessions (under the guidance of thera-pists), again voluntarily, designed to promote pro-social peer associations, atti-tudes, and self-control. The program had some of the intended outcomes, with improvements in parenting skills and reductions in antisocial behavior among the youth, but formation of peer-focused groups in which older delinquents were included increased deviant behavior among the younger youth in the group, which is not a surprising outcome when modeling and imitation effects are considered (Dishion, Patterson, and Kavanagh 1992; Dishion et al. 1999).

The participants in the OSLC's Multidimensional Treatment Foster Care (MTFC) program were chronic, high-frequency, and serious youthful offenders who had been adjudicated by the juvenile court as delinquents (Chamberlain, Fisher, and Moore 2002; Eddy and Chamberlain 2000). The judge allowed them to be assigned randomly to regular group home foster care or to foster-care parents who had been specially recruited and trained by the OSLC to use "behavior management methods . . . to implement and maintain a flexible and individualized behavior plan for each youth within the context of a three-level point system that made youth privileges contingent on compliance with program rules and general progress" (Eddy and Chamberlain 2000, 858). The foster parents were trained "to notice and reinforce youngsters" for proper behavior in a positive way. In addition, each youth took part in weekly sessions "focused on skill building in such areas as problem solving, social perspective taking, and nonaggressive methods of self-expression" (Chamberlain, Fisher, and Moore 2002, 205–206), working directly with behavioral therapists. All aspects of the intervention program were coordinated and supervised by case managers to monitor the participation of the youth and to insure that the procedures and techniques were carried out as intended by the program design. After the youth completed the program, they were returned to their biological or stepparents, who also received support and training in parenting skills to help them manage the youths' behavior and maintain the behavioral and attitudinal gains made in the MTFC. Evaluation of the program found that the treatment group had sig-nificantly lower levels of both self-reported and official delinquency than the control group up to three years later. Moreover, the research showed that the effects of the intervention procedures on program outcome were mediated by their effects on the social learning variables—that is, reductions in differential association with delinquent peers and increases in parental supervision of the children's behavior and positive reinforcement for good behavior (Chamberlain, Fisher, and Moore 2002; Eddy and Chamberlain 2000).

While the MTFC was a treatment program for court-adjudicated delin-quents, Linking the Interests of Families and Teachers (LIFT) was an OSLC delinquency-prevention project. While high-risk areas of the community were targeted, LIFT used a "universal strategy" in which services were made available to all first- and fifth-graders (as the transitional grades into elementary and middle schools, respectively), their parents, and teachers in those areas. No attempt was made to identify individual youth at risk and single them out for preventive intervention. LIFT secured the cooperation of schools serving the high-risk neighborhoods and the voluntary involvement of children and families in those neighborhoods. The program was based on the theoretical principle that "the driving force in a child's conduct problems are the reinforcement processes that occur in his or her day-to-day relationships. . . . [A]ntisocial behavior develops as an interaction between the child's antisocial behavior and the reactions of those with whom he or she interacts on a daily basis" (Reid and Eddy 2002, 222). Therefore, the program focused on modifying the ways in which the youth interacted with peers, with parents and siblings, and with teachers and classmates at school. "The three major components of the LIFT are (a) classroom-based child social and problem skills training, (b) playground-based behavior modification, and (c) group-delivered parent training" (Eddy, Reid, and Fetrow 2000, 165). The program had some modest to strong effects almost immediately on reductions in physical aggression on the playground and improved behavior in classrooms in the participating schools. Also, in the longer term, by the time the fifth-graders were in middle school and the first years of high school, the LIFT participants had experienced significantly fewer police arrests, lower levels of self-reported drug use, and fewer associations with deviant peers (as observed by the teachers) than did the youth in the control group.

Two Programs of the Seattle Social Development Research Group

As can be seen from these descriptions, and as is fully evident from its name, these and other projects of the OSLC are transparently and explicitly predicated on social learning principles. However, the training of parents in good practices for supervising and disciplining their children to prevent delinquent behavior is also consistent with principles of self-control (Gottfredson and Hirschi 1990) and social bonding (Hirschi 1969) theories. Indeed, much to my consternation, control theorists often refer to the work of the OSLC as supportive of social bonding or self-control theory while usually neglecting to point out that it is the Social Learning Center, not the Social Control Center. Although the implications of the two theories for intervention in peer groups are very different (control theory would advise paying no attention to foster learning of conforming, non-deviant behavior in peer groups and concentrate only on enhancing attachment to peers), there are commonalities in the practical implications of social learning and social bonding for family interventions (and to some extent for school-based interventions). The Social Development Model (SDM) programs are explicitly formulated on a combination of social learning and social bonding theories. This model has been developed and implemented in a series of delinquency and substance-use prevention programs by J. David Hawkins, Richard F. Catalano, and their associates in the SDRG at the University of Washington, Seattle (Brown et al. 2005; Hawkins, Von Cleve, and Catalano 1991; Hawkins et al. 1992, 1999, 2005; Weis and Hawking 1981). The SDM combines strengthening social attachment and commitment (social bonding theory) with positive reinforcement, modeling, and learning pro-social attitudes and skills and avoiding learning delinquent patterns (social learning theory) as applied in families, schools, and peer groups.

The first major program applying the SDM by the SDRG was the Seattle Social Development Project (SSDP). The SSDP was designed to enhance opportunities, develop social skills, and provide rewards for good behavior in the classroom and in families. The teachers in the intervention classrooms were trained to use "proactive classroom management," in which teachers were trained to "establish consistent classroom expectations and routines; . . . give clear, explicit instructions for behavior; recognize and reward desirable student behavior and efforts to comply; [and] keep minor classroom disruptions from interrupting instruction" (Hawkins et al. 2005, 27), as well as practice "interactive teaching" (e.g., state explicit learning objectives and model skills to be learned). Small groups of students were formed to participate in "cooperative learning" teams that were given positive recognition for both individual and group improvements, and other innovative techniques were used to strengthen bonds to school and teach the students academic and social skills for interacting properly with others. These included interpersonal problem solving and "refusal" skills to help the children recognize peer and other social influences on their behavior, identify consequences of behavior, and involve peers in conforming behavior. Parenting-skills training was also offered on a voluntary basis to parents of students that included learning ways to monitor their children's behavior, to teach and support pro-social and anti-delinquent definitions and attitudes, to discipline with proper application of punishment for their children's misbehavior and of positive rewards for their good behavior (differential reinforcement) while providing a positive family environment and encouraging commitment to school (differential association and social bonding).

The program was evaluated by comparing the intervention and control groups when they were in the fifth grade (Hawkins et al. 1992) and then again when they reached 18 (Hawkins et al. 1999). The findings on outcomes in the fifth grade show that the intervention group (20 percent) was somewhat less likely than the control group (27 percent) to have initiated alcohol use. Also, relatively fewer students in the intervention group (45 percent) than in the control group (52 percent) had engaged in some other forms of misconduct or problem behavior. By the time the students were 18, the two groups did not differ in self-reported nonviolent delinquency, smoking, drinking, and use of other drugs or in official arrest and court charges. However, the two groups did differ significantly in self-reported violent delinquency (48.3 percent versus 59.7 percent), heavy drinking (15.4 percent versus 25.6 percent), and sexual activity (72.1 percent versus 83 percent) with multiple partners (49.7 percent versus 61.5 percent). Participants were then followed into young adulthood (age 21) with both self-reported and court record data collected. "Full-intervention group participants were significantly less likely to be involved in a high variety of crime, to have sold illegal drugs in the past year, and to have an official life-time court record at age 21 years" (Hawkins et al. 2005, 28–29).

The SDM has also been applied in the SDRG's Raising Healthy Children (RHC) project (Brown et al. 2005) in the middle- and high-school years:

> As a theory-based intervention, RHC is guided by the social develop-ment model (SDM) which *integrates empirically supported aspects of social control, social learning, and differential association theories into a framework for strengthening prosocial bonds and beliefs.* Within this framework, the SDM emphasizes that prevention should (a) begin before the formation of antisocial beliefs and behaviors; (b) recognize the importance of individual and family characteristics as well as larger social contexts of community, school, and peer influences; and (c) iden-tify and address the changing needs of its target population with regard to risk and protective factors that change in influence during the course of development. . . . [F]our distinct points of intervention were targeted by RHC: (a) opportunities for involvement with prosocial others (e.g., family, teachers, and peers who did not use substances); (b) students' academic, cognitive, and social skills; (c) positive reinforcements and rewards for prosocial involvement; and (d) healthy beliefs and clear standards regarding substance use avoidance. (700; emphasis added)

Five schools were randomly assigned to the intervention program and five schools were assigned to the control group. The teachers in the intervention schools were given training in teaching and classroom management strategies and techniques for developing positive learning, reading, social, and problem-solving skills to promote students' bonding to school and pro-social peer asso-ciations. During the time, the students were in the elementary school and in the first year of middle school. The approach to intervening with individual students was to offer after-school opportunities for academic tutoring, studying "clubs," and other individual and group sessions to develop "healthy behavior" and "pro-social beliefs" (Brown et al. 2005).

Parents were given the opportunity to participate in sessions that sought to reduce family conflict and enhance family bonding while countering associations with deviant peers and deviant attitudes. The RHC program seemed not to make a difference in using or abstaining from, but it did significantly lower the frequency of use of alcohol and marijuana during the middle-school to high-school years.

Social Learning and Cognitive-Behavioral Approaches: Overview of Evidence on Effectiveness

To a greater or lesser degree, the theoretical foundation for these earlier and more recent treatment and prevention programs just reviewed (one or more of the principles of differential association, definitions and attitudes, role modeling and imitation, differential reinforcement, and other dimensions of the social learning process, sometimes in combination with other theoretical principles) have also been reflected, although often less explicitly, in a range of other group therapies; positive peer counseling programs; gang interventions; family and school programs; teenage drug, alcohol, and delinquency prevention and education programs; and other private and public programs (see Akers 1992; Andrews and Bonta 2003; Hersen and Rosqvist 2005; Lundman 1993; Morris and Braukmann 1987; Pearson et al. 2002.)

No program has been found always to be highly effective, and even the successful programs have modest effects. However, as D. A. Andrews and James Bonta (1998, 2003) report, the preponderance of evaluation research findings show that the *"cognitive behavioral and social learning approaches* [are more effective than] nondirective relationship-oriented counseling or psychodynamic insight-oriented counseling [and that] behavioral treatments had a substantially greater average effect [mean effect size of .25] on recidivism than did non-behavioral treatments [mean effect size of .04]" (Andrews and Bonta 1998, 262–263, 267–268, 282–290; emphasis added). Meta-analysis and other research literature support the same conclusions. There is "strong and consistent support for theories, such as differential association/social learning theory, that link offending to antisocial associations and to the internalization of antisocial values. A consistent finding across meta-analyses, including cross-cultural studies, is that 'cognitive-behavioral' programs tend to achieve higher reductions in recidivism than other treatment modalities" (Cullen et al. 2003, 353). Assessments of the research literature and meta-analysis of findings have led many others to reach similar conclusions about the effectiveness of applied program grounded in social learning principles (Ellis and Sowers 2001; Gendreau, Smith, and French 2006; Lipsey and Landenberger 2005; Losel 2007; Pearson et al. 2002; Triplett and Payne 2004).

"The core criteria of successful programs in developmental prevention are similar to those in offender treatment. For example, such programs have a sound theoretical basis in social learning theory, follow a cognitive-behavioral approach, are well structured, and address multiple risk and protective factors" (Losel 2007, 4). And R. Ellis and K. Sowers write:

> The use of cognitive-behavioral interventions is consistent with the conclusion of other meta-analyses that intervention based on *social learning theory* is particularly effective (Losel 1996). Social learning theory asserts that behavior is learned through several processes, including modeling, *imitation,* and differential reinforcement (Bandura 1977). In *modeling* a child observes an adult engaging in a behavior. If the child sees that the adult experiences positive consequences, he is likely to imitate the behavior. . . . He is also likely to associate with people who encourage his violent behavior (*differential association*). Eventually, he develops ideas (cognitions) that support violence. . . . Cognitions that support specific behaviors are known as '*definitions*' (Akers 1985). Definitions justify those behaviors by explaining why they are useful, necessary, or merited. Definitions, then, could be seen as one form of the problematic cognitions that the therapist needs to address. (2001, 91–92; emphasis in the original)

Two Programs with Police Officers in the Classroom: Unstated and Unclear Theoretical Rationales

All of the programs described thus far have clearly stated, or readily observable, links to principles and processes of social behavior as found in my and others' social learning models of the causes of criminal and delinquent behavior (and sometimes to those of other theories such as social bonding). This linkage is most strongly and clearly made by the OSLC and the SDRG in their programs. In each of these, the theoretical perspective and assumptions in the design of the programs and the specific ways in which the practical actions taken relate to theory are explicit, sound, and well made. The linkage is also apparent in other treatment and prevention programs that take a cognitive-behavioral approach. There are many other treatment and prevention programs, both long-standing and newly developed, however, for which theoretical principles or assumptions are left unstated or poorly articulated by their designers and implementers. I will briefly review two well-known and well-funded examples: Gang Resistance Education and Training (GREAT) and Drug Abuse Resistance Education (DARE). Both of these rely on uniformed police officers' going to school classrooms over a period of time to teach a curriculum that is meant to educate preadolescents and adolescents so that they will "refuse" or "resist" influences that can lead them into gang activity (GREAT) or substance use (DARE).

GREAT is a gang- and delinquency-prevention program that originally consisted of nine officer-run classroom sessions, including lessons on conflict resolution, resisting peer pressure, and recognizing the negative effect of gangs on the quality of life in the community. Based on disappointing evaluations of effectiveness (Esbensen 2004; Esbensen et al. 2001), GREAT was later modified to include an expanded school curriculum and a family component (see http://www.great-online.org). It entails no direct intervention in gang activity or efforts to work directly with youth or with their families. The school programs have police officers teach the students about gangs, violence, and drugs to foster pro-social attitudes and to teach "refusal skills" that, it is hoped, allow the youth to avoid gangs and other deviant peer groups. Police officers also deliver the family component of the program, attempting to teach parents to apply good parental skills, provide pro-social role modeling, and control their children's access to television, movies, video games, and the Internet. Neither the original nor the revised program descriptions delineate social learning or any other specific theory of adolescent or delinquent behavior as guiding the curriculum for students or parents. It would seem that GREAT includes at least some implicit recognition of the social learning principles that differential peer association and attitudes (definitions favorable and unfavorable), modeling, and learning in the family are relevant to joining gangs and committing delinquency. At the same time, the parental monitoring and supervision taught in the program seems to be fashioned on social bonding theory. Moreover, some GREAT activities do not follow from, or even run counter to, what one would expect from social learning theory. What principle of learning is invoked in placing both school and family instruction in the hands of uniformed police officers? Social learning theory (backed by network analysis of gang membership and peer relationships) would suggest direct intervention with individual gang members or potential gang members, especially those who occupy central "cut points" (sole connecting links between different individuals and groups), as a potentially more effective approach (McGloin 2005; McGloin, Pratt, and Maahs 2004).

DARE is the largest and longest-running youth drug-use prevention program in the United States, with programs in other countries (see http://www .dare.com). Like GREAT, DARE is a cooperative effort between local police departments and school districts. This cooperation involves the schools' allowing uniformed police officers to come to the school classroom and teach a curriculum over a seventeen-week period in the fifth and sixth grades (e.g., social skills, drug knowledge, and self-esteem), with shorter sessions in middle school or junior high school (e.g., resisting peer pressure and resolving conflict) and senior high school (e.g., making choices and managing anger). Opportunities are also provided for some after-school activities and for programs for parents

(Sherman et al. 1998). As the name implies, DARE is designed mainly to equip students to recognize, and develop the ability to "resist," peer influence to use drugs and alcohol, with the expectation that this will also prevent or reduce other forms of delinquency. Police officers are assigned full time to the project and present one-hour classroom lessons that stress the consequences of using drugs and teach students how to say no to drugs and alcohol. The activities in the program from the beginning have included not only instruction but also student role-playing to demonstrate strategies for resisting "peer pressure" and other influences to take drugs, group discussions about ways to enhance self-esteem, behavioral alternatives to drugs, decision making, and understanding media influences (Bureau of Justice Statistics 1988; DeJong 1986; Triplett and Payne 2004).

Although unequivocal claims of DARE's high level of effectiveness are often made, it has been difficult to find clear, scientifically valid evidence that the program has reduced the problems of adolescent substance use and delinquency in the communities where it has been instituted (Akers 1992; Rosenbaum 2007; Triplett and Payne 2004). The fairly long history of disappointing findings with regard to the central goals of affecting adolescent substance use has led to a reassessment of governmental investment and support for the program and calls by some to discontinue or greatly reduce it. This has been met with resistance from the police, schools, and communities involved in DARE (Rosenbaum 2007).

The DARE curriculum was supposedly "grounded in three main 'psychosocial' approaches to prevention: psychological inoculation, resistance skill training, and personal and social skills training" (Rosenbaum 2007, 816). However, the theoretical assumptions of the program, including assumptions that would lead one to believe that classroom exposure to the range of topics in the curriculum and related activities led by uniformed police officers will prevent adolescent substance abuse, were left unspecified when the program was initiated (Bureau of Justice Statistics 1988) and are still not clearly delineated (see http://www/dare.com). Social skills training and instruction on ways to "resist" or counteract peer influences and efforts to promote anti-drug attitudes would seem at first glance to be based at least implicitly on some aspects of social learning theory (differential peer association and definitions). However, the curricular focus in DARE on teaching adolescents to resist "peer pressure" runs counter both to the concept in social learning theory of differential peer association and to the empirical evidence supporting the predicted effects of peer influence on adolescent substance use in research on the theory (Akers 1992). In addition, training in decision-making skills based on factual information on drugs suggests rational choice theory. A portion of the curriculum that deals with enhancing individual self-esteem and anger management would seem to reflect psychological personality theory or general strain theory (Agnew 1992). The prominence of police officers (and the symbolism of law enforcement functions in apprehending and punishing drug law violators) would imply some reliance on deterrence theory. The reference on the Web site to "stunning brain imagery—tangible proof of how substances diminish mental activity, emotions, coordination and movement" suggests both a return to the old idea that kids will make the right decision if you just "give them the facts" about drugs and the "scared straight" idea that showing "this is your brain on drugs" negative effects will deter use. These are plausible inferences about the theoretical underpinnings of DARE, but there is nothing in the program that shows how teaching of anti-drug attitudes is based on social learning or any other theory of the causes of substance use. Thus, it is difficult to determine at this time what the theoretical assumptions are in the GREAT and DARE programs. Further analysis and more careful examination of the rationale of the programs by those funding and running them might produce a clearer understanding concerning on which, if any, theory the programs rely.

I find little explicit reference to social learning principles in either program, but perhaps closer attention to social learning principles and incorporation of program elements more clearly relevant to those principles in the future would improve effectiveness. I would suggest doing away with or modifying the reliance on in-class curricula taught by police officers and paying more careful attention to how influence, modeling, imitation, and social reinforcement by peers and others truly operate in drug behavior and avoiding sole reliance on the notion of "peer pressure," a popular but inarticulate theoretical construct. I would suggest borrowing from the successful programs of the OSLC and the SDRG with regard to the pro-social modeling and behavioral reinforcement practices and procedures they use in the in-school programs, direct contact with families to train them in effective parenting and socialization of children, after-school programs for youth, and other elements, as well as the more successful cognitive-behavioral approaches to changing attitudes and behavior used in other substance-use and delinquency-prevention programs.

Concluding Observations

A good theory is useful for guiding practice, and good practice both reflects and informs theory. I propose here that social learning theory is such a theory. It is an empirically valid theory on which sound and effective crime and delinquency prevention and treatment programs have been and can be formulated. I have concentrated on examples of American programs that are based, at least in part, on social learning principles but have given a couple of examples of programs for which it is uncertain which theoretical principles inform them. There is a body of evidence that supports the conclusion that past and current applications of the cognitive-behavioral principles in social learning theory have at least a modest impact and are more effective than alternative programming. That does not mean that all programs with discernible social learning elements in them have been effective or even that one can always determine the theoretical underpinnings of applied programs, whether successful or not. As Ruth Triplett and Brian Payne (2004) point out, even sound theory can be misunderstood or misapplied in a way that inhibits programs from producing the effects they could have. Starting with social learning theory does not guarantee that the goals of a program, policy, or strategy meant to prevent or change criminal, delinquent, and deviant behavior will be achieved. However, I would hypothesize that the more explicitly and directly the design of the prevention or treatment strategy is predicated on or informed by all of the social learning principles (alone or in combination with principles from other compatible theories), the greater the "fidelity" to the theory (Reid, Patterson, and Snyder 2002) of the actions taken by the operators and participants in the program to that design and the greater the extent to which midstream modifications in the program (whether induced externally or precipitated internally) moves it closer to really affecting the targeted social behavioral processes, the more likely it is that the programs will have some success in preventing and treating delinquent and criminal behavior. In short, I would say that social learning theory is a prime exemplar of the maxim with which I began: There is nothing as practical as a good theory.

References

Abrams, L. S., K. Kim, and B. Anderson-Nathe. 2005. Paradoxes of treatment in juvenile corrections. *Child and Youth Care Forum* 34:7–25.

Agnew, R. 1992. Foundation for a general strain theory of crime and delinquency. *Criminology* 30:47–88.

Akers, R. L. 1973. *Deviant behavior: A social learning approach.* Belmont, Calif.: Wadsworth Publishing.

———. 1985. *Deviant behavior: A social learning approach.* 3rd ed. Belmont, Calif.: Wadsworth Publishing.

———. 1992. *Drugs, alcohol, and society: Social structure, process and policy.* Belmont, Calif.: Wadsworth Publishing.

———. 1994. *Criminological theories: Introduction and evaluation.* Los Angeles: Roxbury Publishing.

———. 1998. *Social learning and social structure: A general theory of crime and deviance.* Boston: Northeastern University Press.

———. 2005. Sociological theory and practice: The case of criminology. *Journal of Applied Sociology/Sociological Practice* 22:24–41.

———. 2006. Aplicaciones de los principios del aprendizaje social. Algunos programas de tratamiento y prevencion de la delincuencia. In *Derecho penal y criminologia como fundamento de la politica criminal: Estudios en homenaje al professor Alfonso Serrano Gomez.* Ed. J. G. Dalbora and A. S. Maillo, 1117–1138. Madrid: Dykinson.

Akers, R. L., and G. F. Jensen (Eds.). 2003. *Social learning theory and the explanation of crime: A guide for the new century.* Vol. 11, *Advances in criminological theory.* New Brunswick, N.J.: Transaction Publishers.

————. 2006. Empirical status of social learning theory of crime and deviance: The past, present, and future. In *Taking stock: The status of criminological theory.* Vol. 15, *Advances in criminological theory.* Ed. F. T. Cullen, J. P. Wright, and K. R. Blevins, 37–76. New Brunswick, N.J.: Transaction Publishers.

Akers, R. L., M. D. Krohn, L. Lanza-Kaduce, and M. Radosevich. 1979. Social learning and deviant behavior: A specific test of a general theory. *American Sociological Review* 44: 635–655.

Akers, R. L., and C. Sellers. 2004. *Criminological theories: Introduction, evaluation, and application.* 4th ed. Los Angeles: Roxbury Publishing.

Andrews, D. A., and J. Bonta. 1998. *The psychology of criminal conduct.* 2nd ed. Cincinnati: Anderson Publishing.

————. 2003. *The psychology of criminal conduct.* 3rd ed. Cincinnati: Anderson Publishing.

Bandura, A. 1977. *Social learning theory.* Englewood Cliffs, N.J.: Prentice Hall.

Barlow, H. (Ed.). 1995. *Crime and public policy: Putting theory to work.* Boulder, Colo.: Westview Press.

Braukmann, C. J., and Wolf, M. M. 1987. Behaviorally-based group homes for juvenile offenders. In *Behavioral approaches to crime and delinquency: A handbook of application, research, and concepts.* Ed. E. K Morris and C. J. Braukmann, 135–159. New York: Plenum Press.

Brown, E. C., R. F. Catalano, C. B. Fleming, K .P. Haggerty, and R. D. Abbott. 2005. Adolescent substance use outcomes in the raising healthy children project: A two-part latent growth curve analysis. *Journal of Consulting and Clinical Psychology* 73: 699–710.

Bureau of Justice Statistics. 1988. *An invitation to project DARE: Drug Abuse Resistance Education.* Program brief. Washington, D.C.: U.S. Department of Justice.

Burgess, R. L., and R. L. Akers. 1966). A differential association reinforcement theory of criminal behavior. *Social Problems* 14:128–147.

Chamberlain, P., P. A. Fisher, and K. Moore. 2002. Multidimensional treatment foster care: Applications of the OSLC Intervention Model to high risk youth and their families. In *Antisocial behavior in children and adolescents: A developmental analysis and model for intervention.* Ed. J. B. Reid, G. R. Patterson, and J. Snyder, 203–218. Washington, D.C.: American Psychological Association.

Cressey, D. R. 1955. Changing criminals: The application of the theory of differential association. *American Journal of Sociology* 61:116–120.

Cullen, F. T., J. P. Wright, P. Gendreau, and D. A. Andrews. 2003. What treatment can tell us about criminological theory: Implications for social learning theory. In *Social learning theory and the explanation of crime: A guide for the new century.* Vol. 11, *Advances in criminological theory.* Ed. R. L. Akers and G. F. Jensen, 339–362. New Brunswick, N.J.: Transaction Publishers.

DeJong, W. 1986. Project DARE: Teaching kids to say "no" to drugs and alcohol. Report, National Institute of Justice, U.S. Department of Justice, Washington, D.C.

Dishion, T. J., J. McCord, and F. Poulin. 1999. When interventions harm: Peer groups and problem behavior. *American Psychologist* 54:755–764.

Dishion, T. J., G. R. Patterson, and K. A. Kavanagh. 1992. An experimental test of the coercion model: Linking theory, measurement, and intervention. In *Preventing antisocial behavior: Interventions from birth through adolescence.* Ed. J. McCord and R. E. Tremblay, 253–282. New York: Guilford Press.

Eddy, J. M., and P. Chamberlain. 2000. Family management and deviant peer association as mediators of the impact of treatment condition youth antisocial behavior. *Journal of Consulting and Clinical Psychology* 68:857–863.

Eddy, J. M., J. B. Reid, and R. A. Fetrow. 2000. An elementary school based prevention program targeting modifiable antecedents of youth delinquency and violence: Linking the Interests of Families and Teachers (LIFT). *Journal of Emotional and Behavioral Disorders* 8:165–176.

Ellis, R., and K. Sowers. 2001. *Juvenile justice practice: A cross-disciplinary approach to intervention.* Belmont, Calif.: Wadsworth/Brooks Cole Publishing.

Empey, L. T., and M. L. Erickson. 1972. *The Provo experiment: Evaluating community control of delinquency.* Lexington, Mass.: Lexington Books.

Esbensen, F. D. 2004. Evaluating G.R.E.A.T.: A school-based gang prevention program. National Institute of Justice Research for Policy, U.S. Department of Justice, Washington, D.C., June.

Esbensen, F. D., W. Osgood, T. J. Taylor, D. Peterson, and A. Freng. 2001. How great is G.R.E.A.T.? Results from a longitudinal quasi-experimental design. *Criminology and Public Policy* 1:87–118.

Gendreau, P., P. Smith, and S. K. French. 2006. The theory of effective correctional intervention: Empirical status and future directions. In *Taking stock: The status of criminological theory.* Vol. 15, *Advances in criminological theory.* Ed. F. T. Cullen, J. P. Wright, and K. R. Blevins, 419–446. New Brunswick, N.J.: Transaction Publishers.

Gibbons, D. 1965. *Changing the lawbreaker: The treatment of delinquents and criminals.* Englewood Cliffs, N.J.: Prentice-Hall.

Gottfredson, M., and T. Hirschi. 1990. *A general theory of crime.* Palo Alto, Calif.: Stanford University Press.

Hawkins, J. D., R. F. Catalano, R. Kosterman, R. Abbott, and K. G. Hill. 1999. Preventing adolescent health-risk behaviors by strengthening protection during childhood. *Archives of Pediatric and Adolescent Medicine* 153:226–234.

Hawkins, J. D., R. F. Catalano, D. M. Morrison, J. O. O'Donnell, R. D. Abbott, and L. E. Day. 1992. The Seattle Social Development Project: Effects of the first four years on protective factors and problem behaviors. In *Preventing antisocial behavior: Interventions from birth through adolescence.* Ed. J. McCord and R. E. Trembley, 139–161. New York: Guilford Press.

Hawkins, J. D., R. Kosterman, R. F. Catalano, K. G. Hill, and R. D. Abbott. 2005. Promoting positive adult functioning through social development intervention in childhood: Long-term effects from the Seattle Social Development Project. *Archives of Pediatric Adolescent Medicine* 159:25–31.

Hawkins, J. D., E. Von Cleve, and R. F. Catalano. 1991. Reducing early childhood aggression: Results of a primary prevention program. *Journal of the Academy of Child and Adolescent Psychiatry* 30:208–217.

Hersen, M., and J. Rosqvist (Eds.). 2005. *Encyclopedia of behavior modification and cognitive behavior therapy.* Vol. 1, *Adult clinical applications.* Vol. 2, *Child clinical applications.* Vol. 3, *Educational applications.* Thousands Oaks, Calif.: Sage Publication.

Hirschi, T. 1969. *Causes of delinquency.* Berkeley: University of California Press.

Jensen, G. F., and R. L. Akers. 2003. "Taking social learning global": Micro-macro transitions in criminological theory. In *Social learning theory and the explanation of crime: A guide for the new century.* Vol. 11, *Advances in criminological theory.* Ed. R. Akers and G. Jensen, 9–38. New Brunswick, N.J.: Transaction Publishers.

Laub, J. 2004. The life course of criminology in the United States. The American Society of Criminology 2003 presidential address. *Criminology* 42:1–26.

Lipsey, M. W., and N. A. Landenberger. 2005. Cognitive-behavioral interventions. In *Preventing crime: What works for children, offenders, victims, and places.* Ed. B. C. Welsh and D. P. Farrington, 57–71. Dordrecht: Springer.

Losel, F. 1996. Changing patterns in the use of prisons. *European Journal of Criminal Policy and Research* 4:108–127.

———. 2007. It is never too early and never too late: Toward an integrated science of developmental intervention in criminology. *Criminologist* 32, no. 5 (September–October): 3–8.

Lundman, R. J. 1993. *Prevention and control of juvenile delinquency.* 2nd ed. New York: Oxford University Press.

McGloin, J. M., T. C. Pratt, and J. Maahs. 2004. Rethinking the IQ–delinquency relationship: A longitudinal analysis of multiple theoretical models. *Justice Quarterly* 21:603–631.

Morris, E. K., and C. J. Braukmann (Eds.). 1987. *Behavioral approaches to crime and delinquency: A handbook of application, research, and concepts.* New York: Plenum Press.

Patterson, G. R. 1975. *Families: Applications of social learning to family life.* Champaign, Ill.: Research Press.

Patterson, G. R., D. Capaldi, and L. Bank. 1991. The development and treatment of childhood aggression. In *The development and treatment of childhood aggression.* Ed. D. Pepler and R. K. Rubin, 139–168. Hillsdale, Ill.: Erlbaum.

Patterson, G. R., and P. Chamberlain. 1994. A functional analysis of resistance during parent training therapy. *Clinical Psychology: Science and Practice* 1:53–70.

Patterson, G. R., B. D. Debaryshe, and E. Ramsey. 1989. A developmental perspective on antisocial behavior. *American Psychologist* 44:329–335.

Patterson, G. R., and T. J. Dishion. 1985. Contributions of families and peers to delinquency. *Criminology* 23:63–79.

Patterson, G. R., J. B. Reid, and T. J. Dishion. 1992. *Antisocial boys.* Eugene, Ore.: Castalia Publishing.

Pearson, F. S., D. S. Lipton, C. M. Cleland, and D. S. Yee. 2002. The effects of cognitive-behavioral programs on recidivism. *Crime and Delinquency* 48:476–496.

Reid, J. B., and M. Eddy. 2002. Preventive efforts during the elementary school years: The linking of the interest of families and teachers (LIFT) Project. In *Antisocial behavior in children and adolescents: A developmental analysis and model for intervention.* Ed. J. B. Reid, G. R. Patterson, and J. Snyder, 219–233. Washington, D.C.: American Psychological Association.

Reid, J. B., G. R. Patterson, and J. Snyder (Eds.). 2002. *Antisocial behavior in children and adolescents: A developmental analysis and model for intervention.* Washington, D.C.: American Psychological Association.

Rosenbaum, D. P. 2007. Just say no to D.A.R.E. *Criminology and Public Policy* 6:815–824.

Sellers, C. S., and R. L. Akers. 2006. Social learning theory: Correcting misconceptions. In *The essential criminology reader.* Ed. S. Henry and M. M. Lanier, 89–99. Boulder, Colo.: Westview Press.

Sherman, L. W., D. L. Gottfredson, D. L. MacKenzie, P. Reuter, and S. D. Bushway. 1998. *Preventing crime: What works, what doesn't, what's promising. Research in brief.* Washington, D.C.: National Institute of Justice.

Snyder, J. J., and G. R. Patterson. 1995. Individual differences in social aggression: A test of a reinforcement model of socialization in the natural environment. *Behavior Therapy* 26:371–391.

Sutherland, E. H. 1947. *Principles of criminology.* 4th ed. Philadelphia: J. B. Lippincott.

Triplett, R., and B. Payne. 2004. Problem solving as reinforcement in adolescent drug use: Implication for theory and policy. *Journal of Criminal Justice* 32:617–630.

Warr, M. 2002. *Companions in crime: The social aspects of criminal conduct.* Cambridge: Cambridge University Press.

Weeks, H. A. 1958. *Youthful offenders at highfields.* Ann Arbor: University of Michigan Press.

Weis, J. G., and J. D. Hawkins. 1981. Preventing delinquency: The social development model. *Preventing delinquency.* Washington, D.C.: U.S. Government Printing Office.

Welsh, B. C., and D. P. Farrington. 2006. Evidence-based crime prevention. In *Preventing crime: What works for children, offenders, victims, and places.* Ed. B. C. Welsh and D. P. Farrington, 1–7. Dordrecht: Springer.

Zetterberg, H. L. 1962. *Social theory and social practice.* New York: Bedminster Press.

6

MARCUS FELSON AND RONALD V. CLARKE

Routine Precautions, Criminology, and Crime Prevention

When reflecting on society's defenses against crime, criminologists and sociologists usually distinguish between two main systems of control: formal and informal. Formal social control has the purpose of defining, punishing, and deterring crime and is exerted principally through the law and the criminal justice system. Informal social control attempts to induce conformity through people's routine supervision of each other's behavior, reinforced by rule making, admonition, and censure.

It is well understood that these two principal forms of social control are interdependent. The law and the criminal justice system define and regulate the outer limits of unacceptable conduct, most of which is kept within bounds by the day-to-day exercise of informal controls. If they were not backed up by the law and the criminal justice system, however, these informal controls would soon lose their force.

It is also widely recognized that as society evolves into more complex forms, informal control increasingly has to be supplemented by formal systems of control. This is because informal controls depend greatly on people in a community knowing one another and knowing who are each other's neighbors, relations, and work mates. People may know each other this well in agrarian or rural societies but not in urban and industrial societies. Consequently, these latter societies come to rely increasingly on widely promulgated laws and a developed system of law enforcement.

Less well understood, however, is that informal and formal social controls are intertwined with and dependent on a third important control system: routine precautions taken against crime by individuals and organizations.[1] Every day, we all do such things as lock our doors, secure our valuables, counsel our children, and guard our purses and wallets to reduce the risk of crime. To this end, we also buy houses in safe neighborhoods, invest in burglar alarms and firearms, and avoid dangerous places and people.[2] Similarly, schools, factories, offices, shops, and many other organizations and agencies routinely take a host of precautions to safeguard themselves, their employees, and their clients from crime.

Whole industries and sectors of employment exist whose sole purpose is to supply or service this need for personal and organizational security: manufacturers of alarm and surveillance systems, weapons makers, locksmiths, safe makers, guards and custodial services, security consultants, store detectives, guard-dog handlers, and ticket inspectors, to name but a few. According to Robert Mikos (2006), who draws on studies by John Dilulio (1996) and Tomas Philipson and Richard Posner (1996), the costs of these private precautions exceed the costs of the entire public law enforcement budget. One study estimates that U.S. citizens spend nearly $90 billion worth of time each year simply locking their doors and searching for keys (Anderson 1999). Even if there is a large margin of errors in these estimates, it is clear that without this system of routine precautions, the task of informal social control would be immeasurably more difficult, and the criminal justice system would be swamped by a flood of additional crimes.

Routine precautions will grow in importance with the decline of formal and informal controls.[3] Marcus Felson (2002) has listed some of the factors in the decline of informal control in modem society, including working mothers, larger schools, more casual employment, increased economic power of teenagers, and the separation of home and workplace. Many of the same factors have weakened the power of the criminal justice system. Offenders have become more anonymous and less detectable (most detections are the result of leads to the

---

[1] The words "routine precautions" merit some definitional attention. The word *precaution* is itself interesting, for it implies that efforts can be made in advance to thwart danger. This does not include purely unplanned efforts to dig oneself out of trouble after having fallen into it. The word "routine" implies that such precautions require continued action, such as locking doors, trimming hedges, and avoiding dangerous places or excessive drinking. Thus, buying an alarm or designing an environment will not succeed as one-time actions without follow-up activities. Routine precautions are not identical to routine activities. Much of the security or danger produced by routine activities is inadvertent. By contrast, routine precautions constitute only conscious efforts to prevent crime.

[2] Since precautions cannot interfere too much with basic sustenance activities, all people face some limitations on the precautions they can routinely take. Thus, those who work late cannot easily avoid coming home after dark, and those who are raising families have to go shopping where they can afford to buy.

[3] Routine precautions are influenced by formal and informal control. Some jurisdictions fine people for leaving keys in cars or failing to take other routine precautions. Families and friends exert informal social control to remind one another of their precautionary duties. However, these three aspects of crime control remain analytically distinct.

identity of perpetrators provided by victims and others). Their opportunities for theft and vandalism have greatly expanded with the growth in possessions. Their greater mobility has reduced the value of preventive patrol, which relies for much of its effect on the police knowing who should and who should not be present in particular places.

The job of the police has also been made more difficult by the increases in nighttime activity resulting from more transportation and electricity. In addition, the police have a wider range of behavior to regulate as more misconduct is brought within the purview of the criminal law. The criminal justice system is therefore deluged with offenses, many of a petty nature. It is increasingly ineffective as a deterrent and is becoming prohibitively costly. As the criminal justice system is less able to cope with the flood of crime, people turn increasingly to ways of protecting themselves. They become consumers of books and television programs purveying crime prevention advice. They learn self-defense and purchase car alarms and Mace. In the same way, organizations adopt more sophisticated ways to screen employees and provide surveillance of their properties. They engage in background checks and drug screening. They install surveillance cameras and employ doormen. This demand for additional security is reflected in the tremendous growth of private policing, which in terms of numbers employed now outstrips the public police (Nalla and Newman 1990).

The increased reliance on routine precautions is assisted by technological development, which results in a proliferation of low-cost security devices and systems designed for particular offenses and particular settings. Harbingers of things to come are provided by the breathalyzer, by electronic personal identification numbers (PINs), by Caller ID, and by photo radar. Hardly dreamed of thirty years ago, these devices developed for use against specific crimes are now routine.

While we have mentioned the security precautions taken by organizations, our primary concern in the chapter is with the routine precautions taken by ordinary people. We will discuss why criminologists have neglected them in the past and outline a program of research intended to make their use more effective. We will close by contrasting the use made of everyday problem solving in criminology and in medicine.

Routine Precautions and Criminology

Electronics may greatly expand the scope of routine precautions, but technology has always served to protect people from crime. Consider medieval times, when, long before the development of a recognizable criminal justice system, moats, drawbridges, and portcullises protected castles and cities. Swords were routinely worn by nobles, and when the nobles were absent, chastity belts were worn by their ladies.

These routine precautions represented the technology of the day. They are integral to our conception of the Middle Ages and an important component of our cultural heritage. It is all the more remarkable, therefore, that only a few criminologists (e.g., Marx 1995; Reiss 1967; Skogan and Maxfield 1981; Suttles 1972) have paid any attention to routine precautions. Perhaps the causal link between precautions and reduced crime is too simple to attract the interest of sociological theorists. Or they may find distasteful the individual and collective preoccupation with protecting possessions, preferring to leave these matters to the security industry. According to Lawrence Sherman (1993), many criminologists see police efforts to control crime as being reactionary and opposed to due process, and they may see routine precautions in similarly negative terms. When discussed at all, these precautions are generally treated not as an indispensable part of society's defenses against crime, but as an undesirable response to fear, which, if unchecked, will lead limit people's freedom and encourage a "fortress" mentality. Research has been mostly limited to studies examining whether those most afraid of crime or most recently victimized are most likely to take precautions. These studies that have produced mixed results (Hope and Lab 2001). With a couple of notable exceptions, including Martie Thompson and colleagues (1999) and recent British Crime Survey analyses of precautions against burglary (see below), little research has been undertaken to determine whether routine precautions have any positive value in conferring protection against crime.

The main reason, however, for the academic neglect of routine precautions is that, when thinking about the causes and the control of crime, criminologists focused too exclusively on offenders and insufficiently on the situations in which they operate. Thus, it is no surprise that the focus of both formal and informal social control is the offender, whereas for routine precautions, which generally have been ignored by criminologists, the focus is the situation.

A body of criminological theory has now been developed, however, that gives due weight to the situation of crime, including routine activity theory (Cohen and Felson 1979; Felson 2002), the "lifestyle" theory of victimization (Hindelang, Gottfredson, and Garofalo 1978), the rational choice perspective (Cornish and Clarke 1986), "strategic thinking" (Cusson 1986), and "pattern theory" (Brantingham and Brantingham 1993). Despite their different points of departure, these all lead to a similar point of convergence: the need to explain crime by focusing on the immediate situation in which crime occurs (Felson and Clarke 1998).

This can be illustrated by the two theories with which we are associated: routine activity theory and the rational choice perspective. The routine activity theory deals with the ebb and flow of human activities in time and space and how these interrelate to produce a physical convergence of the three minimal elements of crime: a likely offender, a suitable target, and the absence of a capable guardian. The focus of the theory is therefore the situation that gives rise to crime. The rational choice perspective also focuses on the crime situation but concentrates on how it is perceived and evaluated by a potential offender who is seeking some benefit through illegal action.

Together with these advances in theory, developments in thinking about crime control have taken place that also focus on the crime situation, including Crime Prevention through Environmental Design (Jeffery 1977), "defensible space" architecture (Newman 1972), problem-oriented policing (Goldstein 1990; Clarke and Eck 2005), and designing out crime (Clarke and Mayhew 1980; Clarke and Newman 2005). These approaches all focus on reducing opportunities for crime and are subsumed under the more general label of "situational prevention" (Clarke 1983, 2005).

In one sense, situational prevention is the attempt to apply science to the routine taking of precautions. This does not simply mean improving the effectiveness of such things as locks, lights, and alarms through better technology. That is the province of the security industry, whereas situational prevention falls clearly in the realm of criminology. It consists of three main components: the developed body of theory, referred to above, concerning the role of opportunity in crime; a standard approach to the analysis and solution of specific crime problems based on the action research methodology (Lewin 1947); and a set of distinct opportunity-reducing techniques (Clarke 1997, 2005). It can be thought of as a systematic method of finding ways to reduce opportunities for highly specific categories of crime. This can be contrasted with our definition of routine precautions against crime as actions that the general populace applies in everyday life. Although some overlap between the two categories may occur, many routine precautions are not really situational prevention measures—or, at least, they are not among the more desirable of such measures.

Routine Precautions and the Role of Governments

Governments have not known whether, or how much, to encourage routine precautions among citizens. The danger of doing so is that they might be criticized for avoiding their primary responsibility to protect people from crime through the provision of a well-funded and well managed criminal justice system. They might even be charged with "blaming the victim." Moreover, governments know little about the effectiveness of routine precautions, and those they promote could prove useless or even counterproductive. Indeed, the general consensus in the legal and economic literature (but not in the criminological literature, as we discuss below) is that routine precautions simply displace crime from some victims to others (see Mikos 2006). If so, routine precautions bring no societal benefit, and governments have little reason to promote them. Indeed, it is possible that displacement could produce a net increase in the harms of crime—

for example, by diverting crime from wealthy people who are less harmed by it to poor people who will suffer more greatly. As a result of these concerns, governments have tended to treat crime prevention publicity campaigns as public relations efforts, mostly of value in demonstrating official and ministerial concern about crime. Similarly, the police investment in "crime prevention" has usually been limited to small units' dispensing crime prevention advice, often as part of larger public relations departments.

Fortunately, there is now a considerable body of evidence from situational prevention that reducing opportunities for crime does not displace crime nearly to the extent argued by legal scholars and economists and that substantial real societal benefits can result (Hesseling 1994; Clarke and Newman 2007). Much of this evidence results from research funded by the British government's Home Office and, in recent years, the Home Office has taken an active role in promoting routine precautions. One good example of this is *Your Practical Guide to Crime Prevention,* a Home Office booklet for the public that has been in print with small revisions and updates since 1994. The 1994 edition lists precautions designed to protect people from crime in a range of everyday locations and situations, such as "on public transport" and "when away from home," along with "keeping children safe from molesters" and "strangers at the door." All together, the booklet provides more than three hundred fifty tips, a sampling of which, for "when driving," is presented in Figure 6.1. As large as this number is, it almost certainly underrepresents the routine precautions in regular use and the number of situations in which they are employed. For example, we recently discovered a flyer produced by the Munich Trade Fair Center (Messe München International) listing sixteen precautions for exhibitors to take to protect themselves against theft (see Figure 6.2).

Modern governments have realized that they cannot control crime without help from citizens, and it seems likely that they will increasingly promote routine precautions. This will require them to invest in programs of research to examine the range and prevalence of routine precautions, the public and private and resources they represent, their inconvenience and opportunity costs, their effectiveness and efficiency as crime prevention measures, and their possible other benefits in terms of feelings of empowerment or control. In more detail, the questions that governments will need to examine include:

1. What are the range and the extent of routine precautions taken by the public?
2. How do precautions taken vary with age, sex, place of residence, occupation, etc.?
3. How much cost and effort do these precautions entail?
4. How does the public perceive the benefits and value of these precautions?

5. What are the actual benefits? (For example, do those taking precautions in high-crime neighborhoods have lower levels of victimization when other risk factors are taken into account?)
6. Do some widely taken precautions lack any real benefit, and are some rare precautions highly effective?
7. Are some precautions so widespread that further promotional efforts would be redundant?

Crime Prevention Tips When Driving

1. Before a long trip, make sure your vehicle is in good condition.
2. Plan how to get to your destination before leaving.
3. Choose main roads if you can.
4. Make sure you have enough money and petrol [gasoline].
5. Take change and a phone card in case you need to make a phone call.
6. If you travel frequently in your car, consider getting a car phone.
7. Carry a torch [flashlight].
8. Before you leave, tell anyone you are planning to meet what time you will get there and the route you are taking.
9. If someone tries to flag you down, drive on to a service station, or somewhere busy, and call the police.
10. Do not pick up hitchhikers.
11. Keep doors locked when driving.
12. Keep bags, car phones, and valuables out of sight.
13. If you keep the window open, only wind it down a little—not far enough so someone can reach in while you are stopped in traffic.
14. If you think you are being followed, flash your lights and sound your horn and keep driving till you come to busy place.
15. After dark, park in a well-lit, busy place.
16. Look around before you get out.
17. If you are leaving the car in daylight, think about how things will look in the dark.
18. Have your key ready when you go back to the car.
19. Make sure there is no one in the car.
20. If your car develops problems, find a telephone.
21. If this happens on the freeway, follow the marker arrows to the nearest phone. (Never cross to the other lane.)
22. While on the shoulder or while telephoning, keep a lookout.
23. Don't accept lifts from strangers.
24. Don't wait beside the car. Stand well away from traffic with the passenger door open.
25. If you feel threatened by a stranger, lock yourself in the car and speak through a small gap in the window.

FIGURE 6.1   Twenty-five Crime Prevention Tips When Driving
Source: Your Practical Guide to Crime Prevention, Home Office, London, 1994.

Theft Prevention Advice for Exhibitors, Munich Trade Fair Center

When planning your trade fair stand

1. Design your trade fair stand in such a way that you always have a good view of all your exhibits.
2. When planning your trade fair stand, please make sure you include lockable and covered-in booths (if necessary, in conjunction with a stand kitchenette).

During assembly

3. Never leave your trade fair stand unattended. A member of staff should always be at the stand, even during breaks.
4. Keep an eye on items that can be moved easily, such as tools, bags, electric appliances, etc. Secure smaller exhibits or stand equipment with chains with a lock.
5. When deliveries are made to your trade fair stand (e.g., by courier services, forwarding agents, etc.), make sure that someone you trust is always available to receive the goods properly.
6. The risk of theft is particularly high the night before the trade fair opens. Therefore, we strongly recommend hiring a guard for your stand.

During the trade fair

7. Never leave your trade fair stand unattended. Staff your trade fair stand in good time and do not leave it too early in the evening. We strongly recommend hiring a guard for your stand at night.
8. When the trade fair closes in the evening, lock up all valuables that can be moved easily.
9. Do not leave any electronic business aids, such as mobile phones and laptops, at the trade fair stand overnight. Consider the damage that could be caused if important customer data, working documents, appointments, etc. were suddenly irretrievably lost.
10. Adopt a healthy mistrust even of people who are well known in your sector. Keep a particularly watchful eye on people who spend time at your trade fair stand but are obviously not customers.
11. Please remember that big events always attract pickpockets. Therefore, it is particularly important to avoid showing that you have large amounts of cash with you.

During dismantling

12. You should be particularly vigilant during the first night of dismantling when levels of activity tend to be frenetic and large numbers of outside helpers are required in the trade fair halls. It is particularly easy for thieves to "do good business" in this environment.
13. Never leave your stand unattended during dismantling. Secure your exhibits, valuables and other items that can be moved easily as soon as the trade fair closes.
14. If you have rented furniture for your trade fair stand from our service partners, make sure that it is collected only by the authorized staff of the rental company concerned. Remember: You can be held liable for the damage or loss of rented items.
15. Make sure that only the forwarding agents or stand construction firms you commissioned and authorized take your exhibits and stand components away.
16. If necessary, hire a guard for your stand for the first night of dismantling.

FIGURE 6.2 Theft Prevention Advice for Exhibitors at the Munich Trade Fair Center

Source: Messe München International, 2007, *Opportunity Makes the Thief,* available online at http://download .messe-muenchen.de/media_pub/mediacenter/messe-muenchen.de/documents/pdf/gelegenheitmachtdiebe 2005_engl.pdf (accessed November 10, 2007).

8. What seem to be the most effective means of ensuring that people take necessary precautions?
9. Which kinds of crime prevention publicity campaigns are most effective in drawing attention to the need for routine precautions?
10. To what extent do these have the negative consequences of provoking fear of crime and resentment about "victim blaming"?

Answers to these questions would help governments (1) broaden the available repertoire of routine precautions for the public; (2) learn how to encourage the public to make use of these precautions; and (3) accumulate knowledge about the value of the routine precautions.

Broadening the Repertoire of Routine Precautions

We have noted the distinction between situational prevention and routine precautions. As our knowledge of both increases, we need to move citizens as far away as possible from the ineffective and counterproductive prevention methods toward those that work at minimal cost. This means broadening the public repertoire and finding simple ways to communicate knowledge. However, this does not mean ignoring everything the public thinks and does. Many people have good ideas about prevention that are probably correct, from staying away from groups of young men drinking in the park to avoiding urban nooks and crannies. One of the main research challenges is to collect more detailed information from citizens on their repertoire of ideas about and experiences with prevention. Much research could then be done to verify the effectiveness of these techniques. Crime prevention research is essentially clinical research: It investigates the application of scientific principles toward solving crime problems. Such clinical research could be greatly enriched by drawing from citizens their various ideas about prevention. However, this could not be accomplished by taking only a handful of popular methods. Rather, one needs to derive from many observant people a more varied repertoire of ideas, even if most of those are employed by only a small proportion of the population.

Encouraging People to Take Routine Precautions

Even when citizens have in mind effective routine precautions against crime, they do not necessarily follow their own precautions. Many people forget to lock doors; they park in dangerous spots, walk down risky streets, stay out late and drink too much, and so forth.

How can society encourage people to follow their own best judgments? Several methods come to mind:

1. *Formal social control.* We have already mentioned the dangers of overburdening the criminal justice system, but sometimes laws can be enacted that promote routine precautions. Curfews for juveniles not only keep potential offenders in at late hours; they also keep potential victims of crime inside and, presumably, safe. Closing hours for bars and liquor stores provide citizens with less to do out late, thus encouraging their compliance with routine precautions.

2. *Informal supervision.* This is a specific kind of informal social control that occurs when family and friends keep an eye out and remind each other to lock the door, park under the light or closer to the destination, not stay out late, turn on the alarm, leave the jewelry in a safe place, and so on. This day-to-day supervisory control needs to be distinguished from socialization, which teaches people what they should do in the hope that they will do it later.

3. *Signage and instructions.* Signs can be posted reminding people to lock office doors when leaving at night or to guard their purses on the subway. Hotels can remind guests to deposit valuables for safekeeping and provide them with information about safe areas to walk. In these and many other ways, people are reminded of the need for precautions. These reminders should not be overdone, however, or they will lose their force.

4. *Product design to facilitate routine precautions.* Cars may buzz when keys are left in the ignition. Entrance doors to apartment blocks may be fitted with self-closing springs. PINs that include numbers chosen by the PIN holder are more easily remembered and thus more secure. All of these design features encourage people to act more safely.

5. *Design to improve natural surveillance.* Public street lights—at least in theory—make a street safer, even if residents forget to turn on their private lights. Trimming hedges and avoiding solid fences also facilitate natural surveillance.

Knowing Which Routine Precautions to Promote

Some routine precautions against crime do not in fact prevent crime for the people who take those precautions because matters can be complicated. For example, putting lights on when away from home might not fool potential burglars, who have plenty of other indicators of residential absence. Similarly, citizens already know to lock their doors, but they think wrongly that the lock by sheer strength will prevent intrusion. Most locks are not that strong. Rather, they force intruders to make noise on entry. If the residents do not also trim their hedges, the neighbors will not hear the noise or be able to see what is happening. Thus, trimming hedges is an important co-factor in locking doors. Some routine precautions against crime may do the job but are costly to buy and install, are complicated or unreliable mechanically, or create problems for the user or others. For example, car alarms and home alarms can be very costly, often go out of kilter, and send out false alarms. Finally, some routine precautions may totally backfire, producing more rather than less crime. For example, walls around backyards in suburban areas may provide cover for burglars to enter. And guns bought for self-defense kill many more family members than intruders.

In truth, we know very little about which routine precautions work and which do not, and research agencies would face considerable difficulties in producing the needed information. The difficulties result from the sheer number of routine precautions that people employ—far too many to be evaluated separately—and the fact that these precautions constantly change and evolve as a result of social and technological developments. In addition, routine precautions will work in some crime situations and not in others, and their effectiveness may depend on other precautions being deployed at the same time. A program of work to sort out all these issues would quickly absorb the budgets of the relevant government research agencies; indeed, the only realistic approach might be to evaluate the effectiveness of "bundles" of precautions—say, those taken by citizens to protect themselves from being victimized when traveling or as tourists.

This was the approach taken in a recent Home Office report. Using British Crime Survey data from more than 47,000 face-to-face interviews, the report examined the effectiveness of a bundle of simple security measures (e.g., deadlocks and window locks) in preventing residential burglaries. It found that the failure to take precautions was by far the strongest predictor of residential burglary—22.5 percent of households that had "no home security measures" were burgled compared with a national average for all homes of 2.5 percent (Table 6.1). The next strongest predictor of burglary, household head age 16–24, was only a third as powerful as no home security. Multivariate analysis that took account of the influence of all other variables showed that having no security measures was independently associated with a higher risk of burglary (Walker, Kershaw, and Nicholas 2006).

This study needs to be repeated for the bundles of precautions that citizens routinely take to protect themselves from other forms of victimization. As we learn more about what works, we need to feed back into practice information about crime prevention, thus helping to broaden the repertoire of good ideas and abandon the worst of routine precautions against crime. In the ideal world, routine precautions and situational prevention will begin to converge, with the general public drawing on better prevention ideas and putting them into action. One hopes that well before that ideal state occurs, criminologists in general

TABLE 6.1   Residential Burglary in England and Wales, 2006–2007

Average occurrence of burglary for England and Wales	2.5%
Among households experiencing a burglary:	
Local authority tenants	4.1%
Less than one year at address	4.6%
Perceived physical disorder in local area	5.1%
Household head long-term unemployed	5.1%
Household head homemaker	5.4%
Single adult and child or children	5.5%
Household head temporarily unemployed	6.0%
Household head student	6.4%
Household head age 16–24	6.7%
No home security measures	22.5%

Source: Nicholas, Kershaw, and Walker 2007.

will realize that situational crime prevention offers much more than locks and alarms and that the routine precautions taken by citizens in everyday life offer an important means for preventing crime. Perhaps then society will not have to turn to draconian punishments or to utopian social philosophies.

Lessons from Medicine

In closing, it is illuminating to compare the history of criminology with the history of medicine. Criminology emerged largely from philosophy. Crime was seen as aberrant behavior and hence raised questions about human nature. These philosophical discussions then led to the examination of the philosophy of punishment and, in time, to treatments of crime as subfields of various social sciences.

Medicine, in contrast, derived largely from folk remedies. The latter consisted of a body of advice to people on how to avoid illness and to overcome it when it struck. Folk medicine ranged from learning various bits of information about herbs and diet to treatments that were highly intrusive. Although much folk medicine was administered by ordinary people to their family and themselves, some was administered by specialists (such as witch doctors or shamans) and was closely linked to religion.

One could easily dismiss all folk medicine as myth. Yet as human civilization proceeded to grow in its knowledge, some folk medicine proved to be correct or partly correct. Some herbs from the past are used today, albeit in purified forms and more careful dosages. Some falsehoods from the past led to some truths as more experience accrued. Most important, folk medicine kept theory and practice somehow linked. If folk medicine claimed to solve problems in the real world, there was always a chance to demonstrate such claims to be false or partly false. That possibility in time helped produce improvements in the science itself. Folk medicine was superseded mainly because modern medicine offered such improvements.

Most of modem criminology is far behind even folk medicine. It does not solve crime problems, and it does not even try to. Thus, it avoids the opportunity for its own improvement. Most crime theories are so remote from real life that such evasion is built into their very structure. For example, the policy implication of strain theory is a complete restructuring of society, which in reality is not likely to occur anywhere. Biological theories do not at present identify genes or how to change them; nor is there any practical way to alter the gene pool. Rehabilitation theories could hardly be applied in practice on a scale large enough to succeed. Despite claims by some "practical policy" advocates, it is not practical to apprehend and punish or incapacitate a large enough share of the pool of offenders in a large modern society to reduce crime. Nor is it practical to abandon punishment to please labeling theorists, who never seem to think about protecting society and victims. In the end, all of these theories become untestable in practice and thus unverifiable, leaving out for the moment the evidence and arguments against them in the first place.

Only by finding truly clinical criminology can we at last bring crime theory and crime prevention into the same world. By making promises of the latter we can also help verify or reject the former and thus develop criminology as a science. In doing so, we should not lose sight of a remarkable generality that emerges from the history of medicine: Public health measures have had far more impact on morbidity and mortality than has treatment of individual patients. For example, many public health measures—such as building sewers, treating water, modernizing plumbing, spraying swamps, inoculating children, and inspecting food production and distribution—have far surpassed surgery and other patient-centered methods in significance. This fact is well known in the fields of demography and public health but not so well known to a population brought up to revere individual physicians.

In the field of crime prevention, we need to put this lesson into practice. It is difficult to teach each citizen to take better routine precautions against crime, and it may be more efficient to apply situational prevention on a public health basis, "inoculating" a facility against burglary by removing its nooks and crannies, designing safer automated teller machines (ATMs), arranging convenience stores to reduce theft and danger to clerks and customers, and so forth. It is easier to change the minds of a few thousand organizations than to change the minds of 250 million individuals. By working with organizations rather than individuals, it may be possible to bring prevention to fruition more quickly while feeding back what is learned into improved criminology. That is the essence of science, and perhaps in time, the lessons will filter to individuals, as well.

References

Anderson, D. A. 1999. The aggregate burden of crime. *Journal of Law and Economics* 42: 611–642.

Brantingham, P. J., and P. L. Brantingham. 1993. Environment, routine, and situation: Toward a pattern theory of crime. In *Routine activity and rational choice,* Vol. 5, *Advances in criminological theory.* Ed. F. Cullen, J. Wright, and K. Blevins, 259–294. New Brunswick, N.J.: Transaction Publishers.

Clarke, R. V. 1983. Situational crime prevention: Its theoretical basis and practical scope. In *Crime and justice: A review of research,* Vol. 4. Ed. M. Tonry and N. Morris, 225–256. Chicago: University of Chicago Press.

———. 1997. *Situational crime prevention: Successful case studies.* 2nd ed. Albany, N.Y.: Harrow and Heston.

———. 2005. Seven misconceptions of situational crime prevention. In *Handbook of crime prevention and community safety.* Ed. N. Tilley, 39–70. Cullompton, U.K.: Willan Publishing.

Clarke, R. V., and J. Eck. 2005. *Crime analysis for problem solvers—In 60 small steps.* Office of Community Oriented Policing Services, U.S. Department of Justice, Washington, D.C.

Clarke, R. V., and P. M. Mayhew. 1980. *Designing out crime.* London: Her Majesty's Stationery Office.

Clarke, R. V., and G. R. Newman. 2005. *Designing out crime from products and systems.* Crime Prevention Studies, Vol. 18. Monsey, N.Y.: Criminal Justice Press.

———. 2007. Police and the prevention of terrorism. *Policing* 1:9–20.

Cohen, L. E., and M. Felson. 1979. Social change and crime rate trends: A routine activity approach. *American Sociological Review* 44:588–608.

Cornish, D. B., and R. V. Clarke. 1986. *The reasoning criminal.* New York: Springer-Verlag.

Cusson, M. 1986. L'analyse strategique et quelques developpements recente en criminologie. *Criminologie* 19:51–72.

Dilulio, J. J. 1996. Help wanted: Economists, crime and public policy. *Journal of Economic Perspectives* 10:3–11.

Felson, M. 2002. *Crime and everyday life.* 3rd ed. Thousand Oaks, Calif.: Pine Forge Press.

Felson, M., and R. V. Clarke. 1998. *Opportunity makes the thief.* Police Research Series, Paper 98. London: Home Office.

Goldstein, Herman. 1990. *Problem-oriented policing.* New York: McGraw-Hill.

Hesseling, R. B. 1994. *Displacement: A review of the empirical literature.* Crime Prevention Studies, Vol. 3. Monsey, N.Y.: Criminal Justice Press.

Hindelang, M., M. R. Gottfredson, and J. Garofalo. 1978. *Victims of personal crime: An empirical foundation for a theory of personal victimization.* Cambridge: Ballinger.

Hope, T., and S. P. Lab. 2001. Variation in crime prevention participation: Evidence from the British Crime Survey. *Crime Prevention and Community Safety: An International Journal* 3:7–21.

Jeffery, C. R. 1977. *Crime prevention through environmental design.* 2nd ed. Beverly Hills: Sage.

Lewin, K. 1947. Group decisions and social change. In *Readings in social psychology.* Ed. T. M. Newcomb and E. L. Hartley, 340–344. New York: Henry Holt.

Marx, G. T. 1995. The engineering of social control: The search for the silver bullet. In *Crime and inequality.* Ed. J. Hagan and R. Peterson, 225–246. Stanford, Calif.: Stanford University Press.

Mikos, R. A. 2006. "Eggshell victims," private precautions, and the societal benefits of shifting crime. *Michigan Law Review* (November): 307–351.

Nalla, M., and G. Newman. 1990. *A primer in private security.* Albany, N.Y.: Harrow and Heston.

Newman, O. 1972. *Defensible space: Crime prevention through urban design.* New York: Macmillan.

Nicholas, S., C. Kershaw, and A. Walker. 2007. *Crime in England and Wales 2005/6.* 4th ed. Home Office Statistical Bulletin. London: Home Office.

Philipson, T. J., and R. A. Posner. 1996. The economic epidemiology of crime. *Journal of Law and Economics* 29:405–433.

Reiss, A., Jr. 1967. Public perceptions and recollections about crime, law enforcement, and criminal justice. In *Studies in crime and law enforcement in major metropolitan areas.* Vol. 1, sec. 2, 1–114. Washington, D.C.: U.S. Government Printing Office.

Sherman, L. W. 1993. Why crime control is not reactionary. In *Police innovation and control of the police.* Ed. D. Weisburd and C. Uchida, 171–189. New York: Springer-Verlag.

Skogan, W. G., and M. Maxfield. 1981. *Coping with crime: Individual and neighborhood reactions.* Beverly Hills: Sage Publications.

Suttles, G. D. 1972. *The social construction of communities.* Chicago: University of Chicago Press.

Thompson, M. P., T. R. Simon, and L. E. Saltzman. 1999. Epidemiology of injuries among women after physical assaults: The role of self-protective behaviors. *American Journal of Epidemiology* 150:235–244.

Walker, A., C. Kershaw, and S. Nicholas. 2006. *Crime in England and Wales 2005/6.* Home Office Statistical Bulletin 12/06. London: Home Office.

II

The Policy Implications of
Theory Applied to
Specific Crime Types

HUGH D. BARLOW AND SCOTT H. DECKER

Introduction to Part II

*Impact of Theory and Policy on
Key Criminological Issues*

There is no debate that criminal justice policy and practice include attention to illegal drug use and trafficking, youth gangs, violent crime, and (at least since 9/11) terrorism. It is also clear that these crimes are not discrete; rather, they are overlapping and are often mutually reinforcing. For example, much terrorism is financed by the international drug trade, and youth gangs participate in drug use and trafficking and in violent crime, though perhaps not as extensively as is generally believed. These convergences illustrate important overlaps in policy and theory.

It should come as no surprise that criminologists have weighed in with various attempts to explain the origin, character, and persistence of these crimes (terrorism belatedly). Yet policymakers may not be paying as much attention to these efforts and their implications. In the so-called war on drugs, for example, federal drug-control policy is firmly committed to reducing the supply of illegal drugs, while the policy implication of criminological theory in this area leans toward reducing demand through treatment, education, rehabilitation, and community building. It is disheartening to learn that from 1996 to 2008 the percentage of federal drug-control dollars spent on reducing demand dropped from 52.6 percent to 36.5 percent, while the percentage spent on reducing supply, including international interdiction, grew from 21.5 percent to 38.5 percent.[1] Worse still, there is little evidence that the supply-side approach is working, to say nothing of the human and political costs of U.S.-led interdiction efforts.

---

[1] See *Sourcebook of Criminal Justice Statistics*, available online at http://www.albany.edu/sourcebook, table 1.14.

The disconnect between much policy work and theoretical conceptualizations of specific types of crime is the major focus of this section of the book.

In fairness, policymakers operate under intense political pressure and are often faced with confusing recommendations from the scientific community. The situation is made even worse when scholars say one thing and practitioners say another. Not surprisingly, the inclination is to follow the recommendations of those on the front lines rather than those who write theory or do policy analysis. All this makes it important for theorists to spell out the policy implications of their ideas and the evidence that supports them. Some of this evidence comes from the work of practitioners and feedback from the front lines that can be immensely important for theory building itself. Building an iterative process whereby theory and policy inform each other in an ongoing interaction is crucial.

More than one hundred years ago, Emile Durkheim observed that crime and punishment are inseparable, two sides of the same coin. He meant that each affects the other, and therefore a theory of crime that does not include reactions to it will be inadequate, as will a theory of punishment that fails to incorporate a theory of crime, and vice versa.

The chapters in Part II address the policy implications of theories applied to specific types of crime, including reactions to crime. Chapters 7–10 address theory and policy as they relate to criminal activity—theft, gangs, state crime, white-collar crime. The last four chapters examine the other side of crime—the criminal justice response. Importantly, all eight chapters demonstrate that Durkheim was right.

In Chapter 7, for example, Neal Shover and Heith Copes show how the routine activities of street-level thieves revolve around "life as party," where crime is pursued as a rational means of supporting a lifestyle that includes not only the avoidance of unpleasant conditions such as drug withdrawal but also the enhancement of pleasurable activities such as drug use, sex, and risk taking. Despite periodic trips to prison, some thieves maintain this lifestyle for many years. Shover and Copes conclude that, for many thieves, far from deterring crime or reducing it, the prison experience helps improve the rationality of criminal decisions, making them less impulsive and emotional.

In their analysis of the formation, activity, and persistence of gangs in Chapter 8, Jean M. McGloin and Scott Decker demonstrate the importance of integrating levels of analysis to maximize the range of variables that may be targeted in interventions guided by such integrated theory. Using evidence and insights from specific gang-intervention programs, the authors conclude that careful integration of levels in gang theory will lead to more relevant and successful programs. This analysis reinforces the links between theory and practice.

In Chapter 9, Dawn Rothe and David Kauzlarich demonstrate yet again the importance of integrating levels of analysis. Genocide and ethnic cleansing carried out by or on behalf of states or rebel groups within them are examples of state crime. Despite millions of deaths and personal injury and property losses during the twentieth century, state crime remains a relatively neglected area of criminological theory and research. Looking at the motivations and opportunities that promote state crime and the constraints and controls that inhibit it, Rothe and Kauzlarich show how an integrated model of international, state–institutional, organizational, and interactional variables furthers understanding of recent events in Darfur and the U.S. invasion of Iraq. Among the policy implications is the need to develop a "true international community and common identity," and the authors suggest an important role here for non-governmental organizations (NGOs) and social movements.

The study of white-collar crime occupies an important place in the development of criminology, yet it has received considerably less theoretical and policy attention than might be imagined. In Chapter 10, Nicole Leeper Piquero and Andrea Schoepfer examine the causes of white-collar crime against the backdrop of definitions, contrasting offender- and offense-based definitions. They argue in the end that situational approaches that examine life-course issues may be most appropriate. Such theories offer strong links to policy interventions.

Chapters 11–14 examine the practical and policy implications of theories that deal with reactions to crime, or—more specifically—lawmaking and law enforcement. Chapter 11 looks at how the application of law in drug enforcement affects the likelihood of violent retaliation in drug conflicts. Chapters 12 and 13 address gender issues and the differential treatment of people of color, and Chapter 14 uses a prominent model of police practice as a template for reform of restorative justice programs.

It would be difficult to find a better illustration of the interrelationship of crime and reactions to it than Donald Black's theory of law. In Chapter 11, Scott Jacques and Richard Wright apply this important sociological theory to the world of drug enforcement and drug-related conflicts and the amount of violent retaliation (new and dangerous crime) they produce. They focus on the importance of offenders' and victims' social status in determining the amount of law applied to them in drug-offense situations. In general, the lower the offenders' status, the more law is applied against them, and the higher the victims' status, the more law is applied against offenders. Jacques and Wright show that as the amount of drug-law enforcement increases (consistent with the lower status of drug participants), so does the amount of drug-related violence. Since social status is dependent on social information, they then propose a controversial idea: Discrimination in drug-law enforcement might be reduced by reducing access to social information about offenders. The policy implications of this approach are novel and potentially of great importance.

In Chapter 12, Marie Griffin applies feminist theories of crime to the complex problems of prisoner reentry. She notes that the "imprisonment binge" since the 1990s has resulted in significant increases in female inmate populations, most of it a result of the war on drugs and most of it affecting women of color. She proposes policies that address the factors that produce and sustain female criminality: physical and sexual abuse, mental illness, economic marginality, child-care stresses, and homelessness. This analysis forms a strong link between aspects of theory and policy.

In December 2007, a long-advocated and long-awaited change in federal sentencing guidelines was made to equalize the sentences for offenses involving powder and crack cocaine. In Chapter 13, Katharine Tellis, Nancy Rodriguez, and Cassia Spohn call this a "significant and noteworthy policy change that addresses race disparities" in criminal justice. The authors examine three theoretical perspectives on the differential treatment of minorities—critical race theory, conflict theory, and attribution theory. The first two contend that the law and the criminal justice system have been used to promote and maintain white privilege, while attribution theory explains the racial disparities that stem from the way criminal justice officials assess and evaluate offenders and their crimes. The authors focus on attribution theory and show how perceptions of minority blameworthiness and "ability to do time" and concerns about community protection lead to higher rates of criminal justice intervention and incarceration for people of color.

Police are the first-line responders among criminal justice officials. Their policies and practices—and the associated discretionary decision making in the field—are important in shaping the character of reactions to crime and thus to crime itself. This is recognized in so-called problem-oriented policing (POP), an attempt to address the underlying causes of recurring crime incidents so that police resources and interventions are allocated in the most useful way. In Chapter 14, Gordon Bazemore and Rachel Boba apply the POP model to restorative justice programs designed to reduce youth crime. Calling restorative justice an inherently collective reaction to crime, Bazemore and Boba show how problem-solving restorative justice can lead to community building and an increase in social capital. This approach links theories of restorative justice to the practice of criminal justice.

Observing that "criminological theory is seldom applied to intervention practice," Bazemore and Boba note that various mainstream criminological and social theories underlie their approach: exchange theory (with its emphasis on reciprocity), social support theory (with its emphasis on building healthy relationships that inhibit criminal activity and help victims recover), and theories of social capital (emphasizing networks of support and collective responses to crime). They also acknowledge a debt to John Braithwaite's prominent theory of reintegrative shaming.

These chapters complement the chapters in Part I on general theories of crime. Both parts describe the link between different kinds and different levels of theory and policy responses. In our view, the best theory addresses issues of policy, and concomitantly the best policies are built on theory.

7

NEAL SHOVER AND HEITH COPES

Decision Making by Persistent Thieves and Crime Control Policy

The closing decades of the twentieth century saw dramatic change in the way policymakers and elite academics talk about crime and what should be done about it. In place of the deterministic explanations that enjoyed support for decades, they turned to and advanced an interpretation of crime as *choice*. In the quest to explain why some citizens commit crime but others do not, this approach resurrects an answer advanced by philosophers nearly two centuries ago: They choose. As with all choices, criminal ones are said to be preceded by a decision-making process in which individuals assess options and their potential outcomes, paying attention particularly to the odds and severity of aversive consequences. Economists, cognitive psychologists, and many in the criminological mainstream offered models of criminal decision making grounded in these assumptions.

Rational choice theory stimulated numerous studies of decision making by criminal offenders, and *persistent thieves* are the focus of many. Reasons include the fact that they repeatedly commit robberies, burglaries, and acts of theft—the crimes that invariably and immediately come to mind when the subject of crime is raised in conversation or featured in the media. By definition, persistent thieves commit crime over several years, and many serve multiple jail or prison terms in the process. Despite having at least one adult conviction for robbery, burglary, or theft, they characteristically return to crime commission.

This chapter reviews what is known about criminal decision making by persistent thieves and some policy implications of it. It draws primarily from ethnographic research to examine how persistent thieves perceive and experience state-imposed sanctions and the extent to which their decision making approximates the systematic and careful deliberative process suggested by rational choice theory. The primary source of materials is research carried out by investigators in North America and Europe, although we draw heavily from several ethnographic studies carried out by investigators at the University of Tennessee (Cherbonneau and Copes 2006; Copes 2003; Copes and Hochstetler 2003; Hochstetler 2001, 2002; Shover 1985, 1996; Shover and Honaker 1992). We also use materials from published autobiographies by offenders (e.g., McCall 1994). We begin by examining the lifestyle of street-level persistent thieves. Next we explore temporal changes in their criminal calculus and decision making as they experience punishment and get older. This is followed by description and discussion of the potential efficacy of deterrence-based crime control policies in light of what is known about decision making by persistent thieves and patterned changes in it as offenders get older and experience confinement. The chapter concludes by suggesting that manipulating the schedule of prison years threatened for street-level crimes of acquisition probably is a crude and clumsy tool for deterring these offenders. We suggest instead that more attention should be focused on increasing the situational risks of crime, improving rehabilitative programs, and raising estimates of the likely payoffs from conforming behavior.

Lifestyle as Decision-Making Context

Enhanced understanding of criminal decision making by persistent thieves can be gained by examining it in context of the lifestyle characteristic of most of them: *life as party* (Shover 1996). The hallmark of this lifestyle is enjoyment of "good times," with minimal concern for obligations and commitments external to the person's immediate social setting. It is seen, for example, in the behavior of men who at 3 P.M. on any day perhaps leave the place where they spent the night with a promise to return "later," only to disappear into drug use and indolence for days or weeks. Life as party is distinguished in many cases by two repetitively cyclical phases and corresponding approaches to crime. When efforts to maintain the lifestyle (i.e., party pursuits) are largely successful, crimes are committed to sustain circumstances or a pattern of activities they experience as pleasurable; crimes are "part of a continuing satisfactory way of life" (Walsh 1986, 15). By contrast, when offenders are less successful at party pursuits, crimes are committed to forestall or avoid conditions experienced as unpleasant, precarious, or threatening. Generally this is represented by involuntary sobriety or the discomforting effects of withdrawal from drug use.

Because it is enjoyed in the company of others, life as party generally includes shared consumption of alcohol or other drugs in bars and lounges, on street corners, or while cruising in automobiles. A wealth of studies from the United States and Europe show that persistent thieves spend much of their criminal gains on alcohol and other drugs (Figgie International 1988; Gibbs

and Shelly 1982; Hearnden and Magill 2004; Maguire 1982; Shover 1996;
Wright, Brookman, and Bennet 2006). Put differently, their criminal proceeds
"typically [are] used for personal, non-essential consumption (e.g., 'nights out'),
rather than, for example, to be given to family or used for basic needs" (Walsh
1986, 72). Interviews with thirty active burglars in Texas caused investigators
to observe "that . . . only one . . . reported a primary need for money for something other than to purchase drugs or alcohol or for other 'partying' activities"
(Cromwell and Olson 2004, 16).

In the venues where life as party is enjoyed, participants celebrate and
affirm values of spontaneity, independence, and resourcefulness. Spontaneity
means that rationality and long-range planning are eschewed in favor of enjoying the moment and permitting the day's activities to develop in an uncon-
strained fashion. This may mean, for example, getting up late, usually after a
night of partying, and then setting out to make contact with and enjoy the
company of friends or associates who also are predisposed to partying. A young
robber explains:

> I just wanted to be doing something. Instead of being at home, or some-
> thing like that. I wanted to be running, I wanted to be going to clubs
> and picking up women and shooting pool. And I liked to go to [a nearby
> resort community] and just drive around over there. A lot of things like
> that. . . . I was drinking two pints or more a day. . . . I was doing Valiums
> and I was doing Demerol. . . . I didn't want to work.

Party pursuits also appeal to offenders because they permit conspicuous
displays of independence (Persson 1981). This generally means avoidance of
the world of work, freedom from being "under someone's thumb," and the ability
to avoid or escape restrictive routines. As John MacIssac (1968, 69) puts it, "I
was always quite candid in admitting that I was a thief because I enjoyed the
stimulation of crime and because I had a marked aversion to the 40-hour week."
Likewise, in the words of a subject in one of our studies:

> I can't see myself, you know, staying home. Basically, I'd rather have
> fun—hang out. I see that on the corner, you know. They have fun. They
> got everything they need. Wild, you know. I got that mentality. Why sit
> here and do nothing? I ain't never been to school, so I ain't gonna have
> a good job. The only kind of job that will hire me is construction. Damn
> man, I ain't liftin' them heavy bricks [laughs].

Pursuit and enjoyment of life as party is expensive, largely because of the
cost of drugs. As one of our research subjects remarked: "We was doing a lot

of cocaine, so cash didn't last long, you know. If we made three thousand dollars, two thousand of it almost instantly went for cocaine." Another subject echoed these comments:

> It's hard to go to work and work twelve hours a day when you got a two hundred dollar drug habit a day. You only make two hundred dollars a day at best, you know. That's at sixteen or seventeen dollars an hour, when I went to industrial carpentry. [But] you still can't support a drug habit and a family.

The need to maintain the appearance of "getting over" successfully on the world of squares (e.g., Wiersma 1996) is important in pursuit of life as party. A portion of the illicit income of persistent thieves also may be used for ostentatious display and enjoyment of luxury items or activities that probably would be unattainable on the returns from blue-collar employment. Typical of what has been learned about the profligacy of persistent thieves, investigators who interviewed fifty residential burglars in Ireland remark that "the general impression given . . . was that [they] went through a lot of cash" (Nee and Taylor 1988, 107).

For persistent thieves, no method of generating funds allows enjoyment of life as party for more than a few days. Consequently, the emphasis on spontaneity and independence is matched by the importance attached to financial resourcefulness, as demonstrated by the ability to sustain the lifestyle over a period of time. Doing so earns for persistent thieves a measure of respect from peers for their demonstrated ability to "get over" and translates into "self-esteem . . . as a folk hero beating the bureaucratic system of routinized dependence" (Walsh 1986, 16). The value of and respect for those who are impressively resourceful means that criminal acts as a way of sustaining life as party generally are not condemned by peers. They enable persistent thieves simultaneously to enjoy the lifestyle and to demonstrate commitment to values shared by peers. Disdain for conventional rationality and resourcefulness affirm character and style.

The dynamics and calculus of criminal decision making when the party goes well have distinctive qualities. The risks of crime are approached blithely but confidently in the same spontaneous manner as are the rewards of life as party. Interaction with partners that precedes criminal acts is distinguished by circumspection and the use of rhetorical devices that relegate risk and fear to the background of attention (Hochstetler and Copes 2006). Rarely are confederates asked bluntly if they want to "steal." Instead, they are asked if they "want to go out," if they are "game tonight," or if they "want to make some money."

Q: OK. So, then you and this fellow met up in the bar. . . .Tell me about the conversation.

A: Well, there wasn't much of a conversation to it, really. . . . I asked him if he was ready to go, if he wanted to go do something, you know. And he knew what I meant. He wanted to go make some money somehow, any way it took.

To the external observer, inattention to risk at the moment when it would seem most appropriate may border on irrationality. For those engaged in party pursuits, however, crime is but one aspect of behavior that is rational in other respects. The decision-making calculus and process mutate noticeably, however, when offenders find themselves in other circumstances.

Party Pursuits and Eroding Resources

Party pursuit can be appreciated and enjoyed to the fullest extent only if participants moderate their involvement in it while maintaining identities and routines in the square world. This ensures their "escape value" but requires an uncommon measure of discipline and forbearance; enthusiastic and extended party pursuit threatens constantly to deplete the resources needed to sustain enjoyment. Most commonly, offenders become ensnared by the chemical substances and drug-using routines that party pursuit features. The meaning of drug consumption changes in the process; physical or psychological tolerance increases and drugs are consumed not for the high they once produced but, instead, to maintain a sense of normality by avoiding withdrawal and sickness.

Party pursuit also can erode legitimate fiscal and social capital. It cannot be sustained by legitimate employment, and it typically undermines both the inclination and ability to hold a job. Even if persistent thieves were willing to work at the kinds of employment available to them—and evidence suggests that many are not—the physical demands of work and that of party pursuit conflict. It is nearly impossible to do both well; few people can spend their nights drinking and playing in bars and routinely rise early for work. Also, the best times of the day for committing street-level property crimes are the times when blue-collar workers are at work; days spent searching for suitable businesses to rob or homes to burglarize cannot be spent on the job (Rengert and Wasilchick 2000). Consequently, for those who pursue life as party, legitimate employment often is sacrificed, which reinforces the need to find alternative sources of money (Akerstrom 1985).

Prolonged pursuit of life as party also can affect participants' relationships with legitimate significant others. Many offenders manage to enjoy the lifestyle only by exploiting the concern and largesse of others. This may take the form of repeated requests for and receipt of personal loans that go unrepaid, occasional thefts, and other forms of exploitation. Eventually, friends and even family members may come to believe that they have been manipulated or that continued assistance will only prolong a process that, if not ended, may continue indefinitely. Gradually they may come to believe also that continued moral support and cash may do more harm than good. As one of our subjects told us, "Oh, I tried to borrow money and borrow money and, you know, nobody would loan it to me. Because they knew what I was doing." After first refusing further assistance, acquaintances, friends, and family members may avoid contact with the party pursuer or sever ties altogether. This is not always an asymmetric dynamic, however. When party pursuit is not going well, feelings of shame and self-disgust are not uncommon, and unsuccessful party pursuers may elect to manage these emotions by distancing themselves from conventional others. The resulting social isolation reduces legitimate interpersonal constraints on their behavior.

When the party assumes qualities of difficulty and struggle, offenders' utilities and risk perceptions change. Increasingly, crimes are committed not to enjoy or sustain the lifestyle so much as to forestall unpleasant circumstances. Those addicted to alcohol or other drugs, for example, must devote increasing time and energy to the quest for money to purchase their chemicals of choice. The criminal calculus for many becomes simplified, and the frequency of their criminal acts may increase (Chaiken and Chaiken 1991; Johnson et al. 1985; Makkai and Payne 2003; White et al. 2002). For them, as for others, the inability to draw on legitimate or low-risk resources eventually may precipitate a crisis. A research subject told of a time when he faced a court appearance on a burglary charge and needed funds to hire an attorney:

> I needed some money bad or if I didn't, if I went to court the following day, . . . the judge was going to lock me up. Because I didn't have no lawyer. And I had went and talked to several lawyers and they told me . . . they wanted a thousand dollars, that if I couldn't come up with no thousand dollars, they couldn't come to court with me. . . . So I went to my sister. I asked my sister, I said, "Look here, what about letting me have seven or eight hundred dollars?". . . And she said, "Well, if I give you the money you won't do the right thing with it." And I was telling her, "No, no, I need a lawyer." But I couldn't convince her to let me have the money. So I left. . . . I said, shit, I'm fixing to go back to jail. . . . So as I left her house and was walking—I was going to catch the bus—the [convenience store] and bus stop was right there by each other. So I said, I'm going to buy me some gum. . . . And in the process of me buying the chewing gum, I seen two ladies, they was counting money. So I figured sooner or later one of them was going to come out with the money. . . . I waited on them until . . . one came out with the money, and I got it.

Confronted by crisis and preoccupied increasingly with relieving immediate distress, offenders eventually see themselves propelled by forces beyond control. Behavioral options may be dichotomized into ones that hold out some possibility of relief, however risky, and others that promise little but continued pain. Legitimate options are few and are seen as unlikely while crime offers hope of relief. Thus, acts that earlier were chosen with blithe lack of concern for risk over time are committed out of determination to master or reverse what is experienced as desperately unpleasant circumstances; inattention to risk gives way to belief that one has *nothing to lose*:

> It . . . gets to the point that you get into such a desperation. You're not working, you can't work. You're drunk as hell, been that way two or three weeks. You're no good to yourself, and you're no good to anybody else. Self-esteem is gone. [You're] spiritually, mentally, physically, financially bankrupt. You ain't got nothing to lose.

Desperate to reestablish a sense of normality, offenders pursue emotional relief by choosing to act decisively, albeit in the face of potentially severe legal consequences.

The threat posed by arrest and imprisonment, however, is attenuated for many desperate offenders. As compared with their marginal and precarious existence, it may be accompanied by a sense of relief: "When I [got] caught—and they caught me right at the house—it's kind of like, you feel good, because you're glad it's over, you know. I mean, a weight being lifted off your head. And you say, well, I don't have to worry about this shit no more, because they've caught me. And it's over, you know." When asked what he thought when he was arrested, one of our research subjects said:

> It was, I would have to say, a relief at that point. At that point it was just a relief. I think I knew that it was coming. I was getting well out of hand with the money I was spending, the way I was spending it and stuff like that. So I think that I knew it was coming, and I was getting a little more sloppy in the end, not keeping track of this and that. It was just kind of a relief.

In sum, because of offenders' eroding access to legitimately secured funds, their diminishing contact with and support from conventional significant others, and their efforts to forestall withdrawal and maintain themselves physically, crimes that once were committed to achieve recreational goals increasingly become desperate attempts to head off or reverse uncomfortable situations. When pursuing the short-term goal of enjoying party pursuits, legal threats are remote and improbable contingencies, but they become acceptable risks for offenders whose lives are marked by social isolation, penury, and desperation.

The challenge of constructing effective crime control policies grounded in notions of crime as choice would be less difficult if not for this contextual variation in the meaning of and attention paid to legal threats. It helps explain why for persistent thieves "definitions of costs and rewards seem to be at variance with society's estimates of them" (Walsh 1980, 141). Men and women who choose deviant lifestyles are decision-making, albeit distant, kin to Rotarians, but their metrics and calculus must be seen through their eyes and with some awareness of the circumstances of their lives. This does not mean that decision making by persistent thieves is incompatible with the language and theory of crime as choice, but it does highlight the complexities of the process. Offenders do calculate in some manner, but the process is constrained severely by their prior choice of lifestyle, and while they calculate potential benefits and costs, they do so differently or weigh utilities differently from the cocksure way these are sketched in decision-making models. Information collected in eighty-three interviews with Dutch thieves, for example, led the investigator to remark that, to conventional observers, "the way the profits of burglary are spent does not seem to be rational" (Wiersma 1996, 223).

Experience and Aging

Their lifestyle is not the only factor that constrains decision making and conditions the effectiveness of threat for persistent thieves. Both the meaning of crime and the calculus of stealing change with the experience of incarceration and getting older.

Rationalization of Crime

A taste of "the joint" affects criminal decision making in large part because exposure to a measured dose of confinement following a criminal conviction is meant to nurture the *rationalization of crime*. This is the process by which people develop and bring to bear in decision making a more precise calculus and metric of crime and punishment than they employed before incarceration. The prison experience hastens the process and helps replace an emotion-laden and impulsive decision-making process with a more careful and prudent one.

Juveniles typically use minimal deliberation before committing crime. They often become involved in stealing without having developed an autonomous and rationalized set of criminal motives. Questioned retrospectively about their decision making when they were juveniles, forty-nine imprisoned armed robbers reported using little or no sophistication in planning the offenses they committed. Peer influence, anger, and a quest for excitement or revenge are commonplace motives for crime by juveniles; they often commit offenses for these and other "expressive" reasons (Petersilia, Greenwood, and Lavin 1978). As a result, the potential repercussions of crime to some extent are blunted. As important, juveniles neither possess nor bring to bear a precise, consistent metric for assessing the potential consequences of delinquent episodes, and they fail to see or to calculate carefully their potential losses if apprehended. For many youth, crime is a risk-taking activity in which the risks are appreciated and calculated dimly.

Imprisonment can be an important catalyst in the rationalization of crime. It does so because by clarifying previously inestimable variables in the offender's criminal calculus, the calculus is transformed. In causing offenders to see more clearly that criminal definitions and crime control are rational matters, the prison experience improves their ability to calculate before acting. By familiarizing thieves with the definitions and penalty tables at the heart of the criminal code, it promotes a keener awareness of the potential costs of criminal behavior and a more clearly articulated understanding of the price of crime. A former thief has written: "When I first began stealing I had but a dim realization of its wrong. I accepted it as the thing to do because it was done by the people I was with; besides, it was adventurous and thrilling. Later it became an everyday, cold-blooded business, and while I went about it methodically . . . I was fully aware of the gravity of my offenses" (Black 1926). This process begins in jail and continues in prison:

Q: Did you know of the penalties [for crime]?
A: Well once you get to prison you learn. . . . You learn a lot of things in prison. What other people was doing and got caught at and stuff like that.
Q: How did you come to know about [the] penalties?
A: [From] a combination of friends being arrested . . . and then by me being arrested, you know. When you're in jail you learn a lot of things, you know. You've got guys—everybody has got their own problems and everybody is trying to tell you, you know, "You've got your problems, but I'm trying to tell you how I got busted and why I got busted" and what, you know, I should do. And we're exchanging views. You're tell[ing] me, "Well man, here's all they can do to you is this, that and the other. Here's what they did to me on the same thing." (254)

In the recounted experiences of their peers, prisoners learn the range of sentences and the "going rate" for common crimes. They learn to think of the criminal code as a table of specific threats to which specific, calculable punishments are attached. Never mind that the entire criminal justice apparatus is clumsy and non-rational in operation: The claim of rationality that underpins and justifies it is not lost on thieves.

Another way that imprisonment promotes the rationalization of crime is by helping elevate *money*, the most calculable of payoffs, to the forefront of criminal motives. Prison conversations are laced with depictions of criminal acts as a means of acquiring money—"big money," perhaps. This talk is not without effect, and as thieves experience confinement and get older, money increasingly assumes importance as a criminal objective. After serving a term in the National Training School, a research subject and his friends began robbing gamblers and bootleggers. He was asked,

Q: Did the desire for excitement play any part in those crimes?
A: No, I think the desire for excitement had left. . . . We recognized that it was a dangerous mission then because we knew that gamblers and bootleggers carried guns and things like that. And it was for, you know, just for the money.

Generally, as they get older prisoners learn the importance of assessing opportunities and committing crimes on the basis of an increasingly specific metric of potential benefits and costs. In the words of one of our research subjects: "Whatever started me in crime is one thing, but at some point I know that I'm in crime for the money. There's no emotional reason for me being into crime." Another subject stated: "I wouldn't get caught for just joyriding. No, indeed. I got a lot of partners they'll steal [a car] and joyride in it, but I would never take that type of chance. Because like I said, if we didn't make no dollars, shit, I ain't doin' it."

The prison world is filled with talk of crime as a rational pursuit, some of it pushed by administrators, but most by prisoners. Men who are abject failures at crime talk as if they are successful and well-informed professionals. Many of the men we spoke with bragged about their criminal expertise, as in "I'm the best at what I do" and "To my knowledge I'm the best who ever did it, you know." To those who do not know better, prison conversation makes criminal success seem easily attainable as long as offenders plan and execute carefully. Other inmates admonish them to use their heads and commit crime in ways that tip the odds in their favor—in short, to be rational about crime.

In fact, as in the fantasies of prisoners, the odds of being arrested for any specific criminal act are not great (Felson 2002; Walker 2006). Inmates analyze past offenses to perfect criminal techniques and success as if there is a finite, manageable number of ways that crimes can fail. An interview with a British thief reveals this process:

Q: When you're arrested, what are your reactions at that moment?

A: I think the first thing's annoyance—with myself. How could I be so stupid as to get nicked? What's gone wrong, what have I forgotten, where have I made the mistake? (Parker and Allerton 1962, 149)

Imprisoned thieves may come to believe that once the full array of errors and "mistakes" is learned, prison is a thing of the past: "Every person who ever did time can tell you what he did wrong to get caught. Everyone feels that all he has to do is rectify that one mental error and he's on his way. I knew what had gone wrong in the McDonald's stickup. We hadn't planned carefully. I knew I could do it right this time" (McCall 1994, 22).

The rationalization of crime is one reason some young prisoners develop the belief that crime can be both a lucrative and a low-risk enterprise as long as they "play it smart." Paradoxically, for some the prison experience seduces them into thinking they can avoid arrest. Those who return to stealing after leaving prison often do so with confidence because they now appreciate the importance of planning their crimes:

I didn't worry too much about getting caught because, like I said, I put a lot of planning and forethought into it. . . . The potential gain that I saw increased substantially. The risk diminished because I was a lot more aware of my capabilities.

I was aware of what could happen now, if I got busted again, how much time that I could receive in prison by me being locked up and incarcerated that first time. . . I learned about different type crimes that would get you the most time. . . . I'd always weigh my chances of being captured, being caught, and I'd always have an escape plan.

Forty-nine imprisoned armed robbers said that during their young adult years they developed new confidence in their ability to avoid arrest for their crimes, and their concern about arrest declined significantly (Petersilia, Greenwood, and Lavin 1978, 69–70). Those who continue to commit crimes after their first incarceration think about the possibility of legal sanction more than in the past, and they show marginally improved planning and care in doing so (Petersilia et al. 1978, 60; Wiersma 1996).

If the rationalization of crime were the only consequence of imprisonment, it arguably could be considered an effective and efficient crime control strategy for persistent thieves. But in other ways, as well, the experiential consequences of imprisonment go beyond those envisioned by advocates of crime as choice. Given life in state programs and entrusted to bureaucracies, crime control policies often produce unplanned or unintended consequences that diminish their effectiveness (Kovandzic, Sloan, and Vieraitis 2002). This is the case with imprisonment. Even as it makes offenders more rational about crime, it causes them to believe either that the odds of being captured may not be great or that the pain of penalty is not excessive in any case. How does this happen?

Reassurance

Despite the fact that many have previous experience with juvenile confinement and jail, nearly all men approach their first prison sentence with trepidation. Their assumptions about the world they are about to enter has been formed from old movies, sensational media reports, and conversations with jail inmates who have prison experience under their belt. Those on their way for the first time see prison as a test of their mettle, one that they understand must be endured "like a man." Although many are confident, others fear involuntary segregation from the outside world and the violence and exploitation related in stories about jail and featured in media exposés. Impending imprisonment is never experienced with greater anxiety than by the uninitiated.

Confinement in a penitentiary tends to polarize prisoners. Some recoil from it and resolve, if possible, never again to do anything that will put them back in that situation. Those who can count on strong interpersonal support and financially and personally satisfying employment may avoid returning to prison, particularly if they lack identification with crime as a way of life. For other prisoners, the reaction is different: They adapt and grow acclimated to their surroundings as they learn about prison sentences, prison lifestyles, and the mechanics of criminal justice (e.g., the reduction of sentences for "good and honor time"). Some, for example, are reassured by learning that they will not have to serve their maximum sentence:

> Q: When I asked you how much time you did, you said, "Nothing, 18 months." Did that not seem like much time to you?
>
> A: I always thought it wasn't nothing because I went and did it and come on back here. But it really wasn't eighteen months; it was thirteen months and something. See, they give me eighteen months . . . [and] they give me so much off for good behavior. Just like this time I'm doing now. To you fifteen years would be a lot of time, because you don't quite understand it. But after you get into the system here, then they give you so many points for this and so many points for that . . . and when you get through looking at that you really don't have to stay as long as you might think.

Those new to the world of jail and prison undergo a process of adaptation that effectively decreases the shock and suffering they experience if they are confined again (Irwin 1985). Confinement erodes conventional sensibilities, teaches inmates how to cope successfully with a depriving and dangerous environment, and acclimates them to deviant norms, adaptations, and others. The harshness of prison life is diminished also by the presence of friends from the streets or acquaintances from other institutions. The prison experience will leave many of those who pass through it once less fearful of and better prepared for a second trip, if that should happen. Put differently, some aspects of imprisonment may limit its specific deterrent effect:

Q: Did you, did you actually think at [the time you passed forged checks], "Hey, I could go to jail for this?"

A: I think I thought about it, but I didn't care if I went to jail. Jail was just, I was used to jail. Jail wasn't a threat to me.

Q: Before you went to prison the first time in your life, was it a threat to you?

A: Yeah, it was, the first time was. It was a change.

Q: Was prison something that you were kind of scared of?

A: Scared of! I was even scared for the first year that I was in prison. Because I knew nothing about the lifestyle. But now I do know about the lifestyle, and it doesn't scare me. I would rather not be locked up. I'd rather get out and get my head screwed on right, and stay away from alcohol where I didn't do anymore crime, but I'm not able to do that.

Conservative political leaders are quick to point out that imprisonment is not meant to be a pleasant experience. And it is not, at least for the overwhelming majority of those subjected to it. Even for those who have spent more than one stint in prison, "it's a terrible thing to have to put up with" (Crookston 1967, 96). But those who discover that they can survive satisfactorily or even thrive in the prison world are changed by this; they have learned the potentially important lesson that they can "handle it" (Martin and Sussman 1994, 23). By allaying doubts and uncertainties, this can lessen the threat of imprisonment:

Q: Prison must not be much of a threat to you.

A: It's not. Prison wasn't what I thought it was. . . . When I went in, . . . well, at that point in time it was kind of an awful thing to go to prison. That's what I had always heard. But when I got there and then found out that, "Well hell, look who is here. . . I didn't know he was here or they was here." Then I seen that I'm a man just like they are and I can make it.

Q: What kind of effect did that first time you were incarcerated have on you?

A: I was seventeen years old, and they sent me to a men's prison, you
   know. And I went down there, and I made it, you know. I survived
   it. And I come out, I thought, a man. . . . It just showed me that
   what, you know, what I had been afraid of happening wasn't nothing
   to be afraid of.

In several ways, experience with incarceration teaches thieves that they have
the personal qualities and social support to endure if it should happen again.

Dependence

Offenders who are not hardened by gratuitous, excessive punishment in the
name of crime control may be depleted psychologically by the experience and
left dependent. The overwhelming majority of street-level thieves hail from
blue-collar or underclass worlds where a distinctive cultural capital is acquired
(Shover 1996). Working-class culture, like all human cultures, "can be visual-
ized, if only in part, as a kind of theater in which certain contrary tendencies
are played out" (Erikson 1976, 82). For every prisoner who aids official control
by exaggerated displays of independence at least one other opts for *dependence*.
Describing the appeal of incarceration, a subject in one of our studies said that
in prison,

   I can kick back if I want. I can do as much as I feel comfortable doing,
   or as little as I want to do. They're still gonna feed me and they're still
   gonna give me a warm place to sleep. I can get institutionalized real
   easy. It's comfortable.

Like him, many who are forced to accommodate to subordination and enforced
dependence manage to create from the experience aspects that are satisfying.
If it does nothing else it frees one of the responsibilities and uncertainties of
self-direction. A sixty-five-year-old man who was interviewed in prison expressed
ambivalence about returning to the free world:

   In a way, I'm looking forward to getting out, and another way it don't
   much matter to me. . . . I know everybody here. . . . I do almost like I
   want. I go to early chow. [Earlier today] I went down to the law library
   and used their copying machine. I can do fairly well what I want to do
   without anybody buggin' me about it, 'cause all the officials know me.

Despite the normative call of independence and autonomy, men of
working-class background adapt easily to hierarchical supervision. Surveying

his options, which he acknowledged were bleak, a middle-aged persistent offender commented:

> I don't care much about being in the free world. Too tough, too tough for me. I'm too institutionalized, been in prison too much, been taken care of too much as a youngster and as an adult by the state and it kind of gets into your system. . . . See, I do fine when I'm in institutions. . . . I help cook, I help do this, I help do that, but you let me out on my own, I won't do a goddamn thing for myself. (Cardoza-Freeman 1994, 179–181)

He is not alone in this response to the undertow of regimentation and freedom from the need to provide for material sufficiency.

Lessons for Crime Control Policy

The ascendant popularity of rational choice interpretations of offending in recent decades was matched by dramatic changes in American criminal justice. Political leaders seized on citizens' growing anxiety about economic and life-quality issues to cast street offenders as enemies in a "war on crime." Crime control policies justified by theories of rehabilitation were jettisoned and replaced by policies that increased the risks of criminal behavior by increasing the odds and severity of aversive consequences (Garland 2001; Gordon 1990). The crime control apparatus now provides increased punishment across its operating spectrum of jails, training schools, and prisons; institutional populations have soared to historically unprecedented levels (Austin and Irwin 2001; U.S. Department of Justice 2006, 2007a, 2007b).

The challenge of minimizing noncompliance with law is similar in some respects to the challenge of minimizing the socially harmful consequences of sexual attraction between human beings. Every solution comes at a price. This is as true of threat-based approaches as of all the others. What has been learned about the calculus of persistent thieves shows that fear and its effects on criminal decision making vary situationally and with criminal experience. One-size-fits-all delivery of penalties largely ignores this. It also costs an enormous sum of money, which perhaps could be spent better elsewhere. Alternative or complementary crime control policies may offer more cost-effective responses to the threat of crime by street-level persistent thieves.

Situational Deterrence

Most persistent offenders give little thought to the possibility of a lengthy prison sentence but focus instead on the potential rewards of crime and the technical challenge it poses; potential arrest is approached as a problem to be overcome, not something to get hamstrung over or weighed in fine detail (Nee and Taylor 2000; Shover and Honaker 1992). Some are so addicted to drugs that they are willfully inattentive to legal threats in the hope of minimizing the immediate discomforts of drug addiction. Some become accustomed to the risks and reconcile themselves to occasional failure. Offenders who believe they have little to lose are not deterred easily. Other thieves enjoy the adrenaline "rush" of crime, likening it to the effects of chemical stimulants, speeding, high-stakes gambling, or fighting (Gove 1994; Gove and Wilmoth 1990). This is common particularly among young offenders, for whom increasing the threatened penalties paradoxically may increase the emotional high provided by transgression.

Fear perception in settings that spawn criminal acts differs considerably from what is commonplace in more solitary and deliberative settings, where clear-headed potential offenders look at crime and its long-term prospects. But the deterrence lessons of the penitentiary world and the policies contained in complex sentencing tables are remote and easily lost sight of when thieves weigh the risks and potential rewards of criminal acts. The message embedded in threatened criminal penalties are refracted and discounted in the contexts where street-level thieves choose crime. Here formal threats and repercussions are pushed to the background of attention or, alternatively, are seen as improbable or acceptable contingencies. Effective deterrence requires that the message get through to potential offenders. The challenge is to imagine and create circumstances in which fear works.

Research conducted or sponsored by the British Home Office, for example, has shown the effects on crime reduction of manipulated situational elements on offenses as diverse as identity theft, pay-phone-toll fraud, and drive-by shootings (Clarke 1997; Dedel 2007; McLennan and Whitworth 2008; McNally and Newman 2008). This approach is no less applicable to street-level theft, because despite what is true of their criminal decision making, persistent thieves are noticeably attentive to risk when selecting specific targets (Ashton et al. 1998; Nee and Taylor 1988; Wiersma 1996; Wright and Logie 1988). At this stage of crime commission, the focus is no longer whether to commit crime but how to select targets and reduce technical challenges to avoid detection and arrest. In the words of one offender, "You don't think about getting caught; you think about how in the hell you're going to do it *not* to get caught."

Greater emphasis, therefore, should be placed on understanding the risks of crime that are present during criminal events and the techniques offenders use to manage these risks. Risks are present at all stages during the criminal event, and perceptions of these risks do affect behavior. Legal threats assume more importance when offenders begin "rooting" once inside burglarized premises (Wright and Decker 1994). Fear of discovery causes many to minimize the amount of time they spend doing so, even if this means settling for smaller returns (Cromwell and Olson 2004; Rengert and Wasilchick 2000; Wright 2001). Although offenders manage to overcome the threat of the law and choose to commit crime, the possibility of arrest is recognized squarely at subsequent stages of the criminal event and understandably constrains how offenders behave.

Fear and anxiety are salient emotions during the commission of crime (Cusson 1993; Lejeune 1977). Offenders must learn to manage these feelings, because learning to do so is a large part of what it means to be a skilled and experienced thief. By actively engaging in arrest-avoidance strategies, offenders gain the peace of mind that comes from having control over a situation, and "as long as the thief keeps everything under control, he will not panic" (Cusson 1993, 64). These strategies give offenders the confidence that they will be successful and allow them to control the negative emotions associated with crime (Cherbonneau and Copes 2006). Disrupting offenders' arrest-avoidance strategies may lead to long-term crime prevention. By manipulating environmental cues and aspects of criminal opportunities, both the risks and the efforts associated with crime can be released, thereby making the decision to offend less attractive to thieves. For example, when selecting homes to burglarize, offenders are concerned primarily with whether or not the homes are occupied; they pass by occupied homes in favor of those where there is no danger of confronting residents (Shover 1991). Knowledge of this is the basis for advice to homeowners to simulate occupancy when no one is at home, perhaps by leaving interior lights burning or by insuring that uncollected mail does not accumulate in the mailbox.

Rehabilitation and Increased Legitimate Opportunities

Traditionally, advocates of rational choice interpretations of offending question the effectiveness of rehabilitation efforts and leaned toward simple models of deterrence (Cullen et al. 2002). Rational choice perspectives lend themselves most easily to state policies that adjust costs of crime and are distant from perspectives that focus on what is wrong with offenders. One reason is the presumed difficulty of altering a person's values. Investigations into the world of street offenders and their decisions to engage in illegal behavior may call these biases into question. There is reason to believe that it takes considerable preparation to commit even spontaneous crime, and most costs can be minimized in the offender's mind as long as there is a reasonable chance of success. This suggests that criminals' confidence in the face of fear is not the result of some intractable and deep-seated preference for risk and may expose penetrable chinks in the armor of thieves.

The trend in rehabilitation is to teach offenders through training and exercises how to recognize their past mistakes and errors in thinking. The hope is that through changes in thinking and simple cognitive training offenders will recognize their responsibilities and apply these lessons when confronting criminal opportunity when they are released. This method has proved to be effective in helping offenders who are prepared to make a change in their lives. Offenders can be taught lessons that change their thinking, and these lessons help them to avoid situations that lead them to crime. There may be other things that they can be taught to recognize in their own thinking, including the devices that enable crime. Thus, cognitive restructuring programs based on what we have learned from decision-making research may prove to be effective in transforming offenders into ex-offenders (Vaughan 2007).

Like pain, a full sense of fear and terror and how it is experienced is difficult to articulate. In the abstract, offenders remember well fearful sensations and how they learned to manage them. They recall the labor of getting past fear, including the procedures and suppression of thought that allowed them to do something that they thought was "not quite right" in the first place. To recognize that they share this experience with others who should have known better, like many rehabilitative lessons, might make clear that the route to prison operates against an almost natural better judgment. Knowing that they scouted multiple crimes before coming to one with a suitable target suggests that the lingering effects of anxiety created in aborted crimes, if interpreted properly, could throw cold water on criminal plans for the evening. If there is time to switch targets, there is time to reflect self-consciously on fear-reducing tactics and the dangers they create. Using the same sort of cognitive training that characterizes other programs, offenders could be taught to recognize fear as a warning mechanism and to respond appropriately. They could learn to recognize the moods, rhetorical devices, and interpersonal dynamics that made it possible for them to cope with fear and to offend in the past. Learning to interpret and respond differently to fear may be part of rehabilitation.

Rational choice theory highlights offenders' prospective comparative assessment of both the risks of crime and other opportunities available to them. Crime control policies constructed on the basis of the theory, however, have been confined almost exclusively to increasing risk. In doing so, policy advocates ignore the theoretically obvious: Offenders' behavior can be changed also by increasing legitimate opportunities. Providing more legitimate opportunities extends the choices available to offenders and increases the risk associated with decisions to commit crime. Our review of research on decision making by persistent thieves shows that risk is hardly a consideration in their calculus, but profits and opportunities are. It is possible that an increase in legitimate opportunities would influence the outcome of their decision making; offenders may be more likely to choose profitable legitimate opportunities than criminal opportunities.

Deterrence-based crime control policies generally are premised on the belief that the meaning of legal threats is invariant across contexts and situations.

This is not the case. Moods of desperation, reckless thrill seeking, and indifference can distort severely the calm and thorough calculus imagined by policymakers. At other times, persistent thieves' decision-making processes are distorted by the influence of drugs, co-offenders, or a combination of the two. Nothing said here is meant to imply that legal threats do not have *some* deterrent effect. We are saying only that tinkering with them on the assumption that offenders are aware of and behaviorally sensitive to the changes is naive or even disingenuous.

Research on criminal decision making proceeds from the premise that "there can be no more critical element in understanding and ultimately preventing crime than understanding the [offender's] perceptions of the opportunities and risks associated with [criminal activities]" (Rengert and Wasilchick 1989, 1). What has been learned from ethnographic studies into these matters makes clear that state crime control policies grounded in notions of deterrence take insufficient account of factors and conditions that constrain decision making by persistent thieves and thereby limit the rationality they employ. They do calculate to some degree and in some manner, but the process is bounded severely by the lifestyles they pursue; when they make decisions to commit crime, persistent thieves are not attuned to nuances of threatened penalties. It comes as no surprise, therefore, to learn from research on residential burglars that they make "hurried, almost haphazard, decisions to offend while in a state of emotional turmoil" (Wright and Decker 1994, 211). For those who are caught—and most persistent thieves will be at some time or other—the experience of incarceration erodes its perceived harshness and reassures many that it can be endured. Time spent in confinement causes younger thieves to rationalize crime and to believe they can be successful at it by perfecting criminal techniques. This and what is known about the dynamics of criminal decision making mean that we should be wary of crime control proposals that promise significant reductions in crime by increasing threat and repression. It is past time for greater modesty by those who stump for crime control policies justified by theories of crime as choice.

References

Akerstrom, M. 1985. *Crooks and squares: Lifestyles of thieves and addicts in comparison to conventional people.* New Brunswick, N.J.: Transaction.

Ashton, J., I. Brown, B. Senior, and K. Pease. 1998. Repeat victimization: Offender accounts. *International Journal of Risk, Security and Crime Prevention* 3:269–279.

Austin, J., and J. Irwin. 2001. *It's about time: America's imprisonment binge.* 3rd ed. Belmont, Calif.: Wadsworth.

Black, J. 1926. *You can't win.* New York: A. L. Burt.

Cardoza-Freeman, I. (Ed.). 1994. *Chief: The life history of Eugene Delorme, imprisoned Santee Sioux* Lincoln: University of Nebraska Press.

Chaiken, J. M., and M. R. Chaiken. 1991. Drugs and predatory crime. In *Crime and justice: A review of research*, Vol. 13. Ed. M. Tonry and J. Q. Wilson, 203–240. Chicago: University of Chicago Press.

Cherbonneau, M., and H. Copes. 2006. Drive it like you stole it: Auto thieves and the illusion of normalcy. *British Journal of Criminology* 46:193–211.

Clarke, R. V. 1997. *Situational crime prevention: Successful case studies*. Guilderland, N.Y.: Harrow and Heston.

Copes, H. 2003. Streetlife and the rewards of auto theft. *Deviant Behavior* 24:309–332.

Copes, H., and A. Hochstetler. 2003. Situational constructions of masculinity among male street thieves. *Journal of Contemporary Ethnography* 32:279–304.

Cromwell, P. F., and J. N. Olson. 2004. *Breaking and entering: Burglars on burglary*. Belmont, Calif.: Wadsworth.

Crookston, P. 1967. *Villain*. London: Jonathan Cape.

Cullen, F. T., T. C. Pratt, S. L. Miceli, and M. M. Moon. 2002. Dangerous liaison? Rational choice and theory as the basis for correctional intervention. In *Rational choice and criminal behavior: Recent research and future challenges*. Ed. A. R. Piquero and S. G. Tibbetts, 279–296. New York: Routledge.

Cusson, M. 1993. Situational deterrence: Fear during the criminal event. In *Crime prevention studies*, Vol. 1. Ed. R. V. Clarke, 55–68. Monsey, N.Y.: Willow Tree Press.

Dedel, K. 2007. *Drive-by shootings*. Problem-Oriented Guides for Police, Problem-Specific Guide No. 47. Office of Community Oriented Policing Services, U.S. Department of Justice, Washington, D.C.

Erikson, K. T. 1976. *Everything in its path*. New York: Simon and Schuster.

Felson, M. 2002. *Crime and everyday life*. 3rd ed. Thousand Oaks, Calif.: Sage.

Figgie International. 1988. *The Figgie Report part VI—The business of crime: The criminal perspective*. Richmond, Va.: Figgie International.

Garland, D. 2001. *The culture of control: Crime and social order in contemporary society*. Chicago: University of Chicago Press.

Gibbs, J. J., and P. L. Shelly. 1982. Life in the fast lane: A perspective view by commercial thieves. *Journal of Research in Crime and Delinquency* 19:299–330.

Gordon, D. 1990. *The justice juggernaut: Fighting street crime, controlling citizens*. Rutgers, N.J.: Rutgers University Press.

Gove, W. R. 1994. Why we do what we do: A biopsychosocial theory of human motivation. *Social Forces* 73:363–394.

Gove, W. R., and C. Wilmoth. 1990. Risk, crime, and neurophysiological highs: A consideration of brain processes that may reinforce delinquent and criminal behavior. In *Crime in biological, social, and moral contexts*. Ed. L. Ellis and H. Hoffman, 261–287. New York: Praeger.

Hearnden, I., and C. Magill. 2004. *Decision-making by house burglars: Offenders' perspectives*. Home Office Research Study No. 249. London: Home Office.

Hochstetler, A. 2001. Opportunities and decisions: Interactional dynamics in robbery and burglary groups. *Criminology* 39:737–764.

———. 2002. Sprees and runs: The construction of opportunity in criminal episodes. *Deviant Behavior* 23:45–74.

Hochstetler, A., and H. Copes. 2006. Managing fear to commit felony theft. In *In their own words: Criminals on crime*. 4th ed. Ed. P. Cromwell, 102112. Los Angeles: Roxbury.

Irwin, John. 1985. *The jail*. Berkeley: University of California Press.

Johnson, B. D., P. J. Goldstein, E. Preble, J. Schmeidler, D. S. Lipton, B. Spunt, et al. 1985. *Taking care of business: The economics of crime by heroin abusers*. Lexington, Mass.: D. C. Heath.

Kovandzic, T., J. J. Sloan III, and L. Vieraitis. 2002. Unintended consequences of politically popular sentencing policy: The homicide promoting effects of "three strikes" in U.S. cities. (1980–1999). *Criminology and Public Policy* 1:399–424.

Lejeune, R. 1977. The management of a mugging. *Urban Life* 6:123–147.

MacIssac, J. 1968. *Half the fun was getting there.* Englewood Cliffs, N.J.: Prentice Hall.

Maguire, M. 1982. *Burglary in a dwelling: The offense, the offender, and the victim.* London: Heinemann.

Makkai, T., and J. Payne. 2003. *Drugs and crime: A study of incarcerated male offenders.* Australian Institute of Criminology Research and Public Policy Series 52. Canberra: AIC Press.

Martin, D. M., and P. Y. Sussman. 1994. *Committing journalism: The prison writings of Red Hog.* New York: W. W. Norton.

McCall, N. 1994. *Makes me wanna holler.* New York: Random House.

McLennan, D., and A. Whitworth. 2008. *Displacement of crime or diffusion of benefits: Evidence from the New Deal for Communities Programme.* Oxford: Social Disadvantage Research Centre, University of Oxford.

McNally, M., and G. Newman. 2008. *Perspectives on identity theft.* Monsey, N.Y.: Criminal Justice Press.

Nee, C., and M. Taylor. 1988. Residential burglary in the Republic of Ireland: A situational perspective. *Howard Journal of Criminal Justice* 27:267–295.

———. 2000. Examining burglars' target selection: Interview, experiment, or ethnomethodology? *Psychology, Crime, and Law* 6:45–59.

Parker, T., and R. Allerton. 1962. *The courage of his convictions.* London: Hutchinson.

Persson, M. 1981. Time-perspectives amongst criminals. *Acta Sociologica* 24:149–165.

Petersilia, J., P. W. Greenwood, and M. Lavin. 1978. *Criminal careers of habitual felons.* Washington, D.C.: National Institute of Law Enforcement and Criminal Justice, U.S. Department of Justice.

Rengert, G. F., and J. Wasilchick. 1989. Space, time and crime: Ethnographic insights into residential burglary. Final report submitted to the National Institute of Justice, U.S. Department of Justice, Washington, D.C.

———. 2000. *Suburban burglar.* 2nd ed. Springfield, Ill.: Charles C. Thomas.

Shover, N. 1985. *Aging criminals.* Beverly Hills: Sage.

———. 1991. Burglary. In *Crime and justice: An annual review of research,* Vol. 14. Ed. M. Tonry, 73–114. Chicago: University of Chicago Press.

———. 1996. *Great pretenders: Pursuits and careers of persistent thieves.* Boulder, Colo.: Westview Press.

Shover, N., and D. Honaker. 1992. The socially bounded decision making of persistent property offenders. *Howard Journal of Criminal Justice* 31:276–293.

U.S. Department of Justice. 2006. *Juvenile offenders and victims: 2006 national report.* Washington, D.C.: Office of Juvenile Justice and Delinquency Prevention.

———. 2007a. *Prison and jail inmates at midyear 2006.* Washington, D.C.: Bureau of Justice Statistics. Available online at http://www.ojp.usdoj.gov/bjs/abstract/pjim06.htm.

———. 2007b. *Prisoners in 2006.* Washington, D.C.: Bureau of Justice Statistics. Available online at http://www.ojp.usdoj.gov/bjs/abstract/p06.htm.

Vaughan, B. 2007. The internal narrative of desistance. *British Journal of Criminology* 47: 390–404.

Walker, S. 2006. *Sense and nonsense about crime and drugs: A policy guide.* 6th ed. Belmont, Calif.: Wadsworth.

Walsh, D. 1980. *Break-ins: Burglary from private houses.* London: Constable.

———. 1986. *Heavy business.* London: Routledge and Kegan Paul.

White, H. R., P. C. Tice, R. Loeber, and M. Stouthamer-Loeber. 2002. Illegal acts committed by adolescents under the influence of alcohol and drugs. *Journal of Research in Crime and Delinquency* 39:131–152.

Wiersma, E. 1996. Commercial burglars in the Netherlands: Reasoning decision-makers? *International Journal of Risk, Security and Crime Prevention* 1:217–225.

Wright, R., and R. Logie. 1988. How young house burglars choose targets. *Howard Journal of Criminal Justice* 27:92–104.

Wright, R. T. 2001. Searching a dwelling: Deterrence and the undeterred residential burglar. In *Contemporary issues in crime and criminal justice: Essays in honor of Gilbert Geis*. Ed. H. Pontell and D. Schicor, 407–418. Upper Saddle River, N.J.: Prentice-Hall.

Wright, R. T., F. Brookman, and T. Bennet. 2006. The foreground dynamics of street robbery in Britain. *British Journal of Criminology* 46:1–15.

Wright, R. T., and S. Decker. 1994. *Burglars on the job*. Boston: Northeastern University Press.

8

JEAN M. McGLOIN AND SCOTT H. DECKER

Theories of Gang Behavior and Public Policy

James Short (1985, 1998) has argued that criminology suffers from a "level of explanation problem." In particular, he suggests that criminology ignores the extent to which our implicit level of explanation influences the way we create theory and conduct research and, by implication, the way we create policy. The literature on street gangs serves as one of the best examples of the tendency for researchers to adopt different implicit paradigms (Short 1985). The roots underlying the spectrum of gang theories extend from *macro-level* sociological factors (e.g., social disorganization, poverty, subcultural norms), to *micro-level* explanations focused on social interactions and processes (e.g., differential association), to *individual-level* variables (e.g., self-control and social control). These different perspectives, combined with the fact that the term "gang" contains considerable heterogeneity (Sullivan 2006), set the stage for "talking past each other," potentially handicapping theoretical and empirical growth, as well as policy effectiveness.

Short recognized the importance of considering all levels of explanation during the course of his field research with gangs in Chicago with Fred Strodtbeck (Short and Strodtbeck 1965). Relying on an array of data sources, including observations by detached workers, they initially set out to investigate individual and macro-level explanatory factors. However, it became clear over the course of the project that group processes were at least as responsible, if not more responsible, for producing most of the delinquent behavior (see also Short 1985). For example, Short and Strodtbeck discovered that aggression between gangs was often instigated by gang leaders who believed that their status was tenuous or under threat. In the end, this research revealed that structural and individual variables intersect at the process level, which ultimately produces behavior. In addition, social interactions at the micro-level have consequences for future interactions, since behavioral processes can affect and transform the group culture. In effect, just as researchers have argued for theoretical integration, Short (1985) noted that his work in Chicago highlighted the need for integration among levels of explanation as a means of understanding gang behavior.

More recent work also has recognized the intellectual insight such integration affords when attempting to understand gangs' characteristics and behavior. For instance, like Short and Strodtbeck, James Vigil's (1988) discussion of multiple marginality recognized the interplay between macro-level (e.g., low socioeconomic status and social disorganization) and individual-level factors (e.g., self-identity) in supporting interactional processes that defined and shaped gang life. Furthermore, he found it difficult to disentangle these levels of explanation when attempting to understand gang events and the behavior of gang members. As Vigil stated, "Socialization to *cholo* ways, especially for those who go on to become gang members, is strongly influenced by family life and peer groups in interaction with the schools and law enforcement agencies" (42–43).

Building on such work, we do not suggest that researchers, practitioners, or stakeholders adopt a single level of explanation for the sake of efficiency. Instead, it is the collective integration of all three that provides theoretical advances. Although viewing a theory or a policy from all three levels may be difficult, it forces the discussion to be comprehensive and to acknowledge the multifaceted character of street gangs and other topics of theoretical attention. To demonstrate the utility of this framework, this chapter examines the manner in which theory, empirical work, and policy can be viewed from these three levels of explanation, which, in turn, provides further insight into the understanding of gangs, gang theory, and gang policy.

Theory and Levels of Explanation

Many theories that discuss gang formation and behavior are primarily rooted in macro-level factors. This largely reflects the trend toward sociological positivism, the apparent concentration of crime in the poor, and the resultant Progressive movement (Lilly, Cullen, and Ball 2002; Matza 1969). For example, Clifford Shaw and Henry McKay (1942) proposed that social disorganization—defined as urbanization, residential mobility, poverty, and ethnic and racial heterogeneity—was the key contributing factor to gang formation and maintenance. This premise was supported empirically by Frederick Thrasher's (1927) work. He found that the "gangland represents a geographically and socially interstitial area in the city"—that is, gangs were prominent in converging areas where there were breaks in social organization and cohesion (6). Thus, the essential proposition from the Chicago school (see Park and Burgess 1925; Shaw and McKay

1942; Thrasher 1927) was that the etiology for gang formation and continuation rested in the social cohesion and normative organization of the community. Although this appears to be a straightforward macro-level explanation of street gangs, it also extends to micro- and individual levels of explanation. Exploring these levels provides a deeper and more comprehensive understanding of theory.

First, the reason that these macro-levels are implicated in explanations of gang presence and gang crime is that they affect local networks, which in turn affect a community's capacity to solve issues and meet common goals (Bursik 1986, 1988; Sampson and Groves 1989). Residential instability, urbanization and changing land use, and heterogeneity can undermine a neighborhood's capacity to leverage resources for formal and informal social control, largely because they facilitate anonymity, weak social networks, and minimal social cohesion. There is a growing literature on these social processes and their impact on neighborhood crime, largely in response to the work of Robert Sampson and colleagues (e.g., Sampson and Groves 1989; Sampson, Raudenbush, and Earls 1997) on collective efficacy. To be sure, contemporary investigations of social disorganization are typically viewed as ill-conceived or mis-specified if they fail to account for these key micro-level processes as mediators.

This suggests that the concept of social disorganization is a key theoretical context for understanding street gangs unless it extends past a single level of explanation. Indeed, another theoretical view argues that understanding these micro-level processes provides insight not only into the etiology of gangs, but also into the nature or form of these gangs. Richard Cloward and Lloyd Ohlin (1960; Cloward 1959) took issue with the notion, which they attributed to Shaw and McKay, that economically deprived areas characterized by gangs and crime were inherently socially disorganized. Drawing largely on the ethnographic work of William F. Whyte (1943), they argue that some neighborhoods can have strong, interconnected networks yet remain oriented around unconventional norms. Through his portrayal of "Cornerville," it became clear that high crime rates can emerge in the face of cohesive networks of social reciprocity. Intense social interactions defined the boundaries of the gangs and the links among gangs and other groups, as well as the cohesion of the gangs and the individual roles within them. Whyte's fieldwork suggests that social cohesion arguably allowed for and facilitated the emergence and persistence of gangs focused on criminal enterprise (see Chin 1996, a more recent work on Chinatown gangs, for a similar theme). Moreover, the interconnectedness of the neighborhood may allow it to control violence largely because it threatens the success of an enterprise.

In contrast, disadvantaged neighborhoods characterized by the absence of social cohesion, stability, and the integration of legitimate and illegitimate networks do not provide the opportunity for more coherent criminal enterprises.

Instead they facilitate the emergence of conflict groups. In this micro-level context, legitimate and illegitimate opportunities to deal with strain are constrained, so neighborhood youth turn to violence as a means to achieve status and garner respect. At the same time, fractured social cohesion and instability result in a neighborhood's having minimal capacity to manage and control violence. In this way, Cloward and Ohlin (1960; Cloward 1959) assert that understanding and attending to a neighborhood's micro-level processes can facilitate an understanding of why and where gangs emerge and provide insight into such things as the structure and crime repertoire of the gang (see also Schreck, McGloin, and Kirk forthcoming).

One is also able to (and, we argue, *should*) extend the discussion of social disorganization to the individual level, although most scholars do not to elaborate on this level of explanation. In returning to one of the core works in both the gang literature and the social disorganization literature—Thrasher's in-depth look at gangs in the Chicago landscape—it becomes clear that this third level of explanation is also important. Thrasher (1927) found not only that gangs emerged in "interstitial" areas, but that the members themselves had an "interstitial" character for their lives. During the course of his observations, he noted that many youth were trying to negotiate a place between the norms, expectations, and even language of their immigrant families and those of their newly adopted home. Furthermore, most gang members were at an age when they were no longer children but were not quite adults, further cementing a feeling of not having a clear place or social role. The gang fills these social voids and reinforces the adolescent desire for excitement: "Gangs represent the spontaneous effort of boys to create a society for themselves where none adequate to their needs exists. What boys get out of such an association that they do not get otherwise under the conditions that adult society imposes is the thrill and the zest of participation in common interests" (Thrasher 1927, 12). Although Thrasher's primary interest was in macro- and micro-level factors, extending the discussion to these individual-level notions provides a deeper and more comprehensive understanding of social disorganization as a theoretical framework for gangs.

This is but one theoretical example and does not capture the array of explanations for the emergence, proliferation, or behavior of gangs. Yet it does demonstrate the benefit of taking care to address all three levels of explanation. Whether one emphasizes subcultural explanations of gangs (e.g., Cohen 1955; Miller 1958), socialization and micro-level perspectives (Akers 1998; Sutherland 1947), or individual-level viewpoints (e.g., Gottfredson and Hirschi 1990), considering the issue from a variety of perspectives certainly deepens knowledge and provides a conceptual framework for empirical work and intervention programs.

Empirical Work and Levels of Explanation

An extensive literature exists on a number of empirical lines of inquiry with regard to street gangs, including the role of gender in gangs, gang structure and organization, drug sales and use, and the nature of gangs' growth and proliferation, among others. One of the fundamental areas of interest remains the extent to which gangs serve to facilitate or prompt violent behavior among their members, and we use this as an example. A number of potential explanations exist for this notion. Again, however, researchers are best served by considering the question from all three levels of explanation.

A number of studies have found that gang members engage in more criminal behavior than do their non-gang delinquent counterparts (see Curry and Decker 1998; Klein 1995; Spergel 1995; Thornberry 1998). Terence Thornberry and James Burch (1997) found that 30 percent of the subjects in the Rochester Youth Development Study revealed that they were gang members, yet they were responsible for 65 percent of the reported delinquent acts. Though research generally suggests that gang members are involved in a variety of criminal activities (Klein 1995 referred to this as "cafeteria-style" offending), the disproportionate tendency to engage in crime clearly extends to violence (Battin et al. 1998; Thornberry 1998). For example, in the Rochester Youth Development Study, the same 30 percent of the sample (i.e., the cumulative prevalence of reported gang membership) was responsible for 68 percent of the cumulative self-reported acts of violence. Furthermore, in a sample drawing from Los Angeles, Chicago, and San Diego, Jeffrey Fagan (1990) found that 23 percent of his sample identified as gang members, yet they accounted for 66 percent of robberies and approximately 67 percent of assaults. On a related note, Mark Fleisher (1997) highlighted the prominent role that guns play in gang culture. To be sure, gang membership or involvement has been established as a correlate and predictor of gun ownership, possession, and use (see Bjerregaard and Lizotte 1995; Decker and Van Winkle 1996; Lizotte et al. 1997, 2000; Luster and Oh 2001).

Hypothetical reasons for this nexus of gangs and violence emerge within all three levels of explanation. With regard to a macro-level focus, a number of scholars call attention to the power of subcultures to evoke and shape behavior (e.g., Cohen 1955; Miller 1958). For example, Marvin Wolfgang and Franco Ferracuti (1967) argued that some groups of people (who were rooted in disadvantaged areas) were enmeshed in a subculture of violence. In this subculture, violence is a normative way to manage social life and basic interactions. Situations that may seem trivial can easily escalate to demonstrations of serious violence, whether between parent and child, between husband and wife, or among peers. Elijah Anderson's (1999) work on the "code of the streets" further illustrates the notion of a violent subculture. Through his observations of social life on the streets of Philadelphia, he noted that an oppositional culture existed within disadvantaged African American communities. This subculture structures the appropriate and expected way to behave and interact on the street and draws heavily on demonstrations of dominance and aggression. Even "decent" people who do not subscribe to this code often must be primed for defensive violence as they navigate public life. In short, there are neighborhood-based "scripts" for proper behavior, which value conflict and violence as a way to establish, negotiate, and maintain social standing (see also Fagan and Wilkinson 1998). Importantly, Anderson (1999) argued that this subculture emerged from even larger structural factors, such as economic deprivation and anomie, systematic racism, and a sense of cynicism toward public institutions, especially the criminal justice system.

Thus, street gangs embedded in these neighborhoods may generate violent crime because they emerge from a subculture oriented toward violence. Indeed, when considering the various community- and family-level risks implicated in joining gangs, they often line up nicely with Anderson's (1999) description of individuals who are most inclined to embrace and reinforce the code of the streets. These risks, such as low parental supervision, low expectations about school by parents, positive views of drug use, and low parental attachment to the child (see Thornberry 1998) do not characterize the children of "decent" families. These families actively struggle against the subculture through strict parental supervision and involvement in conventional activities (although they also may be skilled at negotiating norms and scripts of the street). Thus, part of the reason for the connection between violence and gangs is rooted in social ecology (e.g., Kubrin 2005).

Other discussions of the connection between violence and gangs and gang membership argue that a focus on micro-level processes provides the most insight. For instance, Scott Decker (1996) proposes that gang violence, including homicide, is an expressive result of group processes. Relying on interviews with gang members in St. Louis, he described a seven-step process in which perceived threats from symbolic or actual enemies sparked an escalation of conflict, which typically ended in violence, sometimes fatal. In support of this premise, Decker and Van Winkle (1996) found that most gang homicides were spontaneous, expressive, or retaliatory in nature. Malcolm Klein and Cheryl Maxson (1989) also found that gang violence in Los Angeles was largely the product of escalating actions and reactions among rival gangs. Finally, Jesenia Pizarro and Jean M. McGloin (2006) recently found that collective behavior was the most robust predictor of gang-related homicides in Newark, New Jersey. This research demonstrates that interactions among groups and individuals can build on each other and, akin to a contagion-like process, generate violence. It is the social exchanges themselves and their perceived meaning that shape behavior; without a focus on micro-level processes, this perspective argues, one would be unable to understand gang violence.

The more traditional micro-level processes implicated in discussions of deviant peers are also relevant to a consideration of the relationship between violent behavior and street-gang membership. The core proposition advocated by learning theorists (see Akers 1998; Sutherland 1947) is that gang members are disproportionately involved in violence because of socializing processes endemic to the gang. The gang provides the context for core behavioral processes—they expose members to definitions and values, to behavioral models for imitation, and to sources of differential reinforcement. If violence is part of the gang's identity, it facilitates violent behavior among its members. Simply, under such circumstance, gang members are regularly exposed to a group culture that values and supports violence, they witness fellow gang members engage in violent behavior, and their own aggressive acts are reinforced, all of which facilitate disproportionate levels of violence among gang members.

In addition to these traditional peer processes, Mark Warr (2002) notes that groups can facilitate violence and crime through diffusion of responsibility and anonymity, techniques that help members justify and neutralize their behavior (see also Sykes and Matza 1957). This is somewhat consistent with D. Wayne Osgood and colleagues' (1996) discussion of routine activities and how basic peer interactions facilitate delinquency, independent of whether the peer group is deviant (see also Haynie and Osgood 2005). Osgood and colleagues assert that when adolescents spend time together in unsupervised and unstructured settings, they are at increased risk of engaging in delinquency. "They argued that the presence of peers makes deviant acts easier and more rewarding, the absence of authority figures reduces the potential for social control responses to deviance, and the lack of structure leaves time available for deviance. Therefore, individuals who spend more time in unstructured socializing activities will also more frequently engage in delinquency and other deviant behavior" (Haynie and Osgood 2005, 1112). Given that research has affirmed that gang members spend the bulk of their time "hanging out" (Decker and Van Winkle 1996; Klein 1995), presumably in an unstructured and unsupervised manner, it may simply be that social processes make it easier to commit, excuse, and reward violent acts, regardless of how prone individual members may be to commit violent crime. This discussion focuses on micro-level interactions among people, but interactions among gangs are also important. For example, gang rivalries can drive and shape violence (see Papachristos 2006), adding another layer for consideration, and further suggesting the importance of the group-process level of explanation.

Additional research examines the connection between gangs and violence by focusing on the individual level of explanation. Michael Gottfredson and Travis Hirschi (1990), adopting a population heterogeneity approach, argue that low self-control underlies an individual's predisposition to engage in criminal behavior. Simply put, they propose that individuals who are impulsive, short-sighted, prone to physical expression rather than verbal communication, and driven to take risks will succumb to the temptations offered by crime. Indeed, such individuals will repeatedly fall victim to such temptations and will express their low self-control in a variety of impulsive acts, from shoplifting to sexual promiscuity, substance use, car racing, and violence. Gottfredson and Hirschi (1990) also argue that there are many social consequences to low self-control, such as poor academic performance and having delinquent peers (Evans, Cullen, and Burton 1997). Thus, in a manner consistent with other control theories, they assert that people "self-select" into deviant peer groups and gangs. Because gang membership is simply a product of low self-control and because low self-control promotes high levels of versatile crime (of which violence is part), the connection between gang membership and violent crime is therefore spurious, as the gang does not facilitate violent behavior. As Gottfredson and Hirschi (1990, xv) firmly state at the start of their text: "Crime does not require . . . peer influence or the gang." Instead, insight on the finding that gang members are responsible for a disproportionate amount of violent crime comes from drilling down to the individual level of explanation.

Considering all three levels of explanation independently provides an understanding of an empirical relationship, but integrating all three may provide the most accurate and complete explanation. For instance, despite the apparent competitive stance of the socialization (i.e., micro-level explanation) and selection (i.e., individual-level explanation) models, viewing them as complementary lines up more closely with much empirical work (see Pratt and Cullen 2000). This viewpoint is perhaps best demonstrated by Thornberry's (1987) interactional theory. This view begins from the assumptions that (1) behavior, including violent behavior, occurs in the context of social interaction; and (2) the connection between deviant peer groups and delinquency was, in all likelihood, not unidirectional. Instead, a reciprocal relationship exists between selection and socialization, a viewpoint in the gang literature termed "enhancement." Under this premise, gang members may be predisposed to delinquency and violence prior to entering the gang, but the gang nevertheless has a social impact and serves to enhance or amplify this behavior. In this way, there is an interaction between the person and his or her social environment (see also Wikstrom 2006).

In general, empirical findings are consistent with the view that the majority of gang members initiate their criminal careers before they join a gang, but the gang also imparts its criminally oriented norms to its members (Esbensen and Huizinga 1993; Thornberry et al. 1993, 2003). Selection may guide gang membership and a predisposition for violence and delinquency; the gang amplifies this proclivity for delinquent behavior. For instance, using data from the

Pittsburgh Youth Study, Rachel Gordon and colleagues (2004) found that gang members were more likely to be delinquent (and violent) than non-gang members prior to membership, but violence (along with other forms of delinquency) increased when they were part of the gang. Moreover, the increase in criminal involvement dropped off precipitously when individuals left the gang. This pattern emerged across self-reports, parent reports, and teacher reports of behavior. Finn-Aage Esbensen and David Huizinga (1993) found similar results with data from the Denver Youth Study, as did Sara Battin and colleagues (1998) with data from the Seattle Social Development Project (see also Lacourse et al. 2003).

Furthermore, someone whose proclivity toward violence is amplified by the gang can be further entrenched in a macro-level violent subculture, given that the neighborhood is also an active participant in promoting violence, as discussed earlier (Sampson and Groves 1989). Economic deprivation and constrained legitimate opportunities provide few alternative social options to the street gang in many communities. Decker (1996, 246) notes that gang members are often, "isolate[d] . . . from legitimate social institutions such as schools, families, and the labor market. This isolation, in turn, prevents them from engaging in the very activities and relationships that might reintegrate them into legitimate roles and reduce their criminal involvement." Thus, macro-level factors are also part of this complex, integrative, and reciprocal mechanism that drives the linkage between violence and street-gang membership. In this way, all three levels of explanation are necessary to understand this single empirical relationship and to shape any intervention or strategy aimed at affecting gang violence.

Gang Intervention and Levels of Explanation

We believe that the most accurate description of the relationship between gang theory and gang policy is that they have often worked parallel to each other, but that theory has rarely guided policy or interventions. That is, there is consistency among many of the theoretical explanations (and perhaps with so many theories there has to be *some* level of convergence) and what occurs in the gang-policy and gang-intervention worlds. However, there is seldom an explicit recognition of the theory behind the intervention and use of the theory to actually develop or guide an intervention. Where there is such an effort, however, theory has been drawn from macro-level explanations. Here we highlight two of the best-known and most widely imitated gang interventions: the Spergel model and the Boston Gun Project.

Comprehensive approaches to street gangs combine suppression and intervention (typically social service) tactics in a holistic strategy that typically relies on an array of partners operating in collaboration. Cloward and Ohlin (1960) in particular provide conceptual inspiration for the attempts to address fundamental causes of gangs, what Irving Spergel (2007) and the Office of Juvenile

Justice and Delinquency Prevention (OJJDP) would call "opportunities provision." Such strategies focus on improving the opportunities for employment and education that plague underclass youth. For example, the Spergel model—known formally as the Comprehensive Community Wide Approach to Gang Prevention, or the OJJDP Comprehensive Strategy—calls for a team of community organizations to deliver five core strategies through an integrated approach: community mobilization; social intervention, including street outreach; provision of opportunities; suppression; and organizational change. This model has been piloted under a variety of federal initiatives, including the Little Village Project in Chicago; the SafeFutures program across several locations, including St. Louis, Missouri; the Rural Gang Initiative in four communities, including Elk City, Oklahoma; and the Five City initiative in Riverside, California, San Antonio, Texas, Mesa and Tucson, Arizona, and Bloomington, Illinois. Because it is comprehensive, the model attempts to address each of the three levels—individual, group, and macro-level—arguing that without integration across all three, intervention cannot be successful.

At the individual level, counseling, crisis services, and other services are provided to gang members and fringe members. At the group level, street outreach workers target gangs and subgroups of gang members for intervention. Organizational change is also an important part of this stage of the intervention. Suppression can be viewed as an individual-level strategy. At the macro-level, as noted, the provision of opportunities responds to the more fundamental needs of gang members for jobs, job training, and education. The dilemma with this strategy is that successful implementation is hard to find (Klein and Maxson 2006). Although Spergel (2007) argues that the model was successfully implemented in the Little Village neighborhood of Chicago, the level of oversight and investment of resources suggest that it is quite difficult to implement and sustain. That said, there is no other evidence that this model was successfully implemented and sustained (Klein and Maxson 2006).

Perhaps there is a need to reflect on the quality of theory at this point. First, the failure to implement the model successfully might in part be due to a failure of theory to accurately specify the links between each of the levels and fully explicate their interdependence. Second, even if the links are well specified, failure might reflect the difficulty of implementing one of the key levels, most likely the group level. Klein and Maxson (2006, 20) argue that the Spergel model is "a statement of a conceptual or theoretical approach to gang control." But perhaps it is a stronger conceptual statement about the organizations that serve gangs and gang members than about the behavior of gang members or gangs. The explicit failure to address the mid-range theoretical issues (e.g., group context) is particularly important here. The amplification of the seriousness and incidence of crime attributable to gang membership represents an important theoretical and empirical premise about gang behavior. Under the

Spergel model, social intervention—typically in the form of street outreach workers but also in the form of suppression—is designed to affect gangs as a group and group process. But as Spergel (1995) and Klein and Maxson (2006) note, this can be the most difficult part of gang interventions and often fails.

Perhaps this is a failure of practice: the inability to hire the right outreach workers; train them appropriately; monitor their behavior; and maintain an appropriate balance of relationships with gangs, gang members, community, police, and agencies. Of course, it might also be that the policies represented by the Spergel model fail to grasp the group context of gangs. In this sense, the implementation and outcome failures of the Spergel model may reflect the lack of a solid conceptual understanding of the micro-level of explanation. Indeed, in perhaps no other area are groups more misunderstood than in characterizations of their organizational structure.

Much of the gang "literature" characterizes gangs as hierarchical formal structures in which communication and relationships are highly structured. This "literature"—often reflected in the popular press or the pronouncements of the criminal justice system—stands in stark contrast to an accumulating body of research showing that gangs as groups reflect the age-graded characteristics of their members, are largely flat, and are ineffectual mechanisms for accomplishing tasks in a rational manner (e.g., Klein 1995; McGloin 2005). This understanding of the micro-level characteristics of gangs certainly seems disconnected from suppression efforts targeted at gangs and may vary from the perceptions of outreach work and other forms of social intervention. Thus, it would seem that theory and practice are not joined effectively and it is theory that has failed policy.

Another useful example of a comprehensive gang model is the Boston Gun Project, which began with the goal of addressing the marked increase in local youth violence in Boston (see Braga et al. 2001). The partners involved in this program included local, state, and federal criminal justice agencies (e.g., police, probation, parole, prosecution), social service agencies, academic researchers, and community and faith-based groups. Each of these partners provided a unique perspective and expertise on local youth violence, which allowed the researchers to address the crime problem at all three levels of explanation. Information about the micro-level processes among gangs, particularly the rivalry-based interactions, provided insight on the mechanisms that drive gang behavior. A network analysis based on the relationships among rival gangs served to identify the gangs that were particularly attractive targets for an intervention focus (i.e., those gangs at the core of the rivalry network) and explained why certain geographic areas experienced high levels of violence (i.e., such locations had proximal territories of rival gangs). This focus on group process was one of the strengths and unique features of the Boston intervention and may lie at the root of why some analyses have shown it to be successful. This focus reflects the attempt to specify a "theory" of gangs that could be used to guide the intervention. To be sure, this conceptualization of the nature of gangs and the sources of their violent behavior served to orient suppression and outreach efforts, two key components of micro-level interventions.

The intervention operated at many levels and provided a multitude of services, all intended to "match" the various problems and issues identified at the analysis stage. Two components in particular came to characterize Operation Ceasefire, the operational intervention component of the Boston Gun Project. First, researchers recognized that a majority of the chronic violent offenders, by nature of their past behavior, were vulnerable to an array of sanctions from the criminal justice system (e.g., violation of probation or parole, enhanced sentences, federal prosecution and incarceration). If these offenders engaged in violent behavior, the criminal justice partners would bring every resource to bear in a unified manner against them. This deterrence strategy came to be known as "pulling levers" (Kennedy 1997). What made it different from most criminal justice interventions against gangs was its comprehensive nature: It did not just talk about using multiple intervention points; it used them. Second, the fact that small, cohesive gangs were generating much of the violence provided an additional avenue for deterrence. Operation Ceasefire used the social cohesion among gangs as leverage against them by relying on "collective accountability." According to this strategy, if any one member of a gang or group engaged in a violent offense, it would bring the attention of law enforcement on the entire group. Thus, this part of the intervention program relied on the micro-level, informal social processes internal to the gang as an additional means of controlling behavior. This was particularly important for the role of revenue-generating activity (mostly street-level drug sales) by gang members. When violence was attributed to a gang or to gang members, high-visibility interventions by law enforcement followed that effectively shut down drug markets. Thus, the gang members in a sense became partners in keeping the lid on violence if they wanted less interference in their revenue-generating activities. This approach to gang policy included an explicit recognition of gang micro-level process and behavior on the use of network theory.

For a variety of reasons, such comprehensive activities are rare. They are expensive, require a large commitment from a number of individuals over time, and often require political alliances that are difficult to establish or hold together (Decker and Curry 2002). The norm in gang policy is smaller-scale efforts that rely almost exclusively on law enforcement and suppression. For a variety of reasons, some supported by a solid reading of gang theory, such interventions are not likely to be successful. Suppression strategies typically focus on the individual criminal behavior of gang members as individuals are targeted for arrest, prosecution, and sentencing. There are some exceptions to this, however. Racketeer Influenced and Corrupt Organizations Act (RICO) prosecutions against gangs are one example, but there is too little evidence to assess their utility. However, some (Klein 1995; Klein and Maxson 2006) have suggested that most street gangs lack the level of organization to be appropriate targets for such prosecutions, which typically require months of investigative work and legal preparation to establish. The use of suppression to enforce Civil Gang Injunctions (CGIs) is a suppression tool that has the group as its focus. CGIs were piloted in California and establish a pattern of behavior in which gang members engage that creates a public nuisance. Once a civil order is filed against the named members of a gang, they are enjoined from a variety of behaviors, such as talking on cell phones, congregating with each other, selling drugs, and playing loud music. When they are observed participating in these behaviors, they are subjected to a civil sanction, which can result in short-term jail stays. Maxson and colleagues (2005) argue that the results for such interventions in terms of crime reduction are mixed, but that they do have a measurable impact on community solidarity. This suggests that there are conceptualizations between gang theory and gang policy at the micro-level.

Conclusion

More than twenty years ago, Short (1985) argued that criminology had a "level of explanation" problem. The level of explanation was critical for criminology in that it affected the problems selected for study, as well as the approaches and theoretical developments associated with those problems. We believe that Short's assessment is particularly true in the area of gangs and the links among theory, empirical work, and gang policy and intervention. We have described the relationship between gang theory and gang policy as parallel and complementary, yet hardly directive. This is the case because of two failures. First, criminologists have not effectively developed micro-level group process theories of gangs. Their inability to do so is in part a shortcoming of data: Very few direct measures of processes or relationships are available. But the failure is also a reflection of the stagnant nature of theory development at the micro-level. Similarly, policies and programs, with few exceptions, have failed to capitalize on the available theory and findings regarding group process and other micro-level issues. The development, implementation, and monitoring of gang policies and programs would benefit considerably from a more complete understanding of this critical level of explanation.

In the end, whether one is interested in studying gangs or having an impact on them, a comprehensive understanding should be the necessary first step. To achieve this, scholars and practitioners alike would benefit from heeding Short's advice to view the question of interest from all three levels of explanation. Not only does this reduce the chance of talking "past each other," but it also underlies a deep and careful analysis of the problem at hand. Just as gangs can affect local communities in broad and diverse ways, so, too, must researchers and practitioners begin to view street gangs with a broad and inclusive lens.

References

Akers, R. L. 1998. *Social learning and social structure: A general theory of crime and deviance.* Boston: Northeastern University Press.

Anderson, E. 1999. *Code of the streets.* New York: W. W. Norton.

Battin, S. R., K. G. Hill, R. D. Abbott, R. C. Catalano, and J. D. Hawkins. 1998. The contribution of gang membership to delinquency beyond delinquent friends. *Criminology* 36: 93–115.

Bjerregaard, B., and A. J. Lizotte. 1995. Gun ownership and gang membership. *Journal of Criminal Law and Criminology* 86:37–58.

Braga, A. A., D. M. Kennedy, A. Piehl, and E. J. Waring. 2001. Reducing gun violence: The Boston Gun Project's Operation Ceasefire. Research report. National Institute of Justice, U.S. Department of Justice, Washington, D.C.

Bursik, R. J. 1986. Delinquency rates as sources of ecological change. In *The social ecology of crime.* Ed. J. M. Byrne and R. J. Sampson, 63–74. New York: Springer-Verlag.

———. 1988. Social disorganization and theories of crime and delinquency: Problems and prospects. *Criminology* 26:519–551.

Chin, K. L. 1996 *Chinatown gangs: Extortion enterprise and ethnicity.* New York: Oxford University Press.

Cloward, R. A. 1959. Illegitimate means, anomie, and deviant behavior. *American Sociological Review* 24:164–176.

Cloward, R. A., and L. E. Ohlin. 1960. *Delinquency and opportunity: A theory of delinquent gangs.* New York: Free Press.

Cohen, A. K. 1955. *Delinquent boys.* Glencoe, Ill.: Free Press.

Curry, G. D., and S. H. Decker. 1998. *Confronting gangs: Crime and community.* Los Angeles: Roxbury Publishing.

Decker, S. H. 1996. Collective and normative features of gang violence. *Justice Quarterly* 13:243–264.

Decker, S. H., and G. D. Curry. 2002. Gangs, gang homicide and gang loyalty: Organized crimes or disorganized criminals. *Journal of Criminal Justice* 30:1–10.

Decker, S. H., and B. Van Winkle. 1996. *Life in the gang: Family, friends, and violence.* Cambridge: Cambridge University Press.

Esbensen, F. A., and U. Huizinga. 1993. Gangs, drugs, and delinquency in a survey of urban youth. *Criminology* 31:565–587.

Evans, T. D., F. T. Cullen, and V. S. Burton. 1997. The social consequences of self-control: Testing the general theory of crime. *Criminology* 35:475–504.

Fagan, J. A. 1990. Social processes of delinquency and drug use among urban gangs. In *Gangs in America.* Ed. C. R. Huff, 183–222. Newbury Park, Calif.: Sage Publications.

Fagan, J. A., and D. Wilkinson. 1998. Guns, youth violence and social identity in inner cities. In *Crime and justice: Annual review of research,* Vol. 24. Ed. M. Tonry and M. Moore, 105–188. Chicago: University of Chicago Press.

Fleisher, M. S. 1997. Guns, drugs, and violence: Kids on the streets of Kansas City. *Valparaiso University Law Review* 31:485–500.

Gordon, R. A., B. B. Lahey, E. Kawai, R. Loeber, M. Stouthamer-Loeber, and D. P. Farrington. 2004. Antisocial behavior and youth gang membership: Selection and socialization. *Criminology* 42:55–88.

Gottfredson, M. R., and T. Hirschi. 1990. *A general theory of crime.* Stanford, Calif.: Stanford University Press.

Haynie, D., and Osgood, W. 2005. Reconsidering peers and delinquency: How do peers matter? *Social Forces* 84:1109–1130.

Kennedy, D. M. 1997. Pulling levers: Chronic offenders, high-crime settings, and a theory of prevention. *Valparaiso University Law Review* 31:449–484.

Klein, M. W. 1995. *The American street gang.* New York: Oxford University Press.

Klein, M. W., and C. L. Maxson. 1989. Street gang violence. In *Violent crime, violent criminals.* Ed. M. E. Wolfgang and N. A. Weiner, 198–234. Newbury Park, Calif.: Sage Publications.

———. 2006. *Street gang patterns and policies.* New York: Oxford University Press.

Kubrin, C. E. 2005. Gangstas, thugs, and hustlas: Identity and the code of the street in rap music. *Social Problems* 25:360–378.

Lacourse, E., D. Nagin, R. E. Tremblay, F. Vitaro, and M. Claes. 2003. Developmental trajectories of boys' delinquent group membership and facilitation of violent behaviors during adolescence. *Development and Psychopathology* 15:183–197.

Lilly, J. R., F. T. Cullen, and R. A. Ball. 2002. *Criminological theory: Context and consequences.* 3rd ed. Thousand Oaks, Calif.: Sage Publications.

Lizotte, A., G. J. Howard, M. D. Krohn, and T. P. Thornberry. 1997. Patterns of illegal gun carrying among young urban males. *Valparaiso University Law Review* 31:375–394.

Lizotte, A. J., M. D. Krohn, J. C. Howell, K. Tobin, and G. J. Howard. 2000. Factors influencing gun carrying among young urban males over the adolescent-young adult life course. *Criminology* 38:811–834.

Luster, T., and S. M. Oh. 2001. Correlates of male adolescents carrying handguns among their peers. *Journal of Marriage and Family* 63:714–726.

Matza, D. 1969. *Becoming deviant.* Englewood Cliffs, N.J.: Prentice Hall.

Maxson, C. L., K. Hennigan, and D. C. Sloane. 2005. It's getting crazy out there: Can a civil gang injunction change a community? *Criminology and Public Policy* 4:577–605.

McGloin, J. M. 2005. Policy and intervention considerations of a network analysis of street gangs. *Criminology and Public Policy* 4:607–636.

Miller, W. B. 1958. Lower class culture as a generating milieu of gang delinquency. *Journal of Social Issues* 14:15–19.

Osgood, W. D., J. K. Wilson, and P. M. O'Malley. 1996. Routine activities and individual deviant behavior. *American Sociological Review* 5:635–655.

Papachristos, A. V. 2006. *Murder by structure: Dominance relations and the social structure of gang homicide in Chicago.* Available online at http://ssrn.com/abstract=855304.

Park, R. E., and E. Burgess (Eds.). 1925. *The city.* Chicago: University of Chicago Press.

Pizarro, J., and J. M. McGloin. 2006. Gang homicides in Newark: Collective behavior or social disorganization? *Journal of Criminal Justice* 34:195–207.

Pratt, T. C., and F. T. Cullen. 2000. The empirical status of Gottfredson and Hirschi's general theory of crime: A meta-analysis. *Criminology* 38:931–964.

Sampson, R. J., and W. B. Groves. 1989. Community structure and crime: Testing social disorganization theory. *American Journal of Sociology* 94:744–802.

Sampson, R. J., S. W. Raudenbush, and F. Earls. 1997. Neighborhood and violent crime: A multilevel study of collective efficacy. *Science* 227:918–924.

Schreck, C., J. M. McGloin, and D. Kirk. A study of the contrast between violent and nonviolent neighborhood crime rates in Chicago: What factors make for a violent neighborhood? Forthcoming in *Justice Quarterly.*

Shaw, C. R., and H. D. McKay. 1942. *Juvenile delinquency in urban areas.* Chicago: University of Chicago Press.

Short, J. F. 1985. The level of explanation of problem. In *Theoretical methods in criminology*. Ed. R. Meier, 51–72. Beverly Hills, Calif.: Sage Publications.

———. 1998. The level of explanation problem revisited. The American Society of Criminology 1997 presidential address. *Criminology* 36:3–36.

Short, J. F., and F. Strodtbeck. 1965. *Group processes and gang delinquency*. Chicago: University of Chicago Press.

Spergel, I. A. 1995. *The youth gang problem: A community approach*. New York: Oxford University Press.

———. 2007. *Reducing youth gang violence: The Little Village Gang Project in Chicago*. Lanham, Md.: AltaMira Press.

Sullivan, M. 2006. Are "gang" studies dangerous? Youth violence, local context, and the problem of reification. In *Studying youth gangs*. Ed. J. Short Jr. and L. A. Hughes, 15–36. Lanham, Md.: AltaMira Press.

Sutherland, E. H. 1947. *Principles of criminology*. 4th ed. Philadelphia: Lippincott.

Sykes, G. M., and D. Matza. 1957. Techniques of neutralization: A theory of delinquency. *American Sociological Review* 22:664–670.

Thornberry, T. P. 1987. Toward an interactional theory of delinquency. *Criminology* 25 (4): 863–891.

———. 1998. Membership in youth gangs and involvement in serious and violent offending. In *Serious and violent juvenile offenders: Risk factors and successful interventions*. Ed. R. Loeber and D. P. Farrington, 147–166. Thousand Oaks, Calif.: Sage Publications.

Thornberry, T. P., and J. H. Burch. 1997. *Gang members and delinquent behavior*. Washington, D.C.: Office of Juvenile Justice and Delinquency Prevention.

Thornberry, T. P., M. D. Krohn, A. J. Lizotte, and D. Chard-Wierschem. 1993. The role of juvenile gangs in facilitating delinquent behavior. *Journal of Research in Crime and Delinquency* 30:55–87.

Thornberry, T. P., M. D. Krohn, A. J. Lizotte, C. A. Smith, and K. Tobin. 2003. *Gangs and delinquency in developmental perspective*. New York: Cambridge University Press.

Thrasher, F. 1927. *The gang: A study of 1313 gangs in Chicago*. Chicago: University of Chicago Press.

Vigil, J. D. 1988. *Barrio gangs: Street life and identity in southern California*. Austin: University of Texas Press.

Warr, M. 2002. *Companions in crime: The social aspects of criminal conduct*. Cambridge: Cambridge University Press.

Whyte, W. F. 1943. *Street corner society*. Chicago: University of Chicago Press.

Wikstrom, P. O. 2006. Individuals, settings, and acts of crime. In *The explanation of crime: Context, mechanisms and development*. Ed. P. Wikstrom and R. Sampson, 61–107. Cambridge: Cambridge University Press.

Wolfgang, M. E., and F. Ferracuti. 1967. *The subculture of violence*. London: Tavistock.

9

DAWN L. ROTHE AND DAVID KAUZLARICH

State Crime Theory and Control

Genocide, human-rights violations, war crimes, illegal war, and crimes against humanity are examples of state crimes, which are defined as crimes committed by individuals acting on behalf of, or in the name of, a state in violation of international public law or a state's own domestic law (Rothe and Mullins 2006b).[1] State crimes are ubiquitous and result in more injury and death than traditional street crimes such as robbery, theft, and assault. Consider that genocide during the twentieth century in Germany, Rwanda, Darfur, Albania, Turkey, Ukraine, Cambodia, Bosnia-Herzegovina, and other regions claimed the lives of tens of millions and rendered many more homeless, imprisoned, and psychologically and physically damaged. Despite the gravity of state crimes, until recently they have been under-studied relative to conventional street crimes. However, in the past decade criminologists have made considerable theoretical, conceptual, and empirical progress specifying the nature, extent, distribution, causal variables, and potential social control of state crime (Rothe and Friedrichs 2006). There have also been major new initiatives to bring perpetrators of state crimes to trial, such as international criminal tribunals on genocide in Bosnia and Rwanda, as well as the establishment

---

[1] Critical criminologists and scholars of state crime have debated for many decades about whether an act or omission must be contrary to codified law to be appropriately classified as "criminal": see Kauzlarich, Mullins, and Matthews 2003; Tifft and Sullivan 1980, 2006. Although we employ a more legalistic approach here, the theory reviewed later can be applied to state crimes of omission and social harms not prohibited by formal law. Indeed, the U.S. government's negligence in the case of Hurricane Katrina and its failure to protect consumers and workers by effectively regulating corporations clearly relate to low social control and widely available opportunities (Faust and Kauzlarich 2008).

of the permanent International Criminal Court (Mullins, Kauzlarich, and Rothe 2004; Rothe 2006; Rothe and Mullins 2006b).

This chapter reviews the main theoretical explanations of state crime and their associated implications for public policy and social control. We begin by providing an overview of related theoretical models of state crime developed to explain how and why the crimes occur. We then provide examples of empirical studies of state crime that illustrate the theories' explanatory power. Finally, we address the social control and policy implications of the theories.

Integrated Models of State Crime

The social forces, actors, and situations involved in state crimes are more complex than with most other forms of crime. Deep historical, cultural, political, ideological, international, legal, and economic factors have an impact on the performance of state crimes such as genocide, crimes against humanity, massive human-rights violations, and illegal war. A theory of state crime must be fluid enough to adapt to and include factors that may be specific to a case (e.g., issues of postcolonial rule in Rwanda, the involvement of militias in the Congo, or conditions within a civil war context such as in Uganda). Simply stated, attention to both distal and proximal temporal-spatial contexts within which state crimes occur is critical for the development of a sufficiently general theory of the phenomenon.

The earliest attempts to generate a theoretical model of state crime date back to Ronald Kramer (1990a, 1990b, 1992) and Kramer and Raymond Michalowski's (1990, 1993) work on state-corporate crime (see Kramer and Michalowski 2006 for a complete history). The theory was later expanded and clarified by David Kauzlarich and Kramer (1998, 148), who advanced the central proposition that "criminal behavior on the organizational level results from a coincidence of pressure for goal attainment, availability and perceived attractiveness of illegitimate means, and an absence or weakness of social control mechanisms." Three catalysts for action—motivation, opportunity, and operationality of controls—were posited as constant factors in the actualization of state crime at the interactional (micro-), organizational (meso-), and institutional (macro-) levels of analysis. At the macro-level, basic modes of economic production are seen as shaping or constraining influences on organizational behavior. At the meso-level, Kauzlarich and Kramer (1998) draw heavily from organizational theorists who maintain that "there is built into the very structure of organizations an inherent inducement for the organization itself to engage in crime" (Gross 1978, quoted in Kauzlarich and Kramer 1998, 145). Finally, at the micro-level of analysis, differential association theory is emphasized, wherein a person in a particular environment may engage in crime if criminal definitions outweigh definitions that are non-criminal. Further, models of interaction are incorporated into an integrated framework suggesting how motivation may be affected by socialization processes within a particular social context.

While Kauzlarich and Kramer's (1998) model has proved useful in examining numerous cases of organizational crime, the theory has been critiqued for its heavy emphasis on the criminogenic nature of capitalist social organization, which limits the theory to those crimes associated primarily with the corporate culture or within the United States (see, e.g., and Mullins 2006b, 2008, 2009). Further, Dawn L. Rothe and Christopher Mullins have suggested that the theory fails to recognize several other key factors associated with crimes of the state, such as weakened and transitional states, the involvement of militias, ideological and religious motivating forces, international relations, and factors associated with postcolonialism. To strengthen and expand the explanatory power of Kauzlarich and Kramer's (1998) theory, and Mullins (2006b, 2008, 2009) proposed an *integrated theory of violations of international criminal laws*. Noting that singular societies are not atomistically separated from each other and that institutional arrangements and forces do not cease their influence at the arbitrary political boundaries on maps, Rothe and Mullins maintain that any theory of state crime must be able to address the larger structure within which states interact. As such, the culture of a state—its economic, political, cultural, and historical environment—is distinct from and often in contradiction to the ideology, politics, and practices at the international level. Rothe and Mullins revised and expanded the original framework to address the additional and equally significant international level of analysis to incorporate the increasingly international nature of state criminality.

Rothe and Mullins also discuss the concepts of opportunity and controls in Kauzlarich and Kramer's model. They suggest that these are often intermingled and potentially represent two separate fundamental catalysts. For example, scholars of state crime have investigated the nature of both external and internal controls, the former of which lie outside a state apparatus and yet are imposed on the state. In contrast, internal controls are those that arise within the state and are directed against itself (e.g., domestic laws and self-regulation; Ross 1995, 2000a, 2000b). Suggested external controls *within* a state have included media organizations, interest groups, and domestic nongovernmental organizations (NGOs). Although it recognizes these control factors as more than just failed opportunities, Ross's model does not account for cases wherein the media, interest groups, and NGOs are often ignored or manipulated via hegemonic discourse or through the use of symbolic political gestures. In response to these inconsistencies, Rothe and Mullins (2006b, 2008, 2009) suggest that these agencies can serve to constrain a state's action yet often fail to control or block such activities. In other words, these constraints differ from formal controls in that they serve as an inhibitor or temporary barrier that occurs at the onset of or during an illegal action.

Rothe and Mullins view controls as a complete blockage to an act or as a criminal sanction that is ideally inevitable after the fact. In other words, a criminal action would not occur due to controls, and if it did, there would be ex post facto legal repercussions. External controls would include the United Nations, the International Court of Justice, the International Criminal Court, and, potentially, other states through the use of their legal systems or international criminal tribunals. Controls at the macro-level are conceptualized as emerging from a number of loci. Clearly, law can serve to control actions, but due to the unique position of a state vis-à-vis its own domestic law and the problematic ways in which it is enforced, law may not hold the same deterrent power over a political body as it does over citizen actors.

Another difference between Kauzlarich and Kramer's (1998) model and that of Rothe and Mullins (2006b, 2008, 2009) is the inclusion of an often ignored component of state criminality—social disorganization:

> Essentially, when strong, functioning social institutions are not present, this creates both motivation and opportunity for organized criminal activity. . . . Weak institutions produce a vacuum of formal and informal social control. A nation unable to adequately police or subdue a paramilitary force in its hinterlands creates a gap of institutional control that simultaneously provides motivation and opportunity for the aris[ing] of organized criminal activity. (Rothe and Mullins 2006b, 2008, 2009, 18)

Informal controls such as modalities of socialization and behavioral controls operating within the family, education, religion, or other institutions are distinctly weakened in these environments. This allows for easier transmission of subcultural values that allow and encourage criminality, as well as other beliefs that can feed into criminogenic forces (e.g., racism aiding genocidal events).

In sum, Rothe and Mullins use many of the theoretical concepts advanced by Kramer, Michalowski, and Kauzlarich but expand the theory to incorporate international variables, factors that are not associated with capitalistic endeavors of corporations and states, Donald Black's (1976) relational distance model, and components of social disorganization to address key factors associated with forms of state crime. In addition, as indicated in Figure 9.1, they propose other factors and theoretical concepts that allow for the adaptation of catalysts that may be unique to specific cases (e.g., paramilitary groups, insurgencies, militias, postcolonial conditions, and weakened or illegitimate governments). Of course, with any theory the utility lies in the empirical evidence. Hence, we turn to recently published case studies of state crime that reveal the efficacy of the theory's core concepts.

An Integrated Theory of Violations of International Criminal Law				
	Motivation	**Opportunity**	**Constraints**	**Controls**
International	• Political interests • Economic interests • Ideological interests	• Interstate relations • Complementary legal systems • Transnational markets	• International reactions • Political pressures • Public opinion • NGOs/social movements • Oversight agencies • Interstate relations	• International criminal law • Intergovernmental sanctions • International financial institutions • International Criminal Court
State/Structural	• Political goals/power • Ideological goals • Economic conditions • Status of government legitimacy • Military goals • Access to resources • Cultural beliefs	• Resource availability • State secrecy • Ideological tools/nationalism • Government structure • Media ownership/censorship • Propaganda • Social disorganization	• Internal political pressure • Media scrutiny • Public opinion • Social movements • Counterinsurgencies • State legitimacy	• Legal sanctions • Domestic law
Organizational	• Operative goals • Institutional isomorphism • Leadership pressure • Bound rationality • Reward structure	• Relationship with state • Economic support • Organizational structure • Local social disorganization • Separation of consequences	• Internal constraints • Bounded placement • Economic sanctions	• Internal controls (e.g., rules) • Legal codes
Interactional	• Social meaning • Indoctrination • Economic pressure • Ideological pressure • Religious beliefs • Situational security • Obedience to authority • Definition of situation • Instrumental rationalization	• Social/structural conditions • Group think • Diffusion of responsibility • Group membership	• Personal morality • Perceived legitimacy of law • Local informal controls • Perceived prosecution	• International and domestic law • Community-level law enforcement

FIGURE 9.1 An Integrated Theory of Violations of International Criminal Law

Source: Adapted in part from Kauzlarich and Kramer 1998; Michalowski and Kramer 2006; Mullins and Rothe 2008; Rothe and Mullins 2006b, 2008, 2009.

Darfur: The Forgotten Ones

Internecine violence within the Darfur region of Sudan has claimed the lives of more than four hundred thousand civilians.[2] More than 2 million people have been displaced, and countless more have been systematically raped, robbed, and intimidated and have suffered other depredations of a collapsed social structure. Since the 1980s, the people of the region have been subjected to national and international military abuse and political marginalization (Mullins and Rothe 2007). International political forces, environmental crises, and widespread institutional disorganization created an environment for the regime of Omar el-Bashir to unite a portion of the Sudanese population at the expense of Darfuris. One cannot reduce the complex events within Darfur and Sudan to political motivations realized in an environment of ethnic hostility or as hostilities arising out of a humanitarian crisis. The evolution of the social conditions behind them and the events themselves are much more complex.

In the case of Darfur, several supranational factors exacerbated the conditions leading up to the genocide—mainly, interstate relations and foreign involvement, including the surrounding international conflicts and civil wars (Mullins and Rothe 2007). Darfur often found itself a pawn in conflicts that involved Chad and Libya, as well as in the civil war between northern and southern Sudan. The civil war often pitted peoples against each other, intensifying existing geographic and "ethnic" differences that were created out of a colonial and postcolonial situation for political power. It also created barriers to a common identity based on shared interest, intensifying the motivational dynamics toward acts of genocide at the state level. As these conflicts spilled into Darfur, they provided an environment that facilitated the violence, masking the actions of the Sudanese military and the Janjaweed militia as a response to the larger external conflict.

Mullins and Rothe (2007) found also that when international involvement in the north–south peace talks over Sudan's ongoing civil war began, Darfur found itself marginalized and omitted from the process. The el-Bashir regime used the peace negotiations to mask its continued repressive actions against the Darfuris. In general, the international community was satisfied that the Sudanese government was doing something to order its own house by fully engaging in the north–south negotiations. It provided a built-in excuse as to why the government was not active in reducing the violence in Darfur: It was taking conflicts one at a time. It should also be noted that the peace talks inadvertently served as a diversion. The international media and diplomatic corps

---

[2] Coalition for International Justice, survey, 2006. The survey has been unavailable since the organization was dismantled in March 2006. See also "Darfur's Real Death Toll," *Washington Post*, April 24, 2005, B06, available online at http://www.washingtonpost.com/wp-dyn/content/article/2005/04/23/AR2005042301032.html.

focused on the peace talks and not the widespread disorder and chaos elsewhere in the country, enhancing the government's ability to maintain its genocidal policy.

Once the Nairobi Peace Negotiation was signed, attention to the Darfur crisis essentially disappeared from international political attention. Without larger political, economic, or security stakes for the Western states, international interest dwindled. In this case, the resolution of the north–south conflict allowed Sudan to represent itself to the world community as a stable country and a responsible global citizen. This provided further opportunities for the Sudanese government to escalate the repression against Darfuris. Confident that global attention had turned its back on what was occurring in Darfur, the government in Khartoum launched new offensives to rid any insurgency from the region at a massive cost in the lives of civilians.

As the theoretical model predicts, the role of the media could act as a powerful constraint against states. However, at the onset of the conflict there were relatively few media accounts of the atrocities. Once media outlets picked up the story of the thousands of deaths, they declared them a result of a humanitarian crisis. While moral indignation occurred, the media's attention was distracted when Asia was hit by a tsunami at the end of December 2004. The tsunami provided the "new" humanitarian crisis and was much easier to report on, as there was no need to establish the complex background of the situation for an international audience. Darfur instantly vanished from the news. As such, the media's failure to act as a constraint reinforced the belief within the el-Bashir government that it could reinstate its repressive policies without scrutiny from the media or political elites. In other words, impunity became a reality. The political and profit-driven nature of international media is strongly highlighted by the wavering coverage of Darfur; this demonstrates the generally weak ability of media as an institution to operate effectively as a constraint against state crime.

NGOs did attempt to constrain the state's illegal behaviors. Amnesty International and Human Rights Watch played a significant role in exposing the atrocities that were occurring in Darfur; however, NGOs' activities were limited by the Sudanese government's ability to allow access within the region and to those who had been victimized by government forces and the Janjaweed. As the sole political power, the Sudanese government was in a position to monitor international military forces and humanitarian aid services.

Today, the United Nations stands as the only international institution with universal jurisdiction to control states' actions. However, the United Nations is only as powerful as the will of its member states, and most of the stronger states were unwilling to define the atrocities as genocide. This severely limited the organization's ability to act as a control or constraint. Once the United Nations failed to define the atrocities in Darfur as genocide, the mandatory moral response of the Security Council was negated. In addition, due to the complementary system and required support of states to the United Nations' mission, it was not in a position to send a large peacekeeping mission to Darfur.

At the state level, Sudan's specific historical experiences facilitated the ongoing economic, social, and political marginalization of Darfur (Mullins and Rothe 2007). Colonialism left behind political and social preference for geographic domination, specifically in Khartoum and the north. Such widespread anomie and institutional disorder was indeed a factor in the Darfur genocide. Weakened political and economic institutions, as well as social control vacuums, established social pressure and tension that aided the genocidal episodes.

These geographically preferential divisions coincided with varying forms of subsistence and tribal divisions. Such divisions were later used as tools for political power, at a time of inter-factional party splits (1968) to create ethnic identities that would compete with each other, thereby weakening the ability of Sudanese populations to unite in their own common interests. This was further reinforced by the position of the government and its economic and social preference for the Arab solidarity and identity associated with northern geographic areas and Khartoum. Factors such as ethnicity and cultural and religious identifications, while initially abstract ideological political categories, can be reified into powerful social forces that are catalysts of genocide, as was the case with Darfur. As such, the inclusion of the factors in the theoretical model for crimes of the state is essential.

The political economy of Darfur specifically, and of Sudan more generally, is tightly enmeshed with its local ecology. Several periods of drought and the process of desertification fundamentally altered ecological dynamics that had a significant impact on local populations' subsistence strategies. The ensuing competition for access to these resources reinforced the newly constructed ethnic identities. Lack of government responses to these growing tensions and tribal feuds over resources enhanced the escalating sense of alienation among the southern and western Darfuris. The macro-level motivation context behind the uprisings that occurred February 2003 is a case in point (Mullins and Rothe 2007).

As a state, Sudan was in the position to create new laws, such as the 2005 constitution that grants immunity to officials. A state entity is in a position to define, and often confine, its political situations and internal conflicts. States are also in a position to define acceptable violence and to create, or ignore, their judicial responsibilities. This was the case with Sudan, as demonstrated by the Special Courts that were put in place. These courts were more a symbolic gesture deigned to appease the international political community than true institutions for justice. Furthermore, attempts to define the situation in Darfur as anything other than the declared state propaganda, or bring attention to the imbalance of power or wealth sharing, were rejected. In addition, the Darfur media is controlled by the state, negating its ability to be an efficient constraint on state activities. The media became little more than el-Bashiri's mouthpiece to counter other discourses on the region's experiences. Although it was not used to organize and coordinate genocidal episodes, as seen in Yugoslavia, Rwanda, Côte D'Ivoire, and the Democratic Republic of Congo, it served no constraining functions at all

According to Mullins and Rothe (2007), the strategies the Janjaweed used to commit crimes resulted from both the general paramilitary structure of militias and the strong ethnic biases that form the core of membership identities within these groups. Because the militias within Darfur are loosely organized groups with no extant chain-of-command or responsibility, the potential for criminal cultures to develop is high. State-supported militias find themselves in a unique position of power to act with total unaccountability and with financial and tactical support. Thus, militias under these conditions serve their own interests while simultaneously fulfilling the state's political goals. The Janjaweed were rewarded with tangibles beyond weapons and money. Personal gain and empowerment is clearly a strong motivation for those in power (e.g., government officials) or in strategic positions (e.g., members of a militia). Recall that rewards and economic gains are highly motivating forces toward criminal activity. The Janjaweed, as a state-sponsored militia, are in the unique position to believe that their actions will have no consequences, which has been reinforced by Sudan's unwillingness to prosecute individuals who commit atrocities in the Special Courts.

The U.S. Invasion of Iraq

Kramer and Michalowski (2005) and Kramer and colleagues (2005) have illustrated the utility of the integrated model to explain crimes of the state that are motivated by imperialism.[3] By using these examples, we can see the capability of the integrated theory to incorporate crimes of the state motivated

---

[3] The illegality of the U.S. war on Iraq has been thoroughly documented by critical criminologists (Kramer and Michalowski 2005; Kramer, Michalowski, and Rothe 2005). At the most basic level, any war that is not clearly in self-defense is prohibited by international law. The UN Charter, a principle source of the laws of war, specifies: "All members shall refrain from the threat or use of force against the territorial integrity or political independence of any state, or in any state in which the United Nations is taking preventive or enforcement action" (Art. 2, Chap. 1:4). The only exception to Article 2(4) is in Article 51 of the Charter: "Nothing in the present Charter shall impair the inherent right of individual or collective self defense if an armed attack occurs against a Member of the United Nations, until the Security Council has taken measures necessary to maintain international peace and security." The intention of this article is to allow a state under direct attack to defend itself. Importantly, however, this right is limited and may be executed only until the Security Council provides an international plan of action. In the history of the United Nations, the specific legal meaning of the Article 51 exception in relation to Article 2(4) has been defined in only one

by capitalistic agendas as well as those that cannot be explained in that context (e.g., Darfur, Rwanda, Uganda, and the Congo).

Kramer and Michalowski (2005) place heavy emphasis on the motivation and opportunity for the United States to invade Iraq at the state/structural level. Specifically, they identify political, economic, and ideological interests as key motivators for the invasion. They suggest that a key component of the motivation was the neo-imperialistic ideology and agenda held by key political actors within the administration:

> The Bush administration skillfully exploited the political opportunities provided by the fear and anger over the 9/11 attacks. By linking Saddam Hussein and Iraq to the wider war on terrorism, the government was able to establish the idea that security required the ability to attack any nation believed to be supporting terror, no matter how weak the evidence. This strategy obscured the more specific geopolitical and economic goals of creating a neoconservative Pax Americana behind the smokescreen of fighting terrorism. (Kramer and Michalowski 2005, 459–460)

Kramer and Michalowski (2005) also underscore the importance of religion and ideology as motivating forces in state policies and at the interactional level of actors within these organizations. They state that the "final factor to consider in understanding the Bush administration's war on Iraq is the fusion of a neoconservative imperial agenda with the fundamentalist Christian religious convictions of George W. Bush—a convergence that has been variously referred to as 'messianic militarism'" (460). They continue by noting that Bush was not the only president to rationalize foreign policy on ideological grounds: "In our historical overview of the American imperial project, many presidents have rationalized the pursuit of empire on the basis of ideological claims such as 'white man's burden' or 'making the world safe for democracy'" (460).

---

case: *Nicaragua v. the United States* (1986). The International Court of Justice ruled that Article 51 applies only when a state has been subjected to an armed attack; thus, the decision reaffirms a fundamental precept of international law: that war must be the very last measure taken in times of international dispute and conflict (Kramer and Kauzlarich 1998). The Bush administration did halfheartedly attempt to gain the UN Security Council's permission to launch a war on Iraq in February 2003 when U.S. Secretary of State Colin Powell presented what is now known to be mostly fictional information about Iraq's alleged possession of weapons of mass destruction and ties to Osama bin Laden, Al-Qaeda, and the September 11, 2001, attacks on the United States. Finding the evidence unconvincing, the UN Security Council voted not to support a U.S. attack on Iraq, but this was ignored by the Bush administration, and the war commenced shortly thereafter in violation of the most basic principles of international law. While the war could be labeled criminal under a variety of non-legal and humanistic definitions, there is no clearer prohibition of the action than that found in the UN Charter (Kauzlarich 2007; Kauzlarich and Matthews 2006).

Kramer and Michalowski also pay particular attention to the specifics of the case and the relevance of time and space. For example, they note that the opportunity to invade Iraq rested on more than the motivating forces of ideology, religion, and economic advancement. "Despite the desire of Bush administration unipolarists to invade Iraq, the military power of the United States and the political opportunities provided by the 9/11 Attacks" were essential for the government to act (460). In addition, opportunity was created through the use of state propaganda in the form of an effective public relations campaign proclaiming the necessity of a war in Iraq. They noted that the propaganda campaign rested mainly on false claims about Iraq's possession of weapons of mass destruction and Saddam Hussein's ties to Al-Qaeda.

At the meso-level, key organizational factors facilitated the opportunity to carry out the goal of invading Iraq:

> The group dynamics involved in the decision making of the unipolarists also demonstrate classic characteristics of "groupthink." The unipolarists were a highly cohesive group with a strong commitment to their assumptions and beliefs about America's role in the world.... But, most importantly for this analysis, the unipolarists within the Bush administration were highly selective in gathering information, ignored, discounted or ridiculed contrary views, engaged in self-censorship and protected the group from examining alternatives to their war plans. (Kramer and Michalowski 2005, 463)

Kramer and Michalowski go beyond international formal controls to include what Rothe and Mullins (2006b, 2008, 2009) refer to as constraints. For example, they note the potential significance of world public opinion, including massive antiwar protests (what Rothe and Mullins call constraints). In the case at hand, these constraints had little to no impact on the administration's desire to invade Iraq. In addition, they point to the potential utility of the media to act as a constraint, noting that an important factor in explaining U.S. public support for the invasion of Iraq was the failure of the media to perform its critical role as "watchdogs" over government.

Also explored are extant formal controls that help explain how the United States was able to carry out its illegal actions. Kramer and Michalowski note that, "at the level of the international system, the United Nations failed to provide an effective deterrent to a US invasion of Iraq largely because it has little ability to *compel* powerful nations to comply with international law if they choose to do otherwise" (461). While the model has been used to explain the illegal invasion of Iraq, the question then arises whether it has utility to explain a component of the larger crime—namely, the use by the United States of torture in Abu Ghraib.

This brief review of recent case studies utilizing the integrated theory of supranational crime to explain the etiological factors of specific state crimes highlights the situational and time-specific potential of the theory. As with any theory, however, there are implied and stated policy implications. We now turn to a discussion of those implications for each of the levels of controls.

Practical Policies and Actions to Control State Crime

A theory does more than explain why or how events occur. It also suggests policies that could reduce or control such events. This section deals with the policies that the theoretical model implies could reduce state crimes. Because policies based on the catalysts of motivation and opportunity revolve around controls and constraints, they are the focus of our attention here. Bear in mind that policy suggestions to reduce or control all motivations or opportunities would be utopian and would necessarily represent idealized assumptions about human nature. In other words, to expect a sweeping policy to reduce all self- or organizational motivations that might lead to state crime is unrealistic. We focus on controls and constraints because they are (1) the most relevant; (2) already extant in some form or other; and (3) have a realistic chance of reducing the incidence of the worst kinds of state crime.

Controls

Rothe and Mullins's (2006b, 2009) integrated theory suggests that controls are formal. They are operationalized as complete blockages to an act, as in the form of general or specific deterrence, or serve as after-the-fact systems of accountability. Nonetheless, there are a variety of controls that operate at multiple levels. The following sections discuss each of these.

INTERNATIONAL LEVEL

At the international level, controls are the catalyst that could most realistically address crimes of the state. Controls include international law, intergovernmental organizations, such as the United Nations, the International Court of Justice, international tribunals, and the International Criminal Court. The cases we have reviewed suggest that each of these institutions currently lacks the ability to address most state crimes. We provide a brief review of their current limitations, followed by several suggested policy implementations.

International Law. International law does indeed have a long history; however, it is only in relatively recent years that it also has become a regular feature of modern political life (Sands 2005). The second half of the twentieth century

marked significant developments within the codification of public law (including the codification of criminal liability for individuals who violate public law)
and the establishment of a permanent institution of international social control,
the International Criminal Court. International rules now codified as criminal
law provide a framework for judging and prosecuting individual behavior and
state actions—and, in theory, put an end to impunity (Sands 2005).

International criminal law is composed of substantive law and procedural
law. The substantive law is the body of rules indicating which acts amount
to international crimes, which elements are required for them to be considered prohibited, and under what conditions states must prosecute or bring to
trial those accused of violating such laws (Cassesse 2002). International
criminal law is a branch of public law. Public law is best defined as the body
of law that comes from treaties, charters, protocols, resolutions, and customary law. It was only after World War II that new categories for international
crimes developed; they included crimes against humanity, genocide, torture,
and, most recently, terrorism. International criminal law is a "hybrid branch
of law: it is public international law impregnated with notions, principles, and
legal constructs derived from national criminal law, human-rights law, and
customary laws" (Cassesse 2002, 19). However, since the International Criminal Court was created in 1998, international criminal law is considered a
full-fledged body of law. As a control the laws are indeed present, and deterrence based on extant laws is more promising for actors who commit state
crime than for those who commit traditional street crime (Rothe and Mullins
2006b).

Thus, the existence of international law is not a problem per se. Rather, it
is the enforcement mechanisms within international law that need to be
addressed. States that hold vast economic, military, and political power within
the international arena have long ignored international law as a frame for their
behavior if that law conflicted with their foreign policy interests. Thus, there
is no realistic threat of prosecution for many forms of state crime. The failure
of international law as a deterrent without enforcement mechanisms was also
evident when Attorney-General Alberto Gonzales discussed international law
in reference to U.S. policy for torture and enemy combatants: He referred to
the Geneva Conventions as "obsolete . . . and rendered quaint" (Gonzales 2002,
1). When law is viewed as irrelevant or illegitimate, it obviously no longer holds
a deterrent value. Likewise, international treaties are structured in such a way
that states may attach reservations to them that undermine the original intent
of a treaty. Further, since the international system of control is based on a
complementary system—meaning that states willingly accept jurisdiction—
many types of crimes go unpunished. To suggest policies that would strengthen
the enforcement of international law as an effective deterrent, we must turn to

institutions that are capable of such actions. No differently from domestic laws associated with traditional street crime, international laws need be enforced through a formal criminal justice system.

International Court of Justice. The International Court of Justice (ICJ) is the principal judicial organ of the United Nations. The ICJ has two functions: (1) to settle legal disputes submitted by states; and (2) to give advisory opinions on legal questions. The ICJ is a court for state arbitration, not for addressing individual criminality. Similar to the International Criminal Court, the ICJ holds jurisdiction only for states that have accepted its dominion. The United States withdrew from the ICJ shortly after it was found responsible for several illegal acts against Nicaragua in 1984 (Rothe 2009). Exceptions to the ICJ's mandate for consensual jurisdiction can occur by "virtue of a jurisdictional clause, i.e., typically, when they are parties to a treaty containing a provision whereby, in the event of a disagreement over its interpretation or application, one of them may refer the dispute to the Court" (ICJ 2005, 1).

The ICJ lacks the ability to enforce its rulings. If parties do not comply with its decision, they can be taken before the Security Council for enforcement action. However, if a judgment is rendered against one of the permanent five members of the Security Council, or against one of their allies, any resolution on enforcement would be vetoed. This occurred, for example, when Nicaragua brought the issue of U.S. noncompliance before the Security Council. Furthermore, if the Security Council refuses to enforce a judgment against a state, there is no alternative method to force the state to comply. It should also be noted that the ICJ is able to require only monetary reimbursements or restitution; it is not a criminal court. Thus, any policy solutions that could address the weakness of the ICJ would have to include the restructuring of the power of the Security Council in relation to the ICJ's decisions and enforcement. In addition, the ICJ could be empowered with the authority to freeze states' assets or monies to retrieve monetary awards for states that have been victimized by another state.

International Criminal Tribunals. International tribunals have addressed atrocities committed in Germany, Japan, Rwanda, and the former Yugoslavia. However, they are ad hoc systems of justice that have proved to be very costly. They are also filled with compromises because they draw on multiple legal systems to achieve international cooperation in trying individuals accused of the worst atrocities of mankind. The first international tribunals—the International Military Tribunals of Nuremberg and Tokyo—were established after World War II; such tribunals were not used again until the 1980s and 1990s, in Yugoslavia and Rwanda. Since then, the UN Security Council has become less willing to continue the process of forming ad hoc tribunals. Nonetheless, they are a potential venue for after-the-fact controls in situations where states are unwilling to prosecute their own actors for atrocities or when they are unwilling to submit themselves to the jurisdiction of the International Criminal Court. For example, an international tribunal could be created to prosecute the U.S. Bush administration for war crimes. The principle of individual criminal responsibility for ordering the commission of a crime is expressly recognized in Article 49 of First Geneva Convention; in Article 50 of Second Geneva Convention; in Article 129 of the Third Geneva Convention; in Article 146 of the Fourth Geneva Convention; and in the Statutes creating the Criminal Tribunals on the Former Yugoslavia (Article 7.1) and Rwanda (Article 6.1). Furthermore, the statutes that created the tribunals in the former Yugoslavia and Rwanda provide that "the official position of defendants, whether as Heads of State or responsible officials in Government Departments, shall not be considered as freeing them from responsibility or mitigating punishment."[4]

In the case of the Chilean dictator, Augusto Pinochet two precedents were established: (1) universal jurisdiction and (2) heads of state as responsible actors. Heads of state no longer enjoy personal immunity when they leave office. They become liable for prosecution if extradited by another state to a location where charges are filed (e.g., Spain in the Pinochet case). Furthermore, for such crimes there may coexist state responsibility that could be addressed at the International Court of Justice and individual criminal liability that could be addressed by an international tribunal (Cassesse 2002, 6).

The recognition of such a possibility by the Bush administration also reinforces the idea that such an outlet does have the potential to be a control if other states are willing to challenge the United States, an economic and military superpower. For example, fear of International Military Tribunal prosecutions was formally discussed within the U.S. State Department. The Federal Bureau of Investigation warned several former U.S. officials not to travel to some countries, including some in Europe, "where there is a risk of extradition to other nations interested in prosecuting them." As Senator Jesse Helms noted:

> This year for the first time we have seen an international criminal tribunal investigate allegations that NATO committed war crimes during the Kosovo campaign. In addition, a month ago, in May, NATO Secretary General Lord Robertson submitted to a degrading written interrogation by a woman named Carla Del Ponte, chief prosecutor of the Yugoslavia War Crimes Tribunal. (Helms 2002, 2)

---

[4] Statute of the International Tribunal for the Prosecution of Persons Responsible for Serious Violations of International Humanitarian Law Committed in the Territory of the Former Yugoslavia since 1991, UN doc. S/25704 at 36, Art. 7, para. 2.

Ideally, the potential for an International Military Tribunal against key Bush administration officials (e.g., George W. Bush, Dick Cheney, Donald Rumsfeld, Alberto Gonzales, Jay Bybee) is possible under rules and precedent. However, the likelihood that this will occur is not great without an increase in other states' willingness to challenge the United States and its sovereignty (Rothe 2006). As such, the promise of deterrence based on these ad hoc tribunals is not as promising as that via the International Criminal Court.

United Nations. The purpose of the United Nations is "to maintain international peace and security" (United Nations 2005, 1). As an institution of social control, however, the United Nations has rather limited potential. For example, only the Security Council, under Chapter 7 of the UN Charter, has the authority to enforce measures to "maintain or restore international peace and security." These enforcement mechanisms or social controls range from economic sanctions to symbolic shaming, as was the case in September 2004, when Secretary-General Kofi Annan denounced the U.S. invasion of Iraq as illegal and called the torture of Iraqi prisoners by U.S. forces an example of how fundamental laws were being "shamelessly disregarded." The United Nations also can order sanctions against a state that violates international laws. Mandatory sanctions are used to apply pressure on states to comply with Security Council objectives, including interstate or intrastate peace, when diplomatic means fail. The range of sanctions includes comprehensive economic and trade sanctions and more targeted measures, such as arms embargoes, travel bans, and financial and diplomatic restrictions. Other targeted sanctions involve the freezing of assets (that the United States has used against alleged terrorist groups) and blocking the "financial transactions of political elites or entities whose behavior triggered sanctions in the first place" (United Nations 2005, 2). However, the structural limitations placed on the Sanctions Committee are great, because the Security Council must approve the measures. It is thus highly unlikely that sanctions will be placed on states that hold veto power (e.g., the United States for its role in the torture at Abu Ghraib and Guantanamo or for the war crimes it committed against Afghanistan and Iraq). Empowering the United Nations would require a restructuring of the powers of the Security Council or enhancing the powers of the UN General Assembly by providing a one-vote-per-state member and allowing democratic decision making in applying sanctions.

Further, although the United Nations should not begin state building, it does need to become more active in addressing the disintegration of states. This is particularly true if it is truly to be a catalyst for world peace (Mullins and Rothe 2008). To address these types of issues, the United Nations must require states to move beyond symbolic gestures of aid and intervention and create a full-time international force that is large enough to meet such demands. It must also be given an agenda that goes beyond humanitarian aid (e.g., in the case of

Rwanda, where UN peacekeepers were under-powered and stood by witnessing the ongoing genocide). This could act to reduce extant social disorganization that is directly related to motivation and opportunity. However, the United Nations must act in a neutral capacity, without considering the political, economic, and ideological interests of key members, which, as we have noted, can be achieved only by restructuring the Security Council.

International Criminal Court. The creation and empowerment of the International Criminal Court significantly changes the landscape of international criminality. The intention of the International Criminal Court is to provide an international system of justice that can address heinous crimes against humanity when a state is unable or unwilling to investigate or prosecute any individual accused of the crimes specified in the Rome Statute. A key distinction between the International Criminal Court and other permanent institutions of social control at the international level is that it addresses crimes of individuals versus those of states. The crimes that are eligible for prosecution by the International Criminal Court are defined in Articles 5 of the Rome Statute and include crimes of genocide, crimes against humanity, war crimes, and crimes of aggression (which is still to be defined by the Assembly of State Parties).

The International Criminal Court's ability to penalize those who offend is limited, however. The court currently has jurisdiction only in those states that are party to the Rome Statue or that voluntarily accept the jurisdiction of the court for crimes that have occurred within their territory or on their vessels or aircraft, or of which a person accused is a national. No person can be held liable by the court unless the crime occurred under the jurisdiction of the court. Compliance by a state that is not party to the statute, of course, is highly unlikely; noncompliance therefore can hamper the International Criminal Court's ability to act as an effective measure of international justice. An alternative route to the International Criminal Court is provided when the UN Security Council unanimously recommends a case to the prosecutor for investigation. Again, given the veto power of the Security Council, it is highly unlikely that crimes committed by the major powers or their allies (such as Israel and the United States) would be recommended for prosecution. However, the International Criminal Court is a project in process—the legitimation of an institution comes not with the ratification of a treaty but with the long process of action. It is through the successful addressing of the initial cases that the International Criminal Court will become more legitimate, and thus more powerful (Rothe and Mullins 2006b). Currently, the International Criminal Court is conducting investigations into situations in the Democratic Republic of Congo, Uganda, and Darfur.

For the International Criminal Court to be truly effective as an agent of social control, it must be given universal jurisdiction, which can happen if the

Rome Statute is recognized as customary law. Further, the court must be empowered with its own policing agency to ensure states' compliance. As the case of Darfur has shown, the el-Bashir regime is not willingly going to hand over its own members or key Janjaweed leaders. Nor are states such as the United States going to surrender sovereignty or hand over past or present state leaders to the court or a third party that is a member of the Rome Statute.

MACRO-, MESO-, AND INTERACTIONAL LEVELS

Control over state crime is strongest at the international level. At the other levels of analysis, policy for effective controls cannot be reasonably proposed with a broad brushstroke. For example, domestic legal sanctions and laws vary from state to state; thus, any policy for internal checks or transparency would necessarily have to take into account specific countries. The same holds true at the meso-level of analysis. For example, policy suggestions that are effective for a corporation within the context of a capitalist state would not be relevant to militias or paramilitary groups. In addition, effective responses and after-the-fact controls need to be varied enough to incorporate the various types of crime. For example, international prosecution of those who committed genocide in Rwanda is highly problematic when one considers the scope of the participants. In other words, it is not feasible to prosecute the thousands of individuals who had an active role in the genocide of the Tutsi in an international court setting due to the location, cost, and time frame. The vast number of offenders also created massive infrastructure problems for the state. In response, Gacacas, based on the tradition of using the local community for dispute resolution, have been put in place to address the crimes, reconciliation, and convictions (Haverman 2007). We also see the need for states to incorporate systems of amnesty to address offenders. Case in point, is the ongoing situation in Uganda and the use of children by the Lord's Resistance Army (LRA) to commit murder, torture, mutilations, thievery, rape, and a host of other crimes. In this case, children were abducted and forced to join the militia in its fight against the government and to participate in the many crimes committed against the general citizenry. As children, and in particular child soldiers, they present a challenge for addressing the atrocities they have been forced to commit. Reintegration is key here more than formal controls; they, too, have been victimized and traumatized by their abduction and actions.

The relevance to time-space specifics is especially true when discussing controls at the individual level. Having said this, the key control at this level is the perceived legitimacy of the law. As has been noted, such potential can be problematic at the state level; however, the potential of the International Criminal Court to provide this in the form of deterrence for the senior leaders of states or militias appears to have the most merit.

Constraints

The core problem with the efficacy of constraints is that they are not expected to control or block criminogenic behaviors engaged in by states or organizations. Instead they serve as potential temporary barriers before or during an act (Rothe and Mullins 2006b, 2008, 2009). In addition, it is difficult to suggest broad policies if we consider that such attempts could have serious latent consequences. For example, it has been suggested that institutions such as the World Bank and the International Monetary Fund (IMF) could act as controls or constraints on states' criminality. However, it has also been noted that their policies have directly and indirectly been at the forefront of state criminality, including the Rwandan government's use of such funds to purchase weapons that were used in the genocide. Moreover, the World Bank and the IMF were both aware that the monies were being used illegally and did nothing and have been criticized for promoting conditions that were ripe for atrocities (see Friedrichs and Friedrichs 2002; Rothe, Muzzatti, and Mullins 2006; Rothe, Mullins, and Sandstrom 2009). Political and economic pressures in this context have produced additional criminogenic conditions.

Needless to say, the failure of constraints could provide opportunities for crime (Kauzlarich and Kramer 1998; Michalowski and Kramer 2006); it may be the case that such failure would further facilitate criminal acts by not blocking them, as controls would be expected to do. Further, suggesting intensifying of international reactions, political pressures, public opinion in the form of social movements would be unrealistic given the realpolitik of international relations at this time. While the process of generating a universal ideology of humanism has been under way for more than five decades, a true international community and common identity is far from being realized (Rothe and Mullins, 2007). However, generating a universal sense of humanism or cosmopolitism may be the only solid policy suggestion that could significantly alter the other key factors within the catalyst of constraint at all levels. Supporting or promoting a common identity based on humanism and a "true" international community that include all peoples is a sound, but perhaps unviable, potential constraint. In addition, such an encompassing ideology could reduce opportunities and motivational factors by enhancing social and economic policies that are not based first on sovereign state interests but on the greater good of humankind; reducing conflicting ideological interests; and providing more equitable access to resources.

The work of NGOs has been crucial in building public awareness, and NGOs have been successful in bringing additional pressure to bear on states to respond to atrocities. They continue to promote, directly and indirectly, an ethos of humanity based on the ideology that the United Nations has been advocating since the 1950s (Rothe and Mullins 2007). However, because of their position within the political order, NGOs cannot act as an international police force. As we have also noted, policies for constraints at the state, organizational, and interactional levels must be specific to time and place. Again, political pressure within a state generally may constrain illegal activities; however, implementing a broad policy that enhances such pressure could result in additional crimes. For example, one cannot ignore that the result of several state crimes has been the attainment or maintenance of political power—take, for example, the multiple coups and overt violence against the political opposition in Uganda or Israel's continued placement of camps within the occupied Palestinian territories. Recent events have also shown that reward structures do not always act as constraints. In the case of the Janjaweed in Darfur, for instance, it is the very reward structures that have motivated violence and genocide against the Darfuris.

Conclusion

Our discussion of the theoretical and empirical literature on state crime along with policy proposals to control the phenomenon has stressed the importance of recognizing the uniqueness of organizational crime in time and space. While common patterns and factors are associated with the catalysts for action identified in the theoretical literature, the specific history, culture, economics, and politics of each state must be taken into account, along with the larger international structure in which each state operates. For this reason, we conclude that the most realistic way to control state crime is by increasing the enforcement of international laws and social control mechanisms. The institutionalization of the International Criminal Court means that for the first time a permanent, international criminal justice system has the official backing of more than half of the states in the world. As a natural extension of the growing ethos of an international "community," human rights and international law, the International Criminal Court should only grow in its reach and legitimacy. Presumably its deterrent effect will grow commensurately. Like traditional forms of crime, however, crimes by states are subject to official labeling processes whereby subjects with less social power are more likely to be certified criminal than the more powerful. This is exacerbated in instances of state crime because of the larger political climate in which sovereign entities operate. Thus, as with white-collar crime, criminalization, punishment, and restitution have been rare and wildly disproportionate. As the reach of the International Criminal Court grows, however, proposals for the control of state crimes such as those offered here should find more expression and political support.

References

Black, D. 1976. *The behavior of law*. New York: Academic Press.

Cassesse, A. 2002. *The Rome Statute of the International Criminal Court: A commentary*, Vol. 1. New York: Oxford Press.

Faust, K. L., and D. Kauzlarich. 2008. Hurricane Katrina victimization as a state crime of omission. *Critical Criminology* 16:85–103.

Friedrichs, D. O., and J. Friedrichs. 2002. The World Bank and crimes of globalization: A case study. *Social Justice* 29:1–12.

Gonzales, A. 2002. Memorandum for the president: Decision re application of the Geneva Convention on prisoners of war to the conflict with Al Qaeda and the Taliban. MSNBC News. Available online at http://www.msnbc.msn.com/id/4999148/site/newsweek (accessed February 2006).

Gross, E. 1978. Organizational crime: A theoretical perspective. In *Studies in symbolic interaction*. Ed. N. K. Denzin, 55–85. Greenwich, Conn.: JAI Press.

Haverman, R. 2008. Gacaca in Rwanda: Reconciliation, conviction and much more. In *Supranational criminology: Towards a criminology of international crimes*. Ed. A. Smeulers and R. Haveman, 357–398. Antwerp: Intersentia.

Helms, J. 2002. Committee on Foreign Relations, U.S. Senate, press release, June.

International Court of Justice (ICJ). 2005. Available online at http://www.icj-cij.org/icjwww/igeneralinformation.htm (accessed October 2005).

Kauzlarich, D. 2007. Seeing war as criminal: Peace activist views and critical criminology. *Contemporary Justice Review* 10:67–85.

Kauzlarich, D., and R. C. Kramer. 1998. *Crimes of the American nuclear state: At home and abroad*. Boston: Northeastern University Press.

Kauzlarich, D., and R. A. Matthews. 2006. Lakoff's framing theory and teaching about the criminality of the U.S. war on Iraq. *Critical Criminologist* 16:4–24.

Kauzlarich, D., C. W. Mullins, and R. A. Matthews. 2003. A complicity continuum of state crime. *Contemporary Justice Review* 6:241–254.

Kramer, R. C. 1990a. State-corporate crime. Paper presented at the North Central Sociological Association and the Southern Sociological Association meeting. Louisville, Ky.

———. 1990b. State-corporate crime: A case study of the space shuttle *Challenger* explosion. Paper presented at the Edwin Sutherland Conference on White-Collar Crime, Indiana University, Bloomington.

———. 1992. The space shuttle *Challenger* explosion: A case study in state-corporate crime. In *White-collar crime reconsidered*. Ed. K. Schlegel and D. Weisburd, 212–241. Boston: Northeastern University Press.

Kramer, R. C., and R. J. Michalowski. 1990. Toward an integrated theory of state-corporate crime. Paper presented at the American Society of Criminology meeting, Baltimore.

———. 1993. State-corporate crime: Case studies on organizational deviance. Unpublished manuscript in the authors' possession.

———. 2005. War, aggression, and state crime: A criminological analysis of the invasion and occupation of Iraq. *British Journal of Criminology* 45:446–469.

———. 2006. *State-corporate crime: Wrongdoing at the intersection of business and government*. New Brunswick, N.J.: Rutgers University Press.

Kramer, R. C., R. J. Michalowski, and D. L. Rothe. 2005. The supreme international crime: How the U.S. war in Iraq threatens the rule of law. *Social Justice* 32:52–81.

Michalowski, R. J., and R. C. Kramer. 2006. *State-corporate crime: Wrongdoing at the intersection of business and government*. Piscataway, N.J.: Rutgers University Press.

Mullins, C. W., D. Kauzlarich, and D. L. Rothe. 2004. The international criminal court and the control of state crime: Problems and prospects. *Critical Criminology* 12:285–308.

Mullins, C. W., and D. L. Rothe. 2007. The forgotten ones. *Critical Criminology* 15:135–158.

———. 2008. *Blood, power and bedlam: Violations of international criminal law in post-colonial Africa.* New York: Peter Lang.

Ross, J. I. 1995. *Controlling state crime.* New York: Garland Publishing.

———. 2000a. *Controlling state crime.* New Brunswick, N.J.: Transaction Publishers.

———. 2000b. *Varieties of state crime and its control.* Monsey, N.Y.: Criminal Justice Press.

Rothe, D. L. 2006. *The masquerade of Abu Ghraib: State crime, torture, and international law.* Ph.D. diss., Western Michigan University, Kalamazoo, Mich.

Rothe, D. L., and D. O. Friedrichs. 2006. The state of the criminology of the crimes of the state. *Social Justice* 33:147–161.

Rothe, D. L., and C. W. Mullins. 2006a. International community: Legitimizing a moral collective consciousness. *Humanity and Society* 30:254–276.

———. 2006b. *Symbolic gestures and the generation of global social control: The international criminal court.* Boston: Lexington Books.

———. 2007. "Darfur and the politicalization of international law: Genocide or crimes against humanity." *Humanity and Society* 31 (1): 83–107.

———. 2008. Genocide, war crimes and crimes against humanity in Central Africa: A criminological exploration. In *Supranational criminology: Towards a criminology of international crimes.* Ed. A. Smeulers and R. Haveman, 135–155. Antwerp: Intersentia.

———. 2009. Toward a criminology for international criminal law: An integrated theory of international criminal violations. *International Journal of Comparative and Applied Criminal Justice* 3 (1): 97–118.

Rothe, D. L., C. W. Mullins, and K. Sandstrom. 2009. The Rwandan genocide: International finance policies and human rights. *Social Justice* 35 (3): 66–86.

Rothe, D. L., S. Muzzatti, and C. W. Mullins. 2006. Crime on the high seas: Crimes of globalization and the sinking of the Senegalese Ferry Le Joola. *Critical Criminology* 14: 159–180.

Sands, P. 2005. *Lawless world: America and the making and breaking of global rules.* London: Allen Lane.

Tifft, L., and D. Sullivan. 1980. *The struggle to be human: Crime, criminology, and anarchism.* Sanday, U.K.: Cienfuegos Press.

———. 2006. Needs-based anarchist criminology. In *The essential criminology reader.* Ed. S. Henry and M. Lanier, 259–277. Boston: Rowman and Littlefield.

10

NICOLE LEEPER PIQUERO AND ANDREA SCHOEPFER

Theories of White-Collar Crime and Public Policy

Unfortunately, the study of white-collar crime does not occupy a central place in the study of crime and criminality (although Travis Hirschi and Michael Gottfredson [1987] argue otherwise) and thus has done little to add to the policy discussion regarding what can and should be done to control crime and criminal behavior. Despite Edwin Sutherland's early attempts to debunk the myopic view of crime and criminality as being only a street-level phenomenon engaged in by those of the less privileged classes, the study of white-collar crime still does not command the research attention of the vast majority of scholars working on issues surrounding crime and criminality. White-collar crime does occupy a unique position in criminology, as Gottfredson and Hirschi (1990, 180) point out, and is widely regarded as important (as shown by its coverage in textbooks and at conferences), but its theoretical, empirical, and policy relevance has not received significant research attention. Perhaps even more important, a level of enthusiasm for this important research topic has not been sustained by most scholars in the field.

The general lack of research attention to issues surrounding white-collar crime can be attributed to any number of different reasons. First, some scholars contend that white-collar crime is rare and uncommon (Hirschi and Gottfredson 1987, 360) and "offers little to criminology that cannot be found elsewhere at less cost." Second, a definitional dilemma has long plagued this area of inquiry. Of the scholars who do actively engage in research on white-collar crime, there is little to no agreement about what exactly constitutes this specific crime type or how it should be defined. For example, this heuristic includes occupational crime, or criminal acts committed for the benefit of an individual, as well as corporate crimes, or crimes committed to benefit a corporation or an organization (Clinard and Quinney 1973). Regardless of who is the primary beneficiary of the crime or who is legally held responsible for the act (the individual or the organization), the decision-making process of an individual actor is what one must seek to understand. Finally, the lack of a consensus regarding an operational definition of white-collar crime has stymied empirical research endeavors. This is not to suggest that no empirical research has been undertaken. Rather, the large-scale data collection that is common in other areas of criminological research (e.g., criminal career research) is lacking in the area of white-collar crime. To date, only two publicly available data sets have been made available that are rich with information about offense and offenders' characteristics, and unfortunately both are now more than twenty years old (Forst and Rhodes n.d.; Wheeler et al. 1988) with no current effort underway to gather data on contemporary white-collar offenders.

For the most part, white-collar crime has been studied as an unusual or atypical crime type, where it is used to provide a contrast to street crime and criminals. For this reason, there has been a general lack of attention paid to understanding the causes of white-collar crime and ways to prevent it. As a consequence, much of our understanding of criminal behavior and of policy issues has come primarily from the study of street crimes and criminals. This is not to suggest that much has not been learned. Rather, it is to say that so much more can be learned if criminologists broaden the scope of included criminal behavior to include the study of white-collar crime. Such a body of research has much to offer in understanding a more complete range of causes of criminal behaviors.

This chapter reviews what is known about the causes of white-collar crime and outlines what can be done to control it and more general criminal behavior. First, we define white-collar crime and highlight the sensitive issues that surround such a definition. Second, we examine causes of white-collar criminality. Much of the theorizing about white-collar crime to date has mimicked the more general field, and a great deal of research time and effort has been spent trying to apply existing criminological theories to understanding white-collar criminality. Finally, we review and discuss the lessons learned from the policy implications and findings surrounding white-collar crime—and the lack thereof.

Defining White-Collar Crime

In 1939, during his presidential address to the American Sociological Society, Sutherland (1940) introduced the concept of white-collar crime. Since then, the term has become an everyday part of the American lexicon. It takes little effort to find images of white-collar criminals in popular media and news outlets. The typical image of a white-collar offender tends to be that of "a person of wealth, power, and high social status, who has led an upstanding and otherwise impeccable life" (Piquero and Benson 2004, 155). Images such as these emerged over the years from various case studies that tended to focus on highly publicized, egregious offenders and offenses (Benson 2002). The problem, however, is that despite popular stereotypes of the white-collar offender, there is little to no agreement about what exactly constitutes white-collar crime. In fact, until the Sarbanes-Oxley Act was passed in 2002, the term "white-collar crime" rarely appeared in criminal statutes (Green 2005). While the case-study approach emphasizes and favors the stereotypes, empirical evidence based on samples of convicted offenders challenges such images of white-collar offenders (see Benson 2002; Benson and Kerley 2000; Piquero and Benson 2004; Weisburd et al. 1991). This definitional dilemma and focus on the stereotypical offender has long plagued and divided the study of white-collar crime.

Sutherland (1949, 9) defined white-collar crime as "a crime committed by a person of respectability and high social status in the course of his occupation." His definition highlights two key elements. First, Sutherland stressed the importance of using offenders' characteristics (e.g., respectability and social status) as the key defining criteria of white-collar crime. Second, he outlined the importance of one's occupation in the commission of a crime. Therefore, Sutherland's definition of white-collar crime is often regarded as an offender-based definition—that is, a definition that uses offenders' characteristics as the defining criteria in identifying what constitutes a white-collar crime.

Sutherland's offender-based definition proved useful in challenging the conventional images and criminological theories of his day. At the time, criminals were most commonly depicted as members of the disadvantaged classes who were feebleminded, psychopathic, and from deteriorated families. In addition, Sutherland challenged criminologists to broaden the scope of their research focus to include images of respectable people committing criminal acts. However, offender-based definitions can also be somewhat limiting: Using offenders' characteristics as part of the definition prevents researchers from using those same characteristics as explanatory variables, as is common in criminological theorizing (see Coleman 2006).

Other scholars favor an offense-based definition of white-collar crime. Herbert Edelhertz (1970, 3) provided one of the first of these, defining white-collar crime as "an illegal act or series of illegal acts committed by nonphysical means and by concealment or guile to obtain money or property, to avoid the payment or loss of money or property, or to obtain business or personal advantage." These types of definitions are more in line with the legal codes that are represented in official statistics, such as the uniform crime reports (UCRs). However, offense-based definitions have been criticized for losing sight of the exact population Sutherland wished to underscore and bring to the attention of criminologists. Darrell Steffensmeier (1989, 347), for example, argues that "UCR data have little or nothing to do with white-collar crime" because the typical crimes included (i.e., fraud and forgery) are non-occupational crimes.

The reliance on an offender- or an offense-based definition of white-collar crime is no small issue, in large part because the population of interest varies significantly according to which starting point is used. For example, the case-study approach tends to portray white-collar offenders in terms of the stereo-typical image—that is, a high-social-class individual, usually a high-ranking businessperson, engaging in crimes in the course of his or her occupation. However, quantitative empirical investigations have identified white-collar offenders as coming from the middle sectors of the American economic struc-ture (Weisburd et al. 1991). Thus, white-collar offenders tend to be both similar to (e.g., lack of specialization and presence of prior arrests) and yet different from (e.g., social and background characteristics) street offenders (Benson and Moore 1992).

The use of varying definitions of white-collar crime has raised a broader issue of whether a distinction is, or should be, made between white-collar and street crimes. Despite the different paths and definitions used by white-collar crime scholars, a consensus can be found and built on. The silver lining of this definitional dilemma is that white-collar crime has in fact become a distinct category of crime. Both sides, then, can agree that white-collar criminals are indeed different from street offenders. As Weisburd and his colleagues (1991, 73) concluded, "Whatever else may be true of the distinction between white-collar and common criminals, the two are definitely drawn from distinctly dif-ferent sectors of the American population."

Given the agreement by criminologists in general, and by scholars of white-collar crime in particular, that white-collar crime and criminals are distinct from common crimes and offenders, the question emerges as to whether different theoretical models, interventions, and policies are needed to understand and prevent this type of crime.

White-Collar Crime Theories

Sutherland (1940) not only sensitized criminology to the concept of white-collar crime, but he also explicated a general theory of crime—differential association—to explain its occurrence. He believed that one universal causal process could explain all forms of criminal behavior, including street crimes and white-collar crimes. Building on the belief that one underlying cause of criminality may exist, many scholars have applied extant criminological theories to understand-ing white-collar crime, often with varying results.

Some scholars have argued that deterrence is well suited to explaining and controlling white-collar crimes. For example, William Chambliss (1967) argued that, since white-collar crimes are instrumental rather than expressive and white-collar offenders are not committed to a criminal lifestyle, these offenses and offenders can be more easily deterred than street crimes and criminals (also see Braithwaite and Geis 1982). Empirical research, however, suggests otherwise. It appears that the use of harsh criminal sanctions have no more effect in controlling white-collar crime and criminals than they do in prohibiting street crimes (Braithwaite and Makkai 1991; Makkai and Braithwaite 1994; Simpson 2002; Simpson and Koper 1992; Weisburd, Waring, and Chayet 1995).

Scholars who take a rational choice approach to understanding white-collar crime have had more promising results. Raymond Paternoster and Sally Simpson (1993) have advanced a subjective utility model of corporate offending that focuses on the immediate contextual characteristics of a situation (i.e., the presence or absence of inducements to offend or restrictions within the organizational structure). Their model assumes that individuals will assess the formal and informal costs and benefits of offending for themselves and for their employing organization in deciding whether to engage in illegal behavior. Empirical research assessing their model finds that both individual and organizational factors do significantly influence the decision to engage in a criminal act (Paternoster and Simpson 1996; Simpson 2002; Simpson, Paternoster, and Piquero 1998).

Theories that focus on individual differences have proliferated in the general criminological literature over the past decade. Empirical tests on this body of literature appear to indicate that individual differences do matter by influencing an individual's decision-making process, directly and indirectly. In this vein, Gottfredson and Hirschi's (1990) general theory of crime has received the most research attention. Their theory contends that individuals who lack self-control will be more likely to engage in criminal and analogous behavior (e.g., drinking, sexual promiscuity, and other reckless behaviors). Low self-control has successfully been applied to street crime, with most studies finding the expected positive and significant link between this individual trait and general forms of crime and deviance (see Pratt and Cullen 2000). However, the theory has been less successful when applied to white-collar crimes (see Benson and Moore 1992; Simpson and Piquero 2002).

The lack of empirical support linking low self-control to forms of white-collar crime has led some scholars to search for other personality traits that can better account for this type of offending. Nicole Leeper Piquero and her colleagues (2005) note the incongruence between regular employment and characteristics of low self-control (e.g., impulsiveness, short-sightedness). Focusing on the differences between white-collar and street crimes, they suggest that steady employment is antithetical to low self-control (256). Individuals who are successful in the business world must be able to delay gratification, must be willing to defer to the interests of others (i.e., their employing corporation), and must be future-focused. Therefore, Piquero and her colleagues (2005) turned to the personality trait of the desire for control, or the general need to be in control of everyday life events, to account for acts of white-collar crime. Using data collected from a sample of masters of business administration (MBA) students, their analysis revealed, as expected, a positive and significant relationship between this personality trait and intentions to engage in white-collar crime. They explain the relationship by noting that the intense need to control everyday life events coupled with the disdain for failure pushes individuals "to do something—even if it is criminal—in order to survive, get by and perhaps more importantly, get ahead" (Piquero, Exum, and Simpson 2005, 260).

In addition, theories that focus on societal influences may be more applicable to white-collar crime when the emphasis of the main socializing agent is shifted from society to the organization itself (i.e., an organizational subculture). For example, one might expect the traditional conceptualization of Hirschi's (1969) control theory to have opposite effects on white-collar crime from those it would have on street crime—that is, if an individual is strongly bonded to his or her place of employment (a conventional other), he or she may be more likely to engage in white-collar offending in order to see the company succeed. Thus, criminological theories traditionally used to explain street crimes do provide researchers with a starting point for theoretical explanations of white-collar offending. However, further refinement of these theories may have to be developed to explain this distinct type of crime.

Lessons Learned

While theorizing about white-collar crime has relied heavily on the general criminological literature, the reverse is not true. Extant criminological theories have served as a good starting place to try to understand white-collar criminality. Sutherland himself saw no need for specialized theories of white-collar crime; instead, he, like many of today's theorists, argued for the need for general theories of crime (Agnew 1992; Braithwaite 1989; Gottfredson and Hirschi 1990). Whether or not a truly general theory of crime is possible will surely be discussed and debated by criminologists for years to come. However, one thing is clear if that goal is ever to be attained: Criminology needs to move beyond using white-collar crime theory and research as a contrariety to street crime theory and research. The study of white-collar crime has so much more to offer in terms of understanding the causes of crime and criminality. The exclusion of white-collar crime and criminals in topical discussions within criminology could be regarded as misleading, just as Sutherland (1940) noted years ago, because such discussions would be based on limited information—that is, information from a narrow conception of offenses and offenders (namely, street crimes and criminals).

The study of criminal careers that has done much to advance the understanding of crime over the life course may serve as an example of how the study
of white-collar crime can add to existing knowledge about criminology and help
to better inform policy. Key dimensions of active offenders are now better
understood than ever before. For example, extant research has revealed that
most offenders begin offending in their teenage years (as measured by first
arrest) and have "aged out" of crime by the age of thirty (Piquero, Farrington,
and Blumstein 2007). In addition, it appears that criminals do not favor one
type of crime over another—in other words, they do not specialize. These known
facts about criminals' careers have contributed to developmental theories of
crime, with a popular theory emphasizing two general patterns: those offenders
who begin offending early in life and demonstrate continuous antisocial and
criminal behavior throughout their lives versus those who have a brief flirtation
with crime and antisocial behavior during their adolescent years (Moffitt 1993).
However, caution is warranted in regard to the conclusions, theories, and policies derived from this body of literature, because they have relied on samples
comprised only of street offenders (however, see Weisburd and Waring 2001).

Thus, any excitement about the advancement of knowledge gained from
this criminal career paradigm must be tempered by acknowledging the limited
nature of the groups studied. Established criminal career patterns and theories
cannot account for the patterns of white-collar offending and white-collar criminals. The little research on white-collar criminal careers that has been completed challenges the existing assumptions about the onset and desistance from
crime that are commonly employed within the criminal career paradigm.
Research on white-collar crime shows that this group of offenders begin offending in their late thirties or early forties, when most other offenders are believed
to have "aged out" of crime, and that the mean duration of their criminal careers
is much longer—approximately fourteen years compared with the mean of five
years suggested by extant life-course research (Benson and Kerley 2000; Farrington 1992; Weisburd and Waring 2001).

Therefore, the study of white-collar criminals' careers suggests that existing
developmental theories need to be expanded. Piquero and Michael Benson
(2004) suggest that another pattern of offending must be incorporated into
criminal career theories and discussions. They suggest a pattern of "punctuated
situationally dependent offending" that assumes white-collar offenders follow
an "adolescent limited" trajectory of offending but that, after a period of conformity, offending behavior begins again later in life. The resumed offending is
believed to be "triggered by or dependent on factors external to the offender"
(Piquero and Benson 2004, 158). This newly identified pattern of offending
suggests that alternative explanations of behavior are needed and that perhaps
some existing explanations may need to be revised to account for this group
of offenders.

Some possible avenues have been suggested by white-collar crime research-ers. We discussed one possibility, the desire for control, earlier in the chapter. Drawing a distinction between street crimes and white-collar crimes raises the possibility that different individual factors need to be taken into consideration when dealing with specific types of crimes. Stanton Wheeler (1992) suggested another possible explanation: White-collar offending may be explained by the fear of falling—or, in other words, the fear of losing what one has already attained. While it is commonly believed that the achievements of middle-class success (good job, homeownership, marriage) curb criminal behavior, this explanation suggests that these same stakes in conformity may induce crime for those who have already acquired these possessions. It is important to note that fear of falling applies not only to monetary success. It can also equally apply to the loss of status and prestige (Wheeler 1992). It is important to emphasize that the two approaches illustrated above are not meant to be exclusive to white-collar offending. Rather, they are designed to account for why a group of individuals who presumably have a lot to lose are likely to turn to criminal behavior.

Policy Implications

There is no denying that criminological theories have influenced the develop-ment of public policies aimed at reducing and preventing conventional crime. For example, policies aimed at improving early-childhood development, provid-ing job training for former offenders, incarcerating habitual offenders, treating substance abuse, and encouraging the development of thinking and inter-personal skills have all been shown to reduce or prevent (street) crime when implemented appropriately (see Sherman et al. 1998). Unfortunately, white-collar crime policy has yet to be influenced by criminological theorizing, at least to the extent that the more conventional forms of criminality have been affected. This lack of influence may be due to the lack of long-standing, consistent em-pirical evidence that traditional criminological theories can predict white-collar crime. Perhaps a more important reason for why policymakers have been slow to react to white-collar crime lies in the larger inability to clearly and concisely define the concept, and thus to enrage the public about its existence.

To this end, several scholars have noted the large and influential role the media plays in shaping the public's views of and opinions about crime, as well in shaping their reaction to what is perceived as the most recent crime problem or trend (Benekos and Merlo 2006). When sensationalized storytelling by the media captures the attention of the general public, elected political officials must respond; this usually necessitates actions that are quick, direct, and designed to quell public outrage over a particular social ill. Peter Benekos and Alida Merlo (2006, 7) explain how "quick fixes" of personalized legislation (e.g.,

Megan's Law) may satisfy the emotional needs of a victim's family and the general public but have disastrous effects in framing crime policy. The impetus of gut-reaction policymaking has led to a plethora of single-directed policy initiatives that show little forethought or planning and almost certainly do not consider the underlying cause or causes of criminal behavior.

White-collar crimes do not typically follow the same policy path. Because there are no chalk outlines and the crimes themselves tend to be too complicated to report quickly and easily on the evening news, white-collar offenses do not get the same media attention as street crimes. Therefore—and perhaps most important in terms of affecting crime policy—they also tend not to outrage the public. With the exception of a handful of cases (e.g., Enron and World-Com), white-collar crime is largely under-reported by the media and thus is not generally at the forefront of political or public attention. This does not mean, however, that white-collar crime is not seen as a serious issue. A recent study by Andrea Schoepfer and her colleagues (2007) found that respondents viewed robbery and fraud (a white-collar crime) as equally serious. The lack of media attention, however, may be another factor in the absence of proactive white-collar crime legislation based on theoretical predictions: White-collar crimes have not yet reached a critical moment in the eyes of society.

White-collar crime legislation has not yet been guided by theoretical assumptions or even empirical research. For the most part, white-collar crime legislation has been focused on (1) defining who the victims are and outlining the rights to which they are entitled; (2) defining prosecutorial jurisdiction; and (3) creating funding mechanisms for law enforcement agencies (Green 2005). Furthermore, white-collar crime legislation has come in the form of sentence enhancements, in which crimes committed through the use of fraud or embezzlement would lead to high fines and other penalties that otherwise would not be applied (one example is the "aggravated white-collar crime enhancement" in California Penal Code 186.11[a][1], 2004). Overall, government legislation up to this point has taken a reactive approach to combating white-collar crime rather than a proactive approach to prevent it. This, along with sentence enhancement policies, parallel the current "get tough" approach of our criminal justice system while ignoring the root causes of crime.

Unlike reactive governmental approaches, human-resource specialists are taking proactive policy approaches to recruiting employees. Several companies now look more deeply at job candidates for evidence of cheating or other morally reprehensible behavior in their personal lives, with the idea that such behavior can manifest itself into cheating in the workplace (O'Donnell and Farrell 2004). Many companies use the ESQ, or Employee Screening Questionnaire (Society for Human Resource Management 2007), to assess candidates. The ESQ is a personality test that examines the respondent's work ethic, dependability, future job performance, and propensity for engaging in numerous counterproductive and positive work behaviors. A quick search of the Internet reveals numerous companies that specialize in background checks of job candidates. They offer such services as researching a candidate's criminal background, work history, education, credit and financial status, driving record, drug-screening history, and general character. The idea behind intensive screening procedures is to weed out the candidates who could engage in crime in the workplace.

Since one key component of white-collar crime is that it requires the offender to engage in the offense during the course of legitimate occupation, it raises the question of whether policy should be implemented at the organizational level as opposed to a governmental level. In other words, the question at hand must focus on where policy intervention would be most effective.

While those studying the causes of white-collar crime have relied heavily on extant criminological theories, valuable lessons have been learned that will help inform public policy with regard to white-collar crime. For example, popular theories used to explain white-collar crime have focused on the individual decision-making process. While similarities certainly exist between street-crime and white-collar crime theorizing, white-collar crime research has illustrated that the individual actor takes into account not only his or her own risks and rewards but also organizational influences such as the costs and benefits for the organization as a whole and the culture of the employing organization. It is on the "white-collar" subculture that policy and interventions must focus. Just as Albert K. Cohen and Walter Miller focused on identifying youth-gang subcultures to better understand the causes of delinquent youth behavior, white-collar crime scholars have focused on the influence of the workplace and the decision-making process among those with "social status" to understand the causes of this type of behavior. While some advances have been made, we still have too little research to understand "suite subcultures" and thus develop specific policies. Policy has made great strides in dealing with gangs in the streets. Now, public policy makers need to ask themselves how and what are they going to do about the gangs who rule the suites.

Conclusions

White-collar crime and criminals present a unique and at times frustrating challenge to those who study issues of crime and criminality. While white-collar crime is often used as a contrast to street offending, it also intellectually challenges criminologists to rethink and reconceptualize existing explanations of and means to control criminal behavior. The key policy implication is that criminology and policymakers need to broaden their conceptions of crimes and criminals. It is no longer acceptable to presume that a one-size-fits-all approach will work in understanding or controlling criminal behavior. White-collar crime research has revealed that both similarities and differences exist between street offenders and white-collar offenders; however, the differences tend to emerge on what are believed to be the pro-social preventive factors that reduce street offending. In addition, white-collar crime teaches us that opportunities matter and that they have to be better understood in the decision-making process.

White-collar crime research helps add to the more general criminological literature in ways that can help shape and change public policy. Lessons learned from white-collar crime can and should be applied to street crime, just as lessons learned from street crime have been applied to the understanding of white-collar crime. It goes without saying that research and policy must work hand in hand. Criminology helps to shape policy, and policy helps to refine criminological inquiry. However, to date white-collar crime research has not been included in this research–policy cycle. There is much to be learned from the study of white-collar crime that may help shape and define effective policy for controlling both white-collar and street crime.

References

Agnew, R. 1992. Foundation for a general strain theory of crime and delinquency. *Criminology* 30:47–87.

Benekos, P., and A. Merlo. 2006. *Crime control: Politics and policy.* Cincinnati: Anderson Publishing.

Benson, M. L. 2002. *Crime and the life course.* Los Angeles: Roxbury Publishing.

Benson, M. L., and K. R. Kerley. 2000. Life course theory and white-collar crime. In *Contemporary issues in crime and criminal justice: Essays in honor of Gilbert Geis.* Ed. H. N. Pontell and D. Shichor, 121–136. Upper Saddle River, N.J.: Prentice Hall.

Benson, M. L., and E. Moore. 1992. Are white-collar and common offenders the same? An empirical and theoretical critique of a recently proposed general theory of crime. *Journal of Research in Crime and Delinquency* 29:251–272.

Braithwaite, J. 1989. *Crime, shame, and reintegration.* Cambridge: Cambridge University Press.

Braithwaite, J., and G. Geis. 1982. On theory and action for corporate crime control. *Crime and Delinquency* 31:292–314.

Braithwaite, J., and T. Makkai. 1991. Testing an expected utility model of corporate deterrence. *Law and Society Review* 25:7–39.

Chambliss, W. J. 1967. Types of deviance and the effectiveness of legal sanctions. *Wisconsin Law Review* (Summer): 703–719.

Clinard, M. B., and R. B. Quinney. 1973. *Criminal behavior systems: A typology.* New York: Holt, Rinehart and Winston.

Coleman, J. W. 2006. *The criminal elite: Understanding white-collar crime.* 6th ed. New York: Worth Publishers.

Edelhertz, H. 1970. *The nature, impact, and prosecution of white-collar crime.* Washington, D.C.: U.S. Government Printing Office.

Farrington, D. P. 1992. Criminal career research in the United Kingdom. *British Journal of Criminology* 32:521–536.

Forst, B., and W. Rhodes N.d. *Sentencing in eight United States District Courts, 1973–1978. Codebook.* Interuniversity Consortium for Political and Social Science Research Study No. 8622. University of Michigan, Ann Arbor.

Gottfredson, M. R., and T. Hirschi. 1990. *A general theory of crime*. Stanford, Calif.: Stanford University Press.

Green, S. 2005. The concept of white-collar crime in law and legal theory. *Buffalo Criminal Law Review* 8:1–34.

Hirschi, T. 1969. *Causes of delinquency*. Berkeley: University of California Press.

Hirschi, T., and M. R. Gottfredson. 1987. Causes of white-collar crime. *Criminology* 25: 949–974.

Makkai, T., and J. Braithwaite. 1994. The dialectics of corporate deterrence. *Journal of Research in Crime and Delinquency* 31:347–373.

Moffitt, T. E. 1993. Adolescence-limited and life course persistent antisocial behavior: A developmental taxonomy. *Psychological Review* 100:674–701.

O'Donnell, J., and G. Farrell. 2004. Business scandals prompt look into personal lives. *USA Today*, November 5.

Paternoster, R., and S. S. Simpson. 1993. A rational choice theory of corporate crime. In *Routine activities and rational choice: Advances in criminological theory*, Vol. 5. Ed. R. V. Clarke and M. Felson, 37–58. New Brunswick, N.J.: Transaction Publishers.

———. 1996. Sanction threats and appeals to morality: Testing a rational choice model of corporate crime. *Law and Society Review* 30:549–583.

Piquero, A. R., D. P. Farrington, and A. Blumstein. 2007. *Key issues in criminal career research: New analyses of the Cambridge Study in delinquent development*. Cambridge: Cambridge University Press.

Piquero, N. L., and M. L. Benson. 2004. White-collar crime and criminal careers: Specifying a trajectory of punctuated situational offending. *Journal of Contemporary Criminal Justice* 20:148–165.

Piquero, N. L., M. L. Exum, and S. S. Simpson. 2005. Integrating the desire for control and rational choice in a corporate crime context. *Justice Quarterly* 22:252–280.

Pratt, T. C., and F. T. Cullen. 2000. The empirical status of Gottfredson and Hirschi's general theory of crime: A meta-analysis. *Criminology* 38:931–964.

Schoepfer, A., S. Carmichael, and N. L. Piquero. 2007. Do perceptions of punishment vary between white-collar and street crimes? *Journal of Criminal Justice* 35:151–163.

Sherman, L., D. Gottfredson, D. MacKenzie, J. Eck, J., P. Reuter, and S. Bushway. 1998. *Preventing crime: What works, what doesn't, what's promising*. Washington, D.C.: National Institute of Justice.

Simpson, S. S. 2002. *Corporate crime, law, and social change*. New York: Cambridge University Press.

Simpson, S. S., and C. S. Koper. 1992. Deterring corporate crime. *Criminology* 30:347–375.

Simpson, S. S., R. Paternoster, and N. L. Piquero. 1998. Exploring the micro-macro link in corporate crime research. In *Research in the sociology of organizations: Deviance in and of organizations*, Vol. 15. Ed. P. A. Bamberger and W. J. Sonnenstuhl, 35–68. Stamford, Conn.: JAI Press.

Simpson, S. S., and N. L. Piquero. 2002. Low self-control, organizational theory, and corporate crime. *Law and Society Review* 36:509–548.

Society for Human Resource Management. 2007. Employee screening questionnaire. Available online at http://www.shrm.org (August 4, 2009).

Steffensmeier, D. 1989. On the causes of "white-collar" crime: An assessment of Hirschi and Gottfredson's claims. *Criminology* 27:345–358.

Sutherland, E. H. 1940. White-collar criminality. *American Sociological Review* 5:1–12.

———. 1949. *White collar crime*. New York: Dryden Press.

Weisburd, D., and E. Waring. 2001. White-collar crime and criminal careers. Cambridge: Cambridge University Press.

Weisburd, D., R. Waring, and E. Chayet. 1995. Specific deterrence in a sample of offenders convicted of white-collar crimes. *Criminology* 33:587–607.

Weisburd, D., S. Wheeler, E. Waring, and N. Bode. 1991. *Crimes of the middle classes.* New Haven, Conn.: Yale University Press.

Wheeler, S. 1992. The problem of white-collar crime motivation. In *White-collar crime reconsidered.* Ed. K. Schlegel and D. Weisburd, 108–123. Boston: Northeastern University Press.

Wheeler, S., D. Weisburd, E. Waring, and N. Bode. 1988. White-collar crime and criminals. *American Criminal Law Review* 25:331–357.

SCOTT JACQUES AND RICHARD WRIGHT

Drug Law and Violent Retaliation

Sir Francis Bacon (1939, 56) believed "the true and lawful goal of the sciences is not other than this: that human life be endowed with new discoveries and powers." The goal of *pure science* is to understand behavior, while the goal of *applied science* is to control behavior. These two forms of science can inform each other, as further understanding of behavior can lead to greater control of it, and the outcome of efforts to control behavior can lead to further understanding of it.

The objective of scientists working within the paradigm of pure sociology is to understand *social* behavior (Black 1976, 1995, 1998, 2000), and the objective of this book is to apply theoretic knowledge to criminal justice policy. In this chapter, we draw on the work of the first and foremost pure sociologist, Donald Black (1976, 1983), to provide a purely social explanation of (1) variation in the creation and application of drug law; and (2) how variation in the application of drug law affects variation in the quantity of violent retaliation in drug-related conflicts. We conclude by discussing how Black's theorizing about these matters might inform public policy.

Drug Law

Within any given jurisdiction—city, county, state, or country—the government, or the state, oversees the drug-related behavior of people, pharmacies, factories, crack houses, restaurants, or any drug-involved actors.[1] "Law is governmental social control. . . . It is, in other words, the normative life of a state and its

---

[1] The term "actor" refers to any social unit that interacts on its own behalf. An actor could be a street gang, the police, or any individual or group.

citizens, such as legislation, litigation, and adjudication" (Black 1976, 2). To understand drug law, we find it useful to differentiate cases of drug law according to whether the government is (1) the *complainant*, meaning that law is applied without a citizen's request; or (2) a reactive *mediator*, meaning that one or more disputants ask the government to become involved in the dispute (e.g., with a phone call to the police; see also Black 1980). The quantity of "state-complainant" and "state-mediation" law applied to drug-related behavior varies widely across time and space. Why are some drug-related behaviors defined as illegal while others are not? Why are some actors subjected to more drug-law enforcement than others? Why are all victimizers of drug-involved people not punished equally?

In the seminal work of pure sociology, *The Behavior of Law,* Black (1976) postulates a theory of law that in part uses social status to explain variations in the magnitude of law applied to actors.[2] Any given actor's social status increases concomitantly with gains in wealth (vertical status), community involvement (radial status), organization (corporate status), knowledge or conventionality (symbolic status), and respectability (normative status). Variation in the social status of disputants is, according to Black's theorizing, the source of variation in the quantity of law applied to offenders. We now explore how the social status of drug-involved actors affects "state-complainant" drug law and "state-mediation" drug law in turn.

State as Complainant

Black's (1976) theory of law predicts that, all else equal, offenders with lower social status will have more state-complainant drug law applied to their behavior. Thus, we propose the following relationship between state-complainant drug law and social status:

> *The quantity of state-complainant law applied to a drug-involved actor increases as that actor's social status decreases.*

In other words, drug using, selling, or producing has more law applied to it as the user, seller, or producer decreases in status. This proposition applies to actors involved with different drugs and to actors involved with the same drug. The proposition predicts that the drug behavior of low-status actors is more likely to be criminalized, more likely to lead to arrest, more likely to result in conviction, and more likely to lead to harsh punishment. In the remainder of this section, we explore the effect of social status on drug-law legislation and enforcement, drawing on the five distinct forms of social status.

---

[2] Black (1976) also uses the concept of "social distance" to explain law, but we restrict this chapter to the effect of social status.

Vertical status increases as an individual's wealth increases, whether that wealth resides in drugs, territory, or cash. Black's theory of law predicts that the higher an actor's wealth, the less law is applied to that actor's drug-related behavior. The effect of vertical status can be seen across the Americas. Consider the following situation in Brazil: "Poor users and small dealers are under closer surveillance. . . . In most cases, the justice system merely endorses a discriminatory vicious cycle in which the more modest dealers and users are sentenced to prison while high-level arms and narcotics traffickers seldom are" (Zaluar 2001, 437). Linda Farthing (1997, 267) reports that Bolivia's Antidrug Law 1008 has had especially negative consequences for the poor. Likewise, many American criminologists, sociologists, and philosophers have argued that drug laws have a disproportionate impact on the poor (see, e.g., Husak and Marneffe 2006; Tonry 1995). Legal warrants are customary in the United States for government searches of property, but the "rights" of the poor are more likely than those of the rich to be voided: "In the fall of 1988, the Chicago Housing Authority instituted a new policy designed to rid the city's public housing projects of drug dealers. Dubbed Operation Clean Sweep, the policy authorized warrantless, random searches of tenants' apartments by Chicago police officers and housing authority agents" (Glasser and Siegel 1997, 237).

The more involved an actor is with the institutions of the community, such as family and work, the higher the actor's *radial status*. Black's theory of law predicts that the more integrated an actor becomes with the community, the less drug law is applied to that actor's drug-related behavior. James Spradley's (1970) famous ethnography, *You Owe Yourself a Drunk: An Ethnography of Urban Nomads,* is an exemplary firsthand account of how radial status affects the distribution of drug law. "Urban nomads" are men who travel alone from one American city to the next "bumming," a life of begging and alcohol drinking. When an urban nomad is in court on a "drunk charge," the offender can "make a statement" to beat or lessen the penalty. Spradley writes:

> The tramp learns which factors influence the judge as he sentences a man to jail for public drunkenness, and his statement reflects these concerns. The following questions which judges asked defendants were recorded from court sessions and reflect the kinds of issues to which men's statements will respond:
>
>> Are you employed?
>> Are you married?
>> Do you live with your family?
>> If I suspend your sentence can you find a job?
>> Are you permanently employed?
>> If I give you an opportunity will you go pick apples?

Equal justice for all under the law is the maxim of this court, yet when
we consider to whom the judge gives sentences and who escapes them,
we must conclude that some men are more equal than others. . . . [T]he
man with the *most resources* [i.e., radial status] is rewarded. . . . As a
man moves into the world of tramps he loses many things which middle-
class Americans consider important: steady employment, wife and
family, interest in work, and a sedentary existence. The man who has
retained any of these resources has a better chance of escaping incarceration than others. (183–184)

The more organized a group is, or the more memberships an individual has,
the greater the *corporate status*. According to Black's theory of law, variability
in corporate status results in the differential application of drug law, with more
status garnering better treatment. Perhaps the best illustration of this process
can be found in the interplay between drug law and drug-related behavior of
the state. In modern times, the actors with the highest degree of organization
are often states. Since actors with the most organization have the highest corporate status, law is applied in smaller quantities to the state than it is to less
organized entities. For example, in the Netherlands, government-run pharmacies are permitted to distribute as much marijuana as is deemed necessary for
the patient's well-being, while privately owned coffee shops are legally restricted
to distributing no more than five grams of cannabis to a customer at one time,
even for customers who are prescribed marijuana by a doctor.[3] In a similar vein,
starting in the 1970s British doctors were required to be affiliated (i.e., have a
membership) with the government health system before they were permitted
to prescribe heroin in the treatment of addiction (Stimson and Oppenheimer
1982). Consider the heroin-addiction treatment program that emerged in post-
Soviet Poland:

The 1997 [drug] law . . . specified (Art. 15), that methadone maintenance was generally permissible, but it could be implemented only
within the framework of the, so-called, high threshold programs, run
by selected public health organizations that obtained special permits
from the Ministry of Health. This meant that neither private clinics nor
privately practicing physicians were eligible to obtain such an authorization and prescribe methadone. (Krajewski 2003, 285)

The *symbolic status* of actors increases in tandem with gains in conventionality. As Black (1976, 67) observes: "Some kinds of culture are more conventional
than others: They happen more frequently." Also, symbolic status increases as

---

[3] Coffee shop manager, personal communication, 2006.

knowledge increases. Black's theory of law predicts that an actor who is less conventional and less knowledgeable attracts more drug law.

The effect of knowledge on drug law is clearly evident in the United States, where a person must be "a physician board certified in addiction psychiatry or addiction medicine" (Abood 2005, 168), or have "proof" of knowledge, to prescribe and dispense Schedule III, IV, and V opioids used for the maintenance or detoxification treatment of heroin addiction. Not only does knowledge exempt some from the application of law; it can also decrease penalties for breaking the law:

> [There] is a typical situation in which the pattern of sentencing is strongly biased to provide longer terms to those lower down in the hierarchy of drug dealing. Higher level dealers have more bargaining chips; namely, they can inform on many others in the organization because they simply know more: "The accused, a low-level 'runner' for a drug operation, knew only a very few people in the operation. Therefore, he had nothing to 'bargain' in terms of giving information to prosecutors. He was sentenced to a minimum of 20 years in prison. In the same courtroom, same judge, same drug operation, a drug dealer very high up in the organizational structure could and did name a dozen people around and below him. For his 'cooperation with the prosecution' he received a reduced sentence of only two years in prison." (Duster 1997, 266)

Another indicator of symbolic status is race or ethnicity, with the symbolic status of a particular race or ethnicity increasing as its relative prevalence, or conventionality, in the population grows. The preeminent historian of U.S. drug legislation, David Musto, attributes the origins of American cocaine laws to the low symbolic status of blacks (1999, 7). Smoking opium, Chinese immigrants, and the passage of drug laws predictably came together in the United States (Morgan 1978; see also Reinarman and Levine 1997, 6), the Netherlands (De Kort and Korf 1992), and Australia (Manderson 1997). In each of those countries in the late nineteenth century and early twentieth century, the predominantly— if not entirely—Chinese practice of *smoking* opium was made illegal, whereas other "non-Chinese" or "white-person" forms of opium use remained legal.

Symbolic status also has an effect on drug arrests. Using needle-exchange survey data and ethnographic observations of two outdoor drug markets as indicators of the racial-ethnic composition of low-level drug deliveries, Katherine Beckett and her colleagues (2006) found that in Seattle, Washington, blacks and Latinos are disproportionately more likely than whites to be arrested, and this finding held true even when other variables were controlled for—such as outdoor versus indoor selling (presumably affecting detection) and rates of drug involvement by race.

Variability in symbolic status affects legislation and arrests, but it also has an impact on outcomes at the prosecution level:

> Studies by both the Sentencing Commission and the Federal Judicial Center have found that among offenders who engaged in conduct warranting a mandatory minimum, white offenders were less likely than blacks or Hispanics to receive the mandatory minimum term. In addition, since the mandatory minimums have been enacted, the gap between the average sentence of blacks and those of other groups has grown wider. These racial and ethnic differences indicate that one or more features of the current system have a proportionally greater impact on blacks and Hispanics than on whites. . . . [Furthermore, there is a] significant relationship between sentence length and citizenship. (Vincent and Hofer 1994, 23n70)

The effect of low symbolic status on punishment for drug-involvement was starkly evident in Nazi Germany. The Nazis divided apprehended narcotic addicts into two groups: (1) the genetically inferior, defined by, among other things, a genetically conspicuous family and a moral deficiency (i.e., Jewish); and (2) the reformable, or improvable, defined by a genetically inconspicuous family and racial value (i.e., of "Aryan" descent; Mach 2002, 381). The "reformable" narcotic addicts fared much better than their supposedly "genetically inferior" counterparts, who were "subjected to sterilization and/or commitment to a work or concentration camp" (384).

The more an actor is subjected to social control, the lower that actor's *normative status,* or *respectability.* Law is one form of social control (Black 1976, 1989, 1998), and Black's theory of law predicts that the more drug law that has been applied to an actor in the past, the more law will be applied to that actor's future drug-related behavior. The law's "prejudice" in this respect is so strong that it is actually written into legal codes that call for greater punishments for repeat offenders. In the United States, for instance, a conviction for manufacturing or distributing a kilogram of heroin results in varying penalties for different normative statuses. Those with no prior felony drug convictions are punished with no less than ten years in prison, whereas a second-time offender is penalized with a sentence of no less than twenty years, and offenders with two or more previous drug convictions risk spending the rest of their lives behind bars (21 U.S. Code, sec. 841). Drug users (as opposed to dealers or manufacturers) with previous drug-related convictions also experience worse treatment from the law. For example, a person found in possession of a gram of cocaine for personal use serves no more than one year in prison *if it is a first offense.* But if that same person has a prior drug conviction, he or she faces no less than fifteen days and up to two years in prison, and two or more previous convictions earns that same offender a prison stay of no less than ninety days and no more than three years (21 U.S. Code, sec. 844).

To summarize, the amount of state-complainant drug law that is applied to a drug user, dealer, or producer increases as the wealth, community involvement, organization, knowledge, conventionality, or respectability of the actor decreases.

State as Mediator

The effects of state-complainant drug law do not exist in a vacuum; they have important implications for another aspect of drug law: mediation. "State mediation" refers to any conflict where disputants leave the fate of their case in the hands of the government.[4] Rather than the complainant (e.g., a robbed, burglarized, or defrauded drug seller or buyer) retaliating unilaterally against the offender (Black 1983; Cooney 1998; Horwitz 1990), the government mediates the case and, to some degree, exacts vengeance from the offender on behalf of the victim.

Here we are concerned solely with how normative status affects state mediation because state-complainant drug law directly affects the magnitude of normative status. Remember that normative status is defined by the quantity of social control applied to one's behavior, with being subjected to more social control equating to lower status. This means that the more state-complainant drug law applied to an actor, the lower that actor's normative status. According to Black's theory of law, state mediation varies from one conflict to the next as a function of the victim's normative status:

> In a drug-related dispute, the quantity of state-mediatory law applied to an offender decreases as the normative status of the victim decreases.

In other words, the amount of law applied to an offender in a drug-related dispute will rise as the victim increases in normative status. The above line of reasoning suggests that greater applications of state-complainant drug law leads to less law being applied to offenders in drug-related conflicts, because victims have lower status.

The following case is a prime example of how variation in the normative status of victims affects the quantity of law applied to offenders. In the course of a single incident, the normative status of the victims was lowered, and for that reason, so, too, was the quantity of law applied to the offenders:

> The complainants were a young, white couple. The male was the primary story teller. He stated that he was delivering furniture in the area.

---

[4] Black distinguishes among "mediation, arbitration, and adjudication" (Black 1998, 85), but for simplicity's sake we do not draw such distinctions in this chapter.

His girlfriend accompanied him occasionally on his deliveries and was with him the night of the robbery. As they parked on the street, three individuals approached them, displayed knives, took them inside a building, and robbed them of $80. . . . The police arrived on the scene as the defendants were fleeing the building. The D.A. . . . determined that the [victims] were an innocent young couple; *the case was slated for the grand jury.* About two minutes after the case was sent to the typist, the male complainant returned to the D.A. and stated that he was in the area to buy heroin. He did not want his girlfriend to know about the buy. *The D.A. recalled the papers and reduced the charge to a misdemeanor.* (Stanko 1981–1982, 236–237; emphasis added)

Involvement in a heroin buy lowers an actor's normative status because there are laws prohibiting such behavior. When the victim lowered his respectability by revealing his illicit behavior to the district attorney, the quantity of law applied to the offenders was decreased—from a felony to a misdemeanor.[5]

Violent Retaliation

Thus far we have argued that low-status actors are subjected to more state-complainant drug law, the result of which is less law is applied to victimizers because the drug-involved victims have lower normative status. If the creation and application of state-complainant drug law affects the use of state mediation in drug-related disputes, then perhaps variability in the use of state mediation affects the volume of another form of social control: violent retaliation. In a classic article, "Crime as Social Control," Black (1983) argues that disputants with the least access to law are the most likely to engage in violent retaliation.[6]

As related specifically to the drug world, Black's theory predicts that as more state-complainant drug law is applied to drug-involved actors, more violent retaliation in drug-related conflicts will occur, because disputants will have less access to mediatory law for the reason that they have lower normative status. Thus, we propose the following relationship between state-complainant drug law and retaliatory violence:

> In a drug-related dispute, the quantity of violent retaliation applied to an offender increases as the amount of state-complainant drug law applied to the victim increases.

---

[5] Social information is a variable in itself (Black 1989). This is discussed in detail below.

[6] In truth, Black (1983) provides not a theory of "violent retaliation" but, rather, a theory of self-help, defined as "the handling of a grievance by unilateral aggression" (Black 1998, 74). Nevertheless, the theorizing of Black (1983) applies to the narrower concept of "violent retaliation" (see Phillips 2003).

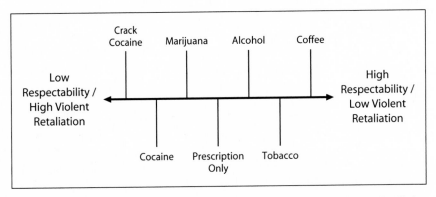

FIGURE 11.1   Hypothetical Impact of Respectability on Violent Retaliation (per Conflict) in Various Psychoactive Substance Markets

Stated differently, as drug-involved people are subjected to more state-complainant drug law, they lose access to state-mediatory law to settle disputes, and their conflicts become more likely to be handled with violent retaliation.

Although we are unaware of any study that documents the rate of mediatory law or violent retaliation per drug-related conflict, we believe that Figure 11.1 is an accurate approximation of the interplay among state-complainant drug law, state mediation, and violent retaliation.

It seems reasonable to speculate that—because the actors involved are less respectable—disputes over crack cocaine turn violent more often than disputes over marijuana, which involve more violent retaliation than conflicts over illicit pharmaceutical drugs, which involve more violent retaliation than conflicts over alcohol, which involve more vengeance than quarrels emanating from coffee use and distribution. According to the proposition above, if the quantities of law applied to, say, alcohol- and marijuana-related behavior were reversed, then alcohol-related conflicts would involve more retaliatory violence than marijuana-related conflicts. Similarly, if the same amount of law were applied to crack- and cigarette-related behavior, then, the theory suggests, there would be similar rates of violence in these two drug markets.

There is evidence in the United States and abroad for the above proposition. In a time-series analysis, Gary Jensen (2000, 31) found that American alcohol "prohibition and its enforcement increased the murder rate." Likewise, in an analysis of 414 homicides in New York City, Paul Goldstein and his colleagues (1997, 117) found that 39.1 percent, or 162, of those deaths were directly attributable to "the exigencies of the illicit [drug] market system." Between-nation variability in drug-related violent retaliation is understandable when viewed in light of the thesis that increased drug law promulgates violence. In Latin America, from Puerto Rico (Montalvo-Barbot 1997)

to Bolivia (Thoumi 2003) and Brazil (Zaluar 2001, 438), there is evidence
that increased law enforcement coincides with increases in drug-related retaliatory violence. In a cross-cultural study of drug law and homicide, Jeffrey
Miron (2001) found compelling statistical support for the thesis that increased
drug-law enforcement increases violence and speculates that "eliminating
drug prohibition would reduce homicide in the United States by 25–75 percent" (Miron 2004, 51).

A comparison of violence and drug law in the United States and the Netherlands, for example, reveals stark contrasts between the two countries. In the
Netherlands, investigations, arrests, and criminal prosecutions for illicit drug
use are relatively rare (Leuw 1991). The relatively high respectability of illicit
drug users and dealers results in relatively little violent social control:

> The relative tolerance of hard-drug use in the Netherlands offers a
> probable explanation for low levels of violence. The police are not
> especially interested in small-time street dealers. Police practices,
> such as undercover purchases or pressuring junkies to serve as police
> informers, are normally not employed at the retail level of the hard-
> drug market. Consequently, the paranoia and retaliation so character-
> istic of drug scenes elsewhere exist to a moderate degree only. (Leuw
> 1991, 240)

The low rates of violence associated with lax drug-law enforcement in the
Netherlands seem to extend all the way up the distribution ladder. In an ethnographic study of the Dutch–Colombian cocaine trade, for example, Damián
Zaitch (2002, 262) reports that he "soon became amazed about the number of
conflicts that did not lead to physical violence." Zaitch (2002) speculates that
this must be related, at least in part, to the tolerant enforcement policy of the
Dutch government:

> Low levels of violence are . . . related, paradoxically, to the lack of an
> American or Colombian model of internal war on drugs. *Traquetos*
> [Colombian drug sellers] in the Netherlands do not have to react against
> military operations, para-legal violence or summary executions, actions
> that would logically expand the number of dead bodies on all fronts.
> Colombian *traquetos* seem to get the implicit message from Dutch
> authorities: "We tolerate you as long as you keep quiet." (270)

Set against the backdrop of the high rates of drug law and drug-related retaliation in the United States, it seems reasonable to suspect that the quantifiably
smaller amount of drug law in the Netherlands has reduced the quantity of
violence in drug markets there.

Policy Implications

This chapter has drawn on Black's (1976, 1983) theorizing to argue that as the social status of an actor decreases, (1) the amount of state-complainant law applied to the actor's behavior increases; and so (2) the amount of state mediation that responds to that actor's victimizations decreases; and therefore (3) the amount of violent retaliation used by the victimized actor against the offender increases. What does all of the above portend for the future of drug-control policy?

Before attempting to answer that question, it is important to point out that practitioners of pure sociology most often see themselves as doing "pure science." Pure science is "that somewhat ephemeral category of research undertaken by men whose immediate goal is to increase understanding rather than control of nature" (Kuhn 1977, 233). The goal of pure sociology is *not* to change social life but, rather, to *understand* it. Pure sociologists, for the most part, take the stance that "sociologists, as sociologists, have no business telling people what moral or political positions they should take" (Cooney 1998, 149), but "provided the pure sociologist does not make the mistake of actually recommending policy, . . . the approach can be used to design novel real-world applications."[7] Below we discuss the policy implications of the propositions outlined in this chapter, but we do not take a moral stance on what policymakers should actually do.

Discrimination, defined as treating actors differently based on differences in their social status, is an important issue for many academics and laypeople. Discrimination, as shown above, is a natural phenomenon in the drug world; it occurs everywhere there is variation in social status (see Black 1989). At least in the near future, differences in social status will not disappear, and neither will discrimination in drug law. Nevertheless, the effects of status variation on discrimination in drug law can be limited to some degree because *social information*—such as knowledge of an actor's status—is a variable unto itself (64–67). Social information is important to understanding discrimination, because in the words of Black, "All discrimination requires social information" (66). If there is no social information, then social status will have a diminished effect on drug law. Conversely, when social information is increased, social status becomes more important.

What this suggests is that to reduce discrimination in drug law, the government could reduce social information. For instance, in any given drug-related trial, the defendant and complainant could be kept out of sight of jurors, and lawyers could be directed not to reveal social information (Black 1989, 68–70). This would limit social information in such way as to reduce both the rate and

---

[7] Mark Cooney, personal correspondence, 2006.

quantity of discriminatory behavior among jurors and judges. But distaste for discrimination is not constant from one dimension of social space to the next. While most regard discrimination against people with low symbolic status, such as ethnic minorities, to be deviant and in need of reduction, these same people often discriminate against those who are low in another form of status—normative status. For example, it seems perfectly reasonable to many that repeat offenders should receive harsher penalties. So if society wants to discriminate on the basis of some forms of status but not others, social information should be reduced accordingly: greater in some places, less in others.

Discrimination in drug law is an important issue, but so, too, is retaliatory violence. Work in the Blackian theoretical tradition suggests that the degree to which drug law is reduced, drug-related violent retaliation will also be reduced. The more state-complainant drug law applied to an actor, the lower that actor's respectability, the less state mediation there is, and the more often violent retaliation occurs. Therefore, less state-complainant drug law—such as legislation prohibiting selling or consumption—leads to greater respectability, more formal mediation in drug-related disputes, and a reduction in the prevalence of violent retaliation.

It seems, however, that the moral climate of the United States is not currently conducive to repealing prohibitory legislation, so perhaps social information could be manipulated to reduce retaliation. As noted by Richard Rosenfeld and his colleagues (2003, 307–308): "Persons who engage in . . . illegal activities . . . make up a disproportionate share of crime victims. Widening their access to legal resources could reduce their reliance on informal means of dispute resolution, and help contain the spread of violence." It may be possible to widen legal access for criminals and thereby reduce violent retaliation by (1) informing citizens of their legal right not to divulge information that could incriminate them; and (2) instituting a "don't ask, don't tell" policy in communities regarding the context of victimization reported to police (see also Black 1989; Cooney 1998; Rosenfeld, Jacobs, and Wright 2003).

The Fifth Amendment of the U.S. Constitution protects people from forced self-incrimination, so those who are victimized while participating in the underworld need not reveal their own lawbreaking before the government will look into the case. In other words, the Fifth Amendment gives citizens the right not to reveal *social information* about their own criminal activities. We wonder, however, what proportion of illicit drug users, dealers, and producers realize that, in fact, the Fifth Amendment protects them from self-incrimination and thereby provides them with the opportunity to report *some parts* of criminal victimization *but not others* to the police. For instance, a drug dealer who is robbed or burglarized of $1,000 in cash and a quarter-pound of marijuana can, in principle, report to the police his or her loss of cash but is not obliged to reveal his or her illicit activities (for an empirical example, see Jacques and

Wright 2008, 217–218). Although this is pure speculation, our interaction with illicit-drug-involved people suggests that they are not fully aware of the implications of the Fifth Amendment for their ability to access the law. Perhaps it is possible to reduce violent retaliation by increasing the use of formal mediation in illicit-drug-related conflicts though a public campaign that informs people of the implications of the Fifth Amendment for reporting victimization. In addition to a campaign to inform victims of their Fifth Amendment right, we also believe that if a "don't ask, don't tell" policy could be agreed to by citizens, police, and prosecutors, then the use of mediatory law would expand among illegal users, traders, and makers because such people would have less reason to worry that their own criminal behavior would be uncovered in the process of reporting victimization. And if resorting to mediatory law becomes more prevalent, then resorting to violent retaliation should do the opposite.

References

Abood, R. R. 2005. *Pharmacy practice and the law.* 4th ed. Sudbury, Mass.: Jones and Bartlett.

Bacon, F. 1939. Novum Organum. In *The English philosophers from Bacon to Mill.* Ed. E. A. Burtt, 3–126. New York: Modern Library.

Beckett, K., K. Nyrop, and L. Pfingst. 2006. Race, drugs, and policing: Understanding disparities in drug delivery arrests. *Criminology* 44:105–138.

Black, D. 1976. *The behavior of law.* New York: Academic Press.

———. 1980. *The manners and customs of the police.* New York: Academic Press.

———. 1983. Crime as social control. *American Sociological Review* 48:34–45.

———. 1989. *Sociological justice.* New York: Oxford University Press.

———. 1995. The epistemology of pure sociology. *Law and Social Inquiry* 20:829–870.

———. 1998. *The social structure of right and wrong.* Rev. ed. San Diego: Academic Press.

———. 2000. Dreams of pure sociology. *Sociological Theory* 18:343–367.

Cooney, M. 1998. *Warriors and peacemakers: How third parties shape violence.* New York: New York University Press.

De Kort, M., and D. J. Korf. 1992. The development of drug trade and drug control in the Netherlands: A historical perspective. *Crime, Law and Social Change* 17:123–144.

Duster, T. 1997. Pattern, purpose and race in the drug war. In *Crack in America: Demon drugs and social justice.* Ed. C. Reinarman and H. Levine, 260–287. Berkeley: University of California Press.

Farthing, L. 1997. Social impacts associated with Antidrug Law 1008. In *Coca, cocaine, and the Bolivian reality.* Ed. M. L. Léons and H. Sanabria, 253–280. Albany: State University of New York Press.

Glasser, I., and L. Siegel. 1997. When constitutional rights seem too extravagant to endure: The crack scare's impact on civil rights and liberties. In *Crack in America: Demon drugs and social justice.* Ed. C. Reinarman and H. Levine, 229–248. Berkeley: University of California Press.

Goldstein, P. J., H. Brownstein, P. J. Ryan, and P. A. Bellucci. 1997. Crack and homicide in New York City: A case study in the epidemiology of violence. In *Crack in America: Demon drugs and social justice.* Ed. C. Reinarman and H. Levine, 113–130. Berkeley: University of California Press.

Horwitz, A. V. 1990. *The logic of social control*. New York: Plenum Press.

Husak, D., and P. de Marneffe. 2006. *The legalization of drugs: For and against*. New York: Cambridge University Press.

Jacques, S., and R. Wright. 2008. The relevance of peace to studies of drug market violence. *Criminology* 46:221–254.

Jensen, G. F. 2000. Prohibition, alcohol, and murder: Untangling countervailing mechanisms. *Homicide Studies* 4:8–36.

Krajewski, K. 2003. Drugs, markets and criminal justice in Poland. *Crime, Law and Social Change* 40:273–293.

Kuhn, T. S. 1977. *The essential tension*. Chicago: University of Chicago Press.

Leuw, E. 1991. Drugs and drug policy in the Netherlands. *Crime and Justice* 14:229–276.

Mach, H. 2002. Exclusion and extinction—the fight against narcotics in the Third Reich. Trans. L. Bollinger. *Journal of Drug Issues* 32:379–394.

Manderson, D. 1997. Substances as symbols: Race rhetoric and the tropes of Australian drug history. *Social and Legal Studies* 6:383–400.

Miron, J. A. 2001. The economics of drug prohibition and drug legalization. *Journal of Law and Economics* 44:615–634.

———. 2004. *Drug war crimes: The consequences of prohibition*. Oakland, Calif.: Independent Institute.

Montalvo-Barbot, A. 1997. Crime in Puerto Rico: Drug trafficking, money laundering, and the poor. *Crime and Delinquency* 43:533–547.

Morgan, P. 1978. The legislation of drug law: Economic crisis and social control. *Journal of Drug Issues* 8:53–62.

Musto, D. 1999. *The American disease: Origins of narcotic control*. 3rd ed. New York: Oxford University Press.

Phillips, S. 2003. The social structure of vengeance: A test of Black's model. *Criminology* 41:673–708.

Reinarman, C. and H. G. Levine. 1997. Crack in context: America's latest demon drug. In *Crack in America: Demon drugs and social justice*. Ed. C. Reinarman and H. G. Levine, 1–17. Berkeley: University of California Press.

Rosenfeld, R., B. Jacobs, and R. Wright. 2003. Snitching and the code of the street. *British Journal of Criminology* 43:291–309.

Spradley, J. P. 1970. *You owe yourself a drunk: An ethnography of urban nomads*. Prospect Heights, Ill.: Waveland Press.

Stanko, E. A. 1981–1982. The impact of victim assessment on prosecutors' screening decisions: The case of the New York County District Attorney's Office. *Law and Society Review* 16:225–240.

Stimson, G. V., and E. Oppenheimer. 1982. *Heroin addiction: Treatment and control in Britain*. London: Tavistock.

Thoumi, F. 2003. *Illegal drugs, economy, and society in the Andes*. Baltimore: John Hopkins University Press.

Tonry, M. 1995. *Malign neglect: Race, crime, and punishment in America*. New York: Oxford University Press.

Vincent, B. S., and P. J. Hofer. 1994. *The consequences of mandatory minimum prison terms: A summary of recent findings*. Washington, D.C.: Federal Judicial Center.

Zaitch, D. 2002. *Trafficking cocaine: Colombian drug entrepreneurs in the Netherlands*. The Hague: Kluwer Law International.

Zaluar, A. 2001. Violence, easy money, and justice in Brazil. *International Social Science Journal* 53:435–441.

12

MARIE GRIFFIN

Feminist Criminology

Beyond the Slaying of Demons

From the start, it was a given that criminology would be the study by men of men, though these men were not to be regarded as interesting because they were men, but rather because they were criminals. Criminology was the study of criminals who happened to mainly be men and so the male criminal was what was studied, though not as a man or masculine being, but as a criminal. This, it seemed, was simply the natural, logical starting point of the discipline.

—Ngaire Naffine, *Feminism and Criminology*

Any discussion of feminist criminology involves the examination of criminological theory and research, as well as the deconstruction of the central elements that serve to buttress most mainstream criminological theories. Such a discussion is as much about what feminist criminology is as it is about what it is not. This is a difficult task indeed, given the multiple perspectives and research foci that make up feminist criminology. Yet Jody Miller and Christopher Mullins (2006) provide a succinct definition with which to begin. "Feminist criminology refers to that body of criminological research and theory that situates the study of crime and criminal justice within a complex understanding that the social world is systematically shaped by relations of sex and gender" (218). Feminist criminology has come to represent multiple perspectives united by the notion that the understanding of women's criminal behavior, as well as the victimization of women and girls, has been omitted—or, worse, misrepresented—within the development of criminological theory. Contemporary feminist perspectives that have explored the significance of gender to the understanding of crime and the criminal justice system include liberal, radical, Marxist, socialist, postmodern, critical race, black feminism, and multiracial feminism. These perspectives represent a diversity of thought and generally are differentiated by the factors that each identifies as the source and nature of women's oppression and gender inequality. Several exceptional reviews have examined these various perspectives and associated assumptions, as well as general debates at varying points in the development of feminist criminology (e.g., Britton 2000; Burgess-Proctor 2006; Daly and Chesney-Lind 1988; Daly and Maher 1998; Miller and Mullins 2006; Naffine 1997). Due to the multi-faceted and interdisciplinary nature of a feminist criminological perspective, such a complete review is not possible here. The purpose of this chapter, then, is to trace the development of feminist criminology, to provide a review of key feminist debates, and finally to discuss what a feminist criminological perspective brings to the understanding of criminal justice policy and social change.

A Feminist Perspective on Criminology

Early studies of the criminal woman were the exception, very much peripheral to the general study of crime. As noted by numerous scholars, the development of the discipline of criminology reflected the study of men by men (e.g., Leonard 1982; Messerschmidt 1993; Miller and Mullins 2006; Naffine 1997). The very fact that women engaged in less criminal behavior than men served to bolster the assumption that the female criminal did not warrant attention; thus, early theorists failed to recognize not only the significance of the relationship between sex and criminal behavior but also the consistency of this relationship over time (Britton 2000). In essence, the study of female offenders was discounted because, relative to men, far fewer women engaged in criminal behavior. The value of exploring the relative absence of criminal behavior among women was largely overlooked and, some would argue, continues to be overlooked by main-stream criminology today (Naffine 1997).

When not ignored, early theorizing on the nature of women and crime was influenced strongly by assumptions regarding the inherent nature of women (Smart 1977). According to Joanne Belknap (2007, 33), early positivist studies were guided by four main assumptions:

> (1) Individual characteristics, not society, are responsible for criminal behavior; (2) there is an identifiable biological nature inherent in all women; (3) offending women are "masculine", which makes them incompetent as women and thus prone to break the law; and (4) the differences between male and female criminality are due to sex, not gender differences.

In various ways, these early researchers (e.g., Freud 1933; Lombroso and Ferrero 1895; Pollock 1950; Thomas 1923) identified a host of factors they believed distinguished the nature of woman from that of man. From this perspective, women and girls were by nature less intelligent than men; unable to feel pain; and more primitive, passive, feminine, loyal, and submissive. Compared with these "good" women, "bad" women were deviants who rebelled against their natural feminine roles (Klein 1980). Unlike male offenders, female offenders were viewed as violating not only the law but, more important, as violating predefined normative standards. The female criminal, then, was not only a lawbreaker but also "abnormal." The nature of this "abnormality" might differ from one theorist to the next; however, women's "deviant" behavior was generally "demonized, masculinized, and sexualized" (Chesney-Lind 2006). At the heart of these assumptions was the failure to distinguish between the concepts of sex and gender and to understand the inflexible nature of the gendered social roles forced on women. Differences between men and women, which are arguably the result of the expected social roles and behaviors ascribed by society, were assumed by these early theorists to be physiologically or psychologically driven (Belknap 2007).

While described elsewhere, it is important to note the ways in which often contradictory ideas regarding the inherent nature of women were used as a foundation to theorize about women and crime. For example, relying on their evolutionary framework to explain female criminality, Cesare Lombroso and Guglielmo Ferrero (1895) argued that women were less evolved than men; female offenders were not only abnormal but also biologically more like men (Belknap 2001). Lombroso and Ferrero (1895, 2004) highlighted what they believed was the link between women and girls' sexuality, or "exaggerated eroticism," and their involvement in crime, suggesting that such eroticism was not normal among women and served as the "starting point for vices and crimes" (185). In a similar vein, W. I. Thomas (1907, 1923) ignored to a great extent the societal restrictions on women's opportunities, explaining prostitution as the inappropriate and socially unapproved means by which women satisfy their "intense need to give and feel love" (Smart 1977, 37). His tendency to confuse criminality with promiscuity and his resulting focus on prostitution illustrates the way in which women's, but not men's, criminal behavior historically has been examined within the context of sexuality in terms of specialization and motivation (Heidensohn 2006). In Freud's analysis, women's inferior anatomical makeup and resulting "penis envy" was used to explain deviant behavior among women. "The deviant woman is a woman who wants to be a man, and she will only end up neurotic in her fruitless search for her own penis" (Belknap 2007, 35). Included in Freud's analysis was the centrality of women's duties as wives and mothers and the need to provide deviant women with the assistance necessary to help re-socialize them to their appropriate gender roles. Arguably, such sentiments were reflected in system policies such as the establishment of the reformatory model of women's incarceration in the United States (Belknap 2007).

Taking a slightly different approach, yet working from many of the same assumptions regarding the innate character of women, Otto Pollak's (1950) very speculative work began with the premise that men and women engaged in similar levels of criminal behavior. According to Pollak, it was women's deceitful nature that allowed them to hide their crimes and only to appear to be engaging in less criminal activity. Women's deceitful nature was reflected in a variety of other behaviors, including what Pollak believed to be women's capacity to fake sexual arousal and to hide their menstruation cycles. According to Pollak, women functioned as both the masterminds and the instigators behind criminal operations; their ability to influence men to engage in crime allowed their involvement to remain undetected (Smart 1977). He believed that even if women were arrested, the chivalry often extended toward them by the criminal justice system would help "mask" the extent of their involvement in criminal activity (Belknap 2007).

The Emergence of Feminist Criminology

It was in response to much of this androcentric theorizing on the nature of women and crime that feminist discourse first distinguished itself as an alternative perspective, providing a critique of mainstream criminology that addressed both its failure to integrate more fully women's experiences and its reliance on misogynist representations of women offenders (Carrington 1998). According to Frances Heidensohn (2006, 1), it was the modern feminist movement that "offered the vocabulary and concepts to criticize and challenge mainstream academic discourse." Scholars point to several noteworthy events that mark the emergence and eventual recognition of the feminist criminological framework. Of course, Carol Smart's (1977) provocative work *Women, Crime and Criminology* represented one of the first significant critiques of "classical" criminological studies on women and crime, as well as an examination of the positivist tradition's continued impact on more contemporary studies of crime and delinquency. Interestingly, Paul Rock's (2007) recent assessment of the historically discredited theories of Lombroso notes the significant role such work played in Smart's ability to establish a feminist critique of criminology—what some have referred to as "foundation by denunciation" (Brown 1986, 360). According to Rock:

> It is certainly the case that there were few enough studies of women in and around crime and criminal justice when, in the late 1960s and 1970s, feminist criminology sought first reflexively to raise itself up as a discrete and challenging theoretical project. The works of [Cesare] Lombroso, Otto Pollak (1950), W. I. Thomas (1923) and Cowie, Cowie, and Slater (1968) seemed to stand out, and were useful, because they admirably condensed in their many ways what a nascent feminist criminology should *not* be. . . . [This] quartet of studies also conveniently encapsulated the analytical, political and ideological demons which must be slain. (2007, 124)

Another signal event was the founding of the American Society of Criminology Division on Women and Crime in 1982 (Chesney-Lind 2006; Rafter 2000). One also could point to the publication of various journals, including *Woman and Criminal Justice*, *Violence against Women*, and, most recently, *Feminist Criminology*, that focus on research related to women and girls as offenders, victims, and professionals working within the criminal justice system, as well as theory testing related to women and crime (Sharp 2006). It is important to note that such efforts to challenge the dominance of mainstream academic discourse have met with resistance (Downes and Rock 2007; Naffine 1997). According to Roger Hopkins Burke (2005, 164), however, in the face of such criticism and trivialization, the feminist project has "challenged the dominance of traditional male-centered knowledge and can be understood as a social and political force."

Distinguishing Feminist Criminology

As noted previously, a discussion of what constitutes a feminist perspective on criminology necessarily entails the need to distinguish a feminist perspective from that of traditional criminological inquiry. In an early essay examining feminist thought and its relevance to criminology, Kathleen Daly and Meda Chesney-Lind (1988, 504) put forth five elements that differentiate feminist thought from other social and political theoretical perspectives:

1. Gender is not a natural fact but a complex social, historical, and cultural product; it is related to, but not simply derived from, biological sex difference and reproductive capacities.
2. Gender and gender relations order social life and social institutions in fundamental ways.
3. Gender relations and constructs of masculinity and femininity are not symmetrical but are based on an organizing principle of men's superiority and social and political-economic dominance over women.
4. Systems of knowledge reflect men's views of the natural and social world; the production of knowledge is gendered.
5. Women should be at the center of intellectual inquiry, not peripheral, invisible, or appendages to men.

Following the publication of Smart's (1977) *Women, Crime and Criminology*, the feminist criminological project continued to challenge the "masculine preoccupation and blinkers of the discipline" (Naffine 1997, 19). The focus, however, shifted as the pioneering work of feminist scholars reframed criminological questions and methods, developing the knowledge base regarding women's and girls' experiences with crime and the criminal justice system and expanding the interdisciplinary nature of criminological inquiry. Scholars have noted how early work by feminist criminologists focused significant attention on the need to make female offenders visible in ways that did not "distort and denigrate" but still assumed as valid the methods and assumptions of conventional empirical science (Gelsthorpe and Morris 1990; Naffine 1997). Heidensohn (1987, 17; 2006, 2) provides four major areas that characterize the findings of early feminist criminologists regarding women's offending:

1. Economic rationality—refuted long-standing beliefs that female offending is specialized and sexually motivated, and found that crimes by women, like their male counterparts, often are economically motivated;
2. Heterogeneity of their offences—found great variety in women's offending;
3. Fear and impact of stigma—drew attention to the notion that criminalized women are viewed as "damaged";
4. The experience of double deviance and double jeopardy—argued that women offenders are punished not only for violating the law, but also for stepping outside their proscribed gender role; as a result, women are subject to both the formal sanctions of the criminal justice system, and the informal sanctions of family and community.

This body of research highlighted the early neglect of women in the theorizing of crime and deviance, as well as the manner by which sexist assumptions permeated criminological theory, criminal justice policy, and criminal justice practice (Daly and Chesney-Lind 1988; Downes and Rock 2007; Gelsthorpe and Morris 1990). Nearly a decade after her initial review, in 1987, Heidensohn (1996) reassessed the state of research on women and offending. She suggested that significant progress was reflected in the way that women were studied, including the broad recognition of terms and concepts such as "feminist criminology" and "gender and crime"; the notable expansion of scholarly writing and research on these issues; the considerable influence of feminist discourse on system and policy debates on such issues as domestic violence and rape; and the recognition of the intersection of race, class, age, and gender and their impact on the life experiences of women.

While it is difficult to draw a timeline signaling the linear development of a feminist perspective of criminology (for there is no one monolithic feminist enterprise and no linearity of development), scholars have identified broad shifts in the nature of inquiry regarding women and crime (Britton 2000; Burgess-Proctor 2006; Daly and Maher 1998). Arguably driving much of the change noted by Heidensohn (1996), a general shift in feminist criminological discourse was reflected in the criticisms that moved beyond the neglect or misrepresentation of women within criminological theory. Early feminist criminologists argued for the application of proper scientific methodology to the study of women, for the need to make visible the neglect of women as criminals and victims. According to Kerry Carrington (1998, 72), early critics challenged the "misogynous content, [but] rarely were these accounts critical enough of the concept of criminality or the discipline of criminology itself." Later work continued the critique, highlighting the problematic nature of empirical research and the traditional concept of objectivity. More pointedly, it recognized the limited relevance of theories developed by men and validated on male subjects for explaining women's criminal behavior (Daly and Chesney-Lind 1988; Morris 1987; Naffine 1997). Naffine (1997) provides an insightful critique of the intellectual roots of criminological research (whether from a biological, psychological, or sociological perspective) and its reliance on empirical scientific method, taking to task the notions of impartiality and objectivity and arguing that the identity of the criminologist cannot be separated from the object of study. She questions the legitimacy of the scientific study that fails mention of the "maleness" of its subjects, arguing that early assumptions of criminological inquiry set the foundation for the study of crime to be a study of men, to view men as the normative standard. She argues that as a consequence, there was "something highly skewed about the criminological enterprise from the outset" (Naffine 1997, 19).

Feminist scholars have pointed to the limitations of many mainstream criminological theories that were developed by men, validated on male subjects, and failed to reflect women's experiences. Such theories, considered "deformed by the almost unrelieved focus on the criminality of males" (Downes and Rock 2007, 264) are viewed by some as weak and invalid (Gelsthorpe and Morris 1988). What is called into question are those gender-neutral findings derived from all-male studies that are used to make general statements about the nature of crime (Britton 2000). From another perspective, to suggest that the study of women and crime is a "special" interest is to say, "in effect, that scientific criminology can still be conducted in a manner which is free from the considerations of gender, and that is it still legitimate to produce vast modern tomes which glide over the sex of the offender under investigation (as long as he is a man)" (Naffine 1997, 20). Merely inserting women into mainstream criminological theories is problematic, since even those theories purported to be gender-neutral often are not (Daly and Chesney-Lind 1988; Downes and Rock 2007; Gelsthorpe and Morris 1988; Heidensohn 1996; Naffine 1997).

Rather than dismissing them in their entirety, however, other scholars have examined closely the relevance of sociological explanations of crime (e.g., anomie, differential association, and social bonding) in explaining criminal behavior among women and girls. Darrell Steffensmeier and Emilie Allen (1996) suggest that gender-neutral theories may provide insight into the less serious forms of offending among women. Recent studies have found that constructs measuring such concepts as social control, attachment, opportunity, and strain are important to the understanding of crime, yet their influence may very well differ by gender (e.g., Alarid, Burton, and Cullen 2000; Griffin and Armstrong 2003; Leverentz 2006; Li and MacKenzie 2002; Simons et al. 2002; Uggen and Kruttschnitt 1998). Yet the concept of "add women and stir" (Chesney-Lind 1988), or the incorporation of gender as yet another variable of interest, has been criticized for its failure to theorize gender. Feminist criminologists have sought to develop gender-based theories by modifying existing criminological theories (e.g., Heidensohn 1985). The discipline also has seen continued development in the theorizing of gender and crime, particularly in the area of feminist pathways research (e.g., Arnold 1995; Belknap and Holsinger 2006; Bloom et al. 2003; Evans, Forwyth, and Gautheir 2002; Maher and Curtis 1992; Richie 1996). This body of research gives voice to girls and women as it explores the sequence of "life-course" events (both childhood and adult) that appear to have led to increased risks for offending (Belknap 2007). Yet clearly, critical distinctions are made between mainstream criminologists who may explore the role of gender within theories of crime and a feminist criminological perspective that considers the relationship between gender and crime using theories of gender, as well as theories of crime (Miller and Mullins 2006).

In addition to these concerns regarding theory construction (e.g., generalizability and gender ratio problems), feminist scholars of minority group status have raised the issue of essentialism within the feminist movement, wherein "a voice—typically a white, heterosexual, and socio-economically privileged voice—claims to speak for everyone" (Sokoloff, Price, and Flavin 2004, 12; see also Burgess-Proctor 2006; Chesney-Lind 2006; Daly and Stephens 1995; Simpson and Elis 1995). With its emphasis on the dominance model, or the notion that patriarchy shapes all facets of gender relations, many in the broader feminist movement accepted with little consideration the idea that all women suffer the effects of patriarchy in a similar manner (Burgess-Proctor 2006). This "shared experience" approach fails to engage the "multiple and cross-cutting relations of class, race-ethnicity, gender, sexuality and age . . . [that] produces a matrix of domination taking a 'both/and' form; that is, shifting and contingent relations of power" (Daly and Stephens 1995, 206–207). This tension between essentialism and the need to consider multiple experiences serves to illustrate the competing considerations of the many feminist perspectives and the need to disentangle the effects of race, gender, class, and other sites of dominance and control on crime.

Contemporary Considerations

More contemporary assessments of the challenges faced by feminist criminological perspectives suggest that feminist scholars have moved beyond such debates as those surrounding essentialism and the emancipation hypothesis "stressing instead the complexity, tentativeness, and variability with which individuals, particularly youth, negotiate (and resist) gender identity" (Chesney-Lind 2006, 8). In their discussion of the current state of feminist criminological theories, Miller and Mullins provide three distinguishing characteristics of a feminist perspective that set it apart from mainstream criminology:

1. The centrality of gender relations to the understanding of crime and criminal behavior; gender is as important to understand and theorize as crime and criminality;
2. The extent to which feminist theoretical perspective is not restricted to the examination of criminal behavior, but offers an exploration of the processing of offenders by the criminal justice system, the interaction of victims with the criminal justice system, the experiences of individuals working within criminal justice occupations;
3. Unlike most criminologists, feminist criminologists face a challenge that is twofold: engaging in research activities that explore the impact of gender and gender inequality in "real life", while at the same time deconstructing the intertwined ideologies about gender that guide social practices. (2006, 218–219)

Theorizing on the relationship between gender and crime has continued to attend to issues of intersectionality, "doing gender," and the construction of masculinities and crime (Chesney-Lind 2006; Miller 2002; Miller and Mullins 2006; Simpson and Elis 1995). For example, criminologists have continued to explore the organizational aspects of crime, tapping into the sexism and racism of the underworld that affect women's access to and opportunity to engage in criminal activity (Griffin and Rodriguez 2008; Steffensmeier 1983; Steffensmeier and Ulmer 2005). According to such research, gendered roles and assumptions regarding women's ability to effectively engage in what is often seen as "masculine" behavior (i.e., use of violence and intimidation) significantly limit women's access to criminal networks. Steffensmeier and Jeffery Ulmer (2005, 221) have argued that "sex-segregation in the underworld is perhaps the most powerful element shaping women's experiences in the illicit economy."

Other theorists have explored the notion of situated social action, or the recognition that men and women engage in gendered behavior in response to "situated normative beliefs about masculinity and femininity . . . such that the performance of gender is both an indication of and reproduction of gendered (as well as raced, classed, generational, and sexed) social hierarchies" (Miller 2002, 434; see also Messerschmidt 1993, 2002; West and Zimmerman 1987). This approach moves beyond a static conceptualization of gender as merely a role. What must be considered instead is the way in which gender is constructed through action. In this sense, crime can be described as "a resource for accomplishing gender . . . as a means to construct masculine identity among urban young men" (Miller 2002, 435). Such theorizing clearly reflects movement beyond considerations of only "women and crime" when examining the relationship between gender and crime, focusing instead on social interactions and the way in which the construction of multiple forms of masculinity and femininity intersect with offending behavior.

Miller and Mullins (2006) suggest that a "gendered lives" perspective remains a critical, although relatively undeveloped, area for continued feminist research. Such a perspective broadens the scope to examine the manner by which women experience society differently from men and how these experiences are uniquely shaped and influenced by race, class, and gender (Daly 1997). Understanding criminal offending is but one part of the analysis that seeks to identify how gender "intersects with cross-cutting structural positions and how ideologies and social practices reproduce structural inequalities" (Miller and Mullins 2006, 242).

Conclusion

Feminist criminology has undoubtedly moved beyond its initial project of "slaying the demons" that served as the foundation of early criminology. A feminist perspective, in its many forms, has brought to the study of crime the language and the theory with which to examine the experiences of women. What must be understood, of course, is that this focus on women is not to the exclusion of men. Feminist criminologists have helped construct a more nuanced and complex understanding of the relationship between gender and criminal behavior by focusing greater attention on what Dana Britton (2000, 73) has referred to as the "screaming silence in criminology": the connection between masculinity and crime. At the same time, it is essential that feminist criminologists continue to provide a critique of mainstream criminological studies that fail to take into consideration the intersection of gender and crime or do so in ways that assume the criminal to be a man and the female offender the exception.

Policy Implications of Feminist Criminological Theory

Historically, feminist scholars have highlighted the absence of women and girls in the theorizing of crime, as well as the role of violence and victimization in the lives of women and girls, and the barriers faced by women entering male dominated criminal justice occupations. These multiple research foci present a range of areas in which to view the intersection of feminist theory and policy. In general, a significant body of research has examined the way in which the social construction of gender, race, and class has affected criminal justice processing, sentencing, and treatment of both women and girls. Feminist scholars have documented the many ways in which the criminal justice response (and non-response) to women and girls as victims of neglect, sexual abuse, rape, and domestic violence has too often resulted in secondary victimization. Less prevalent, but equally important, are studies that explore the historical resistance toward women entering policing, corrections, and law, and the continuing ultra masculine culture of many criminal justice occupations that necessarily contribute to a racist and sexist work environment. For the purpose of this discussion, I have chosen to focus on the issue of prisoner reentry wherein a feminist criminological perspective adds significant insight to the construction and implementation of this criminal justice policy.

Reentry

This country's imprisonment binge has resulted in an increasing number of prisoners, men and women, reentering the community with neither the skills nor opportunities to successfully reconnect with society's institutions. According to the U.S. Bureau of Justice Statistics (2007b), the average annual probation and parole population increased by 2.2 percent each year since 1995. By the end of 2006, 5 million adult men and women were under the control of federal, state, or local probation or parole agencies. Women made up approximately 24 percent of all probationers and 12 percent of the parolees nationwide. During this same year, the number of women incarcerated in prison increased 4.5 percent, reaching a total of 112,498 (U.S. Bureau of Justice Statistics 2007a). A recent recidivism study by the Bureau of Justice Statistics (Langan and Levin 2002) found that more that half of the prisoners released in 1994 in fifteen states were returned to prison within three years for a technical violation or a new offense; approximately 40 percent of those women released were returned to prison. With such an increase in the female prison population, it is important to examine more closely this snapshot of women's incarceration. Additional insight can be found when examining a profile of female offenders, insight that, importantly, dismisses the idea that we have seen an increasingly violent group of female offenders. Barbara Bloom and her colleagues (2003) report the following:

- Drug offenses represent the major factor in the growth of the female prison population.
- The majority of offenses committed by women in prisons and jails are nonviolent drug and property crimes.
- Over half of the women in prison and jail have one or no prior offenses.
- The rate of murder by women has been declining since 1980.

- Three of four women serving time for a violent offense committed simple assault.
- Between 1986 and 1996, the number of women in state prisons for drug offenses rose by 888 percent.

In addition, the majority of incarcerated women are women of color (Richie 2001). Almost two-thirds of those women incarcerated in jail and prison are from non-white ethnic groups (Richie 2001, 369), with African American women representing the greatest increase in the percentage of inmates incarcerated for drug offenses (Bush-Baskette 1999). With the growing number of female offenders incarcerated and a significant portion returning to prison, correctional administrators have to dedicate increasing resources and time to the management of a population that had once seemed relatively invisible.

The concern and interest of policymakers, practitioners, and academics in the critical yet long neglected problem of prisoner reentry is reflected in the incorporation of prerelease reentry strategies within prisons, the substantial federal monies awarded to states and faith-based organizations to develop effective reentry programs, and the increasing number of scholarly publications focusing specifically on prisoner reentry. Much like the general body of mainstream criminological research, however, initial considerations of the problems and particular circumstances encountered by offenders reentering the community has focused primarily on men. The significance of gender has been largely neglected when designing intervention strategies (Bloom, Owen, and Covington 2003; Covington and Bloom 2003; National Institute of Justice 2005; Richie 2001). It is interesting to note that in one of the first comprehensive reviews of the reintegration challenges faced by prisoners reentering the community, only once are women referred to specifically, and this was in reference to the impact of incarceration on family stabilization and childhood development (Petersilia 2001).

Significant strides have been made in terms of identifying the gendered life experiences and needs of female offenders and the obstacles they face upon release from prison and jail. Studies of female offenders, especially those that make use of a feminist pathways and gendered lives perspectives, consistently indicate that the life experiences of women differ significantly from those of men in terms of personal histories, life experiences, and the resulting pathways to crime (Belknap 2007; Bloom et al. 2003; Browne, Miller, and Maguin 1999). When taken as a whole, specific themes emerge suggesting that histories of physical and sexual victimization, drug use and abuse, mental illness, economic and social marginality, educational and vocational deficiencies, homelessness, relationships with criminally involved partners, and primary child-care responsibilities are "key issues in producing and sustaining female criminality" (Bloom et al. 2003, 53; see also Arnold 1990; Belknap 2007; Chesney-Lind 1997; Owen

1998; Richie 1996, 2001). The failure to address these multiple needs and deficits of female offenders while incarcerated merely reproduces and reinforces the difficulties offenders will face once they have been released.

Not surprisingly, many of the barriers women face when they leave prison are related to their status as women and the way in which gender shapes women's lives—that is, the way in which gendered notions are infused into the basic expectations regarding appropriate behavior for women reentering their pre-incarceration lives (Bloom et al. 2003; Richie 2001). In addition, feminist scholars point to the way in which "gender, ethnic identity, and economic status converge to make the situation incarcerated women face very complicated. . . . [A]s such, the challenges that influence successful reintegration are decidedly gendered, and cultural issues play a significant role in successful engagement and program retention" (Richie 2001, 382). Research on the barriers female prisoners face as they reenter the community suggest that the social stigma women face once released from prison is, unlike for men, related to their violation of gender norms as well as their violation of the law. Studies suggest that this stigma, or viewing women as double deviants, has an impact on reentry on many fronts and can contribute to a "lack of social support, ambiguous relationships, and undermine already compromised mother–child relationships following reentry" (Andritti and Few 2006, 105; see also Dodge and Pogrebin 2001; Richie 2001). A recent study found that, compared with their male counterparts, incarcerated women face worse economic conditions upon release (Mumola 2000). In terms of employment, female offenders reentering their communities face significant obstacles. Compared with men, women tend to be less prepared to acquire a job once released, largely because women were less likely than men to have been employed full time prior to incarceration or to have received vocational training prior to or during incarceration (Belknap 2007; Bloom et al. 2003). Women in prison also report significant levels of mental health disorders. Twenty-five percent of those women housed in state prisons have been identified as having a mental illness, including depression, post-traumatic stress disorder, and substance abuse (Bloom et al. 2003; see also Sacks 2004). This intersection of deficits on multiple fronts poses significant obstacles to women's reentry efforts.

The one area that has received a great deal of attention is the process of reunification with children and the stabilization of the family. Too often, female offenders with children are publicly viewed as "bad" mothers. When the guilt associated with their absence from their children's lives is internalized by these women, it adds to the stress associated with the challenges of reintegration (Dodge and Pogrebin 2001). In addition, Beth Richie (2001) concluded from her interviews with women shortly after they were released from prison that they often voiced a sense of rejection from their communities, as if they were the least entitled to the scarce programs and services available within the community. Indeed, the lack of community support exacerbates the multiple strains faced by women reentering the community in that many of these women are mothers who are challenged to meet not only their own personal needs but also the needs of their children (Andritti and Few 2006; Bloom et al. 2003; Brown, Melchoir, and Huba 1999). While the issue of reunification with children is but one of the many challenges confronted by women returning to their communities from prison, it is an issue that delineates the marked differences between the life experiences of women and men. According to Bloom and colleagues (2003), almost three-quarters of all women under correctional supervision have at least one child younger than eighteen, and more than half of the women in prison with children are never visited by their children during their period of incarceration. Moreover, whereas only 25 percent of children with incarcerated mothers live with their fathers, fully 90 percent of children with incarcerated fathers reside with their mother. This difference between women's and men's child custody situation during imprisonment significantly affects single mothers seeking to reestablish custody of their children. Child welfare policies tend to disadvantage those women who, while in prison, have few options for care for their dependent children (Bloom and Steinhard, 1993; Fletcher, Shaver, and Moon 1993; Pollock 2002; Raeder 2003).

Placing reentry efforts within the broader agenda to provide a new vision for a gender-responsive criminal justice system, Bloom and colleagues (2003, vii) suggest several "guiding principles" for a system that will recognize the "behavioral and social differences between female and male offenders that have specific implications for gender-responsive policy and practice":

- An effective system for female offenders that is structured differently from a system for male offenders.
- Policy and practice that target women's pathways to criminality by providing effective interventions that address the intersecting issues of substance abuse, trauma, mental health, and economic marginality.
- Criminal justice sanctions and interventions that recognize the low risk to public safety created by the typical offenses committed by female offenders.
- When delivering both sanctions and interventions, the need for policies that consider women's relationships, especially those with children, and women's roles in the community.

Clearly, reentry initiatives and strategies for female offenders, whether implemented in prison or upon release, cannot be designed as if the male offender is the norm and then fitted without modification to women. Such policies and programs must take into consideration documented differences between men and women, and differences among women, in terms of life experiences and their impact on treatment, service, and supervision needs. In addition, we must continue to revisit and speak critically of those punitive and destructive drug and sentencing policies that have led to increasing rates of incarceration, especially among women.

References

Alarid, L., V. Burton, and F. Cullen. 2000. Gender and crime among felony offenders. Assessing the generality of social control and differential association theories. *Journal of Research in Crime and Delinquency* 37:171–199.

Andritti, J., and A. Few. 2006. Mothers' reentry into family life following incarceration. *Criminal Justice Policy Review* 17:103–123.

Arnold, R. 1990. Women of color: Process of victimization and criminalization of black women. *Social Justice* 17:153–166.

———. 1995. Processes of criminalization: From girlhood to womanhood. In *Women of color in American society*. Ed. M. B. Zinn and B. T. Dill, 136–146. Philadelphia: Temple University Press.

Belknap, J. 2001. *The invisible woman: Gender, crime, and justice.* Belmont, Calif.: Wadsworth.

———. 2007. *The invisible woman: Gender, crime, and justice.* 3rd ed. Belmont, Calif.: Thomson Wadsworth.

Belknap, J., and K. Holsinger. 2006. The gendered nature of risk factors for delinquency. *Feminist Criminology* 1:48–71.

Bloom, B. 2003. *Gendered justice.* Durham, N.C.: Carolina Academic Press.

Bloom, B., B. Owen, and S. Covington. 2003. *Gender-responsive strategies: Research, practice, and guiding principles for women offenders.* Washington, D.C.: National Institute of Corrections, U.S. Department of Justice.

Bloom, B., B. Owen, J. Rosenbaum, and E. P. Deschenes. 2003. Focusing on girls and young women: A gendered perspective on female delinquency. *Women and Criminal Justice* 14:117–136.

Bloom, B., and D. Steinhard. 1993. *Why punish the children? A reappraisal of the children of incarcerated mothers in America.* San Francisco: National Council on Crime and Delinquency.

Britton, D. 2000. Feminism in criminology: Engendering the outlaw. *Annals of the American Academy of Political and Social Science* 571:57–76.

Brown, B. 1986. Women and crime: The dark figures of criminology. *Economy and Society* 15:355–402.

Brown, V., L. Melchoir, and G. Huba. 1999. Level of burden among women diagnosed with severe mental illness and substance abuse. *Journal of Psychoactive Drugs* 31:31–40.

Browne, A., B. Miller, and E. Maguin. 1999. Prevalence and severity of lifetime physical and sexual victimization among incarcerated women. *International Journal of Law and Psychiatry* 22:301–322.

Burgess-Proctor, A. 2006. Intersections of race, class, gender, and crime: Future directions for feminist criminology. *Feminist Criminology* 1:27–47.

Burke, R. H. 2005. *An introduction to criminological theory.* 2nd ed. Cullompton, U.K.: Willan Publishing.

Bush-Baskette, S. 1999. The "war on drugs" a war against women? In *Harsh punishment: International experiences of women's imprisonment*. Ed. S. Cook and S. Davies. 211–229. Boston: Northeastern University Press.

Carrington, K. 1998. Postmodernism and feminist criminologies: Disconnecting discourses. In *Criminology at the crossroads: Feminist readings in crime and justice*. Ed. K. Daly and L. Maher, 69–84. New York: Oxford University Press.

Chesney-Lind, M. 1988. Doing feminist criminology. *The Criminologist* 13:16–17.

———. 1997. *The female offender: Girls, women and crime*. Thousand Oaks, Calif.: Sage Publications.

———. 2006. Patriarchy, crime, and justice: Feminist criminology in an era of backlash. *Feminist Criminology* 1:6–26.

Covington, S., and B. Bloom. 2003. Gendered justice: Women in the criminal justice system. In *Gendered justice: Addressing female offenders*. Ed. B. Bloom, 3–23. Durham, N.C.: Carolina Academic Press.

Cowie, J., V. Cowie, and E. Slater. 1968. *Delinquency in girls*. London: Heinemann.

Daly, K. 1997. Different ways of conceptualizing sex/gender in feminist theory and their implications for criminology. *Theoretical Criminology* 1:25–51.

Daly, K., and M. Chesney-Lind. 1988. Feminism and criminology. *Justice Quarterly* 5: 497–535.

Daly, K., and L. Maher. 1998. Crossroads and intersections: Building from feminist critique. In *Criminology at the crossroads: Feminist readings in crime and justice*. Ed. K. Daly and L. Maher, 1–17. New York: Oxford University Press.

Daly, K., and D. Stephens. 1995. The "dark figure" of criminology: Towards a black and multi-ethnic feminist agenda for theory and research. In *International feminist perspectives in criminology: Engendering a discipline*. Ed. N. Hahn Rafter and F. Heidensohn, 189–215. Philadelphia: Open University Press.

Dodge, M., and M. Pogrebin. 2001. Collateral costs of imprisonment for women. *Prison Journal* 81:42–54.

Downes, D., and P. Rock. 2007. *Understanding deviance: A guide to the sociology of crime and rule-breaking*. 5th ed. New York: Oxford University Press.

Evans, R. D., C. J. Forwyth, and D. K. Gautheir . 2002. Gendered pathways into and experiences within crack cultures outside of the inner city. *Deviant Behavior* 23:483–510.

Fletcher, B., L. Shaver, and D. Moon. 1993. *Women prisoners: A forgotten population*. Westport, Conn.: Praeger.

Freud, S. 1933. *New introductory lectures on psychoanalysis*. New York: W. W. Norton.

Gelsthorpe, L., and A. Morris. 1988. Feminism and criminology in Britain. *British Journal of Criminology*, 221–240.

———. 1990. *Feminist perspectives in criminology*. Buckingham: Open University Press.

Griffin, M., and G. Armstrong. 2003. The effect of local life circumstances on female probationers' offending. *Justice Quarterly* 20:213–239.

Griffin, M., and N. Rodriguez. 2008. The gendered nature of drug acquisition behavior within marijuana and crack drug markets. *Crime and Delinquency*: n.p. [Published online]

Heidensohn, F. 1985. *Women and crime*. New York: Macmillan.

———. 1987. Questions for criminology. In *Gender, crime and justice*. Ed. P. Carlen and A. Worrall. Milton Keynes: Open University Press.

———. 1996. *Women and crime*. 2nd ed. Basingstoke: Macmillan.

———. 2006. New perspectives and established views. In *Gender and justice: New concepts and approaches*. Ed. F. Heidensohn, 1–10. Portland, Ore.: William Publishing.

Klein, D. 1980. The etiology of female crime: A review of the literature. In *Women, crime, and justice*. Ed. S. Datesman and F. Scarpitti, 70–105. New York: Oxford University Press.

Langan, P. A., and D. J. Levin. 2002. *Recidivism of prisoners released in 1994*. Washington, D.C.: U.S. Department of Justice.

Leonard, E. 1982. *A critique of criminology theory: Women, crime and society*. New York: Longman.

Leverentz, A. 2006. The love of a good man? Romantic relationships as a source of support or hindrance for female ex-offenders. *Journal of Research in Crime and Delinquency* 43:459–488.

Li, S., and D. MacKenzie. 2002. The impact of formal and informal social controls on the criminal activities of probationers. *Journal of Research in Crime and Delinquency* 39: 243–276.

Lombroso, C., and W. Ferrero. 1895. *The female offender*. London: Fisher Unwin.

——. 2004. *Criminal woman, the prostitute, and the normal woman*. Trans. N. Hahn Rafter and M. Gibson. Durham, N.C.: Duke University Press.

Maher, L., and R. Curtis. 1992. Women on the edge: Crack cocaine and the changing contexts of street-level sex work in New York City. *Crime, Law and Social Change* 18: 221–258.

Messerschmidt, J. 1993. *Masculinities and crime*. Lanham, Md.: Rowman and Littlefield.

——. 2002. On gang girls, gender and a structured action theory: A reply to Miller. *Theoretical Criminology* 4:461–475.

Miller, J. 2002. The strengths and limits of "doing gender" for understanding street crime. *Theoretical Criminology* 6:433–460

Miller, J., and C. Mullins. 2006. The status of feminist theories in criminology. In *Taking stock: The status of criminological theory*. Ed. F. Cullen, J. Wright, and K. Blevins, 217–249. New Brunswick, N.J.: Transaction Publishers.

Morris, A. 1987. *Women, crime, and criminal justice*. New York: Blackwell.

Mumola, C. 2000. Incarcerated parents and their children. Bureau of Justice Statistics Special Report. U.S. Department of Justice, Washington, D.C.

Naffine, N. 1997. *Feminism and criminology*. Oxford. Polity Press.

National Institute of Justice. 2005. Reentry programs for women inmates. *National Institute of Justice Journal* 252 (July). Available online at http://www.ojp.usdoj.gov/nij/journals/252/reentry.html (accessed December 2007).

Owen, B. 1998. *In the mix: Struggle and survival in a woman's prison*. Albany: State University of New York Press.

Petersilia, J. 2001. Prisoner reentry: Public safety and reintegration challenges. *Prison Journal* 81:360–375.

Pollak, O. 1950. The criminality of women. Philadelphia: University of Pennsylvania Press.

Pollock, J. 2002. Parenting programs in women's prison. *Women and Criminal Justice* 14: 131–154.

Raeder, M. 2003. Gendered implications of sentencing and correctional practices. In *Gendered justice*. Ed. B. Bloom, 173–208. Durham, N.C.: Carolina Academic Press.

Rafter, N. H. (Ed.). 2000. *Encyclopedia of women and crime*. Phoenix: Oryx Press.

Richie, B. 1996. *Compelled to crime: The gender entrapment of black battered women*. New York: Routledge.

——. 2001. Challenges incarcerated women face as they return to their communities: Findings from life history interviews. *Crime and Delinquency* 47:368–389.

Rock, P. 2007. Caesare Lombroso as a signal criminologist. *Criminology and Criminal Justice* 7:117–133.

Sacks, J. 2004. Women with co-occurring substance use and mental disorders (COD) in the criminal justice system: A research review. *Behavioral Sciences and the Law* 22 (4): 449–466.

Simons, R., E. Stewart, L. Gordon, G. Conger, and G. Elder. 2002. A test of life-course explanations for stability and change in antisocial behavior from adolescence to young adulthood. *Criminology* 40:401–434.

Sharp, S. 2006. Editorial. *Feminist Criminology* 1:3–4.

Simpson, S., and L. Elis. 1995. Doing gender: Sorting out the caste and crime conundrum. *Criminology* 33:47–81.

Smart, C. 1977. *Women, crime and criminology*. London: Routledge and Kegan Paul.

Sokoloff, N., B. Price, and J. Flavin. 2004. The criminal law and women. In *The criminal justice system and women*. 3rd ed. Ed. B. R. Price and N. Sokoloff, 11–29. New York: McGraw-Hill.

Steffensmeier, D. 1983. Organization properties and sex-segregation in the underworld: Building a sociological theory of sex differences in crime. *Social Forces* 61:1010–1032.

Steffensmeier, D., and E. Allan. 1996. Gender and crime: Toward a gendered theory of female offending. *Annual Review of Sociology* 22:459–487.

Steffensmeier, D., and J. Ulmer. 2005. *Confessions of a dying thief: Understanding criminal careers and illegal enterprise*. New Brunswick, N.J.: AldineTransaction.

Thomas, W. I. 1907. *Sex and society*. Boston: Little, Brown.

———. 1923. *The unadjusted girl*. Boston: Little, Brown.

Uggen, C., and C. Kruttschnitt. 1998. Crime in the breaking: Gender differences in desistance. *Law and Society Review* 32:339–366.

U.S. Bureau of Justice Statistics. 2007a. *Prisoners in 2006*. Washington, D.C.: U.S. Department of Justice. Available online at http://www.ojp.usdoj.gov/bjs/abstract/p06.htm (accessed December 2007).

———. 2007b. *Probation and parole statistics: Summary findings*. Washington, D.C.: U.S. Department of Justice. Available online at http://www.ojp.usdoj.gov/bjs/pandp.htm (accessed December 2007).

West, C., and D. H. Zimmerman. 1987. Doing gender. *Gender and Society* 1:125–151.

KATHARINE TELLIS,
NANCY RODRIGUEZ, AND CASSIA SPOHN

13

Critical Race Perspectives

Explaining the Differential Treatment of Racial Minorities by the Criminal Justice System

In 2004, the United States celebrated the fiftieth anniversary of *Brown v. Board of Education,* the landmark Supreme Court case that ordered the desegregation of public schools. Also in 2004, the Sentencing Project issued a report entitled "Schools and Prisons: Fifty Years after *Brown v. Board of Education*" (Sentencing Project 2004). The report noted that, whereas many institutions in society had become more diverse and more responsive to the needs of people of color in the wake of the *Brown* decision, the American criminal justice system had taken "a giant step backward" (5). To illustrate this, the report pointed out that in 2004 there were *nine times* as many African Americans in prison or jail as on the day the *Brown* decision was handed down—the number had increased from 98,000 to 884,500. The report also noted that one of every three African American men and one of every 18 African American women born today could expect to be imprisoned at some point in his or her lifetime. The authors of the report concluded that "such an outcome should be shocking to all Americans" (5).

Differential treatment of racial minorities by the American criminal justice system is not confined to sentencing and corrections. Racial minorities are arrested, stopped and questioned, and shot and killed by the police out of all proportion to their representation in the population. Racial minorities, and particularly those suspected of crimes against whites, also are the victims of unequal justice in the courts. Although reforms mandated by the Supreme Court or adopted voluntarily by the states have eliminated much of the blatant racism directed against racial minorities who find themselves in the arms of the law, the race of the defendant continues to affect decisions regarding bail, charging, plea bargaining, and sentencing. The differences are particularly stark with respect to the death penalty. Study after study has demonstrated that those who murder whites are much more likely to be sentenced to death than those who murder African Americans; many of these studies also have shown that African Americans convicted of murdering whites receive the death penalty more often than whites who murder whites.

Criminologists and legal scholars use several complementary theoretical perspectives to explain differential treatment of whites and racial minorities. Critical race theorists (Crenshaw et al. 1995; Delgado and Stefancic 2001) contend that racism (and sexism) are ubiquitous and deeply embedded in laws and criminal justice policies and that the criminal justice system is an institution that reinforces hierarchies in society based on race, class, gender, and other socio-demographic characteristics. Similarly, conflict theorists argue that the administration of criminal justice reflects the unequal distribution of power in society and contend that the more powerful groups (i.e., whites) use the criminal justice system to maintain their dominant position and to repress groups or social movements that threaten it. Other theoretical perspectives focus on the role that race-linked stereotypes or attributions of dangerousness and threat play in criminal justice decision making.

The purpose of this chapter is to provide an overview of three theoretical perspectives that attempt to account for the differential treatment of people of color in the criminal justice system. It begins with a discussion of critical race theory, followed by conflict theory and attribution theory. It concludes with a discussion of the relevance of these theories to public policy.

Critical Race Theory

Historical Development

Critical race theory emerged within the legal academy of the United States in the 1980s as an offshoot of critical legal studies, its predecessor of the 1970s. Critical legal studies spawned from a subsection of predominantly white, male, and left-wing legal scholars who challenged the neutrality and objectivity of American legal liberalism (Crenshaw 2002a, 2002b). Their skepticism was based on consideration of how history informs the current social reality; specifically, scholars within this tradition claim that the law is neither neutral nor objective when it oppresses the poor, women, and people of color, whether directly in terms of content or indirectly through its consequences (Valdes, Culp, and Harris 2002). A series of conferences dedicated to developing critical legal studies was held in the early 1980s. In 1985, scholars from the feminist wing of the critical legal studies movement articulated concern that, despite any reformist intentions, a meaningful analysis of race was missing from the critical legal studies framework, which viewed the law and its consequences through an elite, white, male lens (Crenshaw 2002a, 2002b). These concerns, in conjunction with the influential career and scholarship of Derrick Bell (1992), led to the development of critical race theory in the late 1980s (Valdes, Culp, and Harris 2002).

Critical race theory contends that the substance and procedures of American law, including antidiscrimination law, are structured to maintain white privilege (Valdes, Culp, and Harris 2002; see also McIntosh 2007). Further, it argues that neutrality and objectivity are not only unattainable ideals, but they are harmful fictions that obscure the normative supremacy of whiteness in American law and society (Valdes, Culp, and Harris 2002, 1). The following section examines the assumptions that underlie critical race theory and uses the theory to examine the issue of race and the criminal justice system.

Principal Assumptions of Critical Race Theory

Critical race theory begins with the rejection of three mainstream beliefs about racial injustice: (1) "blindness" to race will eliminate racism; (2) racism results from the behavior of individuals and is not systemic or institutional; and (3) one can fight racism without paying attention to sexism, heterosexism, economic exploitation, and other forms of oppression or injustice (Valdes, Culp, and Harris 2002). The first belief refers to the deeply entrenched individualism that influenced the development of the United States and the concomitant denial of group-based identities (Bell 1992). Critical race theorists reject the notion that ignoring race will eliminate racism. They maintain that racial identities have psychological benefits at the individual level in terms of pride and self-esteem and political benefits at the structural level in terms of influencing policy decisions (Crenshaw 2002a, 2002b). The second belief refers to the tendency of the courts to interpret antidiscrimination law by attempting to ascertain individual offenders and victims, as opposed to seeing racism and its everyday operation in the very structures within which the guilty and innocent are identified (Valdes, Culp, and Harris 2002, 3). The third belief, consistent with the assertions of critical race feminists, centers on the conception of race as socially constructed and emphasizes that race, class, and gender are interconnected. As a result, the particular configuration of these factors is critical to understanding a person's or group's experiences (Anderson and Collins 2007; see also Collins 2000). This intersectional perspective (see also Combahee River Collective 2001 [1972]; Crenshaw 1992), referred to as the "Matrix of Domination" by Patricia Hill Collins (2000), emphasizes that racial stratification is ordinary, ubiquitous, and reproduced in both mundane and extraordinary customs and experience (Brown 2003). In short, critical race theory assumes that race is a socially constructed and historically embedded phenomenon and that race is entrenched in U.S. laws and policies.

The following section considers the historical examples of sexual violence against slave women and the use of the death penalty against black men to examine the criminal justice system through a critical race perspective.

Slavery in the United States:
Examining the Intersection of Race and Gender

Although the transatlantic slave trade began in the fifteenth century, the origins of chattel slavery—the process by which human beings of African descent were smuggled as property to be bought and sold—emerged in British colonies such as Bermuda in 1612 and in Jamestown, Virginia, in 1619 (Lerner 1972; Stevenson 1995). Whites in Virginia attempted to impose their authority on every aspect of slaves' lives, including the family, to subjugate and control their human chattel (Stevenson 1995, 39). For example, Virginia passed a law in 1662 requiring that a child born to a slave woman must take on the legal status of its mother (Stevenson 1995). Throughout the South, state legislatures followed suit, adopting *partus sequitur ventrem* statutes that served two purposes: first, to increase the slave population; and, second, to prevent any confusion as to citizenship status if a white man were to father a slave's child.

The process of dehumanization through objectification was advanced through laws that prohibited slaves from legally marrying, owning property, attending school, and testifying against whites in a courtroom and through forced segregation (Kennedy 1997). Importantly, traditional notions of gender as dictated by white patriarchal culture did not apply to male and female slaves as workers, as the primary focus was on economic exploitation of their labor (Collins 2004; Crenshaw 1992). Angela Davis (1981) argues that African American women were not perceived as women in the accepted (read, white) sense and that the slave system discouraged male supremacy among African Americans to affirm that fathers, mothers, and children were all equally subject to the slave master's power. Practically, this meant that slave women could not be treated as "weaker" and slave men could not be treated as "providers," as all worked alongside one another in the fields, including pregnant women (Collins 2004; Crenshaw 1992; Lerner 1972). Although in border states most slaves were house servants, the "slaveocracy" (Davis 1981) of the Deep South used Africans of both genders primarily for agricultural work. In characterizing the respective roles of female and male slaves, Davis comments:

> Work under threat of the whip in one sense undifferentiated their oppressions, yet sexual abuse was an issue unique to women. . . . Expediency characterized their [white slaveowners'] posture towards female slaves. When it was profitable to exploit them [laboriously] as men they

did so, essentially making them genderless, but when deemed necessary to exploit them in ways suited only for women they were locked into exclusively female roles. (6)

In other words, male slaves dealt with whippings, beatings, floggings, mutilation, torture, and other forms of violent exploitation based solely on color, but the punishment inflicted on slave women exceeded in intensity the punishment suffered by the men, for women were not only whipped and mutilated but also raped (Collins 2000, 2004; hooks 1984; Kennedy 1997; Lerner 1972; Roberts 1997).

Randall Kennedy (1997) argues that the failure to protect female slaves from rape in antebellum America was formalized and deliberate, as illustrated in *George (a Slave) v. the State* (1859), a case that went through the High Court of Errors and Appeals in Mississippi.[1] In *George v. the State,* a male slave was convicted and sentenced to death for having had "carnal knowledge of a female slave under the age of ten." However, his conviction was overturned on appeal under the premise that because slaves had no rights under the common law, it was up to the legislature to decide what rights they might or might not have. Consequently, since no statutes specifically protected slave girls or women from rape, no law was violated by inflicting sexual violence on them (Kennedy 1997, 35).

In response to the *George* case, the Mississippi legislature passed a statute that offered at least some protection for a subsection of the female slave population (Kennedy 1997). It stated that the actual or attempted commission of a rape "by a negro or mulatto on a female negro or mulatto," *under twelve years of age,* is punishable with death or whipping, as the jury may decide.[2] Omitted from this legal conceptualization of victimhood are female slaves over the age of twelve and white male offenders. The fact that these omissions are not explicitly articulated in the statute illustrates the institutionalized nature of white male supremacy. This is further evident in their codified—albeit invisibly—impunity in regard to forced sexual access to women and in the power involved in defining both the victim and the offender. In other words, the criminal justice system served as a social control mechanism through which to maintain white hegemony through its enforcement of laws that disproportionately left African American women unprotected from sexual violence while simultaneously serving the economic needs particular to slavery (Crenshaw 2002a; Kennedy 1997). Consistent with the principles of critical race theory, the laws, which operated to preserve white supremacy, were neither racially neutral nor objective.

---

[1] 37 Miss. Rep. 316, 318 (1859).

[2] 37 Miss. Rep. 320; emphasis added.

The history of lynching provides another example of how race and gender affected the experience of African Americans in the United States (Corzine, Creech, and Corzine 1983; Jacobs, Carmichael, and Kent 2005; Tolnay and Beck 1994). Historical analyses illustrate that during the period of Reconstruction after the Civil War, black men were particularly susceptible to this form of violence at the hands of white mobs (e.g., Kennedy 1997; Walker, Spohn, and DeLone 2007). Kennedy (1997, 45–46) notes that the lynching of black men was justified on several grounds. First, some contended that certain crimes were so heinous—for example, the rape of a white woman by a black man—that they demanded a punishment more swift and sure than the legal process could offer. Others, however, focused on the special threat posed by blacks. One theory suggested that blacks underwent a civilizing process through enslavement that tragically ended with emancipation. In other words, this theoretical perspective suggested that blacks who were freed from the discipline of enslavement would revert to their primitive and brutish ways. Other explanations view lynching and mob violence as part of a more comprehensive attempt by whites to maintain their social, economic, and political dominance. Whites, in other words, lynched blacks "in order to neutralize their threat to the political hegemony enjoyed by southern whites" (Tolnay and Beck 1994, 176).

The juxtaposition of the previously discussed leniency toward white men who raped black women is striking when one considers the public outrage engendered by an accusation of rape by a black man of a white woman. The belief was that black men lusted after white women with such powerful longing that ordinary means of control were insufficient (Kennedy 1997, 45). The assumption that sexual interaction between black men and white women was by default an act of rape illustrates the institutionalized nature of white male supremacy—that is, justifying violence via the goal of protecting white women from black men who were characterized as uncivilized savages. Importantly, this historical context retains significance in the political consciousness of African Americans in the present, particularly with regard to how crimes are processed in the criminal justice system (Kennedy 1997). For example, as Samuel Walker and his colleagues (2007, 299) point out in their discussion of differential treatment of interracial and intraracial sexual assault, 405 of the 453 men executed for rape in the United States from 1930 to 1972 (the death penalty for rape was ruled unconstitutional in 1977) were African American men convicted of raping white women. Research conducted in the past two decades demonstrates that this is not simply an historical fact. Although the results are not entirely consistent, studies continue to find that African American men accused of raping white women are treated more harshly than any other race-of-victim–race-of-offender combination (LaFree 1989).

In summary, critical race theory begins with the premise that race is completely embedded in U.S. laws and policies, which consequentially maintain a structural privilege for whites (white men in particular) to the detriment of people of color. Proponents of critical race theory attribute the paradoxical invisibility of race to the deep-seated individualism that underlies the legal liberalism and culture of the United States, which emphasizes issues of objectivity, neutrality, and color-blindness to promote civil justice. The answer, according to critical race theorists, is to incorporate a commitment to social justice not only in academic discussions but also in the formation of public policy to remedy the detrimental effects of institutionalized discrimination. By examining the policies and practices of the criminal justice system during slavery and beyond, critical race theory accounts for the failure to protect African American women from rape by white slave owners and for the overzealous prosecution of African American men labeled via unsubstantiated accusations of raping white women.

Conflict Theory

Like critical race theory, conflict theory emphasizes the salience of race and class in explanations of social control. In contrast to consensus theory, which views society as consisting of groups with common interests and the state as a means of protecting those interests, conflict theory posits that society is made up of groups with competing norms and values and contends that the authority of the state is used to protect the interests of those in power. Central to conflict theory is the premise that the law is applied to maintain the power of the dominant group to control the behavior of those who threaten that power; the law is applied, in other words, to protect the position and interests of elites from challenges by the powerless, especially racial minorities and the poor (Chambliss and Seidman 1971; Quinney 1970; Turk 1969). Related to this is the notion that the amount of social control imposed by those in power will depend on the degree to which they view the actions of individuals and groups challenging their power as a legitimate threat. As Richard Quinney (1970, 18) noted, "The probability that criminal definitions will be applied varies according to the extent to which the behaviors of the powerless conflict with the interests of the power segments."

The notion of "threat" is central to conflict theory, but the assessment of who or what is threatening varies. Original versions of the theory, reflecting its Marxist origins, emphasized the significance of social class and the importance of economic stratification. Quinney (1974), for example, argued that the dominant economic class used the legal system to protect its economic interests and to control the behavior of lower-class groups that otherwise would threaten the power and position of the economic elite. William Chambliss and Robert Seidman (1971) similarly proposed that legal sanctions are more likely to be imposed on offenders from lower social classes and suggested that the most severe sanctions will be imposed on people in the lowest social class. They also noted that the larger the gap in economic resources between dominant and subordinate groups, the greater the power exerted by the dominant group over subordinate groups. Thus, "the more economically stratified a society becomes, the more it becomes necessary for dominant groups to enforce through coercion the norms of conduct that guarantee supremacy" (Chambliss and Seidman 1982, 33).

Other theorists, while not discounting the importance of class, emphasize that those who threaten the status quo are likely to be members of what is variously referred to as the "surplus population" (Quinney 1977), the "rabble class" (Irwin 1985), or the "problem population" (Spitzer 1975). Conflict theorists also assert that these threatening groups are likely to be composed primarily of racial minorities (especially blacks), the unemployed, the poor, and the young (Box and Hale 1985; Liska and Chamlin 1984). For example, George Bridges and Robert Crutchfield (1988) indicate that criminal stereotypes of offenders as young black men result in more severe punishment for minorities and disadvantaged offenders. Echoing Quinney's (1977, 131) assertion that the criminal justice system "is the modern means of controlling surplus population," they emphasize that members of these groups "are more likely to be subjected to intensified social control—more criminalization, more formal processing by the criminal justice system, and increased incarceration" (Sampson and Laub 1993, 288).

Critical race theorists, and contemporary conflict theorists, contend that although offenders with various combinations of characteristics make up social dynamite, it is the combination of *race* and other characteristics linked to threat that is "its most explosive component" (Chiricos and Bales 1991, 719). Race, in other words, is the critical factor; it affects criminal justice decision making unilaterally *and* in combination with other factors. Studies of sentencing decisions provide compelling evidence in support of this. Darrell Steffensmeier and his colleagues (1998), for example, found that race, gender, and age had a significant direct effect on both the likelihood of incarceration and the length of the sentence. More important, they found that the three factors interacted to produce substantially harsher sentences for one category of offenders—young, black men—than for any other combination of age, race, and gender. Cassia Spohn and David Holleran (2000) similarly found that the offenders most likely to be sentenced to prison were young black and Hispanic men; their research also revealed that unemployed black and Hispanic men were more likely than employed white men to be incarcerated. The results of these studies highlight "the high cost of being black, young, and male" (Steffensmeier, Ulmer, and Kramer 1998, 789), as well as the fact that "offenders with other constellations of characteristics also pay a punishment penalty" (Spohn and Holleran 2000, 304).

Accounting for Anomalies or Inconsistencies

Although there is substantial evidence in support of conflict theory's premise that racial minorities—especially blacks—will be subjected to more formal social control than whites, there also is evidence that racial minorities either are treated no differently from whites or are treated more leniently than whites (for reviews, see Hawkins 1987; Spohn 2000; Zatz 1987). Darnell Hawkins (1987, 721) argues that many of these so-called anomalies or inconsistencies in research on racial bias in the administration of justice reflect "oversimplification" of conflict theory. This is reflected in the fact that many researchers simply test the hypothesis that racial minorities will be treated more harshly than whites, assuming, either explicitly or implicitly, that this will be so regardless of the nature of the crime, the race of the victim, or the relationship between the victim and the offender.

Hawkins (1987, 724) contends that the work of early conflict theorists such as Quinney (1970) and Chambliss and Seidman (1971) does not support the proposition that "blacks or other nonwhites will receive more severe punishment than whites for all crimes, under all conditions, and at similar levels of disproportion over time." Rather, conflict theorists argue that "the probability that criminal sanctions will be applied varies according to the extent to which the behaviors of the powerless conflict with the interests of the power segments" (Quinney 1970, 18). Crimes that threaten the power of the dominant class will therefore produce harsher penalties for blacks who commit those crimes, and crimes that pose relatively little threat to the system of white authority will not necessarily result in harsher sanctions for blacks.

According to this view, blacks who murder, rape, or rob whites will be treated more harshly than blacks who victimize members of their own race. As Ruth Peterson and John Hagan (1984, 54) note, "When black offenders assault or kill black victims, the devalued status of the black victims and the paternalistic attitudes of white authorities can justify lenient treatment. . . . When blacks violate white victims, the high sexual property value attached to the white victims and the racial fears of authorities can justify severe treatment." Gary LaFree makes a similar argument, maintaining that conflict theory is not disproved "if research demonstrates that sanctions are not particularly harsh when relatively powerless persons in society murder and rape each other" (1989, 48).

Conflict Theory and the Concept of Racial Threat

The amount of threat posed by racial minorities also has been linked to macro-level factors. A number of scholars contend that the degree to which the crime control apparatus of the state is used to protect the interests of wealthy and powerful citizens depends in part on the degree of threat that racial minorities *as a group* pose, which in turn depends on such things as the size, visibility, resources, and mobilization of the minority population (Blalock 1967; D'Alessio, Eitle, and Stolzenberg 2005; Eitle, D'Alessio, and Stolzenberg 2002; Stolzenberg, D'Alessio, and Eitle 2004). As their population grows and becomes more visible and their economic and political resources increase, in other words, the threat that minorities present to the dominant majority also increases, triggering increased levels of formal social control.

In the realm of criminal justice, most tests of the so-called racial threat hypothesis have focused on the relationship between the size of the minority population and the level of formal social control (cf. Chiricos, Hogan, and Gertz 1997; Jackson and Carroll 1981; Jacobs, Carmichael, and Kent 2005; Liska, Lawrence, and Benson 1981; Liska, Lawrence, and Sanchirico 1982; Petrocelli, Piquero, and Smith 2003). Researchers argue that whites view the percentage of non-whites in their community as an indicator of the seriousness of the crime problem, are more fearful of crime in communities with large minority populations, and perceive non-whites as more threatening and dangerous, and thus as more in need of formal social control, in communities where minorities make up a sizeable portion of the population. Thus, the larger the minority population, the greater the prejudice and discrimination that population faces. Hubert Blalock (1967), however, suggests that the relationship is not necessarily linear. Rather, there is a "tipping point," or threshold, beyond which further increases in the size of the minority population have little, if any, effect. Intensified social control due to racial threat may manifest in several ways, including discriminatory practices and the use of coercive force against racial and ethnic minorities (Stolzenberg, D'Alessio, and Eitle 2004). The racial threat hypothesis has been used to study the influence of the size of the black population on pretextual traffic stops, arrest rates, incarceration rates, executions, lynchings, hate crimes, and interracial killings.

Three threat-based hypotheses have been used to explain racial threat: the political threat hypothesis, the economic threat hypothesis, and the threat of black-on-white crime hypothesis (Blalock 1967; Eitle, D'Alessio, and Stolzenberg 2002; Stolzenberg, D'Alessio, and Eitle 2004). Each hypothesis predicts that there will be a positive relationship between the size of the black population and the amount of formal social control imposed on blacks, but the nature of the threat posed by the black population varies (Eitle, D'Alessio, and Stolzenberg 2002). Although all three hypotheses are concerned with group conflict, each of them focuses on a different social process. As Allen Liska asserts, "These differences are not just differences of terminology for similar concepts. . . . [T]here are real differences among these theories regarding who and what are threatening to whom" (1994, 63).

To date, studies have produced mixed results regarding the effect of racial threat on criminal justice outcomes. While some studies concluded that there was no direct evidence that blacks face a greater likelihood of arrest in cities with large black populations (Stolzenberg, D'Alessio, and Eitle 2004), others found that blacks are more likely to be arrested in areas where a high percentage of crimes involved a black offender and white victim (Eitle, D'Alessio, and Stolzenberg 2002). There also is little empirical support for the notion that political or economic competition between blacks and whites will lead to increased social control and higher arrest rates for blacks (Eitle, D'Alessio, and Stolzenberg 2002). Studies of criminal court sentencing processes and imprisonment rates have also produced mixed findings. Martha Myers and Susette Talarico (1987), for example, found no evidence that the black proportion of the population or the percentage of arrests involving blacks led to more severe sentences for blacks, but they did find that black offenders were treated more punitively in counties with high levels of unemployment. Other researchers have found that black concentration leads to increased risk of incarceration for all offenders, regardless of race (Britt 2000; Crawford, Chiricos, and Kleck 1998).

Empirical tests of the racial threat hypothesis have been subjected to various criticisms, including the lack of conceptual clarity that "threat" has received in previous studies. According to Liska (1987), because researchers have failed to define key constructs of the threat hypothesis theoretically and operationally, they have produced an array of studies with inconsistent and, in some cases, conflicting, findings. However, the different conceptualizations of threat and the inconsistent findings of research testing the racial threat hypothesis "does not mean that conflict theory is contradictory; it only means that the theory is complex and thus that the implications of both process [i.e., of both positive and negative relationships between racial threat and various types of social control] must be considered simultaneously in a multivariate causal model" (Liska 1994, 65).

Like critical race theory and conflict theory, then, the racial threat perspective posits that members of the dominant culture will use their power to control racial minorities who threaten them politically, economically, or socially. The amount of formal social control exerted by the dominant group, according to this perspective, will depend on the size, visibility, and resources of the racial minority population.

Attribution Theory

Critical race theory and conflict theory, both of which contend that law and the criminal justice system are used to maintain white privilege, focus on systemic factors and macro-level processes. In contrast, attribution theory (Heider 1958), which posits that race-linked perceptions and stereotypes shape decisions, focuses on the micro-level processes through which decision makers assess and evaluate offenders and their crimes. A number of scholars, for example, argue that the decisions made by judges, probation officers, and other criminal justice officials reflect their beliefs about an offender's potential for rehabilitation, which in turn rest on their perceptions of the causes of criminal behavior (cf. Bridges and Steen 1998; Hawkins 1980). According to this perspective, decision makers attribute causality either to *internal* factors (i.e., personal characteristics of the individual, such as an antisocial personality, lack of remorse, refusal to admit guilt, or refusal to cooperate with officials) or to *external* factors (i.e., factors within the environment, such as delinquent peers, a dysfunctional family, drug or alcohol use, or poverty). Individuals whose crimes are attributed to internal factors are viewed as more responsible, and thus as more blameworthy, than those whose crimes are viewed as stemming from external forces; more important, these attributions affect the decisions that criminal justice officials make about the appropriate outcome for the offender. Offenders whose crimes are attributed to internal factors are treated more harshly than are offenders whose crimes are attributed to environmental factors.

George Bridges and Sara Steen (1998, 555), who contend that most studies of racial bias fail to identify the *mechanisms by which* race affects criminal justice decision making, suggest that causal attribution theory can be used to explain "the race–punishment relationship." Building on theories of social cognition, which hold that racial and ethnic stereotypes affect officials' perceptions of minority offenders, Bridges and Steen propose that the harsher treatment of racial minorities may be due to the fact that criminal justice officials attribute their crimes to internal forces while attributing crimes committed by whites to external forces. They further argue that these "differential attributions about the causes of crime by minorities and whites may contribute directly to differential assessments of offender dangerousness" and, thus, to "racial differences in perceived risk and recommended punishment" (Bridges and Steen 1998, 557). John Wooldredge and Amy Thistlethwaite (2004) take this argument one step further, contending that perceptions of minority offenders as chronic and violent often intersect with notions of class, perpetuating stereotypes of "disadvantaged" minority offenders.

A second theory focusing on the linkages between officials' perceptions of offenders and their crimes and their decisions regarding the appropriate outcome in the case is the theory of bounded rationality/uncertainty avoidance (Albonetti 1991), which incorporates both organizational theory and causal attribution theory. Structural organizational theorists (Simon 1957), for example, contend that decision makers rarely have the information needed to make fully rational decisions; because they cannot identify all of the possible alternatives or the costs and benefits of each known alternative, they cannot always select the alternative that will provide the greatest benefit at the lowest cost. Instead, they use a decision-making process characterized by "bounded rationality" to search for a solution that will avoid, or at least, reduce, the uncertainty of obtaining a desirable outcome. According to Celesta Albonetti (1991, 249), "Decision makers seek to achieve a measure of rationality by developing 'patterned responses'" that reflect stereotypes, prejudices, and predictions regarding likely outcomes.

Applied to the criminal justice process, the theory of bounded rationality/ uncertainty avoidance suggests that decisions of criminal justice officials—and, especially, prosecutors, judges, and probation and parole officials—hinge on their assessments of the offender's likelihood of recidivism. Because officials typically do not have the information they need to make accurate predictions regarding the odds of reoffending, they develop patterned responses based on case and offender characteristics that they believe will increase or decrease the risk of recidivism. They attempt to reduce the uncertainty of their predictions by using stereotypes of crime seriousness, offender blameworthiness, and offender dangerousness to classify or categorize offenders and their crimes. Offenders who commit crimes perceived to be more serious are treated more harshly, as are offenders who are deemed more blameworthy and dangerous. Thus, stereotypes linking race, gender, and social class to the risk of recidivism result in harsher treatment for racial minorities, men, and the poor.

Although attribution theory can be applied to any aspect of criminal justice decision making, it is most frequently used to explain sentencing decisions. Another theoretical perspective that has been used to explain differential sentencing of whites and non-whites is the focal concerns perspective, which incorporates and builds on the uncertainty avoidance perspective. As developed by Steffensmeier and his colleagues (1998), this theoretical perspective suggests that judges' sentencing decisions are guided by three "focal concerns": their assessment of the blameworthiness of the offender; their desire to protect the community by incapacitating dangerous offenders or deterring potential offenders; and their concerns about the practical consequences, or social costs, of sentencing decisions.

The first focal concern—offender blameworthiness—reflects judges' assessments of the seriousness of the crime, the offender's prior criminal record, and the offender's motivation and role in the offense. Thus, offenders convicted of more serious crimes or who have more serious criminal histories will be viewed as more blameworthy; consequently, they will be sentenced more harshly. Offenders who have suffered prior victimization at the hands of others or who played a minor role in the offense, by contrast, will be seen as less culpable and will therefore be sentenced more leniently. The second focal concern— protecting the community—rests on judges' perceptions of dangerousness and predictions of the likelihood of recidivism. Like judges' assessments of offender blameworthiness, these perceptions are predicated on the nature of the offense and the offender's criminal history. Thus, judges seek to protect the community by imposing harsher sentences on repeat violent offenders or offenders whose risk of re-offending is high. The third focal concern—the practical consequences or social costs of sentencing decisions—reflects judges' perceptions regarding such things as the offender's "ability to do time," the costs of incarcerating offenders with medical conditions or mental health problems, and the "social costs" of imprisoning offenders responsible for the care of dependent children. It also includes judges' concerns about maintaining relationships with other members of the courtroom workgroup and protecting the reputation of the court.

Like Albonetti's theory of bounded rationality, the focal concerns theory assumes that judges typically do not have the information they need to accurately determine an offender's culpability, dangerousness, or likelihood of recidivism. As a result, they develop a "perceptual shorthand" (Hawkins 1980, 280; see also Bridges and Steen 1998) based on stereotypes and attributions that are themselves linked to offender characteristics such as race, ethnicity, gender, and age. Thus, "race, age, and gender will interact to influence sentencing because of images or attributions relating these statuses to membership in social groups thought to be dangerous and crime prone" (Steffensmeier, Ulmer, and Kramer 1998, 768).

Testing Attribution Theory

The role that racial/ethnic stereotypes play in court processing has been primarily used to address the more severe treatment received by blacks relative to whites (Albonetti 1997; Bridges and Steen 1998; Crawford, Chiricos, and Kleck 1998; Leiber 1994; Leiber and Jamieson 1995; Leiber and Stairs 1999; Sampson and Laub 1993; Steffensmeier and Demuth 2000; Steffensmeier, Ulmer, and Kramer 1998). However, attributions of race and ethnicity that extend those of black offenders have been proposed in the sentencing research. For example, criminal court studies call attention to the attributions that link Latinos to gangs, drugs, and crime and American Indians as "outsiders" that result in more punitive treatment relative to whites (Levy, Kunitz, and Everett 1969; Robbins 1984; Spohn and Holleran 2000; Steffensmeier and Demuth 2000; Zatz, Lujan, and Snyder-Joy 1991).

Policy Implications of Critical Race Theory, Conflict Theory, and Attribution Theory

More than one hundred years ago, the great African American scholar W.E.B. Du Bois (1903, 13) asserted, "The problem of the twentieth century is the problem of the color line." Racism and racial discrimination, according to Du Bois, were the central problems facing modern society. These problems have not disappeared. The blatant, overt and widespread racism that Du Bois decried may be a thing of the past, but racial and ethnic disparity and discrimination have not been banished from the criminal justice system. Although criminal justice scholars and policymakers continue to debate the meaning of the disproportionately high arrest and incarceration rates for blacks and Hispanics—with some contending that they reflect higher offending rates and others that they signal differential enforcement of the law—there is no denying the fact that blacks and Hispanics are arrested and imprisoned at disproportionately high rates. In 2004, for example, 12.6 percent of African American men, 3.6 percent of Hispanic men, and 1.7 percent of white men in their late twenties were in jail or prison (U.S. Bureau of Justice Statistics 2005). There were similar racial disparities among women. Across all age groups, the incarceration rate for African American women was two and a half times greater than the rate for Hispanic women and four and a half times greater than the rate for white women.

As we have shown, critical race theory, conflict theory, and attribution theory offer complementary explanations for the disproportionate number of blacks and Hispanics under the control of the criminal justice system. The principles that form the foundation of these theoretical perspectives also have implications for policy and practice. In the sections that follow, we explore these policy implications, focusing on racial profiling and sentencing.

Racial Profiling

Critical race perspectives, which contend that criminal justice agencies wield their considerable power to control and subjugate those—especially racial minorities—who threaten the political and economic elite and which emphasize the role played by stereotypes linked to race, ethnicity, gender, and class, provide a cogent and convincing explanation of the ubiquitous practice of racial profiling. As used here, the term "racial profiling" has a broader and more comprehensive meaning than the use of race as a reason for pretextual traffic stops. Like Kennedy (1997, 137), we define racial profiling as the practice of using race "as a proxy for an increased likelihood of criminal misconduct." Racial profiling, according to this definition, is therefore not confined to law enforcement officials and traffic stops. All criminal justice officials may attempt to simplify and routinize decision making by using race (and ethnicity) as a sign of an increased likelihood of criminality, with the result that racial and ethnic minorities are subject to more formal social control than whites. The higher level of suspicion that attaches to race means that blacks and Latinos will be subjected not only to "a lifetime of numerous stops" by the police (Kennedy 1997, 157), but also to higher bail and more stringent bail conditions, more severe charges and less favorable plea bargains, harsher sentences and more restrictive conditions of probation, and so on. What this means in practice, according to Kennedy (1997, 157), is that Latinos and blacks are forced "to pay a racial tax for the purpose of more efficient law enforcement."

Viewed in this way, it is clear that racial profiling, whether on the streets or in the courtroom, does not result simply from the prejudice of individual police officers, prosecutors, or judges. Rather, it is an institutional practice that is deeply embedded in the agencies of the criminal justice system and that is widely regarded as a legitimate and effective weapon in the war on crime. It is a practice that labels members of the so-called problem population potential criminals and likely recidivists, without any regard for the presumption of innocence or for the notion that individuals should be judged on the basis of their own conduct and not on the basis of racial and ethnic stereotypes. It is a practice that "does great damage to individuals, to the social fabric of our country, to the rule of law, and to the entire legal and criminal justice system" (Harris 2002, 241).

The difficulties inherent in making informed, rational, and appropriate decisions about individuals who find themselves in the arms of the law, coupled with the pervasiveness of attributions of danger, threat, and criminality that are linked to race and ethnicity, suggest that eliminating racial profiling from the criminal justice system will not be easy. The situation is further complicated by state and federal court decisions that, rather than condemning the practice of racial profiling as a violation of the Equal Protection Clause of the Fourteenth Amendment, place a stamp of approval—albeit a limited one—on its use in the context of law enforcement. Courts have ruled, for example, that the Fourteenth Amendment is not violated if race is only one of several factors taken into account or if race is not the dominant factor used in determining suspiciousness.[3] These rulings, according to Kennedy (1997, 148) are "profoundly wrong . . . even if race is only one of several factors behind a decision, tolerating it at all means tolerating it as potentially the *decisive* factor." David Harris's (2002, 242) critique is even more pointed. He argues that using skin color as evidence of criminal involvement "means, in clear and unequivocal terms, that *skin color itself has been criminalized.*"

Analyzed from a critical race perspective, racial profiling is institutional discrimination. While most visible in the context of law enforcement and traffic stops, it is a practice that affects all aspects of the criminal justice system. It stigmatizes all members of a racial or ethnic group and, the Equal Protection Clause notwithstanding, treats people differently—that is, more punitively—on the basis of the color of their skin. Like the failure to protect black women from rape during slavery or the use of lynching against black men suspected of crimes against whites, racial profiling reflects both a devaluation of the lives of racial minorities and a belief that increased levels of formal social control are required to protect white privilege from the "problem population."

---

[3] *U.S. v. Martinez-Fuerte,* 428 U.S. 543 (1976); *State v. Dean,* 543 P.2d, 427 (Arizona 1975); *U.S. v. Weaver,* 966 F.2d 391 (CA 8 1992).

Sentencing and Incarceration

Although truth-in-sentencing, mandatory minimums, and sentencing guidelines were created to eliminate unwarranted disparity and produce certainly, fairness, and proportionality in sentencing (U.S. Sentencing Commission 2004), the negative impact of sentencing reforms on racial and ethnic groups—especially drug offenders—has been well documented (Crawford, Chiricos, and Kleck 1998; Kramer and Steffensmeier 1993; Tonry 1996). The one-hundred-to-one disparity in the drug-quantity thresholds that triggered lengthy mandatory minimum sentences for offenders convicted of offenses involving crack and powder cocaine resulted in disproportionately longer sentences for black offenders, who were substantially more likely than either white or Hispanic offenders to be convicted of crack cocaine offenses. The crime control policies pursued during the war on drugs and habitual offender laws such as "three strikes" laws also contributed to an unprecedented number of racial and ethnic minorities in the nation's prisons.

After decades of sentencing research documenting the racial and ethnic biases in sentencing processes and outcomes, the U.S. Sentencing Commission, on December 11, 2007, amended the Federal Sentencing Guidelines to address the disparities between crack cocaine and powder cocaine offenses. The commission decided to apply the changes to the guidelines retroactively to deal with the more punitive treatment received by crack cocaine offenders. Although this represents a significant step toward addressing the racial biases of federal sentencing policy, the federal sentencing judge has discretion in deciding whether a crack cocaine offender is eligible for a lower sentence and for how much the sentence should be reduced. As of May 31, 2008, more than seven thousand crack cocaine offenders had been released since the amendment to the guidelines was implemented (U.S. Sentencing Commission 2008). While it is too early to assess the impact of these sentencing reductions, efforts aimed at correcting the biases produced by the federal sentencing guidelines are significant and noteworthy.

Prosecutors' discretion in charging and plea bargaining has also been linked to racial and ethnic disparities in court processes. Although minimal research has been conducted on prosecutorial practices such as charging and dismissal of offenses, researchers have concluded that racial and ethnic disparities are produced by plea bargaining (Kautt and Spohn 2002; Nagel 1990; Rhodes 1991; Roberts 1994; Tonry 1996). Eliminating biases during the prosecutorial phase requires resources and information. To make informed decisions about the appropriate sentences for offenders, especially drug offenders, mechanisms must be in place that reduce uncertainly about a perpetrator's risk of reoffending. Identifying the services that offenders need and implementing effective substance-abuse treatment programs hinges on comprehensive risk assessments and the willingness of court actors to seek alternatives to incarceration. This, of course, requires resources and the collaboration of prosecutors, defense attorneys, and probation services.

As previously discussed, racial and ethnic disparities can also be attributed to probation officers' assessments of offenders (Bridges and Steen 1998). Attributions of offender dangerousness and threat that are linked to race and ethnicity result in limited opportunities to receive services and treatment for the problems related to substance abuse and mental health that plague most offenders in the justice system. As sentencing policies continue to be monitored for racial biases, the examination of disparities that arise from pre-sentencing practices are often difficult to assess, given the few data sets that contain pre-sentencing data (U.S. Sentencing Commission 2004). Whether it is racial and ethnic stereotypes, higher rates of involvement in crime, or incomplete information about offenders' risk, the impact of probation, prosecution, and sentencing practices on minorities will have a lasting, profound effect.

References

Albonetti, C. 1991. Integration of theories to explain judicial discretion. *Social Problems* 38: 47–266.

———. 1997. Sentencing under the Federal Sentencing Guidelines: Effects of defendant characteristics, guilty pleas, and departures on sentencing outcomes for drug offenses, 1991–1992. *Law and Society Review* 31:789–822.

Anderson, M., and P. H. Collins (Eds.). 2007. *Race, class, and gender: An anthology.* 7th ed. Belmont, Calif.: Wadsworth.

Bell, D. 1992. *Race, racism, and American law.* 3rd ed. Boston: Little, Brown.

Blalock, H. M. 1967. *Towards a theory of minority group relations.* New York: Capricorn Books.

Box, S., and C. Hale. 1985. Unemployment, imprisonment, and prison overcrowding. *Contemporary Crises* 9:209–238.

Bridges, G. S., and R. H. Crutchfield. 1988. Law, social standing, and racial disparities in imprisonment. *Social Forces* 66:601–616.

Bridges, G. S., and S. Steen. 1998. Racial disparities in official assessments of juvenile offending: Attributional stereotypes as mediating mechanisms. *American Sociological Review* 65:554–570.

Britt, C. 2000. Social context and racial disparities in punishment decisions. *Justice Quarterly* 17:707–732.

Brown, T. 2003. Critical race theory speaks to the sociology of mental health. *Journal of Health and Social Behavior* 44:292–301.

Chambliss, W. J., and R. B. Seidman. 1971. *Law, order and power.* Reading, Mass.: Addison-Wesley.

———. 1982. *Law, order, and power.* 2nd ed. Reading, Mass.: Addison-Wesley.

Chiricos, T. G., and W. D. Bales. 1991. Unemployment and punishment: An empirical assessment. *Criminology* 29:701–724.

Chiricos, T. G., M. Hogan, and M. Gertz. 1997. Racial composition of neighborhoods and fear of crime. *Criminology* 35:107–131.

Collins, P. H. 2000. *Black feminist thought, knowledge, consciousness, and the politics of empowerment.* New York: Routledge.

———. 2004. *Black sexual politics: African Americans, gender, and the new racism.* New York: Routledge.

Combahee River Collective. 2001 (1972). A black feminist statement. In *Theorizing feminism: Parallel trends in the humanities and social sciences.* Ed. A. Herman and A Stewart, 29–37. Boulder, Colo.: Westview Press.

Corzine, J., J. Creech, and L. Corzine. 1983. Black concentration and lynchings in the South: Testing Blalock's power–threat hypothesis. *Social Forces* 61:774–796.

Crawford, C., T. D. Chiricos, and G. Kleck. 1998. Race, racial threat and the sentencing of habitual offenders. *Criminology* 36:481–511.

Crenshaw, K. 1992. Whose story is it anyway? Feminist and antiracist appropriations of Anita Hill. In *Race-ing justice, en-gendering power: Essays on Clarence Thomas, Anita Hill, and the social construction of social reality.* Ed. T. Morrison, 402–440. New York: Pantheon Books.

———. 2002a. Mapping the margins: Intersectionality, identity politics, and violence against women of color. *Stanford Law Review* 43:1241–1299.

———. 2002b. The first decade: Critical reflections, or "a foot in the closing door." In *Crossroads, directions, and a new critical race theory.* Ed. F. Valdes, J. M. Culp, and A. P. Harris, 9–31. Philadelphia: Temple University Press.

Crenshaw, K., N. Gotanda, G. Peller, and K. Thomas (Eds.). 1995. *Critical race theory: The key writings that formed the movement.* New York: New Press.

D'Alessio, S. J., D. Eitle, and L. Stolzenberg. 2005. The impact of serious crime, racial and economic inequality on private police size. *Social Science Research* 34:267–282.

Davis, A. 1981. *Women, race, and class.* New York: Random House.

Delgado, R., and J. Stefancic. 2001. *Critical race theory: An introduction.* New York: New York University Press.

Du Bois, W.E.B. 1903. *The souls of black folk.* Chicago: McClurg.

Eitle, D., S. J. D'Alessio, and L. Stolzenberg. 2002. Racial threat and social control: A test of the political, economic, and threat of black crime hypotheses. *Social Forces* 81: 557–576.

Harris, D. 2002. *Profiles in injustice: Why racial profiling cannot work.* New York: New Press.

Hawkins, D. 1980. Perceptions of punishment for crime. *Deviant Behavior* 1:193–215.

———. 1987. Beyond anomalies: Rethinking the conflict perspective on race and criminal punishment. *Social Forces* 65:719–745.

Heider, F. 1958. *The psychology of interpersonal relations.* New York: John Wiley and Sons.

hooks, b. 1984. *Feminist theory: From margin to center.* Boston: South End Press.

Irwin, J. 1985. *The jail: Managing the underclass in American society.* Berkeley: University of California Press.

Jackson, P. I., and L. Carroll. 1981. Race and the war on crime: The sociopolitical determinants of municipal police expenditures in 90 non-southern cities. *American Sociological Review* 46:390–405.

Jacobs, D., J. T. Carmichael, and S. L. Kent. 2005. Vigilantism, current racial threat, and death sentences. *American Sociological Review* 70:656–677.

Kautt, P., and C. Spohn. 2002. Crack-ing down on black drug offenders? Testing for interactions among offenders' race, drug type, and sentencing strategy in federal drug sentences. *Justice Quarterly* 19:1–36.

Kennedy, R. 1997. *Race, crime, and the law.* New York: Random House.

Kramer, J. H., and D. Steffensmeier. 1993. Race and imprisonment decisions. *Sociological Quarterly* 34:357–376.

LaFree, G. 1989. *Rape and criminal justice: The social construction of sexual assault.* Belmont, Calif.: Wadsworth.

Leiber, M. J. 1994. Comparison of juvenile court outcomes for Native Americans, African Americans, and whites. *Justice Quarterly* 11:257–279.

Leiber, M. J., and K. M. Jamieson. 1995. Race and decision making within juvenile justice: The importance of context. *Journal of Quantitative Criminology* 11:363–388.

Leiber, M., and J. M. Stairs. 1999. Race, context, and the use of intake diversion. *Journal of Research in Crime and Delinquency* 36:56–86.

Lerner, G. (Ed.). 1972. *Black women in white America: A documentary history.* New York: Pantheon.

Levy, J., S. Kunitz, and S. Everett. 1969. Navajo criminal homicide. *Southwestern Journal of Anthropology* 25:24–152.

Liska, A. E. 1987. A critical perspective on macro perspectives on crime control. *Annual Review of Sociology* 13:67–88.

———. 1994. Modeling the conflict perspective of social control. In *Inequality, crime and social control.* Ed. G. S. Bridges and M. A. Myers, 53–71. Boulder, Colo.: Westview Press.

Liska, A. E., and M. B. Chamlin. 1984. Social structure and crime control among macrosocial units. *American Journal of Sociology* 90:383–395.

Liska, A. E., J. J. Lawrence, and M. Benson. 1981. Perspectives on the legal order: Capacity for social control. *American Journal of Sociology* 87:413–426.

Liska, A. E., J. J. Lawrence, and S. Sanchirico. 1982. Fear of crime as a social fact. *Social Force* 60:760–770.

McIntosh, P. 2007. White privilege and male privilege: An account of coming to see correspondence through work in women's studies. In *Race, class, and gender: An anthology.* 7th ed. Ed. M. Anderson and P. H. Collins, 94–105. Belmont, Calif.: Wadsworth.

Myers, M. A., and S. M. Talarico. 1987. *Social contexts of criminal sentencing.* New York: Springer-Verlag.

Nagel, I. H. 1990. Structuring sentencing discretion: The new Federal Sentencing Guidelines. *Journal of Criminal Law and Criminology* 80:883–943.

Peterson, R. D., and J. Hagan. 1984. Changing conceptions of race: Toward an account of anomalous findings of sentencing research. *American Sociological Review* 49:56–70.

Petrocelli, M., A. R. Piquero, and M. R. Smith. 2003. Conflict theory and racial profiling: An empirical analysis of police stop data. *Journal of Criminal Justice* 31:1–11.

Quinney, R. 1970. *The social reality of crime.* Boston: Little, Brown.

———. 1974. *Critique of legal order: Crime control in a capitalist society.* Boston: Little, Brown.

———. 1977. *Class, state and crime.* New York: David McKay.

Rhodes, W. 1991. Federal criminal sentencing: Some measurement issues with application to pre-guideline sentencing disparity. *Journal of Criminal Law and Criminology* 81:1002–1033.

Robbins, S. P. 1984. Anglo concepts and Indian reality: A study of juvenile delinquency. *Journal of Contemporary Social Work* 85:235–241.

Roberts, D. 1997. *Policing the black body: Race, reproduction, and the meaning of liberty.* New York: Random House.

Roberts, J. V. 1994. The role of criminal record in the Federal Sentencing Guidelines. *Criminal Justice Ethics* 13:21–30.

Sampson, R. J., and J. H. Laub. 1993. Structural variations in juvenile court processing: Inequality, the underclass, and social control. *Law and Society Review* 27:285–312.

Sentencing Project. 2004. Schools and prisons: Fifty years after *Brown v. the Board of Education*. Report. Sentencing Project, Washington, D.C.

Simon, H. 1957. *Administrative behavior: A study of decision making processes in administrative organization*. New York: Free Press.

Spitzer, S. 1975. Toward a Marxian theory of deviance. *Social Problems* 22:638–651.

Spohn, C. 2000. Thirty years of sentencing reform: A quest for a racially neutral sentencing process. In *Policies, processes, and decisions of the criminal justice system*, Vol. 3, *Criminal Justice 2000*, 427–501. Washington, D.C.: U.S. Department of Justice.

Spohn, C., and D. Holleran. 2000. The imprisonment penalty paid by young, unemployed black and Hispanic male offenders. *Criminology* 38:501–526.

Steffensmeier, D., and S. Demuth. 2000. Ethnicity and sentencing outcomes in U.S. federal courts: Who is punished more harshly? *American Sociological Review* 65:705–729.

Steffensmeier, D., J. Ulmer, and J. Kramer. 1998. The interaction of race, gender, and age in criminal sentencing: The punishment costs of being young, black, and male. *Criminology* 36:363–397.

Stevenson, B. 1995. Black family structure in colonial and antebellum Virginia. In *The decline in marriage among African Americans: Causes, consequences, and policy implications*. In B. Tucker and C. Mitchell-Kernan, 27–58. New York: Russell Sage Foundation.

Stolzenberg, L., S. J. D'Alessio, and D. Eitle. 2004. A multilevel test of racial threat theory. *Criminology* 42:673–698.

Tolnay, S. E., and E. M. Beck. 1994. Lethal social control in the South: Lynchings and executions between 1880 and 1930. In *Inequality, crime and social control*. Ed. G. S. Bridges and M. A. Myers, 176–194. Boulder, Colo.: Westview Press.

Tonry, M. 1996. *Sentencing matters: Studies in crime and public policy*. New York: Oxford University Press.

Turk, A. 1969. *Criminality and legal order*. Chicago: Rand McNally.

U.S. Bureau of Justice Statistics. 2005. *Prison and jail inmates at midyear 2004*. Washington, D.C.: Department of Justice.

U.S. Sentencing Commission. 2004. *Fifteen years of guidelines sentencing: An assessment of how well the federal criminal justice system is achieving the goals of sentencing reform*. Washington, D.C.: U.S. Sentencing Commission.

———. 2008. *U.S. Sentencing Commission: Preliminary crack cocaine retroactivity data report*. Washington, D.C.: U.S. Sentencing Commission.

Valdes, F., J. M. Culp, and A. P. Harris. 2002. Introduction: Battles waged, won, and lost: Critical race theory at the turn of the millennium. In *Crossroads, directions, and a new critical race Theory*. Ed. F. Valdes, J. M. Culp, and A. P. Harris, 1–8. Philadelphia: Temple University Press.

Walker, S., C. Spohn, and M. DeLone. 2007. *The color of justice: Race, ethnicity and crime in America*. 4th ed. Belmont, Calif.: Thomson/Wadsworth.

Wooldredge, J., and A. Thistlethwaite. 2004. Bilevel disparities in court dispositions for intimate assault. *Criminology* 42:417–456.

Zatz, M. S. 1987. The changing forms of racial/ethnic biases in sentencing. *Journal of Research in Crime and Delinquency* 24:69–92.

Zatz, M. S., C. C. Lujan, and Z. K. Snyder-Joy. 1991. American Indians and criminal justice: Some conceptual and methodological considerations. In *Race and criminal justice*. Ed. M. J. Lynch and E. B. Patterson, 100–112. New York: Harrow and Heston.

14

GORDON BAZEMORE AND RACHEL BOBA

Problem-Solving Restorative Justice

*From Incidents and Cases to Community
Building and Collective Outcomes in a
New Response to Youth Crime*

In an opening presentation to an international conference on restorative juvenile justice in 1998, Gordon Bazemore read from the paper "Core Challenges Facing Community Policing: The Emperor Still Has No Clothes" (Taylor, Fritsch, and Caeti 1998) but substituted "restorative justice" for each reference to community policing. After about ten minutes of hearing that restorative justice had "failed" in almost every way—because it had not fulfilled, and could never fulfill, the promises made for it—most of the audience seemed relieved to learn that scholars were for the most part *not*, at that time, writing the epitaph for restorative justice (but see Levrant et al. 1999). Yet most also no doubt realized that the reasons for lack of success in community policing provided a template for emerging concerns and cautions for those interested in the future of restorative justice reform.[1] Most notably, the tendency to emphasize one or more "programs" rather than systemic reform has characterized the implementation of both approaches.

In this chapter, we consider what advocates of restorative justice can learn from the successes and failures of another related reform agenda, problem-oriented policing, or POP (Goldstein 1990; Scott 2000). In contrast to traditional policing (and community policing) advocates, problem-oriented policing advocates have pursued systemic change based on a vision of a distinctive prevention

---

[1] Despite some indication of success (e.g., Skogan 1990; Weisburd and Eck 2004), some have concluded that, for a variety of reasons, community policing may never live up to the broad claims made by early advocates (Kelling and Moore 1988; Skolnick and Bayley 1986). In part, community policing has been clear only about the need for community involvement and has been ambiguous about the change in overall goals and objectives that some view as essential to any major criminal justice reform.

and intervention process (Goldstein 2003). The challenge presented by advocates confronts the expectation that rapid response (to individual calls and arrests) is an end in itself. Instead, POP employs a systematic, applied-research approach that focuses limited resources on the larger *source*: the underlying problems behind these "incidents." Similarly, we argue that sustaining restorative justice will require moving beyond the individualized "case-focused" approach associated with people and paper processing (Hasenfeld and Cheung 1985) to a broader *problem-solving,* collective outcome focus on "repairing the harm" of crime to multiple stakeholders, including victims, offenders, and communities (Van Ness and Strong 1997).

This chapter begins with a brief overview of problem-oriented policing, its goals and objectives, practice, and research and evaluation findings. The remainder of the chapter uses the general lessons of this movement (and of noted earlier successes in restorative justice) to assist future restorative reform efforts in the juvenile justice context. While we do not intend to overstate similarities between restorative justice and problem-oriented policing, we highlight the scope and difficulty of substantive challenges faced by both movements in their organizational and community contexts. We suggest that common system- and community-reform objectives of both movements can be achieved only when advocates move from (1) individual to collective *outcomes*; and (2) a strategic process focused on cases and *programs* to a holistic problem-solving model.

Problem-Oriented Policing: Promise and Limitations

In his seminal article "Improving Policing: A Problem-Oriented Approach," Herman Goldstein (1979) argued that police devote too much attention to *means* and not enough to the *ends* of their work, and that underlying causes that give rise to crime incidents and public order concerns should be the focus of police work. The *first* goal of POP is therefore to refocus police efforts on problems rather than incidents, thus using limited resources to address underlying causes of reoccurring problems rather than responding to incidents on a case-by-case basis (Goldstein 1990). "Problems" are a set of related activities viewed as harmful to the community (Clarke and Eck 2005) that should in turn be used to prioritize application of resources and to direct crime prevention activities. By addressing larger problems rather than individual incidents, police have greater, more long-term preventative impact on crime (Goldstein 1990).

The *second* goal of POP is to implement a strategic focus on addressing activity at a higher systems level. Goldstein argued that for police to become "problem-oriented," they must adopt a new, more systemic approach that would demand that they collect new data, develop new methods of analysis, identify innovative crime prevention and reduction strategies, and assess the outcomes of their efforts. This general approach, developed by John Eck and William

Spelman (1987) in their application of problem-oriented policing in Newport News, Virginia, was intended to make the scientific research process palatable to police practitioners, and it has since become the cornerstone of problem-oriented policing. Known as SARA, this process includes scanning, the identification of problems harmful to community life and deemed important by both the police and the community; analysis, or the gathering of data and analysis to understand the nature and immediate causes of the problem; response, or developing and applying both traditional and nontraditional policing techniques to crime prevention and apprehension tailored to the problem and based on the analysis; and assessment, or evaluating the effectiveness of these responses and making adjustments to ensure continued or improved impact. Today the SARA process essentially functions as a set of normative and strategic principles for POP, much like core principles of restorative justice, discussed later in this chapter.

As Goldstein (2003) suggests, the process of problem solving achieves a higher level of focus on the overall "good"—that is, the prevention and reduction of crime. Using this problem-solving process, police can gain broader insight into specific problems, which in turn helps to more directly define the police role in the response. Systematic problem-solving research and practice, according to Goldstein, provides police with effective strategies for dealing with problems, which can reduce current over-dependence on the criminal justice system, as well as with impractical public expectations.

There are also a number of well-documented obstacles to the application of problem-oriented policing, including lack of broad implementation, inadequate problem definition and subsequent analysis, and line officers' assuming too much responsibility for problem-solving work (Boba and Crank 2008; Scott 2000). In a comprehensive review of research, however, David Weisburd and Eck (2004) nonetheless conclude that problem-oriented policing shows promise for reducing and preventing crime over both community-oriented and traditional policing. Moreover, Weisburd and his colleague Anthony Braga (2006) have more recently argued that POP has yet to be implemented as Goldstein originally intended, and that POP advocates have failed to institutionalize the ultimate goal of addressing large scale problems. Nonetheless, they conclude that even *shallow problem-solving efforts, ranging from focused enforcement efforts in high-risk places at high-risk times to problem solving with weak analysis (and mostly traditional responses and limited assessments) are often enough to prevent crime"* (149; emphasis added). They assert that POP strategies focused on "medium-sized problems" and collective outcomes, such as those involving specific locations or small groups of victims and offenders, have been found to be worthwhile, effective, and realistic (Weisburd and Braga 2006).

Interestingly, the effectiveness of POP, even in the case of less-than-perfect implementation fidelity, finds parallels in assessments of restorative justice outcomes. That is, restorative justice evaluation research indicates surprisingly robust impact on recidivism and other outcomes (Bonta et al. 2002; Sherman and Strang 2007), even allowing for the fact that these interventions may often be loosely implemented, short-term encounters that often seem to build on what Mark Granovetter (1973, 1983) referred to as "strength of weak ties" beyond those of family and extended family (Boyes-Watson 2004). Despite this consistent empirical impact and current popularity, however, restorative justice also faces clear threats to sustainability based on the failure of policy and practice to address problems beyond the case level. In the remainder of this chapter, we consider the extent to which restorative justice advocates may employ both the logic of problem solving and sound social theory to address systemic and community-level issues in juvenile justice reform.

Restorative Justice: Origins, Objectives, Practice, and Research

Background and Origins

Restorative justice is not new. Early acephalous human communities, as well as the most highly organized early civilizations, practiced decision-making processes and reparative practices that resemble responses to crime now labeled as restorative justice (Van Ness and Strong 1997).[2] Indeed, some suggest that it was retributive *punishment* that was later "invented" in Western societies as an innovation that essentially formalized the response to conflict resolution by making theft and other offenses crimes against the king or the state (Weitekamp 1999). Although less commonly employed in some eras and cultures, reparation and informal settlement processes, as well as formal and informal restitution and other reparative sanctions (e.g., community service), have nonetheless persisted throughout Western history (Schafer 1970).

Modern interest in what might now be called reparative practice began in the 1970s when monetary restitution, with the support of the emerging crime victims' movement, became popular in U.S. and Canadian criminal courts (Hudson and Galaway 1990), resulting in the development of formal programs

---

[2] Acephalous societies preferred settlement processes that included ritualistic responses to crime that typically sought to restore community peace and harmony as an alternative to blood feuds, which generally had devastating consequences for community life (Michalowski 1985; Weitekamp 1999). In addition, the most advanced ancient state societies—those in Egypt, Babylon, China, Persia, Rome, and Greece, as well as Hebrew and Anglo-Saxon societies—featured formal codes that specified restitution and various forms of reparation (Van Ness and Strong 1997).

for the collection and monitoring of restitution. Community service also became a popular, alternative reparative sanction during this time period (Hudson and Galaway 1990; Tonry 1994). Victim–offender mediation, or "victim–offender reconciliation," programs gained popularity in the 1980s as an informal process to resolve conflicts and to determine restitution and meet other needs of victim and community (Umbreit 2001). Yet it was not until the 1990s that the wide array of non-adversarial decision-making practices (i.e., "restorative group conferencing" programs) began to appear in the United States as an "export" from Australia and New Zealand and soon became viewed by many as the heart of the restorative justice movement (Bazemore and Schiff 2004).[3]

Objectives, Goals, and Principles

Although it is often mistakenly viewed and implemented as an intervention "program," restorative justice is most accurately described as a model of "doing justice" by repairing the harm of crime (Bazemore and Walgrave 1999). Grounded in a principle-based paradigm that provides a clear alternative to now dominant retributive justice models (Braithwaite and Pettit 1990; von Hirsch 1976), restorative justice is compatible with many goals and assumptions of other approaches to juvenile justice, including crime control, rehabilitation, and libertarian/due process models (Bazemore 2001). However, restorative justice views crime as more than lawbreaking and is distinctive in its metric for gauging justice by attention to the extent to which harm is repaired, rather than the degree to which "just deserts" are delivered.

Daniel Van Ness and Karen Strong (1997) articulate three core principles that also suggest standards that provide independent but compatible dimensions for assessing what might be called the integrity, or "restorativeness," of any justice intervention (e.g., Bazemore and Schiff 2004). These principles suggest independent but mutually reinforcing justice goals: (1) *repairing the harm,* assessed by the extent to which all parties identify the damage of a crime that needs to be addressed and develop and carry out a plan to do so; (2) *stakeholder involvement,* assessed by the extent to which victims, offenders, and individuals from the community affected by a crime or harmful action are intentionally and actively engaged in decision making about how to accomplish this repair; and (3) *transforming the community–government relationship,* assessed by the extent to which a response to crime operationalizes a deliberate rethinking and reshaping of the relationship between governmental authority

---

[3] Restorative justice—though broadly focused on all crime and conflict in multiple settings, including international peacemaking, post-conflict healing, and community reconciliation—has become perhaps most widely associated with youth justice reform internationally.

and community members and groups and the role of each in this response (Van Ness and Strong 1997, 8–9).[4] While they provide a normative theory of restorative justice, we later demonstrate that each principle can also be connected to causal theories drawn from criminological and other social-science literature and intervention theories of crime and desistance.

Policy and Practice

Based on these principles, and associated outcomes, any number of responses to crime could be viewed along a continuum ranging from more to less restorative, and *no practice* is inherently restorative. Similarly, a restorative response to crime need not be a formal program or practice at all. For example, a group of neighbors in a primarily white, Protestant, middle-class neighborhood in a Philadelphia suburb placed the Star of David in their windows during the holiday season in solidarity with a Jewish family who had been the victim of group of skinheads who burned a cross in the family's front yard. With input from the family and community, the young men were then diverted from the court with the understanding that they would meet with the victimized family and a rabbi who would also arrange community service and lessons in Jewish history for the boys.

There is, however, a growing list of more structured restorative justice practices that to operationalize the three core principles the greatest extent possible. These practices can be divided into two primary categories: (1) restorative *decision-making,* or "conferencing," processes that seek to maximize stakeholder involvement by enabling victims, offenders, their supporters, and affected community members to have dialogue and input into a plan to repair harm; and (2) restorative *obligations* (or informal sanctions) that are the reparative outcomes of this process. Conferencing practices are non-adversarial processes that may assume many variations within four general structural models: family group conferences; victim–offender mediation or dialogue; neighborhood accountability boards; and peacemaking circles (Bazemore and Schiff 2004). The second category, restorative obligations, are typical intermediate products of the process that require offenders to "make amends" for the crime or harm and demonstrate accountability by taking responsibility through making restitution to victims, community service, apologies, victim service, behavioral agreements, and other means.

---

[4] While each principle is related to the other two and should be mutually reinforcing, each also presumes an independent goal, as well as standards for assessing the strength of restorative justice intervention that are therefore important in their own right. For example, stakeholder participation in the justice process is an essential goal in any democracy and is a fundamental tenet of *procedural justice* (Tyler 1990), regardless of whether it contributes directly to the goal of repairing harm.

Research and Evaluation

The research on restorative justice is promising. In general, it documents the strength of practice in addressing recidivism reduction, victim satisfaction, trauma reduction, and other outcomes for a wide range of participants, including serious adult offenders (Sherman and Strang 2007), as well as low- to moderate-level juvenile offenders (McGarrell 2001; Rodriguez 2004). In addition, several meta-analyses in recent years have demonstrated consistent positive effects across several hundred programs (Bonta et al. 2002; Nugent, Williams, and Umbreit 2003). Perhaps most interesting in terms of the resiliency of restorative justice impact is the surprising persistence of significant positive (if not always large) effects over time, with a variety of offenders and victims in diverse cultures and communities. Importantly, restorative interventions are also generally low cost, short term, and, in the case of restorative conferencing, typically one-time encounters.[5]

Limitations and Promise

Juvenile justice intervention—especially post-arrest—is explicitly individualized and offender-focused. In the attempt to address the needs and risks presented by three stakeholders, restorative justice is inherently collective in outlook. In theory, it offers a process (like POP) aimed at getting to the root of a range of problems. In addition, by breaking down social distance (Pranis 2001), restorative practices may even engage social justice issues and stimulate a kind of "bubbling up" process through which such issues "are increasingly aired in community forums linked intentionally to a vibrant social movement politics" (Braithwaite and Parker 1999, 35).

Yet two primary obstacles challenge efforts to institutionalize a broader, more vibrant restorative practice across systems and communities. First, innovative practices in juvenile justice have often been greatly limited—if not fully "captured"—by the constraints of a casework model aimed at individualized offender assessment, case processing, and referral. It is therefore hard to move beyond this traditional offender-driven treatment model to an intervention paradigm aimed at achieving re-integrative, collective effects for three stakeholders.

Second, restorative justice is often seen as a special *program,* or a specific *process* (Marshall 1996),[6] rather than as a holistic method of understanding and

---

[5] Research on restorative sanctions (e.g., community service, restitution) also indicates robust and significant, if at times modest, impact in terms of recidivism reduction and other impacts (Bazemore 2006; Butts and Snyder 1991; Schneider 1986). The general potency of restorative practice in reducing re-offending may also be related to its connection with a strengths-based or positive youth development emphasis (Saleebey 2002).

[6] This narrow programmatic conceptualization places tremendous limits on the use of restorative resolutions in the vast majority of cases referred to, or diverted from, juvenile courts. In the United

responding to crime that pursues unique, collective healing outcomes (Bazemore and Walgrave 1999). We discuss specific remedies and tools to change this state of affairs and sustain restorative justice after first exploring the broader strategic vision for a "problem-solving" juvenile justice.

Beyond Programs toward Holistic Problem Solving: Implementation Process and Outcomes

The literature of juvenile justice is replete with case studies of failed implementation in prevention, diversion, probation, residential treatment, and so on (see, e.g., Bazemore, Dicker, and Nyhan 1994; Polk 1987). In jurisdictions where restorative justice has been most successful, statutory and policy changes have either mandated use of restorative justice processes for a wide variety of crimes or made referrals to restorative programs a presumptive requirement for large categories of offenses (Masters 2003). Yet, despite the insertion of restorative justice into the juvenile court purpose clauses of some thirty-five American states (O'Brien and Bazemore 2005), no such mandates or incentives to develop restorative processes or refer cases to restorative programs are known to exist in these or any other U.S. jurisdictions. Hence, referral to many restorative programs appears typically to be sporadic, encompassing in most jurisdictions a minuscule proportion of all cases adjudicated in court or diverted to informal programs (Bazemore and Schiff 2004). Countries such as Canada, for example, provide significant statutory support (as well as national and provincial funding) for restorative programs explicitly designated as the preferred or primary option in dispositional and diversion schemes in youth justice. Even in this case, however, the absence of a mandate for use of these programs has led to lower-than-expected levels of referral in some jurisdictions, coupled with concerns about inappropriate use that may result in net widening in some communities (Elliott 2004).[7] Yet such countries represent a great improvement in their systemic support for restorative justice practice compared with the United States.[8]

States, for example, even jurisdictions most active in restorative justice have access to a relative handful of restorative programs that are generally supported by temporary funding streams. Practically, this means that the vast majority of cases will receive standard diversion, probation, or secure placement referrals.

[7] J. Hackler, personal communication, Los Angeles, 2006.

[8] If this net widening is a problem in some locations, this stronger legislation—as also seen in the United Kingdom and in a number of countries in the European Union—explicitly prohibits referral of youth for whom number and seriousness of offenses fall below a certain threshold. Youth below the threshold are to receive only police cautioning, thus ensuring that program slots are primarily reserved for mid- to higher-level offenders. From our perspective, this may also reflect the failure to develop and implement a more participatory, deprofessionalized community-building vision of restorative practices as described later in this chapter, though the policy nonetheless represents a substantial improvement over very limited U.S. policy, and even over more supportive policy of a handful of individual states.

Learning from Success: System and Community Problem Solving

No number of *programs* can provide the basis for a holistic approach to restorative justice in the absence of a systemic commitment to transforming the focus of juvenile justice intervention. The most successful case study of a comprehensive implementation of restorative justice began somewhat inadvertently in the late 1980s in New Zealand as a result of national legislation mandating use of new, non-adversarial dispositional programs: family group conferences (FGCs) in all juvenile cases other than murder and rape. Rather than "alternative" or "add-on" programs, FGCs were meant to displace (or, in some cases, supplement) the dispositional function of the juvenile court (McElrae 1996). The primary lesson of New Zealand's radical reform in juvenile justice decision making, which was grounded in problem solving, was to target restorative practice beyond a focus on the vital needs of individual victims and offenders to a collective-outcome focus. In doing so, policy also addressed chronic system and community issues, the first of which were the overuse of incarceration for juvenile offenders and the disproportionate confinement (DMC) of minority youth (i.e., Maoris). Unquestionably, linked to the latter problem was the related failure to engage important crime prevention, social control, and sanctioning processes already embedded in the Maori extended family culture (Jenkins 2006; Maxwell and Morris 1993).

The adoption of indigenous family and cultural practices into national public policy, which eventually led to a reduction in DMC and the closure of the badly overcrowded youth facility, was itself an unprecedented accomplishment. The New Zealand reforms also clearly illustrate a problem-solving response aimed at empowering a significant minority group in the justice decision-making process. The impact of this wholesale application of indigenous practices at the dispositional (sentencing) stage of the juvenile justice process was to grant substantial decision-making authority to community members and families. Replicated to a less dramatic extent in Australia (Braithwaite and Mugford 1994; Hayes and Daly 2003), this example later prompted training in and implementation of several different versions of FGC practice in Canada, the United States, the United Kingdom, and various European countries.

Yet short of a complete replication of the New Zealand's experience, how might U.S. practitioners design and implement a systemic model of restorative justice in various states or local jurisdictions? Guided by a practical effort to reduce secure confinement and disproportionate minority representation in juvenile justice, one essential strategic focus involves moving away from an "alternative" program approach to a mandated—or, at least, a presumptive first choice—case disposition in specific cases. This outcome would not only maximize informal community input into dispositional/sentencing decision making and other functions but also presumably limit the need for professional involvement in the dispositional function. Judges would then be free to focus more on the due process functions of adjudication, as well as on community leadership and engagement. Juvenile justice practitioners could then begin to develop and apply restorative *principles* and strategies to a full range of cases and system functions rather than simply refer cases to "restorative programs" as one of many "alternatives."

At a micro-level of daily juvenile justice intervention, a systemic restorative *case* strategy aimed at expanding restorative justice should first challenge all juvenile justice professionals and their community partners to find or develop a restorative "way" to respond to any crime or harm, regardless of the seriousness and level of incapacitation required. For example, restorative efforts to "repair harm"—regardless of seriousness of the crime and risk presented by the offender—would always include a response to the needs of victims, families of both victim and offender, and community (as well as some effort to address offenders' needs even in the most secure levels of confinement). At the macrolevel, a restorative *system* model would require that principle-based strategies and objectives be developed as the preferred means to accomplish standard juvenile justice system responsibilities. In addition to the New Zealand example of using restorative approaches as a tool to reduce crowding and improve dispositional decision making, a systemic problem-solving model would define a restorative methodology for increased effectiveness in carrying out multiple juvenile and criminal justice functions and responsibilities. It is possible therefore to envision *restorative models* of: policing youth (McLeod 2003); rehabilitation and treatment (Bazemore and Walgrave 1999); victim services (Achilles and Zehr 2001); restorative probation and community supervision such as diversion (Maloney and Holcomb 2001); discipline and conflict resolution in residential settings and schools (Bazemore, Zaslaw, and Reister 2005; Stinchcomb, Bazemore, and Riestenberg 2006); drug treatment (Braithwaite 2001); gang intervention (Boyes-Watson 2004); changing organizational culture and staff grievances (Carey 2001); and reentry planning (Bazemore and Stinchcomb 2004; Maruna 2001).

Restorative *problem solving* should also involve the application of restorative policies and practices directly to a range of chronic system dilemmas. In addition to overuse of secure confinement at all levels of the system, more mundane, yet important, administrative goals could be addressed using restorative justice principles, including improving staff morale (Carey 2001), disciplining staff, and reducing the courts' workload. In the last case, restorative justice may also engage the growing problem of a new expansion in juvenile justice responsibilities to include non-criminal problems. For example, juvenile justice has become increasingly involved in the criminalization of school disciplinary violations through "zero tolerance" enforcement (Stinchcomb et al. 2006) and the re-criminalization of status offense behavior (curfew violations, under-age drinking, truancy) best addressed in schools, families, churches, or neigh-borhoods (Bazemore, Stinchcomb, and Leip 2004; Clear and Karp 1999). Restorative methods of engaging these problems in a way that does not result in an expansion of system responsibility must also move beyond system change to include a primary focus on *community-building* solutions.

Problem Solving and Community Building

One neglected but increasingly important emphasis of restorative intervention has been efforts to influence the skills and capacities of families, teachers, neighbors, faith community groups, and a range of parochial organizations. In the "community" of the school, for example, a number of education profes-sionals have used restorative justice processes as alternative disciplinary approaches, conflict resolution techniques, anti-bullying practices, and alter-natives to suspension and other, traditional disciplinary approaches (Morrison 2001; Stinchcomb, Bazemore, and Riestenberg 2006). Indeed, much com-munity building of the kind that fosters collective efficacy (Sampson, Rauden-bush, and Earls 1997) and social support also occurs within the conferencing process itself as participants increase their own capacity to resolve and repair conflicts while attending to the needs of victims and offenders (Bazemore and Schiff 2004).

Several examples illustrate use of restorative practice to build community skills and, with some guidance and support, transfer decision-making and intervention responsibilities from juvenile justice programs to various "com-munities." In the small Wisconsin town of Rice Lake, for example, directors of a restorative conferencing program noticed that a very high percentage of their referrals were coming directly from the local high school. School officials supported the program, and the judge appropriately encouraged referrals to conferencing rather than court. The trivial nature of many of these disciplinary cases, however, suggested that the restorative program had become a "dumping ground" expected to provide an individualized response to what were often collective problems that originated in, and would likely return to, the "com-munity" of the school. "Problem students" were referred to the program, yet the conflict, problem, and harm to teachers and other students (and the real needs of the problem students) were not addressed. The compromise solution proposed to school administrators by the conferencing staff was that the pro-gram would continue to take a smaller number of referrals for more serious cases. In return, program staff would train teachers and administrators to con-duct conferences in the school itself. In doing so, school personnel could reduce the need for suspension and other punitive measures while building new disciplinary and conflict resolution skills *within* the school and keeping the settlement of conflict and harm within the community of origin (see Bazemore and Schiff 2004).

One of the most interesting examples of serendipitous neighborhood-driven community building involved several families in a rapidly growing suburban city in the Minneapolis–St. Paul area. In a case involving serious vandalism in which a local teenager had ransacked an elaborately designed tree house open to and used by neighborhood youth, a group of community members took matters into their own hands and with no professional help organized their own neighborhood restorative conference. When police officers, who also ran their own highly effective restorative conferencing program, came to the neighborhood to inform residents that they had scheduled a conference for the youth and all families involved, they were told by several neighbors that one resident (a man whose own son had previously participated in one of the police program's conferences) had "already handled the problem." This community member had acted as a facilitator in a conference held in his basement with the young perpetrator, his mother, several youth and their families, and other neighborhood residents. The conference resulted in restitution paid by the youth and his mother to rebuild the tree house; community service that involved neighbors working with the youth to repair the damage; apologies from the youth and mother; and, later, a neighborhood party to which the police officers were invited.

The common element in both of these quite different case examples was a *collective outcome* that included a just resolution of victim–offender conflict and reparation of harm using a restorative process within the community most affected by the incident. Both cases also provided clear opportunities to *practice* and build skills and capacity for self-regulation. In addition, new, meaningful relationships were built between families, young people, and police (in the second case) and education and juvenile justice professionals (in the first case). Together, these *problem-solving* responses built basic social capital that could be relied on for future informal repair and problem/conflict resolution. In both cases, the interventions also represent collective responses to issues often addressed as individual problems.

Beyond 911 Probation: Community Supervision as Productive Engagement

In today's juvenile justice systems, most staff are overwhelmed with cases and casework. Traditional casework probation, and much diversion case supervision, is best described as the passive monitoring of rules—essentially conducting monthly office visits with juvenile clients, checking to see whether the offender is at home or in school and not violating a range of supervision rules, and occasionally making referrals for available treatment or services. Moreover, just as mainstream law enforcement officers cannot resolve—and may be unaware of—problems that underlie 911 calls, juvenile justice workers responsible for community supervision see only individual cases and focus attention on rule violations rather than pro-social outcomes.

In a restorative model, this passive monitoring and referral approach to supervision would be replaced with a broader vision of the problem. Focused on the needs and input of victim, offender, and community and on collective outcomes, for the offender this would assume active completion of accountability/reparative, competency-development, and public safety outcomes that would go beyond passive compliance with rules and court orders. Youth on community supervision would not be part of a caseload to be "managed" and loosely monitored. Instead, they would have their waking hours productively structured in school, work, community service, victim-awareness education, or (as needed) required treatment programs (Bazemore 2006; Maloney and Holcomb 2001). True restorative intervention focused on a "productive engagement" model of community supervision would therefore also require a new and distinctive intervention model. In essence, this model would require a different unit of analysis to replace the individual "case" with a *place* and *problem* focus on community building aimed at achieving collective as well as individual outcomes (Clear and Karp 1999; Crawford and Clear 2001). The "place-focused," structured, productive engagement approach to community supervision is also about building public support for delinquent youth, who are given a chance to be seen in roles other than predator or victim. It is also about engaging pro-social community members and civic groups in these efforts, ideally working with youth on civic community service and related apprenticeship-type projects (Maruna 2001).

As a key component of a restorative model of community supervision, the role of the probation or diversion officer would be dramatically changed. A "community justice" officer (Maloney, Bazemore, and Hudson 2001) would embrace victim and community, as well as offender and family, as stakeholders, or "customers," of juvenile justice. Freed from most of the burdens of individual casework (some departments have created small, specialized units essentially to manage paper required by courts and other agencies), community justice officers could truly engage victims and their supporters, facilitate restorative conferences with families, neighbors, and youth, staffed to the greatest extent possible by neighborhood volunteers who also assist with individual case follow-up. Community justice officers could then turn much of their attention to community building in schools, neighborhood groups, faith communities, businesses, and civic groups and to working with and supporting employers willing to take risks to employ youth in trouble.

Changes in the community supervision version of 911 probation will not occur overnight and, as we suggest below, will *never* be made unless performance standards (and measures) for probation and diversion supervision are changed to move beyond passive assessment of noncompliance with supervision rules. In a restorative model, "successful completion" of community supervision would be gauged by completion of terms of accountability and productivity-based, pro-social intermediate outcomes, including improvements in school performance and attendance, completion of restitution and community service requirements, meeting with victims or surrogate victims, and completion of other obligations important in their own right or related to re-offending. Indicators of successful completion of community supervision would then be based not on "doing time" but on "doing *good*" (Maloney, Bazemore, and Hudson 2001; Maruna 2001); higher-level outcomes linked to both of these intermediate outcomes would include new pro-social connections and civic engagement (Uggen, Manza, and Behrens 2003).

Measuring and Doing What Matters

If we expect community supervision officers to *engage the community*, it is important, at a minimum, to ensure that barriers to such engagement are addressed. Because "what gets measured, gets done" (Osborne and Gaebler 1992), community corrections leaders in juvenile justice must also develop new incentives and performance standards that in fact *reward* professionals for tasks other than office visits, passive caseload management, and perfunctory home visits. In other words, neither prior efforts to simply change the location of probation offices and officers, new partnerships with other criminal justice agencies, nor even changes in how we view offenders are likely to make much of a difference if staff understand their responsibility only in terms of their "cases."

New performance measures developed in a reform context that envisions collective change, however, could be employed not only to guide and improve impact evaluation and system accountability, but also to drive *change in practice priorities*. For example, dramatic increases in successful completion of restitution, community service, victim–offender dialogue, and other pro-social community supervision obligations (e.g., school attendance) tied to staff incentives have been a result of the use of restorative performance measures, for example, while reductions in supervision have been noted in demonstration efforts (Bazemore 2006). Measuring and *doing* what matters will also require new organizational-change strategies (Senge 1990) that envision, as the skill-building examples of restorative practice in schools and neighborhoods illustrate, targeted reform in "mediating institutions" (Bellah et al. 1985) rather than simply individual change. At the beginning and end of the cycle of community supervision in a restorative model of probation or diversion is an effort to relinquish system responsibility and increase *community* responsibility for social control and social support (see Clear and Karp 1999). A strategy for transforming casework to a capacity-building model, as well as the broader problem-solving change discussed above, will benefit not only from examining existing intervention research and developing performance measures, but also from theory to guide restorative practice and gauge success in completing core intermediate outcomes (Bazemore and Schiff 2004; Braithwaite 2001).

Theorizing Restorative Justice Intervention: Linking Practice and Outcomes

John Hagan's (1989) question "Why is there so little theory in criminal justice?" was in part addressed by Bazemore in his appeal to apply new organization theory (see Weick 1995) to understand the problem of how and when criminal justice agencies collaborated at the "loosely coupled" systems level. At a different level, however, it is even more surprising that criminological theory is seldom applied to intervention practice. Juvenile justice treatment programs in particular seem to be characterized by either an a-theoretical approach focused on simplistic counseling logics based on attitude change or self-esteem improvement or (worse) by an effort to send a "scared straight" message regarding adverse future consequences (Finkenhauer and Gavin 1999). In this context, Hagan's call for theoretical application seems even more urgent.

Restorative practitioners are hardly immune to this absence of theory or to the failure to conceptualize intervention objectives. Indeed, many restorative programs become comfortable and rigid in their own programmatic routines and often become too reliant on what Derek Brookes (2000, 7) calls "service delivery criteria" (e.g., number of agreements completed, amount of restitution collected) as indicators of success. Yet in a field study of restorative decision making in juvenile justice programs in eight states (Bazemore and Schiff 2004), when groups of *experienced* practitioners were asked what they were trying to accomplish at the end of a restorative conference, a number of theoretically coherent immediate and intermediate outcomes were described.

Table 14.1 presents core theoretical dimensions of these objectives and outcomes most commonly viewed by these practitioners as essential to be achieved at the conclusion of a restorative justice conference. These dimensions are essentially the immediate and intermediate outcomes for practice associated with the "theories-in-use" (Argyris and Schon 1974) described. These also mirror assumptions about the importance of intervening processes, or intermediate variables (Agnew 1993; Unnever, Cullen, and Agnew 2006) in core criminological and sociological theories and are briefly considered below as they appear to "line up" with these theories and with the previously discussed core normative principles of restorative justice.

TABLE 14.1   Core Principles of Restorative Justice and Their Dimensions

Repairing Harm	Stakeholder Involvement	Community/Government Role Transformation
Making amends	Victim–offender exchange	Norm affirmation/ values clarification
Relationship building	Mutual transformation Respectful disapproval	Collective ownership Skill building

Source: Adapted from Bazemore and Schiff 2004.

Repairing Harm

Intervention theories and specific intermediate outcomes imply unique objectives and success indicators (Bazemore and Schiff 2004). For example, one core outcome associated with the overarching, principle-based goal of repairing harm in restorative practice is centered on the extent to which the offender is held accountable to victim and community by "making amends" for the harm his or her crime has caused, an outcome dimension grounded in *exchange theories* that emphasize the importance of reciprocity in human interaction (Molm and Cook 1995; see also Putnam 2000). Another outcome, "building or rebuilding relationships" damaged by crime, or building new pro-social relationships, is grounded in *social support* theory (Cullen 1994), which suggests that both emotional/affective support and more tangible instrumental assistance from pro-social adults enables offenders to desist from crime and victims to recover from the trauma of crime.

Stakeholder Involvement

Theories surrounding the principle of stakeholder involvement emphasize different "styles" of restorative process (between or within various restorative conferencing models) and different intervention objectives as most important in various theories of restorative decision making—for example, a theory of *healing dialogue,* which claims that the "victim–offender exchange" in the conference setting (with relevant input from others in the conference), is the most critical dimension (i.e., immediate outcome) of a successful conference (Umbreit 2001). A theory of *common ground,* by contrast, suggests that a kind of "mutual transformation" of victim and offender is an outcome central to resolution of harm and conflict. This outcome is best achieved by close attention to group emotions and to respectful acknowledgment of the "other" (victim of the offender; community member of the victim)—as well as attention of facilitators to subtle phases of the dialogue process (Moore and McDonald 2000). The well-known *reintegrative shaming* theory (Braithwaite 1989) prioritizes a "respectful disapproval" of the offender's behavior that acknowledges the harm caused but distinguishes the offense from the offender himself.

Community/Government Role Transformation

The need for transformation of the community/government role and relationship in the response to crime suggested by the third restorative principle is consistent with theories of *social capital* and informal social control (Putnam 2000; Sampson, Raudenbush, and Earls 1997) and can be operationalized by a focus on the extent to which participants in a restorative process (and their support groups, neighborhoods, and organizations): strengthen "networks of support" as social capital; build skills and commitment to allow for the exercise of informal social control and social support as *collective efficacy*; and promote expansion of a dimension/outcome referred to by some practitioners as "collective ownership" of the response to crime and harm based on a theory of *civic engagement*. This theory suggests that community groups, and the offenders and victims assisted by intervention, are most successful when they take responsibility first for the success of restorative conferences, and then for community problems, while making a commitment to give back to their communities (Bazemore and Stinchcomb 2004; Maruna 2001).

Discussion and Conclusions

We have argued for a new problem-solving and community-building restorative model of juvenile justice reform that is distinctive in its significant effort to move beyond cases toward collective outcomes. Using the case of problem-oriented policing as a more long-standing, somewhat parallel reform, and the New Zealand experience and related experiences as case studies in restorative reform, we argue for the importance of making a leap to a more macro-focus that uses restorative principles to solve chronic system and community problems. We have also argued for a need to go beyond special programs while instead seeking to develop a restorative "approach" to addressing routine juvenile justice functions.

Discussion

Moving beyond passive casework to a productivity and outcome-based community model of intervention will be a requirement of a truly restorative juvenile justice. This implies organizational change and a different incentive structure for professionals and agencies as a whole. Restorative justice practitioners can also learn from the mistakes of POP in focusing most efforts solely on line officers rather than on management—the equivalent in restorative justice of replicating the all-too-common process of building reforms around the efforts of individual caseworkers. We propose a problem-solving and community-building agenda that holds juvenile justice agencies, and the community groups collaborating with them, responsible for achieving theory and research-based restorative outcomes. Finally, we argue that core restorative principles, which should guide all practice, are consistent with social-science theories that set standards for immediate and intermediate outcomes related to repairing harm, involving three stakeholders in the decision-making process, and transforming the community/government relationship to promote community ownership of the justice process.

The group of theories consistent with restorative principles (including even the more micro- and mid-range theories of social support and exchange, reintegrative shaming, and "common ground") are especially relevant to this community-building agenda. It is, however, the more macro–social capital focus on connections between community members and groups that promote the trust and relationships needed for collective action and shared leadership that can make the most important differences in restorative practice. The theory of collective efficacy would further suggest that as community members *practice* justice skills of decision making about harm and repair, learn to resolve conflict, assist crime victims, and exercise both informal support and social control, they make their communities safer. As they participate in restorative processes and gradually share leadership in their operation, they may also develop a sense of ownership of community problems and become defenders of these communities—while also building larger alliances that Robert Putnam (2000) refers to as "bridging social capital."

The value of theory in this context is not simply to legitimize restorative justice—or even primarily to allow researchers to test and also build theory through evaluation. Although such research is needed, the purpose of theory building and testing is ultimately to improve practice by changing course or by replicating positive outcomes in other settings, perhaps with other kinds of offenders and victims. In a field where researchers are continuing to find that restorative justice does often work, we are, however, often unable to say *why and how* it works when it does (Bazemore, Ellis, and Green, 2007; Hayes and Daly 2003). Most importantly, therefore, theories should drive and improve practice by providing standards for gauging the integrity and strength of restorative interventions and pushing practice toward certain intermediate outcomes that link logically and empirically to desired long-term healing outcomes.

Conclusions

The lessons of success and failure of problem-oriented policing and other reforms that struggle to break down adherence to an individualized focus and to create organizational and systemic change hold important lessons for advocates of a restorative juvenile justice. A holistic restorative approach is needed if restorative practice is to become more than an insignificant "add-on" to what is now more mainstream juvenile justice practice. Despite generally positive and robust research findings and use of restorative justice in the response to crimes of severe violence, and even in the aftermath of international conflict (Weitekamp, Parmentier, and Gertis 2007), the overall sustainability of restorative practice in the response to youth crime may well depend on movement toward such an approach.

References

Achilles, M., and H. Zehr. 2001. Restorative justice for crime victims: The promise, the challenge. In *Restorative community justice: Repairing harm and transforming communities.* Ed. G. Bazemore and M. Schiff, 3–17. Cincinnati: Anderson Publishing.

Agnew, R. 1993. Why do they do it? An examination of the intervening mechanisms between "social control" variables and delinquency. *Journal of Research in Crime and Delinquency* 30:245–266.

Argyris, C., and D. Schon. 1974. *Theory in practice: Increasing professional effectiveness.* San Francisco: Jossey-Bass.

Bazemore, G. 2001. Young people, trouble, and crime: Restorative justice as a normative theory of informal social control and social support. *Youth and Society* 33:199–226.

———. 2006. Measuring what really matters: Performance measures for the juvenile justice system. Technical Monograph. Office of Juvenile Justice and Delinquency Prevention, U.S. Department of Justice, Washington, D.C.

Bazemore, G., T. J. Dicker, and R. Nyhan. 1994. Juvenile justice reform and the difference it makes: An exploratory study of the impact of policy change on detention worker attitudes. *Crime and Delinquency* 40:37–53.

Bazemore, G., L. Ellis, and D. Green. 2007. The independent variable in restorative justice: Theory-based standards for evaluating the impact and integrity of victim sensitive process. *Victims and offenders* 2:325–352.

Bazemore, G., and M. Schiff. 2004. *Juvenile justice reform and restorative justice: Building theory and policy from practice.* Cullompton, U.K.: Willan Publishing.

Bazemore, G., and J. Stinchcomb. 2004. Involving community through service and restorative justice: Theory and practice for a civic engagement model of reentry. *Federal Probation* 68:14–24.

Bazemore, G., J. Stinchcomb, and L. Leip. 2004. Scared smart or bored straight? Testing a deterrence logic in an evaluation of police-led truancy intervention. *Justice Quarterly* 21:269–298.

Bazemore, G., and L. Walgrave. 1999. Restorative juvenile justice: In search of fundamentals and an outline for systemic reform. In *Restorative juvenile justice: Repairing the harm of youth crime.* Ed. G. Bazemore and L. Walgrave, 1–14. Monsey, N.Y.: Criminal Justice Press.

Bazemore, G., J. Zaslaw, and D. Reister. 2005. Behind the walls and beyond: Restorative justice, instrumental communities, and effective residential treatment. *Juvenile and Family Court Journal* 56:53–73.

Bellah, R. N., R. Madsen, W. Sullivan, A. Swidler, and M. Tipton. 1985. *Habits of the heart: Individualism and commitment in American life.* Berkeley: University of California Press.

Boba, R., and J. Crank. 2008. Institutionalizing problem oriented policing: Rethinking problem identification, analysis, and accountability. *Police Practice and Research* 9:379–393.

Bonta, J., S. Wallace-Capretta, J. Rooney, and K. Mackanoy. 2002. An outcome evaluation of a restorative justice alternative to incarceration. *Contemporary Justice Review* 5:319–338.

Boyes-Watson, C. 2004. What are the implications of growing state involvement in restorative justice?" In *Critical issues in restorative justice.* Ed. H. Zehr and B. Toews, 215–226. Collompton, U.K.: Willan Publishing.

Braithwaite, J. 1989. *Crime, shame, and reintegration.* Cambridge: Cambridge University Press.

———. 2001. Restorative justice and a new criminal law of substance abuse. *Youth and Society* 33:227–249.

Braithwaite, J., and S. Mugford. 1994. Conditions of successful reintegration ceremonies: Dealing with juvenile offenders. *British Journal of Criminology* 34:139–171.

Braithwaite, J., and C. Parker. 1999. Restorative justice is republican justice. In *Restorative juvenile justice: Repairing the harm of youth crime.* Ed. G. Bazemore and L. Walgrave, 103–126. Monsey, N.Y.: Criminal Justice Press.

Braithwaite, J., and P. Pettit. 1990. *Not just deserts: A republican theory of criminal justice.* Oxford: Oxford University Press.

Brooks, D. 2000. Evaluating restorative justice programs. Paper presented to the UN Crime Congress Ancillary Meeting, Vienna.

Butts, J., and H. Snyder. 1991. *Restitution and juvenile recidivism.* Monograph. National Center for Juvenile Justice, Pittsburgh.

Carey, M. 2001. Infancy, adolescence, and restorative justice: Strategies for promoting organizational reform. In *Restorative community justice: Repairing harm and transforming communities.* Ed. G. Bazemore and M. Schiff, 49–61. Cincinnati: Anderson Publishing.

Clarke, R, V., and J. Eck. 2005. *Crime analysis for problem solvers: In 60 small steps.* Washington D.C.: Office of Community Oriented Policing Services, U.S. Department of Justice.

Clear, T., and D. Karp. 1999. *The community justice ideal: Preventing crime and achieving justice.* Boulder, Colo.: Westview Press.

Crawford, A., and T. Clear. 2001. Community justice: Transforming communities through restorative justice? In *Restorative community justice: Repairing harm and transforming communities.* Ed. G. Bazemore and M. Schiff, 86–112. Cincinnati: Anderson Publishing.

Cullen, F. T. 1994. Social support as an organizing concept for criminology: Residential address to the Academy of Criminal Justice Sciences. *Justice Quarterly* 11:527–559.

Eck, J. E., and W. Spelman. 1987. Problem-solving: Problem-oriented policing in Newport News. Washington, D.C.: Police Executive Research Forum.

Elliott, D. 2004. Restorative justice and Canadian approaches to youth crime. In *Criminal justice in Canada: A reader.* 2nd ed. Ed. J. Roberts and M. Grossman, 26–39. Scarborough, Ont.: Nelson.

Finkenhauer, J., and P. Gavin. 1999. *Scared straight: The panacea phenomenon revisited.* Prospect Heights, Ill.: Waveland Press.

Goldstein, H. 1979. Improving policing: A problem oriented approach. *Crime and Delinquency* 24:236–258.

———. 1990. *Problem-oriented policing.* New York: McGraw-Hill.

———. 2003. *On further developing problem-oriented policing: The most critical need, the major impediments, and a proposal. Problem-oriented policing: From innovation to mainstream.* Monsey, N.Y.: Criminal Justice Press.

Granovetter, M. 1973. The strength of weak ties. *American Journal of Sociology* 78:1360–1380.
———. 1983. The strength of weak ties: A network theory revisited. *Sociological Theory* 1: 201–233.
Hagan, J. 1989. Why is there so little criminal justice theory? Neglected macro and micro links between organization and power. *Journal of Research in Crime and Delinquency* 26:116–135.
Hasenfeld, D., and P. Cheung. 1985. The juvenile court as a people processing organization: A political economy perspective. *American Journal of Sociology* 90:801–824.
Hayes, H., and K. Daly. 2003. Youth justice conferencing and re-offending. *Justice Quarterly* 20:725–764.
Hudson, J., and B. Galaway. 1990. Introduction: Towards restorative justice. In *Criminal justice, restitution, and reconciliation.* Ed. J. Hudson and B. Galaway, 1–16. Monsey, N.Y.: Willow Tree Press.
Jenkins, M. 2006. Gullah Island dispute resolution: An example of Afrocentric restorative justice. *Journal of Black Studies* 37:299–319.
Kelling, G., and M. Moore. 1988. *The evolving strategy of policing.* National Institute of Justice, U.S. Department of Justice, and the Program in Criminal Justice Policy and Management, John F. Kennedy School of Government, Harvard University, Cambridge, Mass.
Levrant, S., F. Cullen, B. Fulton, and J. Wozniak. 1999. Reconsidering restorative justice: The corruption of benevolence revisited? *Crime and Delinquency* 45:3–27.
Maloney, D., G. Bazemore, and J. Hudson. 2001. The end of probation and the beginning of community corrections. *Perspectives* (Summer): 23–30.
Maloney, D., and D. Holcomb. 2001. In pursuit of community justice. *Youth and Society* 33:296–314.
Marshall, T. 1996. The evolution of restorative justice in Britain. *European Journal of Criminal Policy and Research* 4:21–43.
Maruna, S. 2001. Making good: How ex-convicts reform and rebuild their lives. Washington, D.C.: American Psychological Association.
Masters, G. 2003. What happens when restorative justice is encouraged, enabled and/or guided by legislation? In *Critical issues in restorative justice.* Ed. H. Zehr and B. Toews, 227–239. Collompton, U.K.: Willan Publishing.
Maxwell, G., and A. Morris. 1993. *Family participation, cultural diversity and victim involvement in youth violence: A New Zealand experiment.* Wellington: Victoria University.
McElrae, F. W. 1996. The New Zealand youth court: A model for use with adults. In *Restorative justice: International perspectives.* Ed. B. Galaway and J. Hudson, 69–83. Monsey, N.Y.: Criminal Justice Press.
McGarrell, E. 2001. Restorative justice conferences as an early response to young offenders. OJJDP Juvenile Justice Bulletin. Office of Juvenile Justice and Delinquency Prevention, U.S. Department of Justice, Washington, D.C., August.
McLeod, C. 2003. Towards a restorative organization: Transforming police bureaucracies. *Police Practice and Research* 4:361–377.
Michalowski, R. J. 1985. *Order, law, and crime.* New York: McGraw-Hill.
Molm, L., and K. Cook. 1995. Social exchange and exchange networks. In *Sociological perspectives on social psychology.* Ed. K. Cook, G. Fine, and J. House, 241–360. Boston: Allyn and Bacon.
Moore, D., and J. McDonald. 2000. *Transforming conflict in workplaces and other communities.* Sydney: Transformative Justice Australia.
Morrison, B. 2001. The school system: Developing its capacity in the regulation of a civilized society. In *Restorative justice and civil society.* Ed. J. Braithwaite and H. Strang, 195–210. Cambridge: Cambridge University Press.

Nugent, W., M. Williams, and M. S. Umbreit. 2003. Participation in victim–offender mediation and the prevalence of subsequent delinquent behavior: A meta-analysis. *Utah Law Review* 1:137–167.

O'Brien, S., and G. Bazemore. 2005. Introduction to the symposium: Communities, organizations, and restorative justice reform public organization review. *Global Journal* 5: 279–285.

Osborne, D., and T. Gaebler. 1992. *Reinventing government: How the entrepreneurial spirit is transforming the public sector.* Reading: Addison-Wesley.

Polk, K. 1987. When less means more: An analysis of destructuring in criminal justice. *Crime and Delinquency* 33:358–378.

Pranis, K. 2001. Restorative justice, social justice, and the empowerment of marginalized populations. In *Restorative community justice: Repairing harm and transforming communities.* Ed. G. Bazemore and M. Schiff, 31–46. Cincinnati: Anderson Publishing.

Putnam, R. 2000. *Bowling alone: The collapse and revival of American community.* New York: Simon and Schuster.

Rodriguez, N. 2004. Restorative justice, communities and delinquency: Whom do we reintegrate? *Criminology and Public Policy* 4:103–130.

Saleebey, D. 2002. Introduction: Power in the people. In *The strengths perspective in social work practice.* Ed. D. Saleebey, 1–25. London: Allyn and Bacon.

Sampson, R., S. Raudenbush, and F. Earls. 1997. Neighborhoods and violent crime: A multilevel study of collective efficacy. *Science* 77:918–924.

Schafer, S. 1970. *Compensation and restitution to victims of crime.* Montclair, N.J.: Patterson Smith.

Schneider, A. 1986. Restitution and recidivism rates of juvenile offenders: Results from four experimental studies. *Criminology* 24:533–552.

Scott, M. 2000. Problem-oriented policing: Reflections on the first 20 years. Office of Community Oriented Policing Services, U.S. Department of Justice, Washington, D.C.

Senge, P. 1990. *The fifth discipline.* New York: Doubleday Currency.

Sherman, L., and H. Strang. 2007. *Restorative justice: The evidence.* Monograph. Smith Institute, Cambridge.

Skogan W. G. 1990. *Disorder and decline: Crime and the spiral decay in American cities.* New York: Free Press.

Skolnick, J., and D. Bayley. 1986. *The new blue line: Police innovations in six American cities.* New York: Free Press.

Stinchcomb, J., G. Bazemore, and N. Riestenberg. 2006. Beyond zero tolerance: Restoring justice in secondary schools. *Youth Violence and Juvenile Justice* 4:123–147.

Taylor, R., E. Fritsch, and J. Caeti. 1998. Core challenges facing community policing: The emperor still has no clothes. *Academy of Criminal Justice Sciences* 17:1–8.

Tonry, M. 1994. Proportionality, parsimony, and interchangeability of punishment. In *Penal theory and penal practice.* Ed. A. Duff, S. Marshall, and R. Dobash, 318–356. Manchester: Manchester University Press.

Tyler, T. 1990. *Why people obey the law.* New Haven, Conn.: Yale University Press.

Uggen, C., J. Manza, and A. Behrens. 2003. "Less than average citizen": Stigma, role transition, and the civic reintegration of convicted felons. Working paper. Department of Sociology, University of Minnesota, Minneapolis.

Umbreit, M. 2001. *The handbook of victim-offender mediation.* San Francisco: Jossey-Bass.

Unnever, J. D., F. Cullen, and R. Agnew. 2006. Why is "bad" parenting criminogenic? Implications from rival theories. *Youth Violence and Juvenile Justice* 4:3–33.

Van Ness, D., and K. H. Strong. 1997. *Restoring justice.* Cincinnati: Anderson Publishing.

Von Hirsch, A. 1976. *Doing justice.* New York: Hill and Wang.

Weick, K. E. 1995. *Sensemaking in organizations.* Thousand Oaks, Calif.: Sage.

Weisburd, D. L., and A. Braga. 2006. *Police innovation: Contrasting perspectives.* Cambridge: Cambridge University Press.

Weisburd, D. L., and J. Eck. 2004. What can police do to reduce crime, disorder and fear? *Annals of the American Academy of Political and Social Science* 593:42–65.

Weitekamp, E. G. 1999. The history of restorative justice. In *Restorative juvenile justice: Repairing the harm of youth crime.* Ed. G. Bazemore and L. Walgrave, 75–102. Monsey, N.Y.: Criminal Justice Press.

Weitekamp, E. G., S. Parmentier, and M. Gertis. 2007. How to deal with mass victimization and gross human rights violations: A restorative justice approach. In *Large scale victimization and as a potential source of terrorist activities,* Vol. 13, *NATO security through the social sciences.* Ed. U. Ewald and K. Turkovic, 217–241. Amsterdam: IOS Press.

Contributors

Robert Agnew is a professor of sociology at Emory University, where he pursues his interest in teaching and research with a focus on research methodology, social psychology, and causes of crime and delinquency. In addition to serving on the editorial board of the *Journal of Research in Crime and Delinquency,* he has published numerous works, including *Why Do Criminals Offend? A General Theory of Crime and Delinquency* (2007).

Ronald L. Akers is a professor of criminology and sociology at the University of Florida, where he has taught graduate courses since 1980. In addition to serving as president of the American Society of Criminology and holding other influential leadership positions, he has authored more than eighty articles in major sociology and criminology journals and coedited the book *Social Learning Theory and the Explanation of Crime* (2003). His extensive scholarly history includes the development and analysis of research that focuses on policy matters, social learning theory, and deviance.

Hugh D. Barlow is professor emeritus of sociology at Southern Illinois University Edwardsville, where he taught for more than thirty years. After serving as department chair for fourteen years, he directed the new Criminal Justice Studies program, which he designed and implemented in 2001. In 1993 he received the Herbert Bloch Award from the American Society of Criminology for service to the organization and the profession. He is the author of *Dead for Good: Martyrdom and the Rise of the Suicide Bomber* (2007) and coauthor (with David Kauzlarich) of *Introduction to Criminology* (2008) and *Explaining Crime:*

A Primer on Criminological Theory (forthcoming). He now lives in Albuquerque, New Mexico, where he teaches an occasional course at the University of New Mexico.

Gordon Bazemore is professor and chair in the Department of Criminal Justice and Criminology at Florida Atlantic University and director of the university's Community Justice Institute. As an active researcher for more than thirty years, he has trained the staffs of various federal, state, and local agencies and advised them on juvenile justice, restorative justice, public policy, victimization issues, and corrections. He is an active researcher and writer who has published a lengthy list of works, including *Juvenile Justice Reform and Restorative Justice: Building Theory and Policy from Practice* (coauthored with Mara Schiff, 2005).

Rachel Boba is an associate professor in the School of Criminology and Criminal Justice at Florida Atlantic University. She has published in the areas of crime analysis, problem solving, and police accountability, including *Crime Analysis with Crime Mapping* (2008). She is coauthor (with Marcus Felson) of *Crime and Everyday Life* (4th ed., 2009).

Ronald V. Clarke is a professor in the School of Criminal Justice at Rutgers University. Previously, he led the British government's criminological research effort, where he focused on crime prevention strategies. In addition to teaching, he serves as associate director of the Center for Problem-Oriented Policing. He has published various books that examine crime prevention tactics and routine activity and rational choice theories, and he designs and provides training that focuses on problem-oriented approaches for police agencies.

Heith Copes is an associate professor in the Justice Sciences Program at the University of Alabama, Birmingham. As a specialist in symbolic interaction, car theft, white-collar crime, and criminal decision making, he publishes works on corporate and street crime and teaches theories of deviance and criminality. In 2005 he received the President's Award for Excellence in Teaching for his work in the School of Social and Behavioral Sciences.

Francis T. Cullen holds the title Distinguished Research Professor of Criminal Justice and Sociology at the University of Cincinnati. He is a fellow in the American Society of Criminology and the Academy of Criminal Justice Sciences and former editor of *Justice Quarterly*. He has received numerous honors for his scholarship, which includes 9 books and more than 150 articles. His primary research interests include criminological theory, corrections and rehabilitation, and corporate crime.

Scott H. Decker serves as professor and director at the School of Criminology and Criminal Justice at Arizona State University. His academic interests include strategic problem solving, crime control policy, gangs, juvenile justice, and criminology, and he contributes his expertise by writing for scholarly journals and other publications. In 2007 he was recognized as a Fellow of the Academy of Criminal Justice Sciences.

Marcus Felson is a professor of criminal justice at Rutgers University, where he specializes in developing practical crime theory. His routine activity analysis contributes to an understanding of when, where, and how crime occurs and what to do about it. He is the author of *Crime and Nature* (2006) and *Crime and Everyday Life* (3rd ed., 2002); coauthor (with Ronald V. Clarke) of *Opportunity Makes the Thief* (1998); and coeditor (with Ronald V. Clarke) of *Routine Activity and Rational Choice* (2004) and *Business and Crime Prevention* (1997).

Marie Griffin is an associate professor of criminology and criminal justice at Arizona State University. Her research interests include issues of organizational climate in the correctional setting, the use of force in corrections, prison and jail misconduct, and gender and crime. She recently completed an examination of the influence of gender on acquisition behaviors across drug markets (funded by a National Institute of Justice grant). Her work has appeared in *Justice Quarterly, Criminal Justice and Behavior,* and *Criminology and Public Policy.*

Scott Jacques is a doctoral candidate at the University of Missouri, St. Louis, where he serves as research assistant to Professor Richard Wright. He is currently pursuing his interests in pure sociology, drug dealers, and active offender research and is working on a comparative study of middle-status and lower-status drug distributors.

David Kauzlarich chairs the Department of Sociology and Criminal Justice Studies at Southern Illinois University Edwardsville. His academic interests range from peace studies to sociological and criminological theory, with specialization in social control and state and governmental crime. He coauthored (with Rick A. Matthews) "State Crimes and State Harms: A Tale of Two Definitional Frameworks," published in *Crime, Law and Social Change* (2007).

Jean M. McGloin is an assistant professor in the Department of Criminology and Criminal Justice at the University of Maryland, where she also serves as director of the department's undergraduate honors program. Her doctoral dissertation included an examination of the social structure of street gangs; she also specializes in criminological theory, policing, groups and crime, and crime and delinquency. She contributed a chapter on the link between gang involvement and predatory crime to *Violent Offenders: Theory, Research, Public Policy, and Practice* (2008).

Steven F. Messner holds the title Distinguished Teaching Professor of Crime and Deviance in the College of Arts and Sciences at the University of Albany, State University of New York, and serves as deputy editor of the *American Sociological Review*. His primary areas of research include criminology, deviant behavior, and macro-sociology. He was elected vice president of the American Society of Criminology for 2006–2007. He is coauthor (with Jianhong Liu and Susanne Karstedt) of a chapter titled "Economic Reform and Crime in Contemporary China: Paradoxes of a Planned Transition" in *Urban China in Transition* (2008).

Alex R. Piquero is an associate professor of criminology and criminal justice at the University of Maryland. His interests center on lifetime criminality and transitions and factors that alter criminal behavior. He serves on ten editorial boards for scholarly journals and has been appointed by the Bureau of Justice Statistics to reconstruct the government's crime index.

Nicole Leeper Piquero is an associate professor of criminal justice at Virginia Commonwealth University. Her research interests include white-collar and corporate crimes and criminological theory. She is currently coauthoring (with David Weisburd) *Crimes of a Different Class: White-Collar Crimes and Criminals.*

Nancy Rodriguez is an associate professor of criminology and criminal justice at Arizona State University. Her primary areas of research include criminal justice decision making, juvenile justice, and substance abuse. Her research has appeared in *Justice Quarterly, Criminology and Public Policy,* and *Crime and Delinquency.*

Richard Rosenfeld holds the title Curators' Professor in the Department of Criminology and Criminal Justice at the University of Missouri, St. Louis, where he is also the Graduate Program director for the department. His chief concentration is violence and social organization, criminological theory, crime statistics and trends, and crime control policy. He is a Fellow of the American Society of Criminology and coauthor (with Steven Messner) of *Crime and the American Dream* (2007).

Dawn L. Rothe is assistant professor of sociology and criminology at Old Dominion University, Norfolk, Virginia. Her research interests include state and corporate crime, international institutions of social control, classical and contemporary sociological theory, and international humanitarian law. She has published numerous articles and essays, including "The International Criminal Court: Symbolic Gestures and the Generation of Global Social Control" (coauthored with Christopher Mullins), published in 2006.

Andrea Schoepfer is an assistant professor of criminal justice at California State University, San Bernardino. She received a doctorate in criminology and criminal justice from the University of Florida. Her primary areas of research are white-collar and organized crime.

Neal Shover is a professor of criminology at the University of Tennessee, Knoxville. His research interests include career criminals, rational choice theory, and criminal decision making. His latest challenge has been the examination of the features of middle-class child rearing and cultural capital that result in white-collar crime. His most recent book, *Choosing White-Collar Crime* is forthcoming.

Cassia Spohn is a professor of criminology and criminal justice at Arizona State University, where she also serves as the director of graduate studies. She is the author of *How Do Judges Decide? The Search for Fairness and Justice in Punishment* and the coauthor (with Samuel Walker and Miriam DeLone) of *The Color of Justice: Race, Ethnicity, and Crime in America* and (with Julia Horney) *Rape Law Reform: A Grassroots Revolution and Its Impact*. She has published more than seventy-five articles on topics such as the effects of race/ ethnicity and gender on sentencing decisions, the sentencing of drug offenders, prosecutors' charging decisions in sexual assault cases, and the deterrent effect of imprisonment.

Katharine Tellis is a doctoral candidate at the University of Nebraska, Omaha. Her research interests focus on applied academics, such as how the intersection of race, class, gender, and sexuality affect theory and practice in criminology and criminal justice. Her dissertation examines both the overlap of physical and sexual assaults among intimate partners and the dynamics involved in processing sexual assault cases.

Charles R. Tittle serves as professor and Goodnight-Glaxo Welcome Chair in Social Sciences in the Department of Sociology and Anthropology at North Carolina State University. As a researcher, he pursues his interests in the sociology of crime and deviance, sociological theory, and urban sociology. His published works, including *Social Deviance and Crime: A Theoretical Approach* (coauthored with Raymond Paternoster, 2000), focus mainly on theories of social deviance.

Richard Wright holds the title Curator's Professor in the Department of Criminology and Criminal Justice at the University of Missouri, St. Louis. His research interests are in the offender's perspective and emotions and crime. His published works have examined active residential burglars, armed robbers, drug dealers, and carjackers.

Index

Subjects

Cited Authors